Evaluating Networked Information Services

Evaluating Networked Information Services

TECHNIQUES, POLICY, AND ISSUES

Charles R. McClure
and
John Carlo Bertot

asis&t

ASIST Monograph Series

Ess Ess Publications

New Delhi-110002

In Association with

Information Today, Inc.

Medford, New Jersey

Evaluating Networked Information Services: Techniques, Policy and Issues

ISBN 978-81-7000-540-7 (13 digit)
ISBN 81-7000-540-X (10 digit)

Rs.950/-

First Indian Imprint 2008

Published by:
Ess Ess Publications
4837/24, Ansari Road,
Darya Ganj,
New Delhi-110 002.
INDIA
Phones: 23260807, 41563444
Fax: 41563334
E-mail: info@essessreference.com
www.essessreference.com

in arrangement with

Information Today, Inc.
143 Old Marlton Pike,
Medford, New Jersey 08055
United States of America

Printed and bound in India at Salasar Imaging Systems.

Table of Contents

List of Figures

List of Tables

Introduction

Charles R. McClure
John Carlo Bertot

This book is the first of its kind—an attempt to present readers with a number of perspectives on evaluating networked information services and resources. The idea for the book came from the American Society for Information Science's (ASIS) May 1999 Mid-Year meeting in Pasadena, California, entitled *Evaluating and Using Networked Information Resources and Services*. The meeting co-chairs, Charles R. McClure, John Carlo Bertot, and Carol Hert, in working with ASIS staff, decided not to publish conference proceedings for that meeting. Rather, the co-chairs invited attendees to submit chapters based on presented papers and panels for a "post-ceeding" publication. The co-chairs received a number of outstanding submissions, which were then reviewed by external reviewers for inclusion in the publication. The received submissions were of such quality and depth, that the above publication evolved into this edited book.

There is still considerable debate and discussion as to key definitions for *networks*, *networked services*, *evaluation*, and *assessment* in a networked context. It may be too early to determine definitions for these and related terms —although a number of definitions for such terms are proposed in various chapters throughout this book. One problem is that the notion of a network is in itself changing and evolving as the technology changes and as applications and uses of a network change. Thus, to some degree definitions of these terms can be a moving target.

In addition, the notion of evaluation implies *value judgments* offered in a managerial, political, and social context that may vary from setting to setting. Some see assessment as a more objective process in which data are collected, analyzed and reported. Then the evaluation process occurs in which value judgments provide recommendations for how to respond to the findings and offer specific recommendations. Others see the evaluation and assessment process as intertwined and difficult, at best, to separate as different processes.

Regardless of the approach taken in defining these terms by authors in this book, we believe that different definitions and uses of these terms are inevitable at present. Thus, the editors avoid the temptation of prescribing our definitions since the terms are used differently in the various chapters. We expect that as the field of evaluation of networked services expands and evolves, some agreement on terminology and basic definitions will occur. Such is not the case at this time.

IMPORTANCE OF THE TOPIC

The 1999 Mid-Year meeting demonstrated that a number of researchers and practitioners were struggling with understanding the networked environment by asking a series of questions:

- What is a network?
- What is networking?
- Are there models that identify and describe networks?
- Are there identifiable aspects to a network that one can study discretely?
- Can one study the interaction and impact of interaction between various aspects of a network?
- How do organizational, state, and national information policies affect the development and study of networks and the network environment?
- How does one go about studying the networked environment? Do traditional methodologies hold in studying this environment? Does the networked environment require new and/or modified methodologies for systematic study?
- What are the issues, implications, and impacts derived from evaluating networked information services and resources?

Readers will find that these questions recur through the various chapters in this book. While the book does not present definitive answers to the questions, the chapters in the book provide readers with a foundation in understanding evaluation processes, issues, and concerns for the networked environment.

The 1999 ASIS Mid-Year meeting also suggested the wide range of individuals interested in evaluating networks, networked services, and the networked environment. We found that academics, practitioners, researchers in government, network and systems operators, those developing digital libraries, and others had all reached the same conclusion that there was much work yet to be done in the study of networks and the networked environment. Thus, the book is intended to be of interest to a number of different groups and individuals.

BOOK OBJECTIVES

Given this broad interest in topics related to evaluation of networks and networked information services the editors had the following objectives for the book:

- Bring together a range of ideas, studies, approaches, and issues broadly related to evaluating networked information services and resources
- Begin to theorize, conceptualize, and model the networked environment in general and evaluation activities within the networked environment in particular
- Describe current practice, ideas, and methods being used to evaluate networked services
- Assist those developing evaluations of networked services by offering practical examples and techniques for how such evaluations can be done
- Identify key issues and possible solutions to those issues to advance the state of the art in assessing networked services
- Suggest future activities and recommendations that can enhance the quality and impact of evaluations of networked services

Ultimately, the book hopes to draw increased attention to the need for and importance of evaluating networked information services. Equally important is to demonstrate that considerable thinking about these topics is occurring, innovative ideas and techniques are being tried, and new approaches to assess networked services are also being developed.

KEY THEMES AND ISSUES

While this book provides readers with models, tools, techniques, and specific examples of network evaluation activities, it is evident that a number of key themes and issues remain regarding network assessment studies. Identified below are several of these themes.

Rapidly Evolving and Changing Context for Evaluation

The networked environment is one that continually evolves and changes—quickly. As soon as one gets a sense of understanding the technical and social aspects of a particular network or network service, the underlying technology changes, thus substantially changing the interactivity and social structures enabled through technology. As such, researchers and practitioners must be in a constant state of experimentation—experimentation in methods, experimentation in analysis, and experimentation in research design.

The need for experimentation in this evolving field is critical if we are to develop successful evaluation methods. But a corollary of the rapidly changing nature of the field is the need to discard methods and approaches that had been useful in the past but may no longer be appropriate as the technology and services change in the networked environment. Perhaps equally important is determining *when* such methods are no longer useful and when new methods are necessary.

Network Evaluation Requires New and Different Methodologies

The networked environment raises questions regarding traditional positivist approaches to research assumptions, operationalizations, and analysis. While researchers and practitioners should strive to produce valid and reliable research results, the drive for valid and reliable results should not come at the expense of developing new and different methodologies (perhaps) better suited to assessing networked services and resources.

The papers in this book suggest that multi-method approaches and approaches that draw from different epistemologies of scientific research may offer the best chance for innovative evaluation methods in the networked environment. Ethnographic and more naturalistic approaches are but one avenue needing exploration. Also, how best to wed together different types of approaches to offer a more comprehensive assessment of networked services still requires considerable work.

Moreover, as new and innovative methods develop, there will be a need for the training of research professionals in the use, application, and analysis based on such techniques. Such needs will necessitate a rethinking of traditional research methodology courses as well as other means of imparting research methodology expertise. Unfortunately, few educational programs specifically appear to provide education and training in evaluating networked services. Professional associations as well as various educational institutions will need to address this issue if the field is to move forward.

Cross-Discipline Education and Training

The chapters in the book indicate the multi-disciplinary skills required for successful evaluation research. These disciplines include library and information science, telecommunications, communications, public policy and administration, information policy, research methods, management, computer science, and information technology. Few, if any, research programs provide comprehensive education and training activities that cut across these disciplines to prepare evaluators of networked information services and resources.

Thus, successful evaluation of networked services will need to draw upon a team of individuals who bring with them knowledge and expertise from a number of areas. As has been seen in the evaluation efforts of the National Science Foundation-funded Digital Libraries program, learning how to communicate across these disciplines can be a formidable task. Nonetheless, more cross-disciplinary approaches to evaluating networked services are likely to be necessary in the future.

Convincing Organizations of the Importance of Evaluation

A clear theme throughout the book is that of convincing organizations of the value and importance of evaluation activities and the need for an ongoing *program* of evaluation. Despite demonstrated benefits to organizational development, planning, and decision making, some organizations continue to view evaluations negatively—something akin to an audit. The burden still remains on researchers and practitioners who advocate the benefits from evaluation activities to convince organizations to participate willingly in, fund, and plan for assessments of their networked services and resources.

Evaluators can ease this *burden* by offering specific recommendations for how to implement and use the evaluation to improve organizational performance, to increase the usefulness of networked services to users, to reduce or better manage network costs, etc. Too often an evaluation report simply offers evaluation findings without clearly indicating specific options and recommendations that, based on the findings, can improve significantly the overall performance of the network or the usefulness of network services to network users. Evaluations of networked services must offer solutions and recommendations if they are to be seen as valuable to the host organization.

Integrating Technical and Social Evaluation Research Perspectives

Another important theme in the book is the need to integrate the technical and social/behavioral aspects of evaluation of networked services. To some degree, we find evaluations of networked services focus on one view or the other and provide a limited integration of the two perspectives. For example, assessing networked services based on log file analysis alone (technical evaluation) fails to provide the managerial, behavioral, and political context in which those networked services have been provided. Similarly, conducting focus groups of how customers use networks (social evaluation approach) alone fails to determine how the systems configuration and technical infrastructure affects use of the network.

Developing such integrative research perspectives when evaluating networked services is difficult but necessary. Returning to other themes in the book, the need for experimentation and innovation in network services evaluation design to best integrate these perspectives will require considerable additional work. Nonetheless, until these perspectives are better integrated, we will not have realistic and meaningful evaluations of networked services.

Networked Information Services Evaluation: Not an Exact Science

It may be necessary to reconsider notions of precision in measurement and precision in findings and recommendations while studying networked information services. A number of authors in this book suggest that it may be necessary to reassess traditional ideas of precision, validity, and reliability in networked services evaluation. Indeed, the best that researchers may be able to offer, currently, is a good estimate of the quality, use, and impact of networked services. Nonetheless, having good estimates of quality, use, and impact is certainly better than having no data at all. But one is struck by the trade-offs and level of effort that may be necessary to move beyond measures that estimate quality, use, and impact to measurements with more precision.

Need for Additional Research

This book underscores the fact that we do not have the answers to many key research questions in the assessment of networked information services and resources. Indeed, researchers and practitioners are only at the beginning stages of identifying models, methods, assessment techniques, and the implications of findings through such evaluation techniques and approaches. There is a tremendous amount of work yet to do in this rich research area. Researchers rarely get to engage in such a new and exciting area of research that they can shape and guide.

But to shape this emerging area of evaluation research, funding agencies such as the National Science Foundation (NSF), the Defense Advanced Research Projects Agency (DARPA), the Institute for Museum and Library Services (IMLS), foundations, and others need to recognize the importance of incorporating an evaluation component as part of any project or study. The authors' experience is that minimally, 7-10 percent of a total project effort should be dedicated to project or program evaluation. Without such ongoing evaluation future researchers will not have the support to develop innovative evaluation efforts for networked services.

In addition, managers of networked services should also provide direct support to staff to conduct evaluation research for new and ongoing networked programs and services. To implement new networked services without such an evaluation component is poor management at best and mismanagement at worst. Until there is ongoing and meaningful support to conduct and experiment with evaluation methods and techniques to assess networked services we will not be able to successfully plan and develop the next generation of such services.

ORGANIZATION OF THE BOOK

This book presents several views on the evaluation of networked information resources and services—evaluation frameworks, methodologies, techniques, policy, and key issues for future investigation and research. In particular, the book is divided into five themed sections:

Perspectives on Network Evaluation: Frameworks. In this section, Geoffrey Ford, Eliza T. Dresang and Melissa Gross, Ann Peterson Bishop, et al., and R. David Lankes identify several frameworks for assessing the networked environment in general, and information services and resources in particular. The chapters by the authors approach evaluation frameworks from differing user communities, assessment criteria, and assessment goals and objectives.

Perspectives on Network Evaluation: Methodology. William E. Moen, Joe Ryan, et al., and Jonathan Lazar and Jennifer Preece provide readers with a variety of network assessment and evaluation methodologies—electronic surveys, technical standards for interoperability, and multi-method approaches to determine and apply network statistics and performance measures. Each chapter approaches the study of network information services and resources differently, from an underlying and often transparent technical infrastructure to the online assessment of virtual communities to user-based qualitative and quantitative methods.

Perspectives on Network Evaluation: Usability. A specific user-based technique to assessing networked information services and resources is usability. Through evaluating the use, usefulness, and usability of specific aspects of networked information services and resources, evaluators can determine the utility of those services and resources. Carol A. Hert, Joseph Janes, and Jeffrey H. Rubin demonstrate a number of techniques—with direct user contact and unobtrusively through system usage—with which to assess the usability of networked services and resources.

Perspectives on Network Evaluation: Policy. Philip Doty provides an information policy perspective on assessing the networked environment. By describing the policy environment in general, and networked policy environment in particular, Doty lays a foundation for evaluating networked information services and resources in a policy context. Charles R. McClure and J. Timothy Sprehe describe a particular information policy assessment project through their work in developing performance measures for federal agency Web sites. Together, these chapters identify the complexities of network evaluation activities in an evolving policy environment.

Perspectives on Network Evaluation: Future Directions. The book concludes with a forward-looking chapter by Clifford Lynch. Lynch identifies a number of areas for future research regarding evaluating networked information services and resources. Also, Lynch reviews a number of issue areas that require resolution for continued progress in understanding network use and usage in a variety of areas—conceptual, methodological, and philosophical. Finally, Lynch issues researchers and practitioners a number of challenges to consider when conducting research and implementing networked information services and resources.

In all, these chapters demonstrate to readers the importance, complexity, and issues surrounding the evaluation of the networked environment in general, and network-based services and resources in particular. Clearly, a range of additional topics and issues can be addressed in a book such as this. However, the book offers a first step in describing evaluation approaches, identifying selected issues, and offering next steps for future evaluation activities.

EXTENDING EVALUATION RESEARCH FOR NETWORKED SERVICES

Organizations and governments at all levels are committing considerable resources to developing networked services—and this commitment is likely to continue to grow. As more services and resources are put in the networked environment there will be an increased need for more, better, and rapid evaluation of those networked services. The sense that simply putting a service or a resource *up on the network* is in and of itself *a good thing* requires reassessment. The usefulness, quality, and impact of such services and resources still require attention. Ongoing *programs* of evaluation of networked services will only increase in importance in the years ahead.

The stage is set for continued progress for network information services and resources evaluation activities. This book is but a first step in presenting a number of perspectives on what it means to conduct evaluation studies in the networked environment. Currently, evaluation efforts in this area are only in their infancy. Continued work in this area will undoubtedly lead to a greater understanding of the networked environment—something to which researchers and practitioners will look forward.

Chapter 1

Theory and Practice in the Networked Environment: A European Perspective

Geoffrey Ford

ABSTRACT

Forces influencing evaluation generate four approaches: theoretical, analog, dirigiste (French for interventionist), and pragmatic. The main measures proposed or used are evaluated against the criterion of usefulness. A synthesis shows the convergence of interest of funders, professionals and users, and the gaps needing to be filled. Transatlantic collaboration in user evaluation is recommended.

INTRODUCTION

This chapter analyzes some initiatives that illustrate European approaches to performance measurement in the networked environment. These are placed in the context of earlier work on the evaluation of library and information services. I will show that the initiatives in this area derive from three principle forces that influence library activities, and how the influence of these forces converge. Some tentative comparisons are drawn between European and U.S. activities. The already well-developed globalization of the library environment makes it especially important that the North American and European communities be aware of each others activities and understand their differing points of view.

Historical Background

Performance measurement and evaluation of library and information services and procedures have a long history in Europe, in all types of libraries. No single text gives an overview of European activity: from pre-networked days works by Hawgood and Morley (1969), Buckland (1975), Harris (1987), and Winkworth (1991) are representative. *The Effective Academic Library* (Joint Funding Councils Ad-hoc Working Group on Performance Indicators for Libraries, 1995), gives a framework for evaluation and includes a set of more than 30 indicators. Barton and Blagden (1998) takes up the issue of data quality. Ward, et al. (1995) is a comprehensive compilation of measures that represents the state of the art of performance measurement in Europe in the mid-1990s. The proceedings of the University of Northumbria international conferences (1995, 1998, 2000) are rich sources for exploring the take up of ideas (not just in Europe).

In 1992, the national funding bodies for publicly funded universities in the United Kingdom commissioned a study on the provision of library services in universities. The report (Joint Funding Councils Libraries Review Group, 1993), named after its chairman the Follett Report, led directly to the publication of *The Effective Academic Library*, and more importantly spawned the Electronic Libraries programme (eLib, 1993). A number of experimental services and studies were funded to explore all aspects of providing library services in the networked environment, and a useful summary of issues has been published (Rusbridge, 1998), and there is an evaluation report available (Whitelaw and Joy, 2000).

Forces Affecting Evaluation

As with all services, whether or not in the networked environment, the purpose of measurement of any kind depends on the perspective of the evaluator. The three principle forces that influence activities in libraries are the funding bodies, the professional librarians, and the users. Most initiatives in performance measurement come from the funding bodies and the professionals. Some European interest has been generated by professional managerial considerations, some from a more theoretically based research perspective. Much effort has been devoted to standardizing methods, and over the years statistical reporting and compilations of statistics have grown more sophisticated, so that library managers and funding bodies have now respectable amounts of data to inform planning and decision making, such as the Chartered Institute of Public Finance and Accounting (CIPFA) (2000), LIBECON (2000), and the Standing Conference of National and University Libraries (SCONUL, 2000). Some librarians at least have used performance measurement in the context of evaluating the contribution of libraries to the implementation of public policy (Giappiconi, 1998).

The approach to evaluating the networked environment has been evolutionary, and sometimes slow. Librarians often find their colleagues in computing services slow to apply the concepts of performance measurement, and the difficulties of establishing what a statistical count of a computer transaction or event actually means can prove challenging. Discussions between librarians and Information Technology (IT) personnel about statistics have often been characterized by a healthy degree of skepticism (Goldberg, 1997).

The three forces—funders, librarians, and users—have generated four approaches to performance measurement in Europe: the theoretical (librarians, taking account of users), analog (librarians and users), dirigiste (funders), and pragmatic (librarians, funders and users).

THEORETICAL APPROACH

The theoretical approach comes from attempts by professional librarians to define a *model* of the library in the electronic environment. Working on this assumption, models have been developed for networked libraries (Owen and Wiercx, 1996), and for hybrid libraries (Dempsey, et al., 1999). A useful and accessible formulation of a model applicable to traditional, networked, and hybrid libraries was developed by Brophy and Wynne (1997). The authors focus on the manager's requirements for performance measurement. They distinguish between three types of decision making:

- Operational management
- Forward planning
- Evaluation and review

The last of these types of decision making, they suggest, is well served by the kinds of indicators described in the analog approach (below). For forward planning, simple measures of use and indicators of market penetration are needed, which are not specific to the networked environment. For operational management, a range of measures are suggested (see Table 1.1).

Some of these (OM.1/3/4/6/10/11) are simple measures of use. It is not clear whether a manager would want OM.10 and OM.11 to be high or low: too many pages of print could be inefficient, and too many enquiries could signify inadequate user training or poorly designed interfaces. OM.2/5/12 are clearly relevant. OM.7/8/9/13 are helpful to a manager, as it is clear when upward or downward trends are needed. OM.14 is another puzzle: should a manager strive to make this high or low, and how could that be done?

This theoretical model underpinned the early work of the EQUINOX (2000) project, and has led to the formulation of a new generic model (Brophy, 2000). He starts from the premise (surely uncontroversial) that the library is an intermediary between the user and the information universe.

Table 1.1: Measures and Indicators for Operational Management

	Function	Measure or indicator
OM.1	Resource discovery	Sessions per service per month
OM.2		User satisfaction with service results
OM.3	Resource delivery	Items downloaded per service per month
OM.4		Number of *hits* per service per month
OM.5	Resource utilisation	User satisfaction with resource utilisation tools
OM.6		Percentage of users using each tool
OM.7	Infrastructure provision	Queuing times for access to workstations
OM.8		Downtime (as % of total time) per month
OM.9		Availability (as % of attempted accesses) per month
OM.10		Pages of print per month
OM.11		Number of enquiries received per day
OM.12		User satisfaction with help desk service
OM.13	Resource management	Number of sessions on each service/subscription cost
OM.14		Number of help desk enquiries per staff day

In this model, everything except the user universe and Information universe represents the functions and processes that must be strategically and operationally managed. There is much thoughtful analysis underlying the model but, to be useful in performance measurement, it requires a third dimension, which is finance (see Figure 1.1).

Some User Considerations

To this point, I have concentrated on performance as measured from the library manager's perspective. The end user has figured as a bit player, the originator of a session, an enquiry or a request, someone whose opinion is polled or

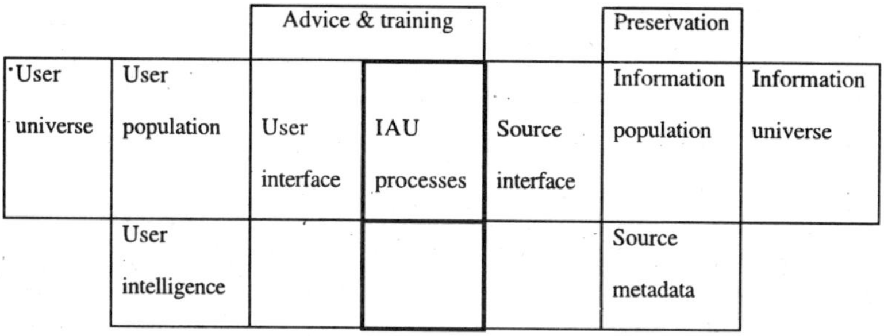

User intelligence: data on individual users

IAU processes: Information access and use processes (browse, discover, locate, request, etc.)

Figure 1.1: The Generic Library Model

canvassed to establish the overall level of satisfaction with a service. But the user has other concerns, which operate at a different level. The advent of the Internet and the World Wide Web has exposed to end users the scale of the information universe. The search engine is such an important information access process that evaluation from the users' perspective is becoming increasingly important. A recent analysis of methods (Oppenheim, et al., 2000) recommends a set of 15 criteria against which Web search engines should be judged. Some of these, such as *options for display of results* are descriptive, but some of the criteria qualify as indicators of performance, that arguably represent the users' point of view (see Table 1.2).

Precision and recall are analogs of those used for many years, particularly by information science researchers, to judge retrieval effectiveness of indexing systems. The difficulty of measuring recall in the Web context (it is impossible to calculate the number of potentially relevant items on the Web that satisfy any specific search query) has led to the concept of relative recall (Clarke and Willett, 1997). In this method, the individual outputs of different searches for the same query are inspected for relevance, and then these results are pooled. The performance of individual search engines is then assessed relative to each other using this pooled set.

To be useful, indicators U.1/2/4/5 need to be calculated regularly by independent auditors, with comparative figures published. Who will do this? A succession of graduate students perhaps. U.3 is a difficult measure: It would be affected by too many components (PC, modem speed, line speed, server capacity, etc.) for it to be meaningful. U.6 would be dependent on the user's own

Table 1.2: Performance Indicators for WWW Search Engines

	Indicator	Definition	Measurement method
U.1	Precision	Ratio of relevant items retrieved to all items retrieved	Relevance judgments made by users
U.2	Relative recall	Algorithm	Relevance judgments by users
U.3	Speed of response	Mean time between initiating search and display of first page of results	Random sampling
U.4	Proportion of dead or out of date links	Ratio of dead or out of date links to all hits	Random sampling of pages
U.5	Proportion of duplicate hits	Ratio of duplicate hits to all hits	Simple count
U.6	Overall quality of results	Rated by users	(for example) Likert scale
U.7	Effectiveness	Algorithm combining number of hits scoring 100%, % score for each hit, and number of items retrieved	Users assign % score to each hit

search strategy and U.7, being an artificial construct, would be difficult for the individual user to interpret.

A measure of potential interest for authors as well as managers and users is the Web Impact Factor (Web-IF). The Web-IF is defined as

> the number of pages linking to a site or area of the Internet divided by the number of pages in that site or area (Ingwersen, 1998).

Web-IFs have been calculated for Web hosts and domains, and the method appears to have some internal consistency. The Web-IF is a relatively crude indicator in practice owing to the variable (and limited) coverage of the Web by search engines (Smith, 1999; Thelwall, 2000).

In summary, the indicators of performance of search engines and the Web-IF seem destined to stay in this theoretical section since they have yet to achieve general recognition as useful.

The strength of the theoretical approach is that it is intellectually satisfying and can be elaborated in a coherent fashion. It readily identifies the areas where work is needed and enables existing work to be placed in a common context. The weakness is that it may fail to engage the funding bodies and the users and, thus, be ignored.

ANALOG APPROACH

The analog method is used by professional librarians looking for measures which parallel those used to assess performance in more conventional libraries.

One of the supporting studies in the eLib programme was an attempt to define needs for management information for electronic libraries (Brophy and Wynne 1997). This assumed that most libraries were going to be *hybrid*—that is active in both print and electronic roles. The project sought indicators which were analogous to those in *The Effective Academic Library*, while also identifying additional indicators where it seemed necessary. The indicators identified were in five categories:

- *P1 Integration*, identifying the level of integration between the mission, aims, and objectives of the institution and those of the library service
- *P2 User satisfaction* with different aspects of the library service
- *P3 Delivery* of service outputs
- *P4 Efficiency* relating outputs to costs
- *P5 Economy* relating resources to Full-Time Equivalent (FTE) student numbers, a long-standing favorite of funding bodies

The size of a library's printed collections has no direct analog in the networked environment. To quote,

> In theory a Conspectus style approach would be rewarding, in which the library's access arrangements were mapped against an authoritative list of possible information sources and services ... the nearest surrogate available to UK academic libraries might be the full set of JISC data services: these have been selected by expert panels for their relevance and are potentially available to all institutions. (Brophy and Wynne, 1997, p. 61)

The Joint Information Systems Committee (JISC), is a U.K. national body that among other things negotiates on behalf of the university sector to acquire access rights to data sets and services at favorable terms. This explains the suggested indicator P3.7A Proportion of JISC data sets available to users. This indicator is by definition only useful in the U.K. context. For more general use, other external services and locally mounted data sets could be included in the statistic.

Table 1.3: Performance Indicators for the Academic Electronic Library

	Indicator	Analogue of or Extension of
P.2.6	User satisfaction with the IT infrastructure	User satisfaction
P.3	Electronic databases—examples of availability targets	Meeting service standards
P3.6A	PC hours used per annum/FTE students	Library study hours/FTE student
P3.7A	Proportion of JISC datasets available to users	No equivalent—see text
P3.7B	Total major electronic subscriptions	No equivalent—see text
P4.7A	Total library expenditure/PC hours used per annum	Total library expenditure/ Study hours per annum
P4.8A	Total major electronic subscriptions/FTE library staff numbers	Volumes in stock/FTE library staff numbers
P4.9A	Total library expenditure/Total major subscriptions	Total library expenditure/ Volumes in stock
P5.3A	PC hours available per annum per FTE student	Space per FTE student
P5.7A	FTE students per networked PC	FTE students per seat

Of the indicators set out in Table 1.3, P4.7A, P4.8A, and P4.9A are difficult to interpret: They are ratios of numbers that happen to be available. On the other hand, P2.6, P3.6A, P5.3A and P5.7A, taken together, do help to illuminate the possible relationships between service provision and outcomes, which is one of the goals of evaluation. P3.7B is not actually a performance indicator.

In addition to those listed in Table 1.3, a number of *standard* library performance indicators relating to inquiries, information skills training and expenditure can all be adapted to include electronic library considerations.

The analog approach has some superficial attractions since it works from the familiar to the (relatively) unknown. Many people with financial power in publicly funded institutions are still relatively uneasy with the concepts of the networked environment—this applies both to senior professionals and to funding bodies. They often suspect that they are being asked to provide new toys for the geeks or are being held over a barrel by the big corporations. So, the strength of this approach is that it is familiar, which helps to engage both other librarians and funding bodies where the network measures look like those they already use. The weakness is that it takes insufficient account of the differences between the networked and print environments, along with the very differing ways in which the infrastructure affects the provision and use of services.

DIRIGISTE APPROACH

The dirigiste method comes from the desire of funding bodies to ensure that money is spent wisely and that *value for money* is obtained from the expenditure of tax revenues. This builds on the long-standing French government tradition of centralization, a tendency that has been spreading in recent years. (For a Belgian example, see Van de Wiele and Van Vaerenbergh, 2000.) In our context, the most significant development has been the Value for Money Initiative (1998a, 1998b). This U.K. study was intended to identify best practice in monitoring expenditure on and use of information technology. The study identified measures that showed which data ought to be collected to enable demonstration of best value. An interesting part of the resulting document was a series of benchmarks derived from a cross-section of 20 institutions. These are reproduced here with the addition of notation (V.1-V.15) to facilitate reference. The absolute values of the numbers are interesting historically and locally (see Tables 1.4, 1.5).

Data are now collected routinely by directors of IT services in U.K universities to enable the calculation of these indicators.

The financial benchmarks (V.1-V.4) are not useful for evaluation: it is entirely a matter of opinion whether these numbers should be high or low. Some of the operational benchmarks suffer from the same defects as some of the analog measures: V.10/11/12 are merely ratios of numbers that happen to be available. The remaining numbers show one-half of the picture—service provision—and they need to be related to measures of use and satisfaction to be useful. The Value for Money Initiative study does recommend the use of a simple survey technique to identify what is important to users and their perception of current performance, and it gives a directional policy matrix to guide managers' actions.

Since coming to power in May 1997, the Labour government in the United Kingdom has placed increasing emphasis on the provision of networked facilities in schools and libraries and has given a commitment that all public libraries, wherever practicable, will be connected to the Internet by 2002. Underpinning this commitment are national funding initiatives contributing to the infrastructure (providing connectivity), digitization of printed materials (providing content), and the training of public librarians in IT skills (providing competencies) (see *Library Technology*, 2000, for a progress report).

Table 1.4: Financial Benchmarks

		Data for 1996-97
	Indicator or measure	**Range**
V.1	Total IS/IT expenditure in relation total institutional expenditure	4.21-5.48%
V.2	Total IS/IT expenditure per student (FTE)	£285-630
V.3	Total IS/IT expenditure per member of staff (FTE)	£1359-2264
V.4	Total IS/IT expenditure per workstation (PC, Mac, etc.)	£876-1688

It is natural that the government should seek an evaluative framework as well. Draft standards for public libraries have recently been published (Department of Culture, Media, and Sport, 2000), and these include reference to application of the new information and communication technologies. Two relevant standards, which can be expressed as performance indicators, are found in Table 1.6: In this context, the term population means resident population—those people who reside within the area of the local government area (U.S. = legal population)—not the enhanced population, which includes potential daytime users who commute from surrounding areas. The interesting thing about these standards is that a lower level has been set, called the Intervention level. Any library that fails to meet the Intervention level will have to demonstrate that it has an achievable strategy for gaining the required level of service within three years.

The great advantage of these indicators is that they are few in number, easy to understand, and make it abundantly clear what has to be done to meet the target.

The strength of the dirigiste approach is that managers know exactly what is required of them. The weakness is that funding bodies are politically driven, can concentrate on only a few issues at a time, and those issues may change with time.

PRAGMATIC APPROACH

I have already mentioned the EQUINOX project. This is funded by the European Union (EU) in the latest stage of a programme of work to identify appropriate indicators for libraries and to develop software tools for reporting and analysis. Among the specific objectives of the EQUINOX project are the following:

- To develop an integrated software tool which will assist European librarians to manage increasingly hybrid (i.e., traditional print-based and electronic) libraries in an effective and efficient manner

Table 1.5: Operational Benchmarks

		Data for 1996-97
Indicator or measure		**Range**
V.5	Number of staff to a staff work station	0.9-1.4
V.6	Number of academic staff to an academic staff workstation	0.66-1.21
V.7	Number of administrative staff to an administrative workstation	0.83-1.3
V.8	Number of students to a student workstation	7.9-13.4
V.9	Hours of availability of workstations in open access computer rooms per student, per year	93-215
V.10	Number of workstations per IS/IT staff member	30-53
V.11	Number of workstations supported by the central IS/IT department per member of the central IS/IT department staff	13-42
V.12	Number of software applications supported by the central IS/IT department per member of the central IS/IT department staff	0.64-1.95
V.13	Number of hours of introductory IT skills training provided to students by the central IS/IT department per student	0-0.04
V.14	Number of hours of user support provided to staff by the central IS/IT department per member of staff	0.22-3.44
V.15	Number of hours of user support provided to students by the central IS/IT department per student	0.13-0.67

Table 1.6: Indicators for Public Libraries

	Indicator or measure	Standard	Intervention level
PL.1	Percentage of service points with access to online catalogue	100%	60%
PL.2	Number of work stations per thousand population	0.7	0.35

- To develop a standard set of performance indicators for the hybrid library and to move towards international agreement on this set

The project has grown from the work on academic libraries reported above (Brophy and Wynne, 1997). In the interests of standardization, the project team have sought to relate the indicators to those familiar with librarians, and in particular those described by the International Standard Organization (ISO, 1998). The indicators now being tested are listed in Table 1.7.

Around 30 libraries have been engaged in testing the methods of data collection. This project is a good example of how professional librarians, both managers and researchers, have combined to produce an internationally acceptable set of measures that have been refined by field testing.

E.1 needs no comment. E.2/3/5/6/8/9 are the kind of indicators that managers like: They make it clear what direction the trend should go. E.10 is in the nature of a warning light, showing that something needs investigation. E.4 is difficult to interpret; given that downloading may incur per transaction costs to the library, the manager would want to be assured that the documents downloaded were actually useful. Similarly, E.12 shows that it should be the aim to deliver services that are intuitive to use, and having a lot of people perceiving the need to be trained could be a sign of failure. E.7 is a problem because it is not clear whether it should be a high or low figure. E.11 is not a measure of performance at all.

Publishers Get Interested

A subset of the pragmatic approach is driven by the owners of proprietary information seeking revenue to satisfy their stockholders. Increasing amounts of content are available on the Internet, and newspaper publishers have been active in research on the use made of the electronic environment. News International, the publishers of *The Times* and *Sunday Times* (both of London) are one group, and some results of investigations are in the public domain

(Nicholas, et al., 1999). The paper discusses some of the methodological problems in collecting data on the use of Web sites and suggests some simple use measures:

- How many users (individual or corporate) use the site per hour, day, week, year
- How many visits users make per hour, day, week, etc.
- How many pages users view per hour, day, week, etc.
- How much time the site/page is used per hour, day, week, etc.

These are of course only the basic statistical measures, and more work needs to be done to establish meaningful indicators of performance. Libraries are interested in this area because of the trend towards replacing print journals by electronic versions: For the first time, data on individual article usage are being collected routinely. Elsevier, for its ScienceDirect service count every mouse click that results in a download of a piece of information. It analyzes the data by type of Web page accessed, ranks the journals in order of popularity, and so on. These data, supplied to subscribing libraries, will be used to generate performance indicators at the level of the individual journal.

An important part of the pragmatic approach is the direct study of users. Research on use, user behavior and user opinion is so commonplace in the traditional library world that it will obviously be important in the digital world also. Nothing about the digital world precludes the application of standard techniques to gather data, and I will merely draw attention to two examples of European studies (Rusch-Feja and Siebecky, 1999 and Whitelaw and Joy, 2000, Appendix C.3).

The strength of the pragmatic approach is that the data exist, and it is easy to prepare a cookbook to tell service managers how to collect and analyze these data. The weakness is the converse: Important aspects may be ignored because data on them cannot be collected routinely.

SYNTHESIS

This rapid overview of the European scene shows a certain amount of convergence of ideas on the performance indicators that are needed and, hence, the kinds of data that need to be collected. Table 1.8 summarizes the situation, using the categories adapted from those originally developed for U.K. academic libraries.

This classification helps to show how the interests of users, funders and professionals converge around some common values. For example, in the *Delivery* category, the measures have been specified by *funders* (PL, V) and *professionals* (E, OM, P) and all provide information that is arguably of interest to *users*.

Table 1.7: Performance Indicators for the Electronic Library

(after EQUINOX, 2000; notation amended)

	Indicator	Category
E.1	Percentage of the population reached by electronic library services	Delivery: subset of ISO 11620 B2.1.1
E.2	Number of sessions on each electronic library service per member of the target population	Delivery
E.3	Number of remote sessions on electronic library services per member of the population to be served	Delivery
E.4	Number of documents and entries (records) downloaded per session for each electronic library service	Delivery
E.5	Cost per session for each electronic library service	Efficiency
E.6	Cost per document or entry (record) downloaded for each electronic library service	Efficiency
E.7	Percentage of information requests submitted electronically	Delivery
E.8	Library computer workstation use rate	Delivery: subset of ISO 11620 B.2.9.2
E.9	Number of library computer workstation hours available per member of the population to be served	Economy
E.10	Rejected sessions as a percentage of total attempted sessions	Delivery
E.11	Percentage of total acquisitions expenditure spent on acquisition of electronic library resources	Financial ratio
E.12	Number of attendances at formal electronic library service training sessions per member of the target population	Delivery

If a measure is to be useful, you must

- know what the measure is for;
- know whether high values are good or bad; and
- know what to do to move it in the desired direction.

As I have commented throughout, some of these measures fail the test of usefulness.

In a further attempt at synthesis, the measures and indicators which have been developed or used in Europe are related to the model developed by Bertot and McClure (1998) in their study of public libraries in the United States.

If my interpretation of the model is correct, then the clustering of measures at the left-hand side is suggestive. It demonstrates graphically that specific measures of quality, impact, and usefulness are still largely awaiting definition.

SOME COMPARISONS

The United States is a single country, with a population of over 270 million sharing a common language and educational system, in which information policy has been on the agenda of the national government for many years. The federal funding agencies sponsor digital libraries research but not the development of large-scale library services. The American Library Association (ALA), with its strong membership base, has ample funds with which to disseminate good practice and influence large numbers of professional librarians and funding bodies of individual libraries; the Association of Research Libraries (ARL) funds its own investigations.

By contrast, Europe, albeit with a population of 370 million, is fragmented, with no common language, common educational system, or common funding models for public and academic libraries although governments fund almost all universities. Not all governments have recognized the need for national information policies, so government funding for information research and development is not guaranteed. However, within individual countries it is possible to tackle centralized projects that would be impossible in the United States. Thus, in the United Kingdom, the JISC provides advanced services to higher education, and a common framework for evaluation of these services can be imposed. As already noted, public library standards can also be imposed. Similar initiatives are possible in other European countries with centralizing tendencies. However, there is no pan-European membership body for library professionals, no pan-European equivalent of the ARL. Bodies like the U.K. Standing Conference of National and University Libraries depend on the voluntary efforts of its members. The European Community (EC), with 15 member nations has potential to fill some gaps, but there are political problems in defining EC-wide information policies. The funds provided by the EC for developing

Table 1.8: Summary of Performance Indicators and Measures for the Networked Environment

Category	Generic description	Indicators and measures
User satisfaction	Satisfaction with infrastructure Satisfaction with tools Satisfaction with support Satisfaction with service results	P2.6 OM.5 OM.12 OM.2, U.1, U.2, U.6
Delivery	Meeting service standards Service usage/population Workstation usage/population Workstation-hours/population Availability of infrastructure Availability of data sets Attendance at IT training/population IT training hours/population User support/population	P.3, PL.1, OM.6, E.1, E.10, U.3 E.2, E.3, E.4, E.7 P3.6A V.9 OM.7, OM.8, OM.9, E.8 P3.7A E.12 V.13 V.14, V.15
Efficiency	Expenditure/workstation usage Electronic resources/staff numbers Expenditure/electronic resources Expenditure/workstation Workstations/IT staff Usage/expenditure Usage/IT staff	P4.7A P4.8A, V.12 P4.9A V.4 V.10, V.11 OM.13, E.5, E.6 OM.14
Economy	Workstation-hours/population Population/workstations Expenditure/population	P5.3A 5.7A, V.5, V.6, V.7, V.8, PL.2, E.9 V.2, V.3
Financial ratio	Network expenditure/total expenditure Electronic acquisitions spend/total acquisitions expenditure	V.1 E.11
Statistics	Basic counts	OM.1, OM.3, OM.4, OM.10, OM.11

Table 1.9: Mapping Indicators to the Network Component Model

	Network Evaluation Criteria						
Network Component	**Extensiveness**	**Efficiency**	**Effectiveness**	**Service Quality**	**Impact**	**Usefulness**	**Adoption**
Technical Infrastructure	V.5, V.6, V.7, V.8, V.9 PL.2 E.8, E.9, E.10 P3.6A, P5.3A P5.7A	V.2, V.3, V.4 V.10, V.11, V.12 OM.7, OM.8 P4.7A	P2.6				PL.1
Information Content	OM.1, OM.3, OM.4 P3, P3.7A, P3.7B	OM.13 P4.8A, P4.9A	OM.2				
Information Services	OM.6, OM.10 E.2, E.3, E.4	OM.9 E.5, E.6, E.10 U.3, U.4, U.5	OM.5 U.7	U.1, U.2, U.6		E.1	
Support	OM.11	OM.14		OM.12			

models of evaluation have been explicitly directed towards the production of commercially viable software with a Europe-wide appeal (Dare, 1998).

Moreover, there is a difference in philosophy in the approach to many projects. In a typical European project, a small group of experts, or project partners, develops a set of measures; then they test them, perhaps in a wider group of organizations. The partners would almost always be those who were already at the leading edge, so this is a kind of top-down approach. A typical U.S. project (Association of Research Libraries, 2000) would start by surveying what measures are currently in use and seek to build a consensus from the bottom up. Nevertheless, the fundamental concerns of the interested parties remain the same world wide, so that the outcomes of different approaches frequently converge. Thus, the indicators developed by Bertot and McClure, in their public libraries study, are very similar in concept, if not in detail, to those emerging from the EQUINOX project.

NEXT STEPS

Given the global scope of networks and information provision, the convergence of ideas and practice in evaluation is not surprising. A collaborative approach in this field could have benefits.

> There is already a high level of international collaboration in digital libraries. This cooperation takes many forms, both at the grassroots and at a government level. ... The value of this international collaboration lies in the different perspectives that the countries bring. ... International collaboration is always fashionable, but it is expensive

> in time and money. Often it is no more than lip service. The National Science Foundation (NSF), JISC and CNI deserve our thanks for taking practical steps to make it happen (Arms, 2000).

One clear need is for agreement on common definitions of the basic units of measurement (e.g., the session), and the work of the International Coalition of Library Consortia (ICOLC) (1998) provides a basis for this. Another need is the identification of indicators of quality, impact, and value: the measures of interest to users. There is scope for cooperation in approaches to user evaluation by developing standardized tools using the Servqual (Hernon and Altman, 1996) and Priority Research, Ltd. (2000) methods. The ISO Library Performance Indicators Working Group is working on a Technical Report that will bring together examples of current practice in this area and identify the emerging consensus between Europe and the United States. Rapid publication of this will encourage libraries to test appropriate measures.

The JISC and NSF should be encouraged to fund collaboration between U.K. and U.S. academic libraries (through the agencies of SCONUL and the ARL), and they should seek other European partners to ensure that a common approach to evaluation is adopted, building on the work of existing projects, to provide a toolkit of standardized measures and methods that can be applied in a variety of contexts.

ABOUT THE AUTHOR

Geoffrey Ford is Director of Information Services and University Librarian at the University of Bristol. His current research interests are the development of measures for the evaluation of information services and systems.

Mailing address: University Library, Tyndall Avenue, BRISTOL, BS8 1TJ, United Kingdom.

E-mail: G.Ford@bris.ac.uk

REFERENCES

Arms, W. Y. (2000). Editorial: the European connection. D-Lib Magazine, 6 (7/8). (retrieved August 6, 2000 from http://www.dlib.org/dlib/july00/07editorial.html)

Association of Research Libraries. (2000). ARL begins e-metrics project. (retrieved August 16, 2000 from http://www.arl.org/stats/newmeas/emnews.html)

Barton, J. and Blagden, J. (1998). Academic library effectiveness: a comparative approach. Wetherby: British Library. (British Library Research and Innovation Report, 120).

Bertot, J. C. and McClure, C. R. (1998). The 1998 national survey of U.S. public library outlet internet connectivity: final report. Washington, DC: National Commission on Libraries and Information Science.

Brophy, P. (2000). Towards a generic model of information and library services in the information age. Journal of Documentation, 56(2), 161–184.

Brophy, P. and Wynne, P. M. (1997). Management information systems and performance measurement for the electronic library (MIEL2). London: Library Technology Centre.

Buckland, M. K. (1975). Book availability and the library user. New York: Pergamon.

Chartered Institute of Public Finance and Accountancy (CIPFA). (2000). Public library statistics. Actuals. London : CIPFA. (Annual publication)

Clarke, S. J. and Willett, P. (1997). Estimating the recall performance of Web search engines. Aslib Proceedings, 49(7), 184–189.

Dare, J. (1998). Introduction to CAMILE. In University of Northumbria, Department of Information and Library Management, Proceedings of the 2nd Northumbria international conference ... 1997 (pp. 413–415). Newcastle upon Tyne: Information North.

Dempsey, L., et al. (1999). A Utopian place of criticism? Brokering access to network information. Journal of Documentation, 55(1), 33–70.

Department of Culture, Media, and Sport. Libraries, Information and Archives Division. (2000). Comprehensive and efficient—standards for modern public libraries: a consultation paper. London: DCMS.

eLib. (2000). The Electronic Libraries programme. (retrieved June 11, 2000 from http://www.ukoln.ac.uk/services/elib/)

EQUINOX (2000). EQUINOX: Library Performance Measurement and Quality Management System. (retrieved June 11, 2000 from http://equinox.dcu.ie/)

Giappiconi, T. (1998). Performance measurement and management strategy: a public library perspective from France. In University of Northumbria, Department of Information and Library Management, Proceedings of the 2nd Northumbria international conference ... 1997 (pp. 21–29). Newcastle upon Tyne: Information North.

Goldberg, J. (1997). Why Web usage statistics are (worse than) meaningless. Cranfield University Computer Centre. (retrieved June 11, 2000 from http://www.cranfield.ac.uk/stats/#whykeep)

Harris, C. (Ed.) (1987). Management information systems in libraries and information services: proceedings of a conference held at the University of Salford, July 1986. London: Taylor, Graham, Hawgood, J. and Morley, R. (1969). Final report on the project for evaluating the benefits from university libraries. Durham: University of Durham Computer Unit. (OSTI Report, 5069)

Hernon, P. and Altman, E. (1996). Service quality in academic libraries. Norwood, NJ: Ablex.

Ingwersen, P. (1998). Web impact factors. Journal of Documentation, 54(2), 236–243.

International Coalition of Library Consortia (ICOLC) (1998). Guidelines for statistical measures of usage of Web-based indexed, abstracted, and full text resources. (retrieved August 16, 2000, from http://www.library.yale.edu/consortia/Webstats.html)

International Standards Organization. (1998). ISO 11620 Information and documentation—library performance indicators. Geneva: International Standards Organization.

Joint Funding Councils Ad-hoc Working Group on Performance Indicators for Libraries. (1995). The Effective Academic Library: A framework for evaluating the performance of UK academic libraries. London: HEFCE.

Joint Funding Councils Libraries Review Group [Chair: Sir Brian Follett]. (1993). *Joint Funding Councils Libraries Review Group Report*. London: HEFCE.

LIBECON. (2000). Fact sheet. (retrieved August 16, 2000 from http://www.libecon2000.org)

Library Technology. (2000). Special issue: Public libraries. Library Technology, 5(4). (http://sbu.ac.uk/litc/lt/ltcover.html)

Nicholas, D., et al. (1999). Developing and testing methods to determine the use of Web sites: case study newspapers. Aslib Proceedings, 51(5), 144–154.

Oppenheim, C., et al. (2000). The Evaluation of WWW search engines. Journal of Documentation, 56(2), 190–211.

Owen, J. S. M. and Wiercx, A. (1996). Knowledge models for networked library services: final report. Luxembourg: Commission of the European Communities. (Report PROLIB/KMS 10119)

Priority Research Ltd. (2000). Priority software. (retrieved August 14, 2000 from http://195.62.205.54/pb_prsoftware.html)

Rusbridge, C. (1998). Towards the hybrid library. D-Lib Magazine, July/August. (retrieved August 14, 2000 from http://www.dlib.org/july98/rusbridge/07rusbridge.html)

Rusch-Feja, D. and Siebecky, U. (1999). Evaluation of usage and acceptance of electronic journals. D-Lib Magazine, October. (retrieved August 14, 2000 from http://www.dlib.org/october99/rusch-feja/10rusch-feja-summary.html)

Smith, A. G. (1999). A Tale of two Web spaces: comparing sites using Web impact factors. Journal of Documentation, 55(5), 577–592.

SCONUL. (2000) Annual library statistics. London: Standing Conference of National and University Libraries. (Annual publication)

Thelwall, M. (2000). Web impact factors and search engine coverage. Journal of Documentation, 56(2), 185–189.

University of Northumbria. Department of Information and Library Management. (1995). Proceedings of the 1st Northumbria international conference on performance measurement in libraries and information services, 31 August to 4 September 1995. Newcastle upon Tyne: Information North.

University of Northumbria. Department of Information and Library Management. (1998). Proceedings of the 2nd Northumbria international conference on performance measurement in libraries and information services, 7 to 11 September 1997. Newcastle upon Tyne: Information North.

University of Northumbria. Department of Information and Library Management. (2000). Proceedings of the 3rd Northumbria international conference on performance measurement in libraries and information services, 27 to 31 August 1999. Newcastle upon Tyne: Information North.

Value for Money Initiative. (1998a). Information systems and technology management value for money study: national report. London: HEFCE. (retrieved June 11, 2000 from http://www.niss.ac.uk/education/hefce/pub98/98_42.html)

Value for Money Initiative. (1998b). Information systems and technology management value for money study: management review guide. London: HEFCE, 1998. (retrieved June 11, 2000 from http://www.niss.ac.uk/education/hefce/pub98/98_43.html)

Van de Wiele, R. and Van Vaerenbergh, J. (2000). Nationwide implementation of performance measurement in Flanders. In University of Northumbria, Department of Information and Library Management, Proceedings of the 3rd Northumbria international conference ... 1999 (pp. 187-190). Newcastle upon Tyne: Information North.

Ward, S., et al. (1995). Library performance indicators and library management tools (PROLIB/PI). Luxembourg: European Commission, DG XIII E3. (EUR 16483 EN)

Whitelaw, A. and Joy, G. (2000). Summative evaluation of phases 1 and 2 of the eLib. initiative: final report. Guildford: ESYS. (retrieved August 17, 2000 from http://www.ukoln.ac.uk/services/elib/info-projects/phase-1-and-2-evaluation/elib-fr-v1-2.pdf)

Winkworth, I. (1991). Performance measurement and performance indicators. In Jenkins, C. and Morley, M. (Eds), Collection management in academic libraries, (pp. 57–93). Aldershot: Gower.

Notes to pages 10, 12

The draft standards for public libraries (Department of Culture, Media, and Sport, 2000) have now been finalized with some changes from the original. There are now three indicators relevant to the networked environment.

	Indicator or Measure	**Standard**
PL.1	Percentage of libraries open more than 10 hrs per week that have access to online catalogues	100%
PL.2	Total number of electronic workstations available to users per 10,000 population	6
PL.3	Number of visits to the Library Web site per 1,000 population	Not yet determined

The concept of the Intervention level has been abandoned in general, but it is expected that libraries will reach the standard before April 2004. (Department of Culture, Media, and Sport 2001).

ADDITIONAL REFERENCE

Department of Culture, Media, and Sport. Libraries, Information and Archives Division. (2001) Comprehensivem efficient and modern public libraries—standards and assessment. London: DCMS.

Chapter 2

Evaluating Children's Resources and Services in a Networked Environment

Eliza T. Dresang
Melissa Gross

ABSTRACT

No comprehensive model exists for planning or evaluating technology-related services and resources provided to children in public libraries. This chapter proposes an outcome-based model to guide the design, development or purchase, and assessment of networked resources and services for children. The model relies on the tools of strategic planning, market research, and outcome-based evaluation.

Children must use networked resources and services effectively in order to acquire information they need now and to prepare for their futures in the work-force. The public library stands as an institution poised to serve children who range from "illiterate" to highly literate in the use of computer resources. In order to provide this service, public librarians must understand how to plan for and evaluate resources and services for children in a networked environment.

Despite widespread funding for computers in the present and more funds committed for the future, no systematic evaluations have been conducted to date to determine what is happening with networked technology and children in public libraries: if they use it, how they use it, and how to improve that use. In the frenzy to provide funds for computers, software, and Internet access, the impact on the recipients has been largely overlooked. For example, the E-rate was established by the 1996 Telecommunications Act to provide affordable access to the Internet in schools and public libraries. So far, no studies have looked at the impact of this massive infusion of connectedness on children. Studies about networked services typically do not single out children as a user group, nor have they examined whether this is necessary. An assumption seems to have been made that the large-scale input of technology in itself will reduce what is known as the digital divide for youth and produce desired outcomes. The complex factors that lead to either success or failure in a young person's use of networked resources in the journey to information and technology literacy have been largely overlooked.[1]

Not only do no data on the topic exist, but also no comprehensive model for planning or evaluating services and resources related to children's use of technology in public libraries exists. Nor has any set of expected or desired outcomes been developed. And finally, no existing model for non-networked resources and services can be adequately adapted to the evaluation of outcomes in the networked environment.

Because of this void and the need to fill it, we are proposing an outcome-based model for evaluating children's use of networked technology in public libraries. This model relies on the tools of strategic planning, market research, and outcome-based evaluation. It is a process model and easily can be incorporated into a library's normal planning and evaluation cycle. The proposal of this model is the beginning of a planned study of children's use of networked resources in public libraries. This chapter, the first step in this research agenda

- gives a brief historical overview of traditional models and methodologies for assessing children's resources and services in public libraries, including how past evaluation of children's services has related to that of overall services;
- identifies assumptions behind the new evaluation model;
- explains the components of the model and provides an example of how the model can be applied in a specific library setting for each phase of the model; and
- ends with suggestions for what should be done with the model and who should do it.

Definitions

The following operational definitions are employed in this chapter.

- **Children's resources and services:** Those resources and services selected and developed for or accessed by users age 18 and younger.
- **Children's networked resources and services:** Digital information resources and/or services that children access using a library network.
- **Input measures:** The measurement of items that lay the groundwork

for services and resources, e.g., number of networked computer workstations accessible to children.

- **Output measures:** The statistical measurement of use of resources and services, e.g., how many children use networked resources and services in a given time period.
- **Outcome measures:** The measurement of impact on the user, e.g., children's increased competence in use of digital resources.

TRADITIONAL ASSESSMENT OF CHILDREN'S SERVICES

Prior to the 1980s, informal evaluation based on casual observation and best professional judgment were the predominant means of evaluating children's services. Children's resources and services were largely assumed to be good if competent librarians planned or selected them and if children and adults used them with what seemed to be adequate frequency. Any formal evaluation consisted of input measures, e.g., how many books, films, and other media were in the collection (perhaps measured per capita), how much space was in the library, how many professional staff existed, attendance at programs.

During the 1980s, however, accountability in public agencies became a theme. As part of this movement, a specific concentration on evaluation of children's services in public libraries became a topic of concern. In 1989, a five-day Leadership Institute on Evaluation Strategies and Techniques for Public Library Children's Services, funded by the Department of Education, was held at the University of Wisconsin-Madison. Participants at the Institute were state consultants for public library children's services as well as coordinators of children's departments in large metropolitan public libraries and public library systems, and educators of future public children's librarians. Proceedings of this conference provide documentation for the state-of-the-art 15 years ago (Robbins, et al., 1990). Scrutiny of the papers in this volume reveals the following:

- No holistic model for the planning and evaluation of children's services existed at the time. Presenters acknowledged the need to incorporate children's services into the overall library planning process, but note that the children's services department has specific requirements of its own.
- Input measures were emphasized. Some speakers suggested measurable objectives and outputs.
- Methodologies new to the arena of children's services, e.g., interviews, were suggested for determining the impact of media use on children.
- No other mention was made of outcomes or impact on the user. This

document continues to be valuable specifically for the explanation of methodologies adapted for use with children and for its data collection and analysis techniques.

The next step forward in the evaluation of children's services occurred in the 1990s. In 1987, a planning process for public libraries, including roles for public libraries and output measures for public libraries, was published (McClure, et al., 1987). Drawing on this planning and evaluation guide, Virginia A. Walter (1992, 1995) developed output measures for children's and young adult services and tested them in public library settings. With the publication of these documents, the necessity for an adequate level of inputs was not negated, but evaluation shifted to how often the resources available were used on a per capita basis. Assessing whether the resulting numbers are good or bad is again left to the best professional judgment of the librarians. In 1998, the public library planning process was revised and in the place of roles, services responses for the public library were established (Himmel and Wilson, 1998).

With the advent of networked resources and services, it has become clear that neither the identification of service responses nor output measures alone are sufficient evaluative tools. The model proposed in this chapter goes more deeply into the development and application of outcomes and focuses on a methodology that allows stakeholders to influence the standards of measurement. The model uses inputs and outputs to develop indicators of success and focuses on children's use of the digital resources in public libraries. Of particular interest are

- which children are using them (by age, gender, ethnicity, etc.);
- how effectively children are able to use them;
- what children themselves want to get from their use of technology;[2] and
- what the community expects and desires from children's use of digital resources and what is actually taking place.

Why Focus on Children as a User Group?

It is important to develop a specific evaluative method for assessing networked services and resources for children because general performance measures do not provide information on the impact of the use of networked resources and services for children. The following observations indicate that there is a need for this information:

- Much of the commentary and statistical data on the digital divide (lack of access) focuses on children (National Telecommunications and Information Administration, 1998a, 1998b, 1999a, 1999b; Benton Foundation, 2000; Benton Foundation and the EDC/Center for Children and Technology, 2000; The Children's Partnership, 1999).

- Much of the corporate and government funding for technology has been aimed at children. (The Bill and Melinda Gates Learning Foundation, 2000; Telecommunications Act of 1996).
- Much of the legislation and the court cases concerning networked resources and services have focused on alleged protection of children versus their protection under the First Amendment. (Communications Decency Act and its court case Reno v. ACLU, 1997; Child Online Protection Act, 2000; Child Online Privacy Protection Act, 1999; Children's Internet Protection Act 2000).
- Youth are responsible for 60 percent of public library use (Heaviside, 1995). In addition to this statistic there is evidence that many adults are in the public library on behalf of children (Gross, in press), and that the public supports providing technology resources and services for children above all other functions (Benton Foundation, 1996).
- Children are a marginalized user group. Adults talk about them but rarely talk to them either in the planning of resources and services or in their evaluation (Druin, 1999; McNeal, 1987).
- Learning about the impact of children's use of networked resources may provide data for the overall improvement of networked library services (Dresang, 1999; Tapscott, 1998).

Despite widespread recognition in government, industry, and the public of the importance of access to networked digital resources for children and generous funding to provide that access for children in public libraries, no one has attempted to collect or analyze data in order to evaluate children's use of networked resources and services or its impact on them.

ASSUMPTIONS BEHIND THE EVALUATION MODEL

All research and evaluation are based on assumptions. In order for the model we propose to be adopted and adapted successfully, those using it must accept these assumptions:

- Evaluation is continuous;
- Children are competent and seek connectivity;
- Children have a right to have access to information;
- Providing the tools alone is insufficient to close the digital divide and to produce the knowledge workers the future economy will demand;
- Input from children, adults, and organizations interested in children is needed both to develop and evaluate the assessment model;

- Desired outcomes for children's technology use can be identified using a market research approach;
- Strategic planning, market research, and outcome-based evaluation are useful tools for assessing children's use of technology in libraries;
- The library staff and the community stakeholders are fully committed to the process;
- The library can and will seek and commit the necessary resources for the process;
- The library can perform adequate data collection and synthesize findings into statements of desired outcomes.

If these assumptions are accepted, then the model proposed is one that we suggest will be comfortable and profitable for its users.

THE OUTCOME-BASED MODEL: COMPONENTS

As shown in Figure 2.1, the outcome-based model is comprised of four phases:

- Data collection (Phase I)
- Outcome-based assessment criteria development (Phase II)
- Products/services production (Phase III)
- Evaluation (Phase IV)

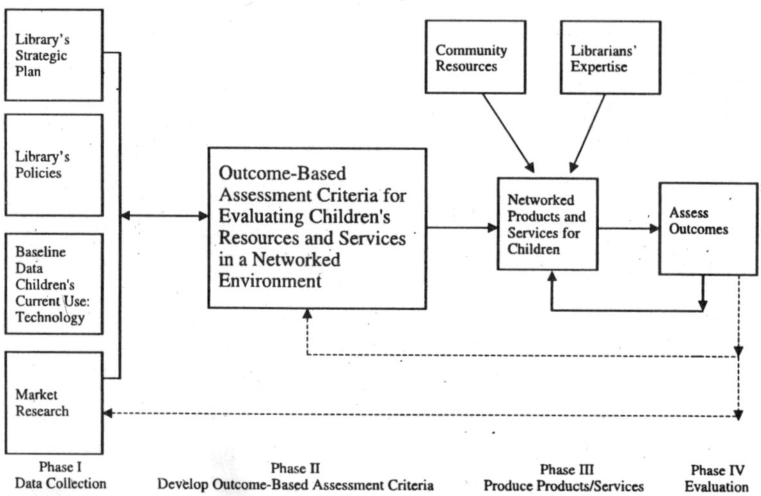

Figure 2.1: Evaluating Children's Resources and Services in a Networked Environment: An Outcome Based Model

Each phase is connected to the others and provides the library with a continuous sense of the extent to which desired outcomes for children are being reached with the networked resources and services the library provides. The model also provides for periodic review of the outcome-based criteria to ensure that the desired benefits it expounds remain synchronized with the needs of children and the perceptions of their advocates in the community.

After an explanation of each phase of the model, a table is presented that provides examples of the components specified in that phase.

Phase I. Data Collection

The outcome-based model begins with the data collection phase, which utilizes the tools of strategic planning, market research techniques, and the collection of baseline data on children's current use of networked products and services in the library. The data collected in Phase I provide the basis for determining the outcome-based criteria, which is developed in Phase II. Phase I also provides important baseline and benchmark data for use in future planning cycles to ensure that the outcome-based criteria remains current and responsive to the needs of children.

The provision of children's resources and services in a networked environment must be integrated into the library's overall strategic plan, just as the provision of other library programs and services are. This is important to ensure that support for these services exists at the highest level in the organization and that the funding, including the commitment of personnel and other needed resources, can be counted on. This means that in all of the steps normally taken to develop the strategic plan, children's networked resources and services must be considered. This includes development of the vision, mission, roles or service responses of the library, and as part of any assessment of the library's strengths, weaknesses, opportunities and threats (SWOTs).

Strategic Planning

It is the function of the library's vision and mission statements to describe the place of the library in the community in terms of benefits to its users and the services it provides (Himmel and Wilson, 1998; McClure, et al., 1987). The vision and mission statements communicate both externally to the community at large and internally to library personnel what the library exists to do. Children's services need to fit within this mantle so that the whole organization can participate in an integrated effort to meet the information needs of the community. Processes like community needs analysis, regular staff interaction with users and other information and social organizations in the community, and the collection of data on library use typically feed the library's understanding of the community's information needs.

The development of vision and mission statements typically occurs early in the strategic planning process. While it is important for children's services to be represented each step of the way, the provision of networked resources and services for children must be specifically represented as well. This must be done to ensure that the commitment and support for children has an integrated place in the library's efforts as a whole. Children's services, including networked services, must be integrated into the planning process, if one currently exists, or included as part of initial planning effort for libraries that are engaging in the process for the first time. This means that when committees are formed to do this work, a representative from the Children's Department must be included as a full participant.

As part of the planning process, the library generally determines what its service responses for the community will be. Himmel and Wilson (1998) outline thirteen potential service responses and some libraries design their own. The choice of service response can affect what happens in the children's room in terms of its networked environment. For instance, the library's decision to support formal learning as a main service response may result in an emphasis on the needs of schoolwork in the provision of children's services. This in turn may lead to a networked environment centered on educational software, World Wide Web links to educational sites, and access to distance education or virtual educational resources. The focus will be on providing homework help and other strategies that support the objectives and curriculums of the local schools.

Choice of service role may also indicate the need for specific kinds of input when it comes time to develop the outcome-based criteria that will be used to design, develop, and evaluate children's resources and services in the networked environment. For instance, an emphasis on formal learning in technology use might indicate the need for outcomes that are tied to improving school performance.

Likewise, as the library assesses its SWOTs, the outcome of that process will also inform what the library wants to do in terms of developing the networked environment and related services for children, the kind of outcomes that can be realistically supported, as well as the kind of outcomes that the library will choose to work toward in service to community needs. For instance, a formal learning service role may allow the library to take advantage of the strength of newly provided technology, but it may also require the library to improve staff training to utilize that technology fully. Likewise, a formal learning service role may allow the library to take advantage of the opportunity to provide a networked environment, when local schools and families have not been able to, and avoid the threat of declining fiscal support by partnering with schools to raise the general educational standard in the community.

Library's Policies

The library's policies, which in turn are influenced by national professional ethics statements and policies set by legislation, must be considered as another input to this process. The policy most germane to the application of the model specifies the library's stance on Intellectual Freedom (IF), usually expressed in a Collection Development or Selection Policy and an Acceptable Use Policy for the Internet (AUP). Guidelines for developing these policies as well as professional ethics statements, all of which support open access for children in libraries, are easily accessible on the American Library Association's Web site. Until late 2000, no national law that curtailed children's access to the Internet in libraries with mandated filtering software had been passed by the U.S. Congress,[3] although numerous pieces of legislation had been proposed. The Children's Internet Protection Act (CIPA) became law as part of the Labor HHS Education Appropriations Bill on December 21, 2000. It requires all libraries receiving federal funds for technology, including the E-rate that supports Internet access, to use Internet filtering software to block obscenity, child pornography, and visual material deemed harmful to minors. Such legislation will have a chilling effect on how children can access and use the Internet. However, prior legislation that had been passed by the U.S. Congress to control (rather than filter) Internet content has been declared unconstitutional. The Communications Decency Act, placing certain restrictions on the Internet, was declared unconstitutional by the Supreme Court on June 26, 1997. On June 22, 2000, the Third Circuit Court of Appeals declared its successor, the Child Online Protection Act, unconstitutional. On March 20, 2001 both the American Library Association and the American Civil Liberties Union filed legal action against CIPA, attempting to block its implementation before the July 1, 2002 date upon which libraries have to state their intention to comply or not. The dynamic nature of the outcome-based model allows it modification when national policies, such as these, and therefore local policies are altered.

Baseline Data

It is critical for libraries to begin the collection of baseline data on children's current use of technology. As noted above, evaluation of children's use of technology is not being widely performed. Most library studies interested in in-house use focus on circulation statistics, program attendance, and reference services. Less work has been done on assessing in-house use of materials, including computers. The use of output measures to evaluate library services has been promoted since the early 1990s. However, output measures tend to look at computers as furniture, focusing more on whether they are being used, than on how, why, and when children use them. Output measures also generally fail to provide data on differences in computer use in terms of age, gender, or ethnic or cultural background. Recent work by Koontz and Jue offers an innovative method to collect baseline data on in-house use of public library resources (1999). Using bar codes and bar code readers (personal digital assistants or PDAs), they were able to code and record in-house use statistics including use of electronic resources at the application level. While some data on children's use of computers were revealed in their investigation, the study they performed was not specifically designed to evaluate children as a user group. It is clear however that their method can be easily adapted to collect in-house data on technology use in the children's room.

Baseline data must include the collection of demographic data such as age, education levels, ethnicity, gender, etc., to determine who is utilizing current resources and services and where gaps in service lie. Children living in poverty, especially those who belong to a minority group and/or live in a rural area, are less likely to have access to computer technology than the general population of children (National Telecommunications and Information Administration. 1998a). A comparison of demographic statistics on children using computers in libraries to the composition of the community is essential to understand how well the public library is serving both users and potential users. This is critical to an overall assessment of outcomes of children's use of computers in a public library setting. These demographic statistics may be incorporated as part of the library's SWOTs.

Market Research

The input box labeled market research data involves collecting much of the same data the library typically does in performing community analysis and needs assessment to support development of its strategic plan. In using a marketing approach however, the process is very focused on the development of products and services specifically intended to meet the needs of a target audience (user or current non-user). The market approach utilizes many familiar techniques, such as the gathering of demographic data and the use of surveys and focus groups, but using them emphasizes the development of specific products and services in partnership with the user, in this case children and adults interested in their welfare. These identified stakeholders in what the library does are asked to provide information about the kinds of products and services they see as valuable and beneficial, how best to deliver the product or service, and how to reach the target audience most effectively to bring these efforts to their attention. The marketing approach can be used to elicit input from children, adults who advocate for children, and representatives of community organizations concerning the outcomes they would like children to experience as a result of their use of and participation in networked resources and related services in the library. For instance, are they interested in the use of networked products in the library to support learning outcomes related to school? If so, what kind of products and supporting programs would they like to see?

Input from children in the design and development of technology products and services in the library and elsewhere has been sorely lacking but can be achieved by including them in the process now (Druin, 1999; McNeal, 1987). On the other hand, the collection of adult views of children's needs has been

Table 2.1: Evaluating Children's Resources

Phase I: Data Collection	
Component	**Example**
Vision Statement	Information for the 21st Century
Mission Statement	To provide equal access to information to city residents and to support their educational and recreational information needs.
SWOTs (Strengths, Weaknesses, Opportunities, Threats)	**S**: Grant from Gates Learning Foundations for technology **W**: Staff training needed to support technology fully. **O**: Schools and public library have history of working together **T**: Declining fiscal support
Service Response	Formal Learning
Baseline Data	Computers heavily used by children. Computers used mainly for email, homework, and games. Children use computers with minimal efficiency and with minimal technical skills.
Market Research	Existing documentation, user survey, and stakeholder focus groups.
Demographic data	40% African-American, 40% White, 15% Hispanic, 5% Other. 10% Unemployed. Less than 10% college educated. Average family income $18,000.
Stakeholder input	Schools can't provide adequate technology to support classroom learning. Low level of computer access in homes. Concerned about children being prepared to enter the workforce. Children express interest in using the Internet.
Library Polices	Acceptable use policy supports unfiltered access to resources for children.

standard practice and continues to be of value (Walter, 1994). Stakeholders like parents, teachers, and organizations such as schools and local community groups serving children must be identified and asked to participate. All of these participants need to contribute to the identification of both the benefits children are currently receiving and the desired outcomes that have not yet been realized from children's use of networked resources and services at the library.

Phase II. Developing the Outcome-Based Assessment Criteria

Phase II uses the data collected in Phase I to develop outcome-based assessment criteria that will be active during the current planning cycle. The objective is to adopt outcomes that take into account the library's place in the community, the resources the library will commit to networked resources and services to children, and the opinions voiced by children and their advocates in the library's service area as discussed in Phase I.

The outcomes to be identified articulate "the result or impact you hope the program to achieve in terms of human benefits" (Institute of Museum and Library Services, 1999). These "may relate to behavior, skills, knowledge, attitudes, values, condition, or other attributes" (United Way, 1996).

The primary question the outcome-based criteria must answer is what do the community and the library want children to achieve in their use of networked resources and services? Desired outcomes may be articulated in terms of impact:

- Skill levels
- Attitudes
- Knowledge
- Behavior
- Status

For instance, formal learning outcomes related to skills might focus on improving critical thinking or increasing technical efficiency, while outcomes related to attitudes might focus on giving children an increased sense of competency in the networked environment. Likewise, outcomes centered on affecting knowledge might concentrate on increasing children's awareness of electronic resources. An example of a desired behavioral outcome is increasing children's ability to learn independently. Status-related outcomes could include efforts to close the digital divide in terms of ethnicity or gender and working to help prepare young people to be the knowledge workers of tomorrow.

The outcome-based assessment criteria can also be developed at various levels of detail depending on the library's needs and experience with strategic planning and marketing techniques. For instance, desired outcomes can be developed to speak to the expected benefits of children's use of networked resources and services in general or they can be developed to reflect desired outcomes at a more detailed level of delivery. In long-term planning it can be beneficial to consider more than one level of desired outcomes that the organization can move toward incrementally as the program is built and as staff gains experience with outcome-based evaluation. It may also make sense to define specifically desired outcomes in terms of children's ability levels in order to most accurately measure changes in skill levels. Table 2.2 provides an example of four levels of one desired outcome a library might want to work toward to support the formal learning service role. The desired outcome in this example is to increase children's ability to use digital resources independently. All of the levels are looking for an increase in the ability of children ages 9–14 to use digital information sources independently when searching for information. At Level I, children are looking for relatively simple facts and are operating at a level of sophistication that is best served by having resources pre-selected for them. Here using resources independently relates to developing the ability to find what they need in a collection of electronic resources tailored for their use. Children's ability to use resources and to move toward the self-selection of resources increases across the four defined levels until at Level IV children are searching for more complex

Table 2.2: Sample Outcome-Based Criteria for Evaluating

Outcome 1: Increased Independent Use of Digital Resources (Behavior)			
Level I: Beginner	**Level II: Advanced Beginner**	**Level III: Intermediate**	**Level IV: Advanced**
Children search for simple factual information in pre-selected digital resources. Children have limited knowledge of the topic they are researching.	Children search for simple factual information using both pre-selected and self-selected digital resources. Children have limited knowledge of the topic they are researching.	Children search for complex information in both pre-selected and self-selected digital resources. Children have basic knowledge of the topic they are researching.	Children search for complex information in a wide range of self-selected digital resources. Children have more in-depth knowledge of the topic they are researching.,
Indicators	**Indicators**	**Indicators**	**Indicators**
• Children go directly to the computer to search for factual information in straightforward sources. • Children ask for information less often when searching for factual information. • Children express more satisfaction with their search results.	• Children self-select more resources. • Children ask for assistance more often as a result of trying to self-select sources. • Children express more satisfaction with their search results.	• Children use more than one resource to locate information. • Children choose multiple types of resources to locate information. • Children ask for assistance more often due to the complexity of their questions. • Children express more satisfaction with their search results.	• Children choose a wider variety of digital resources. • Children ask for assistance less often in searching for information on complex topics. • Children discuss topic they are researching with more sophistication indicating higher level thinking skills. • Children correlate digital information sources with other information sources. • Children express more satisfaction with their search results.

information in sources they have selected themselves. At the fourth level, gaining independence involves the ability to self-identify electronic resources and use them effectively.

This flexibility in determining the outcome-based assessment criteria allows the library to focus on user benefits and recognizes that the defined outcomes may vary from community to community. However, communities may also find that they have similar objectives for their children's use of technology and that some of these can be anticipated. For instance, one goal many share is to have children reach maturity equipped to join the information workforce and to participate fully in the information society. This long-term goal may be supported by shorter-term outcomes that are focused on the development of specific technology-related skills such as the ability to think critically and the development of independent behaviors. However, because communities may share the desire for specific outcomes, they may also benefit from sharing their successes and failures as they develop experience in delivering programs and services using the outcome-based model.

An important part of developing the outcome-based assessment criteria is determining what indicators will be used to determine that the desired outcomes have been obtained. In line with this, Table 2.2 includes examples of indicators a library might use for this purpose at each of the four levels defined in the table. One important indicator associated with all four levels is evidence

Table 2.3: Evaluating Children's Resources

Phase II: Develop Outcome-Based Criteria	
Component	**Example**
Outcomes	Increased competence in use of digital resources (Behavioral)
Indicators	Children express more satisfaction with their search results.
Relationship to Phase I	Outcomes must be based on the data collected.
Specific Resource	Outcome addresses limited availability of networked resources. If digital resources become more widely available in this community identified outcomes should be reassessed.

that the children themselves express increased satisfaction with their use of digital resources.

The development of outcome-based assessment criteria provides a framework for the design, development, and evaluation of products and services whether developed in-house or not. The criteria provide clear definition of objectives to be met that guide the design and development effort during the planning cycle. Products and services thus become oriented from the beginning toward achieving specified goals to improve, enhance, or somehow change the skill level, behavior, or condition of children in terms of using networked resources and services.

Phase III. Products/Services Production

The purpose of Phase III is to answer the question, what will the library do to realize the goals established for children's use of resources and services in a networked environment? In this phase it is time to define the specific products and services to be provided and to relate these to the goals of the outcome-based assessment criteria established for the library based on the mission and goals it has adopted for service to the community.

Because the outcome-based assessment criteria have already been developed, the design of networked products and services takes place within a framework that is focused on achieving specific goals. However, product and service development must also take into account understandings from the community analysis concerning what other similar or complementary resources are available in the community as well as the technical expertise the children's librarians or other children's services staff have or will need to develop.

For example, if the desired outcomes are to increase children's ability to use digital resources independently, one possible service response might be to provide instruction on the use of search engines on the World Wide Web.

Under the structure provided by the outcome-based model, the adoption of technology produced in the marketplace by the library would also be evaluated

Table 2.4: Evaluating Children's Resources

Phase III: Produce Products/Services	
Component	**Example**
Product/Service	Workshops for children on the use of search engines.
Community Support	Local businesses pledge support of the library's children's technology program.
Librarian Expertise	Librarians have excellent searching skills.
Measures	Survey users on changes in confidence levels.
Relationship to Phase II	Products and services developed and/or adopted must help move children toward achieving the outcomes defined in Phase II.
Specific Program Evaluation	Program should result in increased searching skills. If program isn't reaching this goal it will need to be reassessed, modified, or dropped.

for how it might contribute to children's attainment of the specified outcome goals, community resources, and the expertise of the librarian's or other support staff. Using the formal learning example, the decision to purchase software applications or to subscribe to proprietary databases would require an analysis of what they might contribute to attaining the desired outcomes.

Whether the product or service is developed in-house or purchased, it is necessary to be able to identify how it will produce the changes the library hopes to achieve in terms of skills, knowledge, attitude, and/or behavior as relates to the outcome-based criteria established in Phase II.

Assessing Product and Service Outcomes

As part of the product development phase the question of how to evaluate the impact of these products and services must be determined. This entails establishing what the measures, data sources, and data collection points will be. "Measures are opinions, qualities, actions, circumstances or other factors that represent the outcomes" the products or services are intended to provide (Institute of Museum and Library Services, 1999, p.14). They are used to determine whether the desired effect(s) are achieved. For instance, one measure of attitude change is the percent of users who feel an increased sense of competency in the Web-based environment.

Once measures are identified, decisions such as how to collect the data must be made. This choice can include the use of interviews, standardized tests, surveys, or other data collection methods. At this time it is also a good idea to determine when and how often data will be collected to monitor the effectiveness of the networked products and services and to evaluate the effort as a whole. Data collection intervals will vary depending on the nature of the product or service being provided. For instance, when one is providing instruction in the use of search engines it may make sense to collect data at the end of the program to see what changes in attitudes the children evidence. If changes in skill levels are being evaluated pretests and posttests may be needed to evaluate the children's progress.

Phase IV. Evaluation

Use of the outcome-based assessment criteria model means that the evaluation effort is a continuous one. Products and services are developed with outcomes, indicators, and data collection plans in mind. This is purposefully done because the goal of outcome-based evaluation is "not only to demonstrate what works, but also to improve programs" (W. K. Kellogg, 1998). In Phase IV, the products and services developed to achieve the outcomes identified in Phase II are evaluated in the aggregate for how well they are achieving the goals they were designed to attain.

In this phase, evaluation has two aspects. The first focuses on assessing the outcomes of networked products and services for children as they are provided in order to determine if children are receiving the expected benefits and if not, to modify or fine tune the product and/or service offerings as needed. At this level, it is important to know whether the intended outcomes are being realized, whether the measures selected during product/service design or adoption are providing the needed information about outcomes, and to determine whether the data collection methods are effective. Again, this allows for rapid feedback concerning performance and for changes to be made at the product or service level as needed and in a timely way.

At the macro level, evaluation of children's resources and services in a networked environment must also be performed to determine to what extent the technology products and services provided by the children's room are working to make the desired changes in the lives of children. To do this, in addition to evaluation at the product and service level, the effects of electronic products and services in the aggregate must be evaluated using the established indicators associated with the desired outcomes. Data on outcomes are compared to the outcome-based assessment criteria to see how well the library is doing in terms of its target goals, whether or not the target population is being reached, and whether new gaps in services can be identified. Data collection techniques again can include a variety of strategies including surveys, focus groups, and other methods of evaluation. In terms of the children's networked products and services program as a whole, data collection at six-month or even annual intervals may have the greatest utility as this allows time for the new products and services to take effect and for cumulative changes to take place.

The success of the children's technology program is dependent on providing products and services that target the desired outcomes but is also dependent on the viability of the data collected in Phase I. Should it happen that desired outcomes are not being achieved, this may mean that more effective products or services are needed, or it may signal that changes in the community or within the library are impacting the attainment of these goals.

The outcome-based criteria are not a static list of goals, but are expected to be revisited and updated as data are gathered and analyzed and in response to future planning cycles, subsequent community analyses, and future gathering of market data. The double-edged arrow connecting Phase I and Phase II indicates that this is an interactive and iterative process (see Figure 2.1). Changes in inputs must be considered over time for their impact on the outcome-based assessment criteria. Including children's networked resources and services in the overall planning cycle provides a natural vehicle for maintaining this influence. Likewise, the arrow leading back from Phase IV to Phase I illustrates that evaluation is also connected to inputs and that at times the evaluation process itself may reveal the need to re-assess the inputs on which the whole process is based.

Evaluation is critical to understanding the impact of the products and services the library provides. Evaluation allows the library to understand who in the community is being reached, to determine how products and services can be improved to have the maximum positive impact possible, and to ensure that all children are players in the information society in which they live.

Table 2.5: Evaluating Children's Resources

Phase IV: Evaluation	
Component	**Example**
Strategy	Focus groups with children and stakeholder adults.
Relationship to Phase II	Evaluation is used to determine the extent to which the desired outcomes for children are being achieved.
Resulting Action	If desired outcomes are not being achieved, products and services may need to be improved or replaced.
Relationship to Phase I	Evaluation may indicate the need for more data collection.
Resulting Need for More Data	Service utilization indicates community demographics are changing rapidly, perhaps resulting in gaps in service.

LOOKING FORWARD: ADOPTING THE OUTCOME-BASED MODEL

This chapter proposes a theoretical model for evaluating children's networked services and resources in public libraries. In order to determine its viability it will be tested extensively in "real life" situations. It is important to note that analysis of the field tests may result in the need to alter the model and that this is an accepted attribute of the testing process. The application of the model, nonetheless, is expected to yield some real world benefits.

For example, application of this outcome-based evaluation model will enable those involved in public library services to recognize the needs of all youth to be information literate and successful navigators in the technological sea. It will aid understanding of the real complexities of the digital divide. Further, application of the model will help to clarify, through its leveled approach, where the young people with whom we work are and where they desire and need to be in technological competency. It will allow youth some control of their own destiny and assist adult partners to interact with them and encourage and guide them in a productive way.

The knowledge gained through this evaluative process will benefit society, for each of us is contributing to the infusion of technology in public libraries. Each of us wants to get our money's worth and have every young person get his or her value from one of the most comprehensive improvement programs in history. It will keep us from being complacent about an input, only to wake up too late to realize that the input alone was insufficient.

The application of the model and the information it yields will also help public librarians become more proactive in shaping information policy at the national, state, and local levels. The market-based approach gives librarians the information they need in order to advocate for the best handling of the digital divide. Because the users and the community are involved in the process, librarians can be assured that the services provided will be useful in the networked world.

Toward these ends the goals of this research agenda are the following:

- To demonstrate the usefulness to public libraries of an evaluation model that focuses specifically on children as a user group
- To apply and test the model and the sample set of outcomes in various public library settings, making alterations to the model as experience dictates
- To provide a sample set of outcomes for children's use of networked technology that can be adapted in any public library setting
- To clarify how assessment of children's use of technology relates to the overall assessment of networked resources and services
- To develop a manual for outcome-based evaluation of networked children's resources to be used in any public library
- To create a national Web-based statistical and descriptive database on the outcomes of children's use of networked resources in libraries to be used by anyone interested in children's effective use of technology

This agenda requires widespread support by librarians across the country as well as by national organizations as the Association for Library Service to Children of the American Library Association, the Urban Libraries Council, and other non-profit organizations seeking to reduce the digital divide and assure that children achieve the desired outcomes when technology becomes available to them.

ENDNOTES

1. Chapin Hall is conducting an evaluation of 10 public libraries systems funded from 2000–2003 by the DeWitt Wallace-Readers Digest Foundation, but networked technology does not play a major role in this study. How Access Benefits Children: Connecting Our Kids to the World of Information describes interim positive results for eleven innovative-use-of-technology projects funded by the Telecommunications and Information Infrastructure Assistance Program, some of which are still underway (National Telecommunications and Information Administration [NTIA], 1999b). None of these grants, however, involved a public library or emphasis on networked technology.
2. Although the suggestion was made in the 1989 Leadership Institute to interview children about the meaning of a media experience, itself not a common practice, there was no suggestion to interview children during the planning process.
3. The Child Online Privacy Protection Act prohibits sites from asking children for certain private information.

ABOUT THE AUTHORS

Eliza T. Dresang is an Associate Professor at the School of Information Studies, Florida State University, Tallahassee, Florida 32306-2100. Her research interests focus on the information-seeking behavior of children in various formal and informal settings, including evaluation of their resources and services from a user's point of view.

E-mail: edresang@mailer.fsu.edu

Melissa Gross is an Assistant Professor at the School of Information Studies, Florida State University, Tallahassee, Florida, 32306-2100. Her research areas are imposed and shared information seeking behaviors and information service design and evaluation. She has a special interest in children's information needs.

E-mail: mgross@lis.fsu.edu

REFERENCES

American Library Association (ALA). (2000). Minors, Libraries and the Internet. [On-line]. Available: http://www.ala.org/alaorg/oif/minorsinternet.html.

Benton Foundation. (1996). Buildings, Books, and Bytes: Libraries and communities in the digital age. [On-line]. Available: http://www.benton.org/Library/Kellogg/home.html.

Benton Foundation. (2000). The 2001 agenda. [On-line]. Available: http://www.benton.org/News/Extra/dd020800.html.

Benton Foundation and the EDC/Center for Children and Technology. (2000). The E-rate in America: A tale of four cities. [On-line]. Available: http://www.benton.org/e-rate/e-rate.4cities.pdf.

The Bill and Melinda Gates Learning Foundation. (2000). U.S. library program [On-line]. Available: http://www.glf.org/learning/libraries/libraryprogram/default.htm.

Child Online Privacy Protection Act. (1999). [On-line]. Available: http://www.cdt.org/legislation/105th/privacy/coppa.html.

Child Online Protection Act: ACLU v. Reno II. (2000). [On-line]. Available: http://www.eff.org/pub/Legal/Cases/ACLU_v_Reno_II/#moreinfo.

Children's Internet Protection Act. (2000). [On-line]. Available: http://www.ala.org/cipa/legislation.html.

The Children's Partnership. (1999). Kids and families online [On-line]. Available: http://www.childrenspartnership.org/bbar/kids.html.

Communications Decency Act: Reno v. ACLU. (1997). [On-line]. Available: http://caselaw.findlaw.com/scripts/getcase.pl?court=usandnavby=caseandvol=000andinvol=96-511

Dresang, E. (1999). Radical change: Books for youth in a digital age. New York, NY: H.W. Wilson.

Druin, A. (1999). The design of children's technology. San Francisco, CA: Morgan Kaufmann Publishers, Inc.

Gross, M. (In press). Imposed information seeking in school library media centers and public libraries: A common behavior? In Information seeking in context: The third international conference on information needs, seeking and use in different contexts.

Heaviside, S. (1995). Services and resources for children and young adults in public libraries. Washington, DC: United States Department of Education, Office of Education Research and Improvement.

Himmel, E. and Wilson, W. J. (1998). Planning for results: A public library transformation process. Chicago: American Library Association.

Institute of Museum and Library Services. (1999). Outcome-based evaluation for IMLS-funded projects for libraries and museums. Washington, DC.

Koontz, C. and Jue, D. (1999). Market-based adult lifelong learning performance measures for public libraries servicing lower income and majority-minority markets. September 1, 1996–August 31, 1999, final report. [On-line]. Available: http://www.geolib.edu.

McClure, C. R., et al. (1987). Planning and role setting for public libraries: A manual of options and procedures. Chicago: American Library Association.

McNeal, J. U. (1987). Children as consumers: Insights and implications. Lexington, MA: Lexington Books.

National Telecommunications and Information Administration (NTIA). (1998a). Falling through the net: Part I – Household access. [On-line]. From http://www.ntia.doc.gov/ntiahome/fttn99/part1.html.

National Telecommunications and Information Administration (NTIA). (1998b). Falling through the net: Part II – Internet access and use. [On-line]. From http://www.ntia.doc.gov/ntiahome/fttn99/part2.html.

National Telecommunications and Information Administration (NTIA). (1999a). Falling through the net: Part III – Challenges ahead. [On-line]. From http://wwwntia.doc.gov/ntia.home/fttn99/part3.html.

National Telecommunications and Information Administration (NTIA). (1999b). How access benefits children: Connecting our kids to the world of information. [On-line]. From http://www.ntia.doc.gov/otiahome/top/publicationmedia/How_ABC/How_ABC.html.

Robbins, J., et al. (1990). Evaluation strategies and techniques for public library children's services: A sourcebook. Madison, WI: University of Wisconsin School of Library and Information Services.

Tapscott, D. (1998). Growing up digital: The rise of the net generation. New York: McGraw-Hill.

Telecommunications Act of 1996. [On-line]. Available: http://www.fcc.gov/telecom.html/#text.

United Way. (1996). Measuring program outcomes: A practical approach. Alexandria, VA: United Way.

W. K. Kellogg Foundation evaluation handbook. (1998). [On-line]. Available: http://www.wkkf.org/Publications/evalhdbk/default.htm

Walter, V. A. (1992). Output measures for public library service to children: a manual of standardized procedures. Chicago: ALA.

Walter, V. A. (1994). The information needs of children. Advances in Librarianship, 18, 112-115.

Walter, Virginia A. (1995). Output measures and more: Planning and evaluating public library services for young adults. Chicago: ALA.

Chapter 3

Scenarios in the Design and Evaluation of Networked Information Services: An Example from Community Health

Ann Peterson Bishop
Bharat Mehra
Imani Bazzell
Cynthia Smith

ABSTRACT

The Afya participatory action research project employs scenarios elicited from African-American women in the design and evaluation of networked community health information services. This chapter describes and discusses the use of scenarios as a socially grounded technique that both represents authentic experiences and builds capacity related to networked information service use.

INTRODUCTION

Around the world, inequities in health status based on the command of economic power and social resources continues to widen (Moss and Krieger, 1995). A landmark study performed in the United States nearly two decades ago clearly demonstrated that African-American women were at a significantly greater risk of death from cancer, diabetes, and hypertension than the population at large (U. S. Dept. of Health and Human Services, 1985). In the intervening years, little improvement has been achieved. Better healthcare for African-American women remains high on the federal agenda (U.S. Dept. of Health and Human Services, 1990) and current national trends in the inequitable delivery of health care for African-Americans have received attention in the popular press (White, 1999). In addition, those with lower socioeconomic status tend to acquire health information at a slower rate, so gaps in the utilization of knowledge increase over time (Tichenor, Donohue, and Olin, 1970). Moreover, health behavior change models typically used by healthcare professionals are often ineffective in promoting a healthy lifestyle among African-American women because they fail to fit their sociocultural context (Ashing-Giwa, 1999).

Unfortunately, we see an identical pattern in the use of networked information systems. National studies of the "digital divide" highlight wide gaps that occur along socioeconomic fault lines. U. S. Census data reveal that computer ownership and Internet use are less prevalent among marginalized groups: the poor, ethnic minorities, and women (National Telecommunications and Information Administration, 1999). Many fear that the information poor will fall further behind as government, community, and commercial organizations rely increasingly on computer-based formats for communication and information provision. The growing range of digital collections and services in the domain of health include community health information networks (Payton and Brennan, 1999) and interactive health monitors (Berlin and Schatz, 1999). On the Web, consumer-oriented health portals and collections of Web resources vetted by public librarians or health-related organizations are commonplace. While the Internet has proved a useful tool for collective action among Black women (Mele, 1999), women's organizations and groups have typically been behind the curve in technology adoption and use of computers (Balka and Doucette, 1994).

As in community health, the digital divide has been attributed to the lack of knowledge about the sociocultural context of underserved populations and to gaps in the relevance and cultural appropriateness of digital content and its presentation. A recent national report highlighted the lack of "useful content on the Internet—material and applications that serve the needs and interests of millions of low-income and underserved Internet users" (The Children's Partnership, 2000). Perhaps most importantly, the Benton Foundation (1998, p. 12) found that "creative ways will have to be found to make computer networking more a part of the social lives" of traditionally underserved audiences. We know little about the situational or contextual factors that prompt citizens to seek community information online (Pettigrew, Durrance, and Vakkari, 1999).

Real improvements in access and equitable dissemination of information can occur only when "new information needs, created by demographic, social and economic trends" have been recognized and incorporated into the design of community information services, including "not only formal information systems but also human resource networks" (Dosa, 1982). How can we develop information systems and services that marginalized groups, like African-American women, will find both usable and valuable? How can members of marginalized groups participate more fully in the development of digital tools and resources and use them to achieve constructive social change? These are complex questions whose answers involve the synthesis of theories of social action and institutional change, lessons from community organizing, and innovations in system design and evaluation.

The Afya project represents a socially grounded approach to the design and evaluation of networked information services. This chapter discusses how "scenarios" are being used in the Afya project to improve networked information services for African-American women in our community. The Afya project explores the use of scenarios as a design and evaluation technique and does the following:

- Recognizes the links between health and information problems
- Addresses both usability and usefulness of networked information
- Foregrounds social and cultural factors
- Builds the capacity of marginalized groups
- Takes a community-wide approach

This chapter considers the extent to which scenarios provide a technique for system design and evaluation that is well-suited to goals of social equity and change. In the Afya project, scenarios are explored for their power to blur purposefully, make permeable, boundaries that are too often taken for granted or ignored: between haves and have-nots, between system designers and users, between the social and technical. These are boundaries that must be crossed if we hope to address problems related to the inequitable distribution of healthcare, information, and computer technology at the community level.

THE AFYA PROJECT

The Afya project, currently underway, is a collaborative venture undertaken by a range of organizations based in Champaign-Urbana, Illinois. It takes a participatory action research approach to the development of networked health information services at the community level. Participatory action research demands that producing immediate improvements in local conditions for marginalized members of society takes precedence over the needs and interests of academic researchers (McTaggart, 1997). It seeks to empower local community members by giving them control over the research and by building their capacity to address problems confronting them. In participatory action research, action is at the heart of both method and results:

> Participatory action research ... actively involves local residents as co-investigators on a equal basis with university-trained scholars in each step of the research process, and is expected to follow a non-linear course throughout the investigation as the problem being studied is 'reframed' to accommodate new knowledge that emerges. ... Participatory action researchers intentionally promote social learning processes that can develop the organizational, analytical, and communication skills of local leaders and their community-based organizations. (Reardon, 1998, p. 57-64)

Participatory action research, while not common in the development of computer-based information resources and services, has been employed in projects emphasizing social equity and justice at the local level.

For example, in workshops with local community members in Kiepersol, South Africa, researchers hoping to support grassroots initiatives for the redistribution of natural resources collected oral histories related to forced removals, perceptions of land quality and borders, and other aspects of land use (Weiner, Warner, Harris, and Levin, 1995). This "folk" knowledge was integrated in a geographic information system containing more traditional information, such as data on hydrology, topography, climate, and soil quality. Also highlighting issues of community participation and social justice, a participatory action research project introduced computers in New York City neighborhoods as part of a broader initiative to foster creativity, learning, and peace among very poor children and their families (Tardieu, 1999). Researchers collaborated with children to create a computer-based "neighborhood encyclopedia" containing entries that children contributed on whatever topics were important to them.

The primary community-based organizational partner for the Afya project is SisterNet, a grassroots *social* network of African-American women committed to nurturing healthy lifestyles through both their individual behavior and community activism. SisterNet women serve as community action researchers who are working with local providers of healthcare services, librarians, and university researchers to develop networked health information services that African-American women will find both usable and useful. In the Afya project, SisterNet women are initiators in the analysis of information about their own requirements. Their own descriptions of their goals, experiences, and specific situations of use related to health information create the foundation upon which the design and evaluation of networked community health information services rest.

Also playing a key role in the Afya project are staff of Prairienet, the local community network for Champaign-Urbana and the surrounding East-Central Illinois region. Community networks typically provide free or low-cost access to computers and the Internet, offer training and support services, and work actively to develop an online repository of community information (Cohill and Kavanaugh, 2000; Schuler, 1996). Prairienet has been especially active in providing networked information services to members of marginalized groups (Bishop, Tidline, Shoemaker, and Salela, 1999). Its stated mission is to

- strengthen community organizations by helping them provide and retrieve networked information;
- empower individuals (especially those belonging to low-income and disadvantaged neighborhoods) by providing access to networked information and by teaching the skills necessary to access and use this information;
- facilitate information and resource sharing in support of community development efforts; and
- promote equity in access to computer resources for everyone in the community.

Prairienet is participating in the Afya project by providing computers, Internet access, and training. The health information resources and services developed by project members will reside on Prairienet's server and contribute directly to all aspects of its mission.

In pursuing a community-based participatory action research approach for the creation of networked health information services by and for African-American women, scenarios present a tool women can use to critique existing health information services and help formulate design criteria for new services. In the Afya project, scenarios are developed as narratives of specific situations that incorporate African-American women's goals, perceptions, activities, and barriers in their efforts to nurture a healthy lifestyle. Scenarios present a holistic picture based on true-to-life practices and values associated with health information seeking and sharing, and with information technology use. These are the basic steps of the first phase of the Afya project:

- Elicit scenarios from SisterNet women, health care providers, health information providers
- Collaborate to critique existing Web-based health information services based on scenarios that encapsulate their perceptions and experiences (collaboration of SisterNet women and university researchers)
- Develop guidelines for the design of SisterNet's own Web site and create initial prototype (based on the critique of existing services)
- Elicit additional scenarios and begin planning for future improvements to the SisterNet and other local health information Web sites (in assessing SisterNet's prototype Web site). Also, develop other aspects of a "community action plan" for improving the ability of local black women to nurture a healthy lifestyle

The next stage of the Afya project will involve community partners—local librarians and health care providers, university researchers, Prairienet staff—in collaborating with SisterNet women as they develop, implement, and assess outcomes from a community action plan that unites innovation in social and computing technologies.

SCENARIOS: AN INTEGRATED VIEW OF TECHNOLOGY, VALUES, AND SOCIAL PRACTICE

Socially grounded approaches to information system design and evaluation are becoming increasingly common. The collaboration between social scientists and computer and information scientists—a "complex coeducation"—was conceived as an area of academic research in the 1960s in order to understand "how human and technical issues come together in computing systems" (Bowker, Turner, Star, and Gasser, 1997). Since then the diversity of approaches that integrate human and technology research has been enormous. Variations emerging from computer science, sociology, cognitive psychology, anthropology, and organizational research, to name a few, have resulted in multi-disciplinary perspectives on information systems (Monk and Gilbert, 1995). At the technology end of the spectrum, artificial intelligence attempts to improve computer processing by modeling it on human cognition. At the human end, participatory design produces ethnographically informed results geared toward ensuring that the introduction of computers will enrich work environments and benefit workers (Greenbaum and Kyng, 1991).

The field of human-computer interactions (HCI) represents an interdisciplinary approach whose central agenda has clearly been to design computer and information systems that are sensitive to human needs and uses. Scenario building is a unique methodology within HCI research that has been used in the development of a wide range of information technologies. John Carroll, an early explorer of "use-oriented design representations"—or scenarios—presents a clear outline for the development of scenarios as an informal predictive model that tracks particular activities of intended users (1995). In contrast to top-down, technology-driven, abstract and formal approaches, scenarios provide concrete descriptions of use, focus on particular instances, elicit envisioned outcomes, and are open-ended, rough, and colloquial (p. 5). The trick here is to predict who will be a marginalized user and make sure that representatives of those groups are given an equal voice in contributing their scenarios.

The Alexandria Digital Library (ADL) is one project where information need and use scenarios related to geographic information systems were employed to evaluate a system that was innovative and evolving (Hill, et al., 2000). Scenarios were accommodated in an iterative cycle consisting of the following stages: 1) use scenarios were elicited and categorized into a thematic classification system; 2) system designers built certain functionalities based on feedback from the user information need scenarios; 3) users were introduced and made to interact with the new features; 4) users evaluated existing functionalities, and, in the form of new scenarios, suggested additional features based on their previous interaction with the system; and 5) implementers modified the design rooted in suggestions made by users. In addition to eliciting scenarios depicting the needs and circumstances of individuals (see the Alexandria Web Team's collection of use scenarios at http://www.alexandria.ucsb.edu/~hill/scenarios.html), researchers also created more general depictions to characterize an entire set of users. For example, earth scientists are described as the primary intended user group; they work extensively with large data sets and envision the ADL as knit tightly into their high-tech information-processing environment.

By emphasizing social practices, values, relationships, and impacts, other lines of research complement user-centered approaches that focus on individual, cognitive behavior. The term "social informatics" captures the current trend in interdisciplinary research on social aspects of design, use and consequences of information and communications technology (Kling, 2000); even more recently, the term "community informatics" has been introduced (Gurstein, 2000). Also important are new metaphors, such as "information ecology," that help us identify and understand the intertwined relationships among the people, practices, technologies, and values associated with information use (Nardi and O'Day, 1999).

Bruce and Hogan (1998) argue that researchers should undertake situated studies that closely examine how information technologies are realized in given settings and how ideology operates within situations where technology and humans interact. By exploring how and for whom technology becomes so embedded in the living process that it "disappears" (i.e., becomes so easy and natural to use that its use is virtually automatic), we can begin to see how people are marked as full or marginal users. Twidale, Randall, and Bentley (1994) also call for a reframing of evaluation in order to account for how an information system is realized in specific situations of use, noting that ethnographic insights related to authentic contexts of use can be crucial to a system's success.

In fact, authentic insight into social context has become an issue in evaluation throughout the social sciences, especially where educational or social programs for marginalized groups are concerned. When evaluators are too far removed from the authentic experiences of women, the poor, and people of color, they are unable to conduct valid assessments of their experiences. The results they produce are inaccurate and irrelevant and do little to shift existing social practice and power relationships (Stanfield, 1999). Like participatory action research and participatory design, "participatory evaluation" reflects concerns for both social justice and the improved utilization of research results. In this approach, evaluation is seen as developmental process, in which equity and empowerment for those with little control over their situation are explicit goals (Pursley, 1996; Whitmore, 1998).

How can one bring these socially grounded philosophical and methodological threads together to design and evaluate networked information services in a manner that elicits authentic depictions of use situations, as well as fosters capacity-building and positive transformation in individual and institutional practices across a given community? As one strategy for applying participatory action research methods in the Afya project, scenarios elicited from African-American women are being employed for the design and evaluation of networked health information services. Through scenarios, system development becomes a process of identifying enablers and barriers to use. The scenarios women contribute also provide the foundation for the evaluation of outcomes and impact. Perhaps most importantly, scenarios are employed as a developmental tool to build the capacity of local African-American women so that they can participate more effectively in the development of online health information systems.

In the Afya project, the employment of scenarios for the design and evaluation of community health information networks is taken a step further than is typically the case in either scenario-based design or participatory design, in that the aim is no longer to build better technology per se. Concerns for social justice and the immediate improvement of local conditions overshadow concerns for technology innovation and deployment. The ultimate goal of using scenarios during various stages of the Afya project has been nothing less than to overcome national trends of inequitable delivery of both healthcare and networked information services. While this goal is admittedly unattainable in its entirety, one can still look for essential ways to improve health service and information delivery by empowering African-American women to employ technology in the improvement of social conditions and situations.

The remainder of this chapter depicts in some detail the various ways that scenarios have been used in the Afya project to record representative and meaningful user goals and activities early in the system lifecycle. It is important to document and present the procedures involved in the use of scenarios in different contexts, since scenarios have diverse expressions depending upon the nature of a system's users, tasks, and the environment (Karat, 1995). Documenting scenario applications in different milieux also makes sense in terms of facilitating the irreductionist interpretation of social processes associated with the use of networked information systems by different user communities. Social interaction and information processing are "produced through people's ongoing practical action, the concrete day-to-day activity" (Van House, in press) that is obviously not the same in different use contexts.

Hence, recording the details of scenario use in different circumstances not only contributes to a richer understanding of social aspects of information system use, generally; it also pushes the development of the scenario technique by exploring its manifold expressions, its potential and limitations. The employment of scenario building in the Afya project contributes to the growing knowledge base for this particular socially grounded technique for information system design and evaluation.

SCENARIO METHODOLOGY IN THE AFYA PROJECT

Eliciting Scenarios in Focus Groups

An initial set of scenarios related to the use of networked health information services was developed from data gathered in four focus groups conducted in January and February 2000. Three focus groups were conducted with SisterNet women who, based on their age, were assigned into either the "Young Women's," "Prime Time," or "Wise Women" group. In addition, one focus group was conducted with participants who were community healthcare and health information providers. Imani Bazzell, SisterNet Director, served as focus group moderator for all four groups. About six to eight people participated in each group. SisterNet focus group participants discussed the following:

- Their vision of a healthy Black woman
- Important health concerns or situations they recently experienced
- Where and how they typically get and use health information
- Barriers they experience and what works well in using health resources
- Their use of computers
- Actions that they or other Afya project participants could take to improve health information resources and services

Local healthcare and health information service staff addressed similar issues but from their own perspectives as providers. These topics are integral to developing use scenarios for a Web-based community health information service for African-American women because they holistically bring together essential needs, goals, expectations, and practices related to the use of health services, information, and technology.

The focus groups were audiotaped and transcribed, but the transcripts took several months to produce. Therefore, initial progress was made by working from the extensive notes taken by the focus group recorder to: 1) summarize key points within and across the four focus groups; 2) identify specific needs, barriers, and requirements (both implicitly and explicitly stated in the focus groups) related to the use of networked health information services in our community; and 3) craft a preliminary set of scenarios that would represent the most common and important experiences of SisterNet women as well as health care and health information providers.

Summarizing key points across the focus groups helped in understanding the main features of the community's health care system and the primary barriers faced by African-American women in their efforts to nurture a healthy lifestyle. Two types of documents were created to produce basic summaries of the focus group data. One was a simple two-page summary of the discussion in each group. The other was a comparison chart that listed key responses for each focus group topic. What was noted here was the frequency of occurrence of voicing a particular issue by the participants in each of the four focus groups. Exact numbers were not noted; instead, a simple three-point scale was followed where distinctions were made between a general consensus (three or more references), some agreement (two references), and a single reference to a specific issue. In order to point out the differences between the groups, it was also noted when there was no reference to a certain concern in one group as compared to some mention of that issue in the other groups. For example, in the "Prime Time" focus group, there was a general consensus that breast cancer was a major health concern, while there was no mention of breast cancer as an important concern for the participants from the "Young Women's" focus group.

The resulting list of basic issues included some that depict the underlying sociocultural context, for instance, the concern that a history of chronic illness in the Black community leads to a high level of tolerance of disease as a part of life. Other issues depict needs and problems in accessing, exchanging, or using health information. Some examples of these are the following: poor relationships between healthcare providers and patients; the need for information on health topics of particular concern to African-American women (e.g., diabetes, heart disease); and the lack of health information that is convenient, jargon-free, relevant, and culturally appropriate. Some concerns span sociocultural and information domains, such as racial stereotyping in both interactions with, and information created by, providers.

The basic summaries of focus group data were helpful for scenario building in several ways. Since only a limited number of scenarios could be employed to structure the subsequent evaluation of existing networked health information services, the summaries helped in selecting those scenarios which would encapsulate the most critical issues. They also pointed out differences in the perspectives of the four participant groups; discussing these differences helped focus attention on whether and how the differences could be bridged by an online information service.

For example, the differences between the perceptions of African-American women and health care providers suggested the need for online discussion in an amiable and flexible atmosphere. It was felt that, to make a real difference in community practice, there was a need for women and providers to pool ideas, thoughts, perceptions, and resources. Participants from both sides of the fence stressed the need for collaboration among various stakeholders in order to sort out complex connections between health-related problems, information problems, and broader sociocultural, economic, and political problems and begin to mend them.

In addition to summarizing basic findings, the notes from the focus groups were also used to create a "laundry list" of needs and requirements—stated in the form of questions either implicitly or explicitly appearing in focus group discussion—related to the use of networked health information services. The final list included over 100 entries, ranging from open-ended and broad queries, such as "How do I find information concerning the physical/intellectual/emotional/spiritual health of Black women?" and "How can I gain more self-confidence in dealing with local doctors?" to more specific and directed queries, such as "Where can I find a list of bookstores in town that have a special section on Black women's health?" This list was envisioned as a useful tool for both designing and assessing the content and features of online services since it provided a set of "queries" that reflected the real needs of local community members.

The focus group notes themselves contained community members' reports of their specific health needs and practices. The comparison chart described above helped us to see clearly the similarities and differences in the perceptions of community members and understand these in the light of larger sociocultural, political, and economic factors. The laundry list of questions contributed to identifying specific inquiries that attended real life experiences related to the use of community healthcare and health information services. The real challenge was to combine and recombine these ingredients—key health-related issues, specific examples from community members' daily experiences, and the questions that reflected users' needs—in the form of scenarios whose purpose changed somewhat in different steps of the Afya project.

The following scenario is presented to demonstrate how scenarios were constructed early in the Afya project. For this scenario, four comments made by SisterNet women in focus group meetings were brought together: two were comments about diabetes, one was about financial crisis, and one was the report of a search for the appropriate insurance company:

> I have been struggling with diabetes for the past five years (FG#2Ap.4). I don't have any money (FG#2Ap.7) to go regularly for checkups to my doctor and my insurance does not cover more than one trip per month. {Are there any insurance companies that will provide better deals in health care coverage and lower rates than the one I already have (FG#1Ap.2). I also want to know more about diabetes, as well as some information on the Web that will tell me ways that I can do my own checkup and keep a control on my diet, exercises and state of health (FG#1Ap.2)}.

The two comments on diabetes were found in the "Young Women's" Focus Group (FG#1) and the "Prime Time" Focus Group (FG#2), the comment about a lack of money was taken from the "Prime Time" focus group (FG#2), and the narrative about the insurance company was taken from the "Young Women's" Focus Group (FG#1). The location of the comments is recorded by noting the appropriate page numbers (p.4, p.7, p.2, and p.2) in the focus group notes from which they were drawn. The use of the letter "A" designates the original focus group notes as the source of the comments. Curly brackets were used to identify the embedded questions or the needs (i.e., the laundry list queries) about diabetes information and appropriate insurance companies.

The scenario presented above is unauthentic in several ways. It is derived from focus group recorder notes, which may be incomplete or inaccurate. It is constructed from the narratives of several different women, rather than representing a single real life anecdote. The embedded questions may have been explicitly expressed, but may also have been only implied from the SisterNet speaker's remarks. But the Afya project purposely explored the construction and utility of different forms of scenarios for different aspects of system design and evaluation. This particular style of scenario was designed to serve as a kind of prop in the situated user evaluations of existing online resources (described in the following section). The situation depicted in the diabetes scenario was representative of authentic experiences reported by SisterNet women. And it was elaborate enough to hold the interest of, and offer specific criteria against which a particular health-related Web site could be assessed by, a SisterNet evaluator.

For another project purpose, some alternative presentation of scenarios might be more appropriate. As a prompt for discussion among health care professionals about their role in a community action plan, for example, it may be more appropriate to present entries from the compendium of verbatim narratives from local African-American women that were eventually produced from the focus group transcripts:

- "It's hard to know if it is really racism or if the healthcare providers are being pushed. The fact is that if a Black woman presents with abdominal pains the first thing they want to do is run a series of venereal disease tests on her, whether that is the issue or not."
- "My daughter had mono ... and she lost like twenty pounds. ... My mother is a nurse practitioner and the first thing she said was that my daughter needed to go to the hospital and be taken care of. So I did take her to the doctor and the first thing they said was 'well, we ...' I was hitting a brick wall [and] had to take her to the emergency room to get her the care she needs. She was severely dehydrated and was going downhill. You know if you look at the child and that child is being dragged in by the parent because the child cannot walk ... How severe does one have to be before they can get the care they need? Before you can get someone to listen to you?"

- "If your body is not strong, you can't go to work every day and get your finances in order, or it is very hard to do the other things, to go to church, to get your spiritual assets. Physical health is very important, and to go beyond peer pressure, because I can't get on the phone and tell my friends how I do a monthly self breast exam or whatever. Or people laugh at me when they see me put sunscreen on and I'm Black."
- "... I think we find ourselves under so much more stress every day. I know I do. I am in a situation where, this past May I had to take two of my grandchildren rather than have them go into foster care so that is an added stress in my life. ... In fact, since I have had the two kids [one- and two-year olds], they bring home everything [i.e., illnesses] from daycare, you know. ... I have just really been sicker this year than ever. Mainly because of these two babies and the added stress so my whole immune system. ..."

These narratives convey in a forceful manner the types of problems African-American women have experienced and reflect sociocultural elements that may be unfamiliar to some healthcare providers.

Initially, before gathering any empirical data in the Afya project, it was not clear what a scenario would look like. A scenario "template" was drawn up which included elements like topic, purpose, type, mode, qualities, query, format, user, stimulus document, etc. Once analysis of the focus group notes began, a more flexible process and shape replaced this rigid fielded structure. The subsequent formulation of informal anecdotes accommodated evolution to suit each step of analysis. The realization that there was no natural interaction between proposed formal structures for scenarios and the rich data gathered from participants in focus groups was the essential reason for breaking down the rigid template envisioned early on.

Situated User Evaluations

The Afya project is an action-oriented endeavor that involves participation of African-American women for effecting positive change in the design of networked information services that address community health. It promotes collaboration and capacity building between various stakeholders, supports design decisions based on their goals and sociocultural context, and strives to bring about a change in the beliefs, practices, and ways of thinking of all involved, including both African-American women and health and information providers from the community.

One of the main steps of the Afya project was to conduct situated usability testing with local African-American women for the purpose of critiquing national and local Web sites related to women's health in terms of their usability, usefulness, and cultural appropriateness. The following were the objectives outlined during this stage of the project:

- Engage local women in the process of evaluating national and local online health-related resources for African-American women
- Provide local librarians and health information and service providers with constructive critiques of their online health-related resources, based on input from SisterNet participants
- In terms of computer technology, the Internet and Prairienet, increase local African-American women's interest and ability
- Develop a prototype Web site for SisterNet and elicit direct feedback from SisterNet members in the form of their evaluation of the site

The Afya project used the terms "situated user evaluation" or "situated usability testing" for a style of interacting with potential system users that incorporates assessments of usefulness and strives to reveal something of the social context and practice from which the system evaluator's comments arise (Bishop, et al., 2000). In the Afya project, scenarios for African-American women were employed in situated user evaluation sessions in order to gather and understand suggestions for both improving existing networked health information on Prairienet and developing new services. Scenarios were incorporated in the sessions to ground the evaluations performed by SisterNet women. In addition, new scenarios related to their own personal experiences were elicited from the women who participated in the evaluation sessions.

Situated user evaluation sessions were organized as two-hour workshops with volunteer SisterNet community action researchers, with one workshop devoted to assessing each of the following:

- National Web sites on women's health
- Local Web resources related to women's health found on Prairienet's home page
- Communication services on the Internet (online support/discussion groups and mailing lists) related to women's health
- SisterNet's "draft" Web site, which is intended to serve as a primary locus for new networked community health information resources

The first three sessions combined a short training/demonstration component with an evaluation component. Feedback from SisterNet participants in the first three sessions informed Web site development for the fourth session.

The user evaluation tool was custom designed to suit the different requirements of each of the four user sessions. In general, focus group scenarios (both the "composite" and verbatim narratives) were employed in the evaluation of online health information resources in two ways. First, the scenarios created from the focus groups helped the workshop planners. They read the scenarios in order to gain some basic familiarity with the concerns and practices of SisterNet women who would be participating in the workshops. The scenarios also helped the workshop planners identify appropriate Web sites for the SisterNet evaluators to critique. Second, several scenarios were presented to the SisterNet evaluators, who then assessed the Web sites they visited in terms of how successfully they met the needs represented by the scenarios.

To elicit scenarios from SisterNet participants in the evaluation sessions, questions such as the following were asked: "When would you come back to this Web site?" "How would this site be useful to you?" "What would make that kind of feature fit with your daily routine?" This helped to draw direct connections between existing Web resources and community women's actual situations of Web use. Presented here are some examples of the use scenarios generated in our situated evaluation sessions:

- From Workshop 1 (national Web sites): The SisterNet evaluator clicked on links to information on breast implants and cervical cancer and then remarked that the pink text seemed friendlier, it was nice to get some information on topics that she would be reluctant to ask someone about, and that it would be good to have this information before going to her doctor.
- From Workshop 2 (local Web sites on Prairienet): The SisterNet evaluator was looking for information on herbal remedies. She could not find any apparently relevant categories in Prairienet's topically organized "Health and Wellness" area, because the categories were too broad. She then went to an alphabetical listing of organizations and found one called "Alternative Medicine Academy." She commented that she was looking for a natural remedy for her daughter and granddaughter, who both had asthma.
- From Workshop 3 (Internet communication services): In discussing what kind of communication features to implement on SisterNet's own Web site, a SisterNet evaluator commented that she was more interested in sports than working out as part of her fitness routine. She recommended implementing a mailing list or listserv where she could find a partner for tennis or try to get a baseball team together.
- From Workshop 4 (draft SisterNet Web site): After browsing through the site, one SisterNet evaluator said she envisioned using the site to find out about SisterNet activities. She worked long hours running a clothing shop where she sold her own African-inspired designs and operating an after-school recreational/cultural program for children. On occasions when she found herself with a little free time on a Sunday afternoon, she thought it would be nice

> to be able to go to the Web site to see if there were a SisterNet reading group or other activity going on at that moment.

Scenarios were beneficial in several ways as part of Afya's situated user evaluations. They seemed to stimulate the interest of SisterNet evaluators and make them feel that the sessions (and the project as a whole) really were designed "for them." They allowed assessments of both usability and usefulness and supported the identification of links between these two networked information service criteria. Scenarios provided an additional window into the sociocultural context in which the health and information needs of SisterNet members are embedded. They also supplied insights into non-system aspects of designing a community-wide Web site related to African-American women's health. That is, in contrast perhaps to more standard usability testing, scenario-based user evaluations provided substantial data that can help in planning for public access site locations, user support and training, etc.

CONCLUSIONS

The Afya project seeks to create nurturing social ties among local residents, establish effective communication linkages to bridge diversity, and facilitate the development of effective working relationships. It reaches down to the grassroots level to accommodate the inclusion of all relevant stakeholders and enable equitable involvement in decision-making processes and the distribution of resources at the community level. The Afya project exemplifies participatory action research in association with the design and evaluation of networked information services. It follows a systematic approach to learning whose results are applied to making improvements to contemporary social situations and problems (Whyte, 1991). It also presents "a collaborative approach to inquiry or investigation that provides people with the means to take systematic action to resolve specific problems" (Stringer, 1999, p.17).

In the context of community information networks, the Afya project uses scenario building as a strategy for gaining participation and stimulating action related to resolving digital divide issues within a larger sociocultural environment. Scenario building has fostered the active involvement of African-American women throughout early stages of the development of networked health information services. Local women have participated in the analysis of their needs and offered well-grounded assessments of networked health information services. These activities resulted in suggestions—related to content, interface design, and functionality—for the provision of new health information services that would be more usable and useful for African-American women, a group typically marginalized in system design and evaluation.

In the Afya project, scenario building is being implemented as a process in the truest sense of the word. User participation and analysis of community needs is being incorporated at each stage of the process. Each step is shaped via participation of potential and actual users, and this helps to direct inquiry and create the next step, and thus the process continues. Hence, the form of use scenarios is also not seen as a static expression; scenarios are incorporated in different manifestations during the various stages of system design and evaluation.

The Afya project has contributed to the knowledge base of the scenario methodology (Chin, Rosson, and Carroll, 1997; McGraw and Harbison, 1997; Stiemerling and Cremers, 1998; Wilkinson, 1999), since it applied the method in somewhat new ways, with a different kind of information system. In particular, it deepens the social context typically represented in scenario-based research; scenarios helped articulate connections between information, health and broader sociocultural problems in our community.

Through their scenarios, women have shared their painful experiences, making explicit a number of issues related to race and gender in the provision and distribution of health information and services. The scenarios women contributed facilitate a deeper understanding about institutionalized prejudices and other dimensions of belonging to a marginalized and minority group. They have brought to the surface many things that are typically hidden in the remote corners of the dark closet of racist and sexist policies and politicized behaviors—inequality and prejudices based on ethnicity, race, color of the skin, gender, or sexual orientation. It is important that one acknowledges the political hierarchies and power dynamics that shape the distribution of health information and services at the community level, if one hopes to build awareness and work toward changing them. In this light, scenarios are proving helpful in our community's efforts to bridge both social and digital divides in local healthcare.

ACKNOWLEDGMENT

We thank the U.S. Institute of Museum and Library Services for supporting the Afya project.

ABOUT THE AUTHORS

Ann Peterson Bishop is an Assistant Professor at the Graduate School of Library and Information Science at the University of Illinois. Her research focuses on socially grounded research methods and the study of goals and outcomes associated with the use of information systems by disenfranchised groups. Bishop teaches courses in community information systems, information needs and uses, knowledge organization and access, social informatics, and information policy.

Bishop serves as Principal Investigator for the Community-Based Creation of Networked Information Services: Developing Tools and Guidelines for Public Libraries, a two-year Project currently in progress that is funded for over $3 million by the Institute for Library and Museum Services (IMLS). She was also Principal Investigator for the "Community Networking Initiative" (sponsored by the Telecommunications and Information Infrastructure Assistance Program (TIIAP) in the Dept. of Commerce and the Kellogg Foundation), and co-Principal Investigator for the University of Illinois' NSF/ARPA/NASA Digital Libraries Initiative project. Bishop is a co-founder—along with Greg Newby—of Prairienet, the community network that serves East Central Illinois. She served on the national advisory panel for the U.S. Office of Technology Assessment's 1995 study of telecommunications technologies and Native Americans.

Mailing Address: Graduate School of Library and Information Science
University of Illinois at Urbana-Champaign
501 E. Daniel Street
Champaign, IL 61820

Bharat Mehra is a doctoral student at the Graduate School of Library and Information Science at the University of Illinois at Urbana-Champaign. His professional interests lie in mapping human factors in human-computer interactions (HCI). Within this vast domain, he is currently working on projects that evaluate information systems based on user needs and explore the role of social, cultural and behavioral factors (especially of minority and marginalized groups) in the design process of information systems. His work in exploring human behavior and sociocultural patterns of minority and marginalized groups in the context of their influence upon the design of computer-mediated information systems extends his earlier cross-disciplinary research in community development and information exchange. Mehra's prior work on the East St. Louis Action Research Project (ESLARP) involved a close working relationship with the community, analyzing its needs, and making recommendations for re-building the physical and cultural landscape based on positive community participation in the design process. Some areas of interest are in the fields of community information networked systems, social informatics, natural language processing, image databases, and using GIS for spatial mapping of cultural information.

Imani Bazzell is the founder and director of SisterNet, a local network of African-American women committed to the physical, emotional, intellectual, and spiritual health of Black women. Professionally, she splits her time between SisterNet, the Center For Multicultural Education at Parkland College, and independent consultation with public schools, colleges and universities, unions, not-for-profit and state agencies, and community groups on racial justice, gender justice, healthcare access, and leadership development.

Her commitment to institutional change in the area of public education keeps her busy as the coordinator of African-Americans for Accountability in Education (ACE), as well as one of five members of the Champaign School

District's Planning and Implementation Committee representing the Black community. They are charged with the development and implementation of programs and policies designed to address years of discrimination. Bazzell's other membership and organizing activities include: A Woman's Fund; NAACP; Women Against Racism; National Racial Justice Educators and Organizers; National Coalition Against Racism in Sports and Media; and the Black Radical Congress.

Cynthia Smith is pursuing a Master's Degree in Social Work at the University of Illinois at Urbana-Champaign. She has worked for the Decatur School District for many years. Smith received her Bachelor's Degree in Child, Family and Community Services at the University of Illinois in Springfield. Her area of concentration is school social work and her future plans include pursuing a doctorate degree that will enable her to work with children and their families in both the school setting and the community.

REFERENCES

Ashing-Giwa, L. (1999). Health behavior change models and their sociocultural relevance for breast cancer screening in African-American women. Women and Health, 28(4), 53–71.

Balka, E. and Doucette, L. (1994). The Accessibility of computers to organizations serving women in the province of Newfoundland: Preliminary study results. The Arachnet Electronic Journal on Virtual Culture, 2(3).

Benton Foundation. (1998). Losing ground bit by bit: Low-income communities in the information age. Washington, DC: Benton Foundation.

Berlin, R. B. and Schatz, B. R. (1999. Sept. 2). Internet health monitors for outcomes of chronic illness. Medscape General Medicine (MedGenMed), 6 Sections [Available: http://www.medscape.com].

Bishop, A.P.; Neumann, L.J.; Star, S.L.; Merkel, C.; Ignacio, E.; and Sandusky, R.J. (2000). Digital libraries: Situating use in changing information infrastructure. Journal of the American Society for Information Science, 51(4), 394–413.

Bishop, A. P.; Tidline, T.; Shoemaker, S.; and Salela, P. (1999). Public libraries and networked information services in low-income communities. Library and Information Science Research, 21(3), 361–390.

Bowker, G. C.; Turner, W.; Star, S. L.; and Gasser, L. (1997). Introduction. In G. C. Bowker, Star, S.L. Turner, W.; and Gasser, L. (Eds.) Social science, technical systems, and cooperative work: Beyond the great divide (pp. xi–xxiii). Mahwah, NJ: Lawrence, Erlbaum.

Bruce, B. C. and Hogan, M. P. (1998). The disappearance of technology: Toward an epistemological model of literacy. In Reinking, D., Labbo, M. L., and Kieffer, R. (Eds.) Handbook of literacy and technology: Transformations in a post-typographic world (pp. 269–281). Hillsdale, NJ: Erlbaum.

Carey, T. and Rusli, M. (1995). Usage representations for reuse of design insights: A case study of access to online books. In Carroll, J.M. (Ed.) Scenario-based design: Envisioning work and technology in system development. (pp. 165–182). New York: Wiley.

Carroll, J. M. (1995). Introduction: The scenario perspective on system development. In Carroll, J. M.(Ed.) Scenario-based design: Envisioning work and technology in system development (pp. 1–17). New York: J. Wiley.

The Children's Partnership. (2000). Online content for low-income and underserved Americans: The digital divide's new frontier—A strategic audit of activities and opportunities. Santa Monica, CA: The Children's Partnership.

Chin, Jr., G.; Rosson, M. B.; and Carroll, J. M. (1997). Participatory analysis: Shared development of requirements from scenarios. In Pemberton, S. (Ed.) CHI 97—Human factors in computing systems: Conference proceedings (pp. 162–169). New York: Association for Computing Machinery.

Cohill, A. M. and Kavanaugh, A. L. (Eds.) (2000). Community networks: Lessons from Blacksburg, Virginia, 2d ed. Boston: Artech House.

Dosa, M. (1982). Community networking in gerontology and health: A centralized and a decentralized Model. In Special Collections, 53-72. New York: Haworth Press.

Greenbaum, J. and Kyng, M. (Eds.) (1991). Design at work: Cooperative design of computer systems. Hillsdale, NJ: Lawrence Erlbaum.

Gurstein, M. (Ed.). (2000). Community informatics: Enabling communities with information and communications technologies. Hershey, PA: Idea Group Publishers.

Hill, L.L.; Carver, L.; Laarsgaard, M.; Dolin, R.; Smith, T.R.; Frew, J.; and Rae, M. (2000). Alexandria Digital Library: User evaluation studies and system design. Journal of the American Society for Information Science, 51(3), 246–259.

Karat, J. (1995). Scenario use in the design of a speech recognition system. In Carroll, J. M. (Ed.) Scenario-based design: Envisioning work and technology in system development (pp. 109–133). New York: J. Wiley.

Kling, R. (2000). Learning about information technologies and social change: The contribution of social informatics. The Information Society, 16(3), 217–232.

Kyng, M. (1995). Creating context for design. In Carroll, J. M. (Ed.) Scenario-based design: Envisioning work and technology in system development (pp. 85–107). New York: J. Wiley.

McGraw, K. and Harbison, K. (1997). User-centered requirements: The scenario-based engineering process. Mahwah, NJ: Lawrence Erlbaum.

McTaggart, R. (Ed.) (1997). Participatory action research: International contexts and consequences. Albany, NY: State University of New York Press.

Mele, C. (1999). Cyberspace and disadvantaged communities: the Internet as a tool for collective action. In Smith, Marc A. and Kollock, Peter (Eds.) Communities in cyberspace (pp. 291–310). London: Routledge.

Monk, A. F. and Gilbert, N. (1995). Perspectives on HCI: Diverse approaches. In Gaines, B. R. and Monk, A. (Eds.) Computers and people series. London: Academic Press.

Moss, N. and Krieger, N. (1995). Measuring social inequalities in health: Report on the Conference of the National Institutes of Health. Public Health Reports, 110(3), 302–305.

Nardi, B. and O'Day, V. (1999). Information ecologies. Cambridge, MA: MIT Press.

National Telecommunications and Information Administration (NTIA), U. S. Department of Commerce. (1999). Falling through the net: Defining the digital divide. Washington, DC: NTIA [Available: http://www.ntia.doc.gov/ntiahome/fttn99/].

Payton, F. C. and Brennan, P. F. (1999). How a community health information network is really used. Communications of the ACM, 42(12), 85–89.

Pettigrew, K. E.; Durrance, J. C.; and Vakkari, P. (1999). Approaches to studying public library networked community information initiatives: A review of the literature and overview of a current study. Library and Information Science Research, 21(3), 327–360.

Pursley, L. A. (1996). Empowerment and utilization through participatory evaluation. Doctoral dissertation. Cornell University, Ithaca, NY. UMI Dissertation Services.

Reardon, K. M. (1998). Participatory action research as service learning. In Rhoads, R. A. and Howard, J. P. F. (Eds.) Academic service learning: A pedagogy of action and reflection (pp. 57–64). San Francisco: Jossey-Bass.

Schuler, D. (1996). New community networks: Wired for change. New York: ACM Press.

Stanfield, J. H. (1999). Slipping through the front door: Relevant social scientific evaluation in the people of color century. American Journal of Evaluation, 20(3), 415–431.

Stiemerling, O., and Cremers, A. B. (1998). The use of cooperative scenarios in the design and evaluation of a CSCW system. IEEE Transactions on Software Engineering, 24(2), 1171–1181.

Stringer, E.T. (1999). Action research, 2d ed. London: Sage.

Tardieu, B. (1999). Computer as community memory: How people in very poor neighborhoods make a computer their own. In Schön, D. A., Sanyal, B., and Mitchell, W. J. (Eds.). High technology and low-income communities: Prospects for the positive use of advanced information technology (pp. 289–312). Cambridge, MA: MIT Press.

Tichenor, P. J.; Donohue, G. A.; J. M.; and Olin, C. N. (1970). Mass media flow and differential growth in knowledge. Public Opinion Quarterly, 34 , 159–170.

Twidale, M. B.; Randall. D.; and Bentley, R. (1994). Situated evaluation for cooperative systems. In Proceedings, CSCW '94 (pp. 441–452). Chapel Hill, NC: Association for Computing Machinery.

U. S. Dept. of Health and Human Services. (1985). Report of the Secretary's Task Force on Black and minority health. Washington, DC: DHHS.

U. S, Dept. of Health and Human Services. (1990). Healthy people 2000. (DHHS Publication No. PHS 91-50213). Washington, DC: U.S. Government Printing Office.

Van House, N. (in press). Digital libraries and collaborative knowledge construction. In Bishop, A. P., Van House, N., and Buttenfield, B.(Eds.). Digital library use: Social practice in design and evaluation. Cambridge, MA: MIT Press.

Weiner, D.; Warner, T. A.; Harris, T. M.; and Levin, R. M. (1995). Apartheid representations in a digital landscape: GIS, remote sensing and local knowledge in Kiepersol, South Africa. Cartography and Geographic Information Systems, 22(1), 30–44.

White, J. E. (1999, March 8). Prejudice? Perish the thought. Time, 153(9), 36.

Whitmore, E. (Ed.) (1998). Understanding and practicing participatory evaluation. San Francisco, CA: Jossey-Bass.

Whyte, W. F. (Ed.) (1991). Participatory action research. Newbury Park, CA: Sage.

Wilkinson, L. (1999). How to build scenarios. Wired Magazine Online [Available: http://www.wired.com/wired/scenarios/build.html].

Chapter 4

Assessing the Provision of Networked Services: ERIC as an Example

R. David Lankes

ABSTRACT

ERIC is an important component of the U.S. Department of Education's dissemination activity. It has been a source of innovation, and is a powerful tool that supports a range of user services. However, large-scale adoption of the Internet into the program has lead to a fragmented ERIC that finds its greatest value, service, marginalizing its biggest product, the ERIC database. This chapter examines key components of ERIC for assessment and proposes models, key questions and solutions for improving ERIC. The paper suggests that an experiential evaluation approach, combined with deductive modeling, may offer one way to redesign a program such as ERIC.

INTRODUCTION

The Internet has had a significant impact on nearly every sector of the information industry. From e-commerce to libraries to education, the interactive capabilities of the worldwide network have changed users' expectations and organizations' delivery vehicles. Yet, not all aspects of the "Internet effect" are immediately evident. Some organizations that embraced the Internet early are only now discovering the consequences.

While "early" is a relative term, this chapter will focus on Internet adoption after commercialization and popularization of the network. This can be marked at approximately 1993 with the advent of the World Wide Web and removal of commercial restrictions on Internet content and traffic. While certainly the

Internet existed long before the early 1990s and had an impact on research and education, many of the impacts discussed in this chapter can only be seen in the large-scale popular adoption of the Web. An example of an early adopter of the Internet is the Education Resources Information Center (ERIC).

The paper does not attempt to provide a comprehensive literature review about ERIC, evaluation approaches in the networked environment, or key issues in the evaluation of networked services such as ERIC. Other chapters in this book do provide such background reading and will not be repeated here. Instead of a literature-based approach for considering the evaluation of ERIC, the author prefers to rely on a more experiential and deductive approach.

This chapter will examine ERIC and the impacts of Internet adoption in light of assessment. It will identify key aspects of the system that have been affected by a phenomenon known as disintermediation. It will further use post-Internet efforts such as AskERIC and the advances in metadata research to propose a solution to improve the valuable ERIC service. The paper suggests that the existing assessment models for ERIC are inappropriate and that an experiential approach, combined with a deductive model may offer some insights into how best to redesign the ERIC program.

WHY ERIC

ERIC is a particularly revelatory case for examining the provision of networked services for several reasons:

- ERIC is representative of large information resource providers: While having significant funding and structural differences from services like the National Library of Medicine's MEDLINE (http://www.nlm.nih.gov/) and the National Library of Agriculture's AGRICOLA (http://www.nalusda.gov/ag98/), there are many common features. All are federally funded and part of larger national libraries (in ERIC's case, the National Library of Education). Further ERIC has many similar issues with traditional information providers of bibliographic online systems.
- ERIC is government funded and an active member of an emerging market: While the majority of the ERIC creation process is funded by the U.S. Department of Education it plays a significant role in a larger education marketplace. This role can be seen in partners such as Dialog and SilverPlatter, and in standards setting activities such as the Gateway to Educational Materials (GEM) as well as popular Web services such as the National Parent Information Network (NPIN) and AskERIC.
- ERIC's decentralized nature provides a rich environment of Internet

services and resources: As will be discussed in this chapter, ERIC is far from a monolithic service; rather it is a series of subject experts and support components. Each of these ERIC elements has approached the Internet and networked resources in different ways.

- ERIC is at the initial stages of a large-scale evaluation: As ERIC enters into its 35th year it also enters into a two-year evaluation process. The first phase of the evaluation came in the form of five commissioned papers (McClure, 2000). The next phase will be a formal yearlong evaluation looking not only at ERIC's past but setting directions for the future. As the commissioned papers have already demonstrated, the process of evaluating the system and setting direction will be no easy task.

This chapter continues that ongoing ERIC assessment as well as providing an examination of how traditional information resource providers cope with the effects of the Internet.

ERIC BACKGROUND

The ERIC program was founded in 1966 to capture the fugitive, or gray literature (Stonehill and Brandhorst, 1992), in the field of education. The idea was simple: Make the mass of research in education easily available to the field of scholars, and scholarship will improve. ERIC set out to capture dissertations, conference proceedings, white papers, research reports, and the information that was often hard to find (later adding a mission to index and abstract relevant journals). It did so in a revolutionary way for the time. It created a decentralized system of subject specific clearinghouses to build both a digital bibliographic database (a cutting edge concept at the time) and a microfiche archive of the documents themselves.

In the intervening years, ERIC has added an active publication program within the clearinghouses producing both major monographs and small synthesis pieces. The system also has a rich tradition of special projects that have resulted in a rich a varied set of research and development projects including the AskERIC service (Lankes, 1995) and the National Parent Information Network (http://www.npin.org/). In recent years ERIC has become a key player in the Internet environment with each ERIC component hosting a Web site and sponsoring one of the first 100 Web sites and the first Web presence for the U.S. Department of Education.

ASSESSMENT BACKGROUND

In 1999, the ERIC program office in the U.S. Department of Education began a major system-wide evaluation of ERIC by commissioning five papers on different aspects of ERIC (ACCESS ERIC 2000): Mission, Structure, and

Resources; The ERIC Database and Its Technical Processes; Technology and the ERIC System; ERIC User Services; and ERIC Products and Information Dissemination. The papers made a series of observations and discoveries. In some cases they recommended specific technologies, while other papers concentrated on areas for further examination. Across the papers, however, common themes emerged (Lankes, 2000), e.g., that while ERIC is a well-known and successful service with much to be proud of, ERIC was far from a unified system and needed to re-evaluate its users and mission as well as its technology.

> The decentralized model, however, also has caused the system to appear fractured. For instance, the clearinghouses' Web sites are rich with valuable resources, but links to the ERIC system (http://www.accesseric.org) and AskERIC are not consistently provided. Nor do the Web sites provide links to other clearinghouses that may have information relevant to their users' needs. At some sites a visitor would need to be persistent to find information on a clearinghouse's relationship with the central ERIC system. The visitor also may need to know of the existence of another clearinghouse to obtain relevant resources from that clearinghouse. Furthermore, the number of interfaces to the ERIC database, the large number of ERIC components, and the different look and feel of components' Web sites all contribute to users' confusion over the ERIC system. More coordination is needed to give users a more coherent picture of the system. This is one of the easier tasks to enhance ERIC user services. Giving users a clear map of what the ERIC system offers and how a particular clearinghouse relates to the central system and other components will enable users to navigate the system and take full advantage of ERIC services and products. (Hsieh-Yee, 1999)

These themes, particularly the unambiguous call for major changes to the ERIC database and database processes then have formed the basis of a half-million dollar assessment to be conducted in 2000 and 2001. This chapter will seek to add an insider view to the commissioned papers as the assessment gets underway and build a revelatory case for other's assessing information systems adopting the Internet.

A MODEL FOR ERIC ASSESSMENT

What follows is a basic model for assessing ERIC. It can be applied to other large information resource providers. It begins by establishing a basic set of ERIC components and their relations to each other before and after large-scale adoption of the Internet. It then explores these system components in greater detail.

Figure 4.1 represents a simple view of the ERIC system before 1992 and wide-scale adoption of the Web. The key components of the system consisted of

- Users: ERIC users could be characterized as education researchers, librarians, education students, and front-line educators;
- The Database: a coherent collection of bibliographic records managed by the ERIC Processing Facility;
- Clearinghouses: a distributed set of subject experts selecting material for the database, indexing and abstracting this material for the facility and publishing synthesis pieces based on the contents of the database; and
- The ERIC Document Reproduction Service (EDRS): the document delivery service of ERIC that provides microfiche and paper copies of non-copyright documents in the database.

The key relationships of this figure are between the users and the database, the database and the Clearinghouses, and the users and the clearinghouses.

In this model the user's primary interaction with ERIC is through the database and some form of intermediation. The intermediation in this model is

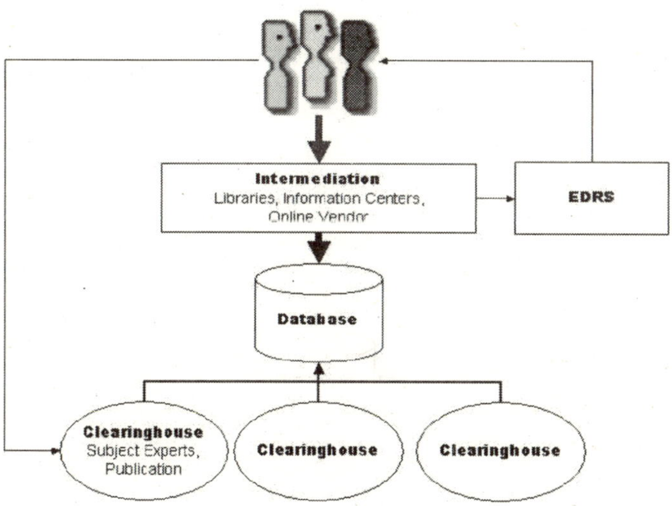

Figure 4.1: ERIC Before Large-Scale Internet Adoption

primarily provided by agents external to ERIC such as libraries or online database providers such as Dialog or SilverPlatter. While there is some minimal interaction directly between users and clearinghouses, this is restricted to database searches, and publication requests. In this model the primary role of the clearinghouses is to feed the database. All information is controlled and processing is centralized. To the end-user, ERIC seems like a coherent system under a single database, and the user population seems to be cohesive.

The current large-scale evaluation of the ERIC system must be careful NOT to evaluate ERIC on this model. As will be shown, this model is no longer a valid representation of the current ERIC system. While ERIC may return to this approach, it does not currently work in this manner. One trap that the evaluation must avoid is assuming that the database still forms the basis on interactions between users and the ERIC system. Another assumption that must not be made is that the majority of intermediation between users and ERIC is done with resources external to the ERIC system (and budget). These assumptions are invalid in light of large-scale Internet adoption.

Wide-scale adoption of the Internet has significantly changed the model offered in Figure 4.1. A new model has emerged as represented in Figure 4.2. As clearinghouses went online, their subject expertise became increasingly available directly to end-users. End-users could go directly to ERIC Clearinghouses they felt best matched their needs (so reading teachers began

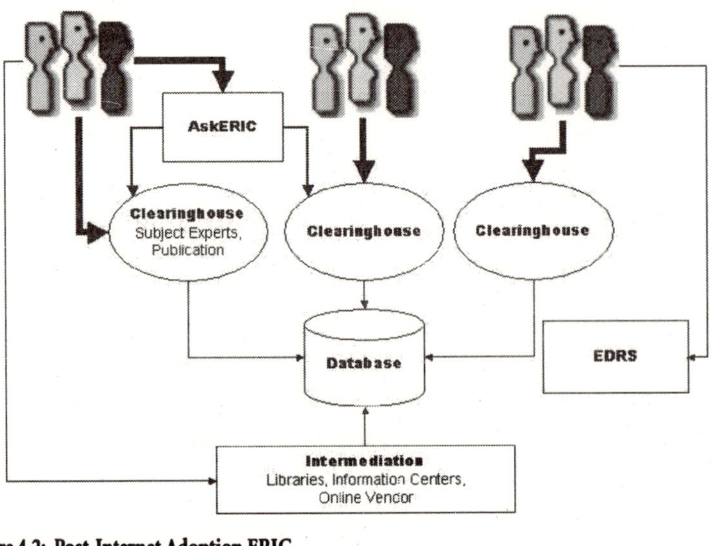

Figure 4.2: Post-Internet Adoption ERIC

to identify with the Reading Clearinghouse while guidance staff began going directly to the Counseling Clearinghouse). Clearinghouses began responding directly to user needs by posting materials and creating services on the Internet. Often these services were seen as small increases in effort, and so clearinghouses mounted Web-based resources with little or no additional resources from the federal government. In the e-commerce literature, this shift of access from user to intermediary to user directly to producer is called disintermediation. The rest of this chapter deals with the impact of a disintermediated ERIC system.

COMPONENTS OF ERIC FOR ASSESSMENT

As previously mentioned there are four key components that must be considered in an assessment of the ERIC system:

- Users
- Database
- The Clearinghouses
- EDRS

In this model, however, a new element is added: AskERIC. AskERIC began as a special project of the ERIC Clearinghouse on Information and Technology but has grown to a system-wide effort involving every clearinghouse and ERIC component. AskERIC consists of a Web site with practitioner-oriented resources such as lesson plans, pointers and response archives, and a digital reference service that takes end-user questions and provides expert answers including ERIC database searches and relevant Internet cites and non-Internet resources.

AskERIC is a significant new component in that

- it is the first ERIC service born after Internet adoption;
- it has attracted large-scale use often from users who know nothing about the larger ERIC system (three million Web hits per month and over 1,400 question per week at peak use);
- it involves all of the ERIC clearinghouses; and
- it does not directly feed the database function.

The author will examine the impacts of Internet adoption and subsequent disintermediation in each of these components.

Users

ERIC began its mission to disseminate education research primarily to education researchers. Over the years this mission was significantly expanded to reach front-line educators such as in-classroom teachers, school librarians and faculty. It has also been expanded to encompass parents and special rural and urban populations. In the pre-Internet adoption model this population, while wide, could still be considered somewhat cohesive. It could be sampled, trained and changes in the ERIC database impacted all user segments equally.

However, considering ERIC users before Internet adoption could be seen as a bit misleading. ERIC's primary users were intermediaries and information organizations that repackaged ERIC for the eventual end-user. Microfiche was produced for libraries. Computer tapes were produced for external organizations, such as universities and online database vendors, to incorporate into their own unique products. The first ERIC produced interface to the database did not happen until nearly 1994. To date there are no controls placed on interface and database manipulation on the part of third-party vendors such as SilverPlatter.

This disconnect between end-users and ERIC had some advantages. Accessibility and technical development, for example, were not concerns of the ERIC system. Third parties handled database technologies and connectivity of end-users to ERIC with little or no cost to the government. With the Internet this disconnect with users is gone. However, as ERIC has taken a greater role in providing direct intermediation, resource issues have become obvious. Clearinghouses have discovered that mounting an adequate Web presence to meet user needs and expectations is a significant new cost from pre-Internet adoption. ERIC has absorbed the work of direct user service without the resources being expended by the previous third parties. Further, the once coherent user population has fragmented based on subject expertise. Parents may be a major user of one clearinghouse but not another. The ERIC system is losing its ability to talk about ERIC users and must now talk about Clearinghouse constituencies. Users of one clearinghouse are often completely ignorant of other ERIC resources.

The ERIC assessment in terms of users must ask these question:

- What are the individual constituencies of each ERIC component (clearinghouses, the ERIC database, EDRS)?
- What is the overlap of these constituencies?
- What impact would limiting these constituencies have on each individual component?
- What is the extent of current and predicted demand on clearinghouse intermediation efforts (Internet services)?

These are all key evaluation questions whose answers are not obvious without a formal ongoing assessment program.

Database

The database lies at the heart of ERIC. While Clearinghouses have become publishers, reference centers, trainers, and Web designers, they still feed from (and to) the database. Furthermore, much of the system-wide approach and history stems from database building, therefore making the database a core element of assessment.

The ERIC database can be seen as having four functions:

- Archive: A collection of objects (cataloging records and digests) that represent the field of education at a given point in time. While one can argue how complete this representation is, it is nonetheless a view of the past. Extensive cataloging acts as a historical record of a document's existence. In this capacity it is not responsible for locating the article, merely marking its existence at a point in time (when it was entered into the database). It is also in this capacity that the database serves educational researchers asking the question "where have we been?"
- Institutional Memory: Strongly related to the concept of archive is that of institutional memory. In a sense the database represents the collective memory of the ERIC system. From the inclusion of ERIC publications and manuals, to implied selection criteria, the database documents ERIC and its changes. This role can be extended to the Department of Education in the system's attempts to capture the publications of the entire department.
- Research/Reference Aid: Possibly the largest use of the database is as a reference aid. Users access the database to find information to be applied to a given circumstance. In this way, the database is merely a finding aid for original documents such as articles or monographs. It is in this capacity that the database serves users asking, "where can I find something?"
- Decision Support: Strongly related to the concept of reference aid is that of decision support system. While information purists may find fault, the truth is a large percentage of users come to the database as a means of supporting action on its own. That is, users aren't looking for the catalogued document but rather use the abstracts and document resumes as documents in and of themselves. Examples of this function might include researchers conducting a literature review or a teacher looking to support technology plans.

All of these roles must be considered as part of an ERIC evaluation. In a disintermediated ERIC all of these roles have been significantly affected by the Web environment, resulting in an increasingly marginalized database. The key to this marganilization is the print orientation of the database. Even

Web materials entered into the database are printed and processed. While this made sense for archiving the gray literature of the past, today an increasing amount of the information to be captured is electronic only. This problem is further compounded by the fact that ERIC Clearinghouses are now producing electronic and non-print resources that cannot be processed into the database. The bottom line is that while the clearinghouses have changed their materials and service to better meet user needs through the Internet, the database has not made any significant changes in light of the World Wide Web.

Clearinghouses

The Internet has signified the dawn of the clearinghouse. While each clearinghouse was always given room for individual innovation and always had some contact with end-users, the Internet has raised the visibility and access by at least an order of magnitude. Each Clearinghouse has its own Web site and a series of Web services aimed at unique constituencies. Since these Web sites and services grew around (and often to circumvent) established quality and consistency standards geared towards the ERIC database, there is very little consistency from clearinghouse to clearinghouse. For example, three of the clearinghouses mount their own versions of the ERIC database. While most clearinghouses mount short synthesis products, some mount larger synthesis pieces as well. Some clearinghouses have even created full-text collection of documents in their subject area separate from the database.

In many ways, the ERIC system has become the ERIC database and a series of semi-autonomous clearinghouses. Each clearinghouse has established partnerships with industry, user associations and other organization with little to no consultation with the other ERIC components. These partnerships have been driven, as mentioned earlier, by a need for resources to support direct user intermediation. It has also lead to fragmentation in mission, vision and certainly operations. These differences are becoming evident as the system wrestles with re-designing the ERIC database, and the system as a whole.

Further, clearinghouses have become more loyal to their individual constituencies than to the database. This is understandable for two linked reasons: ERIC has always been oriented to serving users and clearinghouses see the database as increasingly unable to meet user needs on its own. In a disintermediated environment clearinghouses have moved faster in response to rising user expectations. They also feel that they have a more direct sense of what users want since they have closer interaction to end-users. This is not to say that clearinghouses have abandoned the database. All still see the value of the database, work hard to keep it up to date, and are dedicated to its improvement. It is simply that many clearinghouses are unwilling to wait for changes to the database when they have direct control over their own Web sites and Internet activities. This increased control leads to increased ownership, and increased attention. This has always been true of clearinghouse publications and user services as well.

EDRS

The biggest impact on EDRS with the large-scale adoption of the Internet was the introduction of full-text electronic delivery of ERIC materials. Since ERIC is still a primarily document-based system, document delivery is essential. Pre-Internet document delivery was done through microfiche and paper. The Internet has now brought document delivery of Adobe Acrobat files through the World Wide Web. However, this service provides an excellent example of ERIC caught in two worlds.

Currently non-copyright documents are sent to EDRS where they are photographed for microfiche. These microfiche are then scanned as images into TIFF files that are then converted to PDF files for delivery. The digital files that are sent are images of text, not actual text. This makes the files large and, at best, inconvenient for manipulation. Also, as these electronic documents were created from fiche, not the original document, they wary widely in reproduction quality and lack simple advantages of digital documents such as color. Adoption of full-text has been slow but is increasing. The first roll-outs have been geared at traditional ERIC clients, namely academic libraries, and so marketing and systems to reach in-classroom educators have been limited.

Key questions for an evaluation of ERIC in terms of EDRS include:

- Is fiche still needed?
- If fiche is needed for archival purposes, does it need to be distributed or can it simply become a centralized fiche repository?
- Can the full-text process be improved?
- How can EDRS better handle born-digital documents to speed processing and improve quality?

Once again, answers to these questions will require a careful and ongoing program or assessment.

AskERIC

As previously stated, using the pre-Internet model of ERIC for an evaluation is problematic at best. Aside from ignoring the disintermediation effect, it misses nearly all of ERIC's response to the Internet. The largest scale system-wide response has been the creation and institutionalization of AskERIC. While the service began as a special project of one clearinghouse, it is now part of every clearinghouse contract.

AskERIC, in light of this discussion, can be seen as a model of a post-Internet adoption ERIC. It involves components system-wide not only in answering questions, but in creation of policy and quality criteria. While it provides a central door to the AskERIC service, each clearinghouse can provide its own access and interface. Some clearinghouses, for example, point directly to AskERIC from their Web sites; some point to parts of AskERIC such as a question entry form. Some ERIC projects repackage the AskERIC service, such as the NPIN that uses AskERIC as part of its service called "Parents AskERIC."

AskERIC must be considered in an assessment of ERIC. AskERIC also points at elements that should be part of any ERIC redesign:

- A distributed solution that can be repackaged for specific audiences
- A system-wide solution that builds on the unique subject-level expertise of the clearinghouses
- An Internet-based solution that provides the best of the existing ERIC database, but also materials of direct use to practitioners
- Personalized service controlled by the ERIC system itself

These components have had a significant impact on the operation of ERIC, overall, and have evolved, in part, because of the evolution and development of the Web-based environment.

A PROPOSED SOLUTION: THE ERIC KNOWLEDGEBASE

So, where does the disintermediated ERIC system go from here? Two extreme solutions would be to allow the clearinghouses to continue on their road to autonomy and manage them much as the Education Laboratories (http://www.ed.gov/prog_info/Labs/) run out of the Department of Education now. Each clearinghouse would be given its own audiences, products, and oversight. This approach would require a great deal of oversight on the part of the federal government and would loose the strength of diverse expertise and organizations working together in a comprehensive education dissemination effort.

The opposite extreme would be to corral the clearinghouses into a new version of the pre-Internet model. Clearinghouse expertise would contribute to a new ERIC portal, a single ERIC Web presence that provided a single interface to ERIC information, print, etc. Perhaps the ERIC Web space (a term the author uses to refer to ERIC created/housed information that exists solely on the Web), could be folded into the existing AskERIC service, or system-wide Web site run out of ACCESS ERIC. Both of these approaches seem to sacrifice too much. The question becomes how to preserve to strengths of clearinghouse identity an audience linkage while avoiding a confusing maze of disconnected Web sites.

The Emerging ERIC Knowledgebase

Clearly, a major shift must occur to bring these different information systems, database, Web space and digital reference services into alignment. While this may ultimately lead to a larger price tag for ERIC, the federal government will be assured that their investment makes maximum use of allocated resources.

The author argues that the coordination of ERIC systems comes in the form of an ERIC Knowledgebase. This Knowledgebase can act as a framework for evaluation (to see how close ERIC comes currently) and a vision for strategic planning. The proposed ERIC Knowledgebase would be a multifaceted information system. It would rely on standard metadata and data interchange standards to create an electronic repository of digital objects (full-text articles, software, lesson plans, etc.), object references (to existing fiche, journal articles, non-ERIC Web sites, or other items not stored within ERIC), and services (such as digital reference assistance). ERIC's main purpose would be to add data to the Knowledgebase through its distributed system of clearinghouses and wider network of partners including authors of education related materials. The Knowledgebase itself would be distributed throughout ERIC components, but act as a unified collection with multiple, user-specific interfaces.

Contents of the Knowledgebase

The Knowledgebase would consist of the current ERIC database, however it would directly link bibliographic records to their full text counterparts if they existed in electronic form. In addition to the current bibliographic records, all the contents of the ERIC Web space would be cataloged and harvested to be part of the Knowledgebase. Once again, metadata from the Web space would be directly linked to actual items (Web pages, software, etc.) where possible. Where an ERIC component could secure proper rights, the actual binary objects indexed would be included in the Knowledgebase as well, thereby creating a digital archive. Last, the Knowledgebase would store profiles of subject experts currently available through AskERIC. These profiles could be searched and used to ask questions from within the Knowledgebase. The resulting question/answer sets might also be stored in the Knowledgebase (assuming privacy issues are resolved).

Facets of the Knowledgebase

The Knowledgebase will incorporate a series of facets that will be used to filter information for a given audience and/or interface. For example, instead of a single definition of quality, item quality will vary according to audience and information use. For example, currently ERIC document résumés go through at least two phases of editing before they are entered into the database (one at a clearinghouse, the second at the ERIC facility). This two-step process minimizes typographical and other errors. However, this process also slows the entry of current information into the database. Many clearinghouses have taken to create a *pre-release* Web site that list in-process database items. These would be directly entered into the ERIC Knowledgebase and tagged as *in-process* records. Searchers worried about data quality could filter these records out. Over time, with proper training and software, the second level of editing could become redundant, thereby speeding up database building activities.

Another facet represented in the Knowledgebase would be duration. With the simple addition of document lifespan the ERIC Knowledgebase could become dynamic. Items could be entered into the Knowledgebase knowing they will not be archived (therefore needing to meet a to a different set of quality criteria). These items (such as conference announcements) could be automatically weeded from the Knowledgebase, or brought up for review on a schedule. Further, items with shorter life spans would be subject to a lower level of indexing effort. This notion of cataloging depth then becomes yet another facet for the Knowledgebase. Some documents could have very brief metadata records associated with them (say a title, and short abstract), while other items may have metadata resembling current ERIC document résumés.

A last facet needed in the ERIC Knowledgebase is that of cataloguing intelligence. Here, a record indicates whether or not a human cataloguer created a metadata description. This would allow for the use of automated harvesting of information. Such automation would dramatically increase the amount of information ERIC is able to enter into the Knowledgebase. By indicating whether a record was human catalogued or automatically harvested, users could filter out automated records if they felt they were not indexed well, or wanted better guarantees of accurate metadata description.

Network of Partners

Another significant change enabled by the creation of the ERIC Knowledgebase would be in determining entities allowed to add information to the Knowledgebase. Currently, only ERIC clearinghouses can enter records into the database and, then, only through the centralized facility. In the new Knowledgebase clearinghouses could enter data directly into the Knowledgebase, as could significant non-ERIC partners. Approved publishers, for example, could enter stub records directly, with the system tagging these records for later review, and allowing users to filter these records if they so desired. Further, by using standard metadata approaches, records could be added directly into the Knowledgebase through harvesting. The harvest engine for the Knowledgebase would recognize standard metadata schemes (such as Dublin Core) and translate them into schemes consistent with the ERIC Knowledgebase. Thus, ERIC could utilize the labor of non-ERIC partners.

Interfaces

The key to making the ERIC Knowledgebase successful lies in the interfaces users engage to access the data. Once again, just as no single interface will work for the current ERIC Database, no single interface will work for the new ERIC Knowledgebase. While it will be necessary for ERIC to manage the underlying Knowledgebase structure and systems, interfaces should be plentiful. ERIC should license the right to connect to the underlying Knowledgebase. This license would not be geared towards revenue, so much as control that key filters and fields are always obvious to the user (including clear indication of ERIC's identity). If ERIC manages the underlying Knowledgebase, users will be assured that no matter what interface they use, the underlying data are consistent.

By separating out the interface from the Knowledgebase itself, vendors, partners and the ERIC system will be able to better match the information needs of users with their interface preferences. These preferences may relate to device constraints (connecting to ERIC on a cell phone), experience (simple searches versus professional interfaces), or software selection (embedding ERIC search capabilities directly into word processors for example).

ASSESSMENT RECOMMENDATIONS

This chapter has put forth a series of models, components, and possible solutions for an ERIC assessment. It has concentrated on information flow and organizational structure over such assessment criteria as cost and return on investment. However, the author strongly believes that an evaluation focus on cost, particularly using the old operational assumptions of ERIC is dangerous and misleading. In the old model, ERIC did not cover the cost of user intermediation, it had a single information space it needed to populate (the database) and ERIC was a bargain then. Also using the pre-Internet model for ERIC will put ERIC in a very bad light. By looking at ERIC simply as a database, ERIC will come up desperately short in its ability to innovatively meet user needs. An assessment of ERIC must take into account needed changes to the ERIC database while concentrating on the good work ERIC has done in the Internet. Certainly, means of coordinating these activities and rebuilding the cohesiveness of ERIC must be sought, but it cannot be done by retreating to a marginalized database, or simply seeking to put the Internet genie back in the bottle.

ERIC must be considered as content aggregator, content creator and context provider. The database is content aggregation, and moving to an expanded and distributed Knowledgebase should significantly improve the relevance of this ERIC function. The clearinghouses and their production of synthesis pieces and Web sites can be seen as the strongest aspect of ERIC and should be preserved and strengthened. Finally, content without context is increasingly less useful in these days of information overload. User services and AskERIC providing a human voice and subject area expertise is a vital part of any Internet-based information system and should not be seen simply as an "add-on" function to the database.

SURVIVING THE NETWORKED ENVIRONMENT

ERIC is, in part, a victim of its own success, inventiveness, and desire to serve. The issues the system must face are large and difficult. However, in the face of these problems, ERIC continues to serve users and increase its reputation as a significant and important resource. ERIC stands at the brink of a great opportunity. The system has not sat idly by as the Internet has exploded. It is an Internet-savvy organization. ERIC knows the Internet, and knows how to serve its users on the Internet. ERIC also knows how to serve traditional non-Internet users as well. The problem is its inability to rectify these two missions in its current operations. The system must begin to ask difficult questions and re-evaluate all its services in light of the current information and networked environment.

As the Department of Education's National Library of Education prepares to evaluate ERIC, it is important to identify the key information services of the system. One means to reconcile ERIC's prestigious past, with its entrepreneurial present (and future) is through the advent of the ERIC Knowledgebase. The Knowledgebase would take the current ERIC database, unify it with the ERIC Web space and digital reference activities while creating a more distributed and agile information system. This Knowledgebase would be based on standard metadata and would build a platform for future ERIC activities and priorities. Developing and implementing this model may provide ERIC with the means to fully exploit the Web and networked environment for the benefit of its users.

This chapter suggests that an experiential approach to assessment may be a useful tool when used in combination with other more formal assessment techniques. Too often, formal assessment techniques fail to adequately consider the personal experience and knowledge of those who have actually participated in the development and administration of a program. The experiential approach, combined with an analytical deductive model—in this case the Knowledgebase model—can offer evaluators one means to consider the future development of a program such as ERIC.

ABOUT THE AUTHOR

R. David Lankes works in the area of digital reference and education information. He completed his Ph.D. from Syracuse University, School of Information Studies. He is the co-founder of the AskERIC service, and principle investigator of the Gateway to Educational Materials (GEM) and the Virtual Reference Desk (VRD) projects as well as director of the ERIC

Clearinghouse on Information and Technology. He has also served as a visiting scholar to Harvard's Graduate School of Education. Additional background information can be found at: http://www.askeric.org/~rdlankes.

E-mail: rdlankes@askeric.org

REFERENCES

ACCESS ERIC. (May, 2000). Commissioned Papers on the ERIC System. (WWW Document). From http://www.accesseric.org/papers/index.html.

Hsieh-Yee, Ingrid. (1999). ERIC User Services: Evaluation in a Decentralized Environment. (WWW Document). From http://www.accesseric.org/papers/paper4.doc.

Lankes, R. D. (2000). Grabbing ERIC by the Tail: Introducing the ERIC Commissioned Papers. Government Information Quarterly, 18(1) (in-press).

Lankes, R. D. (1995). AskERIC and the virtual library: Lessons for emerging digital libraries. Internet Research, 5(1), 56–63.

McClure, C. R. (Ed.). (2000). Special Theme Issue: Evaluation Issues Related to ERIC: Issues and Strategies. Government Information Quarterly, 18(1) (in press).

Stonehill, R., and Brandhorst, T. (1992). The Three phases of ERIC. Educational Researcher, 21(3), 18–21.

Chapter 5

Assessing Interoperability in the Networked Environment: Standards, Evaluation, and Testbeds in the Context of Z39.50

William E. Moen, Ph.D.

ABSTRACT

The ability of a broad range of components and processes to work together is an essential characteristic of the networked environment. Interoperability is the concept used to describe this working together. Yet the term interoperability can characterize a range of interactions and capabilities. This paper proposes a framework for assessing interoperability. Based on implementation experience of ANSI/NISO Z39.50 clients and servers, particularly for providing access to online library catalogs, the framework identifies several kinds of interoperability. The paper discusses the extent to which a standard, such Z39.50, can assure interoperability. A review of recent evaluation studies of Z39.50 projects is reported within the proposed framework. One solution path for interoperability problems is the use of Z39.50 profiles. Beyond the specifications, whether in a standard or a profile, there is a need for a testing environment to assure demonstrable interoperability, and the paper concludes with a discussion of a proposed interoperability testbed that could server vendors and consumers.

INTRODUCTION

An underlying assumption of any network is that various components and processes will work together to produce desired results (e.g., data transmission, data interchange, reliability of services). The term interoperability has been used to characterize this working together, especially, the workings of lower-level data communication components. Usage of the term has evolved to refer more generally to the extent to which different types of computers, networks, operating systems, and applications work together effectively to exchange information in a useful and meaningful manner. Miller (2000) suggests a perspective that is even more encompassing: he says that to be interoperable means "one should actively be engaged in the ongoing process of ensuring that the systems, procedures and culture of an organization are managed in such a way as to maximise opportunities for exchange and re-use of information, whether internally or externally."

This broader use of the term brings about new challenges in addressing and assessing the facets of interoperability. In this chapter, we explore the concept of interoperability and the roles of standards, evaluation, and testbeds in addressing and assessing the extent to which diverse systems interoperate. Specifically, this chapter explores issues of interoperability within the context of, and from experience with, the national and international standard *Information Retrieval (Z39.50): Application Service Definition and Protocol Specification (ANSI/NISO Z39.50-1995/ISO 23950)* (National Information Standards Organization, 1995). ANSI/NISO Z39.50 defines a computer-to-computer communications protocol used by systems for purposes of information retrieval. It is increasingly deployed in a variety of information communities including libraries, museums, geospatial and other data centers, and state and national governments. (For background information and a selected list of basic resources about Z39.50, see Moen, 1995; Moen and Lepchenske, 2000).

We use the knowledge gained from identifying Z39.50 interoperability issues to propose a multi-level framework for investigating and evaluating interoperability and to explain the limited role of the standard in assuring interoperability because of other critical factors that affect the "exchange and reuse of information." The framework allows us to identify a range of threats to interoperability and to explore problems of interoperability both from implementor/vendor and user perspectives. This framework is being developed to address Z39.50 interoperability specifically in the context of cross-bibliographic database searching. We suggest, however, that this framework can assist in targeting assessment methods and metrics appropriate to different kinds data and applications where interoperability is a key factor. We exercise the proposed framework by reviewing and discussing several evaluations of Z39.50 projects in terms of the framework.

The networked environment is heterogeneous in that it hosts many different technologies, various data formats, multiple applications, and other networked life forms. A functional goal in this environment is to hide the heterogeneity from users so they may effectively do business, search for information, communicate, and perform other tasks. For example, the centralized Web search engine services appear to hide this complexity from the users. This is done by virtue of centralizing indexes to Web resources and making them searchable through a single system. Contrast this to the way Z39.50 performs searching and retrieval across multiple resources of varying data types, on entirely different information retrieval systems—each with its own peculiar functionality and search structure; this presents a challenge at an entirely different level of magnitude when it comes to hiding the heterogeneity.

Hiding or masking the networked environment's heterogeneity, or at least specific information spaces within the networked environment, and enabling users carry out specific tasks successfully is desired. The concept of interoperability can assist us in characterizing the issues and challenges in reaching the goal of transparent access to information. The experience with Z39.50 has taught us that getting diverse information systems to communicate and interoperate is a challenge. But that experience has also brought us to a point where we can articulate more clearly what is at stake with interoperability and to develop the methods and procedures for evaluating that interoperability.

INTEROPERABILITY

There is little doubt interoperability is a key issue in the networked environment (see for example, Lynch, 1993; Lynch and Garcia-Molina, 1995; Miller, 2000; and Payette, et al., 1999). Interoperability or its absence can affect information access. Technical interoperability can raise important policy and organizational issues (Moen, 2000). Interoperability, however, suffers from a lack of a clear definition (Miller, 2000). Webster's Third International Unabridged Dictionary provides no definition of the term. The Oxford English Dictionary (OED) defines *inter* as "mutually, reciprocally, together; between or among themselves; with each other" and *operable* as "capable of being accomplished; capable of being actually used." Interoperability can be defined simply as the capability of two entities to work together to accomplish some process or task.

Within the information technology and networking context, a number of definitions surface:

- The ability of one machine ... to interact usefully with other machines on a casual, ad hoc basis, without the prior planning or negotiation between the organizations operating those machines (Lynch, 1993, p. 3)
- Components of a system ... communicate with one another

effectively, correctly, and provide the expected services to the user (Preston and Lynch, 1994)

- The ability of different types of computers, networks, operating systems, and applications to work together effectively, without prior communication, in order to exchange information in a useful and meaningful manner (Abbas, et al., 1999)

The context for interoperability in this chapter is the networked environment in which numerous components work together to accomplish some goal. The components can take the form of hardware, software, data interchange formats, protocols, etc. To examine the complexity of interoperability, the focus of this chapter is on the use of Z39.50 to accomplish information retrieval tasks.

We can begin unbundling the concept of interoperability by viewing it in terms of levels and types and arrive at a multi-level perspective on it. Lynch and Garcia-Molina (1995) suggest a continuum of levels of interoperability which vary with individual implementations:

- From common tools and interfaces (navigation and access)
- To syntactic interoperability or the interchange of metadata or the diverse uses of digital objects
- To deep semantic interoperability or the ability to access consistently and coherently similar classes of digital objects and services

They state, "Deep semantic interoperability is a 'grand challenge' research problem; it is extraordinarily difficult, but of transcendent importance, if digital libraries are to live up to their long-term potential."

Based on experience with Z39.50 implementations, several types of interoperability can be articulated:

- Low-level protocol (syntactic): Do two implementations interchange protocol messages according to specifications or a standard?
- High-level protocol (functional): Do two implementations support the common services/functions?
- Semantic level: Do two implementations preserve and act on meaning of information retrieval tasks?
- User Task level: Do two systems support the information retrieval tasks of one or more user groups?

Additional types or levels will likely surface as we look at other network tools, technologies, and protocols, and our understanding of the scope and facets of interoperability problems increases.

In the case of Z39.50, low-level interoperability relates exclusively to syntactic protocol specifications defined in the standard. The other levels relate not only to the Z39.50 standard and its implementation in a system but also to the local information retrieval system and its capabilities. Preston and Lynch (1994) highlight the complexity of interoperable systems and how choices and deployment affect the ability of two systems to communicate meaningfully. The User Task level goes further and focuses not only on the protocol and its function but considers those things that affect an information system user's sense of that system's interoperability with another information system. To further lay the groundwork for this discussion, we review briefly how Z39.50 works and point out the potential threats to interoperability in Z39.50 implementations.

Z39.50 IN BRIEF

The purpose of Z39.50 is to allow a user on one information system to carry out search and retrieval transactions on another information system without prior knowledge of the details of the system. A user is able to interact with the familiar user interface of a local system to access one or more information systems and resources; this reduces the training burden for the user to learn many different search languages. The results of the search are returned and displayed in the familiar user interface of the user's local system.

The Z39.50 protocol provides an intersystem language that allows this communication between systems for the purposes of information retrieval. (Other communications protocols, such as File Transfer Protocol, Simple Mail Transport Protocol serve different purposes.) Z39.50 is an application layer protocol within the seven-layer Open Systems Interconnection (OSI) Basic Reference Model (see Piscitello and Chapin, 1993). Implementations of Z39.50 have used various networking and transport mechanisms, but the majority of implementations currently use the Internet's TCP/IP protocols. (The perceived effectiveness and interoperability of Z39.50 systems can be affected by the lower-level transport and telecommunications mechanisms

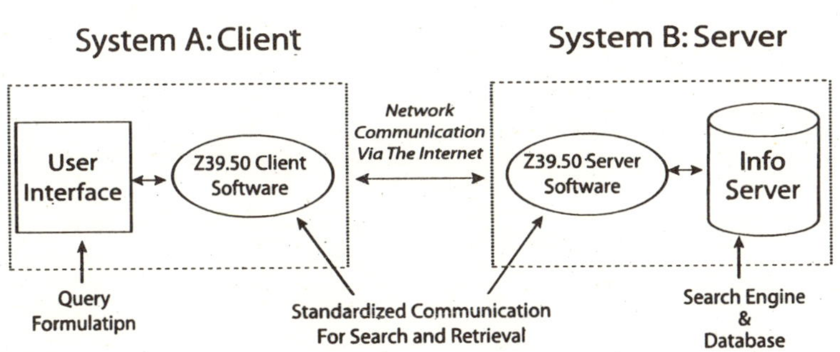

Figure 5.1 Information Systems Communicating via Z39.50

used, but discussion of the impact of these mechanisms is beyond the scope of this paper.)

Z39.50 can be viewed as a protocol and a language two computers use to communicate for the purpose of information retrieval. The protocol provides the rules for using the language (e.g., the sequence of messages). Like any language, Z39.50 provides both syntax and semantics, structure and vocabulary, that comprise the language. This standardized, intersystem language is used to express searches, request information to be returned, and a range of other information retrieval transactions. Figure 5.1 illustrates Z39.50 client and server components for two communicating information systems.

Z39.50 client and server software provides interfaces or front ends to local information retrieval systems. When a Z39.50 server is implemented for a local information retrieval system, a critical programming and configuration task is to provide for the translation or mapping from the local systems languages into the standardized Z39.50 language. An analogy for Z39.50 is Esperanto, which serves as a universal language that allows two people to communicate when they don't share a common language. Figure 5.2 illustrates where in Z39.50 implementations this conversion between local languages and Z39.50 standardized language occurs.

The analogy of Z39.50 as a standard language into which local systems convert their messages helps illustrates the potential problems of interoperability. One must accurately translate from one language into another if meaning (semantics) is to be retained. Current implementations of Z39.50 for online library catalogs (and for other applications) cause users problems when searching and retrieving information because of different interpretations (i.e., mappings) of the standardized language into disparate system schemas and indexing policies. Interoperability is jeopardized by these differences.

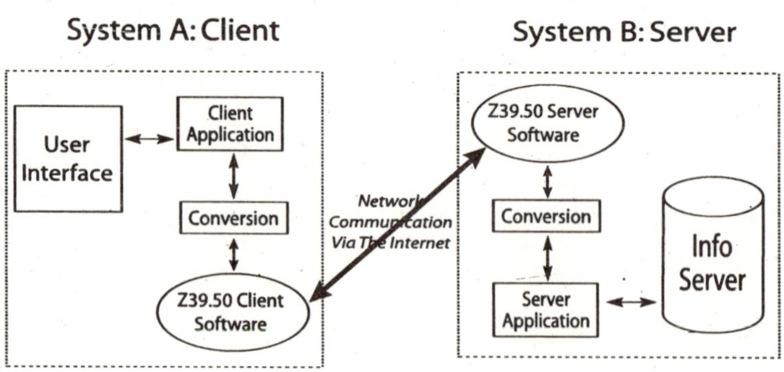

Figure 5.2 Conversion and Translation in Z39.50

The information retrieval systems (and their underlying database search engines) on which Z39.50 is implemented are just as critical when addressing interoperability as the Z39.50 client and server software implementations. Interoperability can be jeopardized by differences in information retrieval systems, their configuration, and their functionality; all of which affect their capability to support information retrieval tasks. For example, System A may support truncation of search terms, while System B does not have that functionality. In this case, System A can use Z39.50 to send a truncation search to System B, but System B will not be able to execute the intended search of the user. Interoperability is jeopardized by these differences. We can refer to the issues and problems in the above example as constituting fundamental interoperability problems within the Z3950 context of search and retrieval.

THREATS TO INTEROPERABILITY

Several critical threats to interoperability exist. A threat to interoperability can be defined as any organizational decision, specification, configuration, or other implementation decision that reduces a user's ability to successfully search and retrieve information in a meaningful way and have confidence in the results. This frames interoperability no longer as a binary "yes, two systems are interoperable" or "no, two systems are not interoperable" but rather proposes a continuum of interoperability. Two systems may be more or less interoperable. In this context, the starting point for evaluating interoperability is the user and the capability provided to his/her by the systems to complete—successfully or adequately—information retrieval tasks.

Three focal technical areas can delineate Z39.50 interoperability:

- The standard
- Implementations of the standard
- Local information retrieval systems

We will look briefly at each of these.

The early development of Z39.50 initially addressed the needs of libraries that wanted their systems to communicate for purposes of information retrieval and resource sharing. From the approval of the first version of Z39.50 in 1988 through 1992, Version 2, and finally with Version 3 approval in 1995, standards developers enhanced and expanded functionality available through the protocol. Additional functionality supported by the protocol provided the basis for broader interoperability.

For example, in the first two versions, the protocol machinery for exchanging anything other than data in the structure of Machine-Readable Cataloging Record (MARC) records was very limited. With Version 3, came the definition of a Generic Record Syntax (GRS-1) that enabled the retrieval of arbitrarily structured data (e.g., data not represented in MARC format).

Inadequacies of available record syntaxes in earlier versions of the standard would have precluded MARC and non-MARC systems from interoperating robustly. Version 3, however, is a fully featured and robust information retrieval protocol.

Current interoperability issues typically relate more to Z39.50 implementation and local information retrieval systems functionality rather than the adequacy of the standard, the protocol it defines, and the features supported by the protocol. Yet Z39.50 has been the object of criticism because to some it represents an outdated technology since it prescribes semantic level interaction between systems and also low-level protocol encoding mechanism. Some think that other available protocols could be used for passing the semantic content of the Z39.50 messages between systems.

Z39.50 implementation is an involved, sometimes modular process. Because Z39.50 is as complex as it is fully featured, an implementor wanting to develop a Z39.50 product needs to make a large number of decisions and choices from the options and features available in the standard. Two implementors independently can develop Z39.50 client and server products that are conformant with the standard, yet the result may be that one implementor's client does not interoperate very well (or at all) with the other's server. Precisely because of the flexibility in the standard (represented by the options and features), interoperability can be reduced or non-existent depending on how it is implemented. Thus, the flexibility provides both benefits and barriers to implementors and interoperability.

Finally, local information retrieval (IR) systems and their functionality are often the deciding factors in the extent of interoperability available. Z39.50 serves as an intermediary between two IR systems, sitting above the local IR system. Each local IR system has its own search and retrieval functionality (i.e., some systems support truncated searches, others don't). Each IR system makes the data in the records searchable according to local needs (i.e., policies for indexing). While this third area is beyond the jurisdiction of the Z39.50 standard, differences between local IR systems threaten interoperability. Z39.50 cannot make a local IR system execute a particular type of search if the underlying IR system doesn't support it.

For example, assume that two IR systems utilize Z39.50 for intersystem communication. A searcher on System A sends a search via Z39.50 for a subject term that it wants truncated (e.g., search is for the subject "comput*") and requests System B execute the search against its database. While the Z39.50 software on System B may understand the request, the local IR system does not support truncation searches. Thus, the user is not able to carry out the IR task as desired. This points to an important fact: The existence and use of a standard is not the only factor in achieving interoperability.

Tying this together in the context of a multi-level perspective on interoperability and with the four types of interoperability introduced above (i.e.,

Low-level protocol, High-level protocol, Semantic, and User Task), we can see more clearly the potential crisis points when two systems communicate. Figure 5.3 illustrates these crisis points.

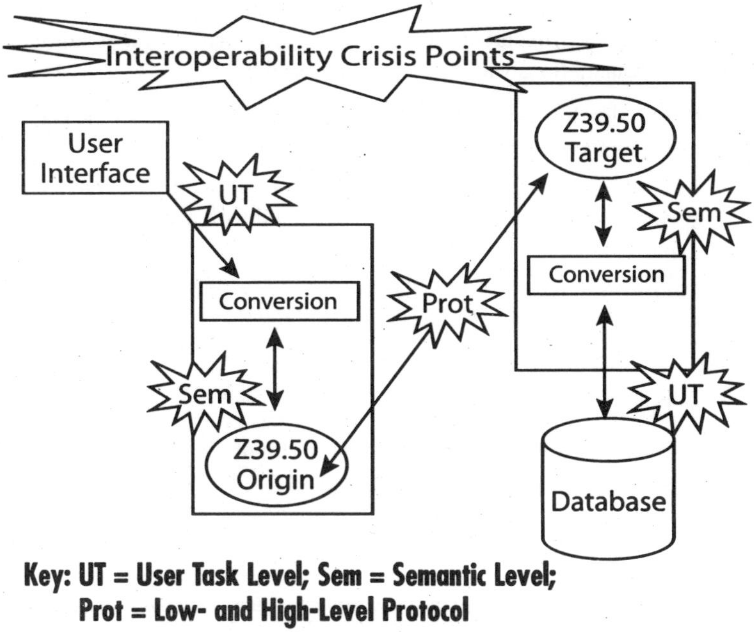

Figure 5.3 Crisis Points in Z39.50 Interoperability

Given the maturity of many of the Z39.50 toolkits and source code, the low-level protocol area usually does not cause much in the way of interoperability problems. The focus at the low level is on the ability of Z39.50 implementations (clients and servers) to construct the appropriately structure protocol messages (Application Protocol Data Units) and send them in the correct sequence. In 1992, the Coalition for Networked Information (CNI) sponsored the first Z39.50 Interoperability Testbed. That testbed resolved many low-level protocol interoperability issues; Clifford Lynch, the coordinator of that testbed, noted that the focus was on getting Z39.50 systems to talk to one another and achieving mechanical interoperability over the Internet (Personal Communication, January 2000).

Z39.50 Version 2 (1992) offered fewer services and less functionality than the current Version 3, and the 1992 Z39.50 Interoperability Testbed focused on the three core Z39.50 services: Initialization, Search, and Present. Conformance to the standard was not the focus of the testbed; it was demonstrable interoperability between systems. Without the foundation of low-level protocol interoperability, however, none of the other levels of interoperability are possible.

The area of high-level protocol interoperability focuses also on the implementation of the standard, but the issues here relate to the specific features or services of Z39.50 supported by communicating systems. At a minimum, Z39.50 implementations will support the following:

- Initialization Service (for the client and server to set up the communications session)
- Search Service (for the client to express a search in the standardized Z39.50 vocabulary and the server respond with a report of the search)
- Present Service (for the client to request records be returned in a suitable syntax and the server complying)

But the standard defines other protocol services:

- Delete: To delete result sets on a server
- Access Control: To support various forms of user authentication
- Sort: To order the records in a result set
- Scan: To browse an ordered list of terms (e.g., an index) to identify search terms

The standard does not specify that any of these newer protocol services must be implemented for a Z39.50 client or server to be conformant. This results in a situation where two systems might each support Initialization, Search, and Present, but only one of the two supports Sort and Scan. In that case a request from System A that supports Sort and Scan to System B that does not will fail the test of interoperability—at least in terms of the Sort and Scan services. A Z39.50 client may be more or less robust that a Z39.50 server, and therefore we need to examine if a specific Z39.50 client or Z39.50 server threatens interoperability. It stands to reason, though, that two systems (i.e., Z39.50 client and server software) must support the same services from the standard to provide a basis for interoperability using those services. This higher-level of protocol interoperability relates to functionality provided by the Z39.50 client and server, but this level also intersects with the local IR system functionality. In the above example, System B may have chosen not to support Sort and Scan precisely because its local IR system does not have the capability to sort result sets and provide a browseable list of its indexes. Although limitations of local systems directly impact interoperability, newer information retrieval systems will likely support the common functions defined in Z39.50, and this issue will begin to resolve itself.

Semantic level interoperability is less amenable to easy solutions in part because of the range of factors affecting it. In the report from the U.S. Government's Information Infrastructure Technology and Applications (IITA) Digital Libraries Workshop, Lynch and Garcia-Molina (1995) noted that the "precise definition of deep semantic interoperability was the subject of some debate, but deals with the ability of a user to access, consistently and coherently, similar (though autonomously defined and managed) classes of digital objects and services, distributed across heterogeneous repositories, with federating or mediating software compensating for site-by-site variations." As noted earlier, they characterized deep semantic interoperability as a "grand challenge" for digital library research.

Going back to the analogy of Z39.50 as a language, the meaning (semantics) of the protocol messages needs to be clear if two systems are to share an "understanding" of the message. Z39.50 provides standardized "vocabularies" to express queries using registered sets of attributes (where attributes are used in the Z39.50 query to characterize a search term). The attribute sets provide the "words" in the vocabulary for searching. Using the vocabulary, we can express—in a standardized Z39.50 query—a query for books *by* Mark Twain (where Twain is the author) as well as a query for books *about* Mark Twain (where Twain is the subject). Compare this to a typical Web search engine where it is not possible to differentiate a search for Mark Twain as author versus Mark Twain as subject (the reasons for this go beyond the scope of this paper).

Z39.50 implementations, however, do not always support (i.e., understand and act on) the same *words* from the standardized vocabulary for searching. Taking an example from searching library catalogs, System A wants to search System B for a corporate author and uses the correct Z39.50 attribute to characterize its search term as a corporate author. But System B does not support that particular Z39.50 attribute. The semantic intention of the user and his/her search cannot be acted upon. However, the System B does support a name search, and in an attempt to be helpful, processes the corporate author search as a name search; the results, however, may include records that are not relevant to the original corporate author search; semantic loss has occurred. In both these cases, semantic interoperability is reduced or does not exist.

The semantic level of interoperability is strongly affected by the local IR systems functionality and indexing policies. Although the standard provides mechanisms for clearly—if not unambiguously—expressing search requests, retrieval requests, and other IR functional requests, the differences in local IR systems can jeopardize semantic interoperability. In the example above, the two systems are online library catalogs (i.e., bibliographic databases) built using standard MARC records. However, System A allows specific MARC fields to be searched for corporate author names while System B, with the same basic set of records, has chosen not to create indexes or is incapable of creating indexes to support the access point of corporate author. There is likely a strong relationship of the search capabilities of the underlying IR system and the Z39.50 attributes it supports in its Z39.50 server software.

The final level of interoperability focuses on the user and his/her tasks. The levels discussed above have become understood fairly well, at least in the library community, through Z39.50 implementation experience. The user task level of interoperability has yet to be investigated and only a tentative outline of this level can be offered here. Users use information systems for a variety of reasons, but one can assume users are interested in searching for information to solve a particular problem, answer a question, or complete a task. The question for users is whether two systems are interoperable to the extent they meet the users objectives. While the Z39.50 community has already and continues to work out protocol (syntactic and functional) and semantic interoperability, those efforts have not been well-informed by an understanding of users' expectations for interoperability. (The evaluation studies and the recent profiling efforts discussed below are implicitly acknowledging these expectations.) When are two systems interoperable enough for users to complete their tasks? The fact is that there are different user groups with differing expectations for interoperability. Take the examples of an undergraduate student searching remote library catalogs via Z39.50 to see if a neighboring library has a copy of a particular book versus a cataloger searching remote libraries for purposes of cataloging a particular edition of a book; the user tasks are different, and the likelihood is that expectations of interoperability, especially at the semantic level, are quite different. Acceptable interoperability for one user group may be insufficient interoperability for another.

Achieving interoperability is a complex challenge. The diversity of IR systems, the variation in conformant implementations of a standard, the numerous levels where threats to interoperability can occur, and the lack of empirical data on users' expectations for interoperability between systems all need to be taken into account when addressing and assessing interoperability. Once we can identify the threats to interoperability, there is a major issue of the cost to solve the interoperability problem. In the case of Z39.50, we now have hundreds, if not thousands of Z39.50 client and server implementations on top of existing online library catalogs. This installed base can be considered part of the interoperability problem. What level of interoperability can we achieve and at what cost?

The multi-level perspective offered above provides a way to understand the challenges to interoperability and can point to levels of interoperability evaluation that can be undertaken. The next section discusses several evaluation reports of Z39.50 projects that can be understood in the context of this multi-level perspective.

RECENT EVALUATION STUDIES OF Z39.50 IMPLEMENTATIONS

In 1998, four studies of Z39.50 use by libraries were released:

- State of Iowa Libraries Online (SILO) initiative (Blue Angel Technologies, 1998)
- Virtual Canadian Union Catalogue project (Lunau, 1998)
- Virtual Electronic Library of the Consortium on Institutional Cooperation (CIC) (Hinnebusch, 1998)
- California Linked Systems Project (Williams, 1998)

These studies were the first published empirical investigations and resulted in important findings about the problems of Z39.50 interoperability. More recently, Williams (1999) provides an update to her 1998 California Linked Systems Project, and Coyle (2000) reports on an evaluation to compare a virtual union catalog using Z39.50 with the University of California's Melvyl catalog. One can surmise from the studies that a standard can provide a context for evaluation, but complex standards such as Z39.50 with its many choices and options, and implemented in conjunction with different IR systems, cannot serve as an evaluation metric by virtue of being a standard.

The common thread among these studies is that they examined and evaluated the use of Z39.50 to search across library catalogs. Although interoperability problems exist when a Z39.50 client communicates with a single Z39.50 server, some relatively straightforward solutions are available to improve interoperability such as gaining knowledge about the server implementation and configuring the client specifically for communicating with that server. Customizing client configuration for each server—an approach used in these projects for improving interoperability—is an option, but whether or not it is an effective approach is an open question. For example, the Virtual Canadian Union Catalogue (vCuc) report indicated that the total process of configuring a client for a specific server—including identifying the server, acquiring details about the server implementation, configuring the client, and testing—took on average 3.5 to seven hours (Lunau, 1998, p. 15).

Designers of the Z39.50 protocol envisioned it for point-to-point communications. Some current Z39.50 clients allow the user to search more than one resource at a time, and in these cases, the Z39.50 client establishes multiple point-to-point sessions with remote Z39.50 servers. These resources may be relatively homogeneous (e.g., searching multiple online library catalogs) or diverse (e.g., searching online catalogs and museum collection management systems). The use of Z39.50 for searching multiple resources at the same time compounds the complexity of the interoperability problems especially when those resources are heterogeneous (e.g., searching library catalogs and museum collection management systems at the same time). The Z39.50 client will have the responsibility for attempting to hide the diversity among the resources being searched (i.e., making this work requires more robust client software). Look again at Figure 5.3 and imagine communication is occurring not between two systems but 20 or more, with an associated multiplier effect on the interoperability crisis points.

Each of the studies had specific purposes and foci, and approached their evaluations differently. For example, the SILO evaluation used questionnaires to librarians and vendors as well as follow-up interviews to collect data on the SILO implementations. The CIC evaluation was an in-depth analysis on the CIC's libraries implementations of Z39.50 (e.g., the Z39.50 services supported, the attribute supported) and the underlying information retrieval systems indexing of MARC records. The vCuc report contained evaluation of Z39.50 implementation but also served as a final report on the entire vCuc Pilot Project. The study of the California Linked Systems Project focused on an assessment of what had been achieved so far and identified challenges and successes of using Z39.50 for searching multiple remote library catalogs. Only the SILO report is called an *evaluation* where the others include evaluative assessments of Z39.50 implementations as part of the larger studies. These differences make cross-study comparability difficult, yet several important common themes emerged and can be discussed in terms of the multi-level perspective on interoperability presented above.

- Low-level protocol interoperability: The studies did not indicate interoperability problems at this level. This reflects the relative maturity of the protocol and implementations at this level.
- High-level protocol interoperability: The implementations discussed by the reports (in 1998) were primarily Version 2 protocol implementations and generally only supported the three core Z39.50 services of Init, Search, and Present. However, the CIC analysis showed a trend toward diversity in other Z39.50 services supported by various servers. Of the eleven Z39.50 servers analyzed, seven support the Scan service and one supports the Sort service. On the client side, five of the six clients supported Scan, and two of the six supported Sort (Hinnebusch, 1998). The other studies did not detail the services supported by the clients and servers. If a client and server do not support the same Z39.50 service, overall interoperability is reduced.
- Semantic interoperability: Most of the interoperability problems identified in the studies fall into this category. This category spans Z39.50 implementation and local IR system functionality and configuration. Two key aspects of this set of problems are differences in support for Z39.50 attribute types and values (Z3.50 implementation), and local

indexing practices and polices (local IR system functionality and configuration). Z39.50 Attribute Support: Although there was common support for the Z39.50 Bib-1 Attribute Set, there were wide differences in support for specific attribute types and values. In Z39.50, the Use attribute type indicates an access point. The vCuc project analyzed server support for Z39.50 use attributes revealed that only two access points were supported in common by twelve separate implementations: Title and Subject (Lunau, 1997). Hinnebusch's analysis of CIC implementations revealed more access points in common with all Z39.50 implementations supporting the following use attributes: Title, ISBN, ISSN, Subject, and Author. In practice, this means that in the vCuc implementations, a user could only be assured that Title and Subject searches would work across all implementations. CIC implementations provided more extensive interoperability for searching given the additional common access points. Whether or not either the vCuc or CIC implementations provide sufficient search interoperability cannot be determined unless we identify specific user task requirements. Another aspect of interoperability at the level of attribute support is the combination of attribute types and values supported by server implementations and how they interpret the attribute types and values. Servers interpret the attributes to determine how to execute a particular query (e.g., is this a truncated author keyword search or some other kind of author search). Hinnebusch noted "it is most assuredly this mismatch of client configuration and server support [for attribute combinations] that lies at the heart of many of the difficulties that CIC libraries have experienced with Z39.50 searching" (1998, p. 8). The SILO report also noted that differences in use attribute and attribute combination support had an impact on the quality of the search results. Local Indexing Policy: The common support for limited Z39.50 Use attributes in server implementations likely reflects the differences in local IR access points or indexes available. Each index is populated with data from one or more fields/subfields in a MARC record. The indexing policy for local IR system determines which fields/subfields will be indexed to support searches. For example, the MARC record has any number of fields/subfields that contain title data. If different IR systems do not index the same fields/subfields, title searches across different systems (even if they hold the same MARC records) may yield different results. The variation of indexing policies of different local IR systems affected the overall quality of searching in the projects. Only the CIC report provides an analysis of systems' indexing policies (see Figures 16 through 23 in Hinnebusch, 1998). The SILO and vCuc reports indicate, however, that this is a key issue to address to improve interoperability.

- User task interoperability: None of the report specifically discussed interoperability in terms of users. As noted above, this type of interoperability has not been articulated well. However, one can glean from the approach in the vCuc project the importance of taking into account user tasks when evaluating interoperability. The vCuc evaluation included controlled searching using a set of test searches (Lunau, 1998, p. 9 and 25+). Participants were also asked to do uncontrolled searches that would reflect searches that are typical for their institutions. Types of searches suggested included: ILL requests, reference questions, searches for cataloging copy, searches to verify bibliographic information prior to ordering a new item, etc. Summary results from the testing indicated that a confluence of factors affected search results including particular characteristics of the client, the database, and the interpretation of attributes. As a result, the report stated, "Users were not confident in the results they received. ... Only 37% felt they were receiving accurate and relevant results" (Lunau 1998, p. 13).

The importance of these evaluations cannot be underestimated. Empirical data confirmed existing anecdotal evidence of Z39.50 interoperability problems. Further, the studies clarified both Z39.50 and non-Z39.50 variables affecting interoperability. As the SILO report indicated, "a number of weaknesses listed by library respondents are not problems associated with the Z39.50 protocol itself, but rather in the inconsistent way in which vendors have implemented many of the open-ended items" (Blue Angel Technologies, 1998). Additionally, including users' perceptions in the evaluation indicate that even more factors may subvert a user's judgment about interoperability, such as quality of a database and system response time. These factors are not related necessarily to the standard or its implementation but can affect the users' perceptions of adequate interoperability to support their tasks.

These studies provided empirical evidence of problems with Z39.50 interoperability, and they also suggested possible solution paths. One key solution path is the use of Z39.50 profiles to improve Z39.50 interoperability.

PROFILES

Profiles are an auxiliary standards mechanism that defines a subset of specifications from one or more standards to improve interoperability. Their use with computer communications protocols stems from the original context of Z39.50 development, namely the Open Systems Interconnection (OSI) framework of the 1980s. OSI protocols typically included many options and choices from which implementors chose. One objective of a profile is to detail a set of specifications from those options and choices in a base standard(s).

Implementors conforming to a profile would produce systems that had an improved likelihood of interoperability.

The motivations for developing Z39.50 profiles can be categorized two ways:

- Prescribing how Z39.50 should be used in a particular application environment (e.g., government information, cultural heritage museums)
- Solving interoperability problems with existing Z39.50 implementations within a community (e.g., libraries) or across two or more communities (e.g., library and museums)

The latter will be the focus of this discussion. (A review of Z39.50 profiles is beyond the scope of this chapter; for a list of Z39.50 profiles see the Library of Congress Z39.50 Maintenance Agency Web site, specifically http://lcweb.loc.gov/z3950/agency/profiles/profiles.html.)

Although the evaluation studies discussed above appeared in 1998, Z39.50 implementors, particularly those within the Z39.50 Implementors Group (ZIG), had acknowledged interoperability problems of searching across library catalogs at least since 1995. In early 1996, the ATS-1 Profile (specifying author-title-subject searching across library catalogs) provided the first attempt to solve some of the problems. The ATS-1 Profile was only a stop gap measure, and problems left unresolved in that profile were addressed by several subsequent profiles built upon ATS-1. These profiles added more specifications to resolve problems not adequately addressed by ATS-1. (For a brief discussion of these profiles and the issues they addressed, see Moen, 1998a.)

Between 1999 and 2000, an international effort produced *The Bath Profile: An International Z39.50 Specification for Library Applications and Resource Discovery* (Bath Profile Group, 2000; for background on the Bath Profile, see Lunau, 2000). The Bath Profile itself was informed by several previous profiles, but most importantly by the *Z Texas Profile: A Z39.50 Profile for Library Systems Applications in Texas* (Texas Z39.50 Implementors Group, 1999; for background on the Z Texas Profile, see Moen, 1998b). These two profiles focused effort on resolving semantic interoperability problems for cross-catalog information retrieval and prescribing specific Z39.50 services required to support various user tasks (e.g., Init, Search, Present, Scan).

As an example, the Bath Profile addresses semantic interoperability for searching by defining a core set of 19 searches; requirements for these cross-catalog searches resulted from discussions among librarians. Defining the searches included naming a search, prescribing IR system behavior to process the query, and prescribing the Z39.50 query vocabulary to unambiguously express the query. For example, the Profile defines an Author Keyword Search with Right Truncation. The semantics (i.e., prescribed IR system behavior) for that search is: "Searches for complete word beginning with the specified character string in fields that contain the name of a person or entity responsible for a resource." The specification of the query using Z39.50 Attributes is the following:

- Use Attribute (1) = author (1003)
- Relation Attribute (2) = equal (3)
- Position Attribute (3) = any position in field (3)
- Structure Attribute (4) = word (2)
- Truncation Attribute (5) = right truncation (1)
- Completeness Attribute (6) = incomplete subfield (1)

This combination of attribute types and attribute values expresses this and only this search.

The Profile also defines an Author Keyword Search (without truncation). The semantics of this search is: "Searches for complete word in fields that contain the name of a person or entity responsible for a resource." And the specification of the query using Z39.50 Attributes is the following:

- Use Attribute (1) = author (1003)
- Relation Attribute (2) = equal (3)
- Position Attribute (3) = any position in field (3)
- Structure Attribute (4) = word (2)
- Truncation Attribute (5) = do not truncate (100)
- Completeness Attribute (6) = incomplete subfield (1)

The only difference between the two Z39.50 queries is the difference in the Truncation Attribute value (1 or 100), but this semantically differentiates one search from the other. Thus, there should not be any ambiguity when the server receives either of these queries as to the search behavior being requested. The Bath and Z Texas Profiles address two kinds of interoperability, high-level protocol and semantic.

Even though the profiles address the Z39.50 aspect of semantic interoperability, the semantic level is also affected by the indexing policies and search functionality in the local IR system. To address variations in indexing in different systems, the Texas Z39.50 Implementors Group (TZIG) is developing recommendations and guidelines for common indexing policies to support the searches specified in the Profile. However, Hinnebusch (1998, p. 3) warns, "the integrated library system vendor community has long used indexing as a market determinant. Attempts at standardizing indexing of bibliographic data have been firmly rejected by the vendors and there is little reason to expect this situation to change." Also, local institutions define indexing policies that address the needs of their users, and these local decisions result in wide variation in available access points across library catalogs. The TZIG believes that the networked environment changes many business models, and the demand for reliable cross-catalog searching may influence or change vendors' business models when it comes to indexing policies and may encourage libraries that want to participate in virtual library catalogs to consider common indexing policies to support certain searches.

Profiles can improve interoperability, but like a standard, they cannot by themselves assure interoperability. Yet, by reducing the diversity of options and choices from the base standard, profiles can provide a more effective evaluation baseline. This leads to the possibility of formal interoperability testing as an evaluation method for assessing compatibility and appropriateness of products through demonstrable interoperability.

INTEROPERABILITY TESTING AND INTEROPERABILITY TESTBEDS

The evaluation studies discussed previously highlighted interoperability as a key problem with Z39.50 implementations. Simply putting in a Request for Proposal (RFP) that a system must be Z39.50 compliant did not result in interoperable systems for many of the reasons already discussed. Profiles provide a solution path to address high-level protocol and semantic level interoperability by specifying configuration of Z39.50 client and server implementations. Requiring compliance to a profile's specification in a RFP may yield systems that are more interoperable. To adequately assure goodness of products, however, another level of evaluation is essential.

Interoperability testing is an appropriate evaluation approach for complex standards in the networked environment. It is a "procedure in which two or more implementations are tested against each other, with the standard [or profile] used primarily as a reference to judge problems and incompatibilities, and secondarily as a guide to the functions that should be tested and the general behavior to be expected" (Preston and Lynch, 1994). Conformance testing is another approach to evaluating a single implementation where it is "compared to the standard [or profile] to be sure that the implementation does what the standard [or profile] specifies. If the implementation conforms to the specifications set out by the standard [or profile], then it is considered to be interoperable" (Preston and Lynch, 1994). We pointed out earlier, however, that two developers of Z39.50 products could produce conformant implementations that may not be interoperable. Demonstrable interoperability rather than conformance to a standard is critical. Lynch (1993, p. 42) stated unequivocally "an interoperable system in the real world is far more valuable to the mission of a library than a system that achieves abstract virtue through the implementation of some specific set of politically or philosophically correct standards."

There are currently, however, no accepted testing methodologies, formal processes, and interoperability benchmarks by which customers and vendors can assess conformance to profile specifications or demonstrate effective interoperability between systems that claim conformance to a standard or profile. An interoperability testbed is an accepted approach for interoperability testing. Preston and Lynch (1994) noted that:

> Because the emphasis is on implementations, testbeds lead to a "whole system" approach to testing rather than one focused on individual standards conformance or interoperability and can be very useful not only in dealing with problems directly related to a given standard but in identifying problems that arise from the interaction between different standards or at the boundaries between standards and implementor agreements often needed to produce real-world interoperating systems.

This holistic approach for interoperability assessment is informing the creation of a formal interoperability testbed at the Texas Center for Digital Knowledge and the School of Library and Information Sciences, University of North Texas.

The testbed will be a technically—and organizationally—trusted environment providing producers and consumers a forum in which to demonstrate and evaluate Z39.50 products. The foundation of the testbed will be reliable, valid testing methods and scenarios using Z39.50 client and Z39.50 server reference implementations. Z39.50 producers and consumers will use the testbed for assessing products/systems that claim conformance to a specific set of Z39.50 specifications (e.g., as represented in a profile). A primary focus will be semantic interoperability testing.

Building upon the success and experience in the 1992 Z39.50 Interoperability Testbed and with the focal goal of assessing semantic interoperability, we have identified a number of components for the proposed testbed. Although this project will focus initially on Z39.50 semantic interoperability, the following testbed components are likely critical in interoperability testing no matter the networked system under evaluation:

- Technical: Hardware and software components of the communicating systems; there is a requirement for flexibility in configuration of the components.
- Reference implementation: A trusted implementation, configured to the extent possible to support a particular set of specifications, and open to inspection and vetting by trusted experts; reference implementations provide the benchmarks for search and retrieval results against which other systems will be evaluated.
- Content: The test corpus or data used by the system (e.g., for a library catalog, a set of bibliographic records); should be of sufficient size to provide a real world environment for testing.
- Test scenarios and Benchmarks: Reliable and validated test scenarios

to provide comparability between systems participating in the testbed. Benchmarks are established by using the test scenarios with the reference implementations; metrics will assess the levels of interoperability achieved by systems.

- Procedural: Procedures of the testbed must be clear and transparent; they should address participation guidelines; security of the test corpus; feedback and challenges; and privacy, conflicts of interest, and trade secret safeguards.
- Organizational: Organization and governance of the testbed must be articulated; the sponsoring organization should be a neutral and trusted party free from conflicts of interest with organizations that might be using the testbed for product testing and evaluation; stakeholder should be represented on an advisory group for the testbed.
- Personnel: Sufficient personnel with suitable expertise to develop and manage the ongoing operation; an advisory group representing a range of the stakeholders that will monitor, assess, challenge, and otherwise help make the testbed a success.

The interoperability testbed will be a vehicle for assessing the extent of interoperability that is achieved between a vendor's implementation of Z39.50 clients and/or servers and the testbed's reference implementations of Z39.50. It must be formal, rigorous, and trusted. But to be successful, the testbed must be used.

MOTIVATING PARTICIPATION IN INTEROPERABILITY TESTING

Evaluation in the networked environment can lead to improved services or abandonment of services and products that no longer provide value to users and organizations. Product developers want their systems to succeed in the marketplace. Rigorous interoperability testing discussed above may dissuade testbed participation if product developers and vendors think that evaluating the extent of their products' interoperability with other vendors' products may adversely affect market share. What will motivate participation in evaluations of networked services and products?

In the context of Z39.50, reference to the standard in RFPs has induced vendors to develop Z39.50 products. Profiles provide additional configuration requirements for vendors. Referencing a profile in a RFP will motivate vendors to configure Z39.50 clients and servers accordingly. But an interoperability testbed offers both producers and consumers a mechanism to demonstrate the appropriateness and compatibility of products. Including a RFP that vendors must demonstrate interoperability of their products in this testbed can serve as a motivation for participation in the testbed.

The testbed itself needs to be attractive to potential participants. Concerns discussed above such as neutral sponsorship, trade secret protection, trustworthiness, and rigor can make the testbed attractive. Add to that an organizational culture of the testbed that emphasizes constructive assistance for product improvement rather than "gotcha!" type evaluations, and the testbed can become a support for product development as well as product evaluation.

All the stakeholders—the consumers as well as the producers—need to perceive the testbed as open, trustworthy, and fair. In developing the testbed, stakeholder input is vital. Participation in an interoperability testbed may hinge on acceptance of the testing methodologies and metrics. The process of developing specific aspects of the testbed such as metrics and test scenarios should involve input, if not consensus, of the stakeholders.

Finally, the ongoing operation of a testbed needs to be supported. For the proposed Z39.50 testbed, initial development and operation of the testbed will rely on grants and contributions. Over the longer term, the stakeholders—consumers and producers—may be the ones to fund its operation. That outcome assumes that the testbed addresses a pragmatic need for effective evaluation.

Based on these considerations, the organization and management of the testbed rather than the technical and evaluative components may offer the larger challenges to its success. Yet, the need for interoperability testing and testbeds appears as a fundamental evaluative need in the networked environment if seamless access to distributed information is to be realized.

CONCLUSION

Interoperability is a term that means different things to many people. Yet, the concept is central in discussions of how components in the networked environment will work together. Assessments of interoperability have become more problematic as the concept has evolved from correctly interchanging data packets to retaining semantic intention of users in networked information retrieval transactions.

This chapter provided a preliminary framework for discussing and analyzing levels of interoperability in the context of Z39.50. It analyzed specific areas of system-to-system communication that threaten interoperability. Some of these areas are better understood than others (e.g., the low-level and high-level protocol areas) but others, such as the semantic level, have not been fully explored from the perspective of evaluation. The interoperability testbed described here will address and explore evaluation methods for semantic interoperability.

We also introduced the User Task level of interoperability. Although this topic has yet to be understood and framed properly for research, we suggest that no matter the extent of interoperability at the other levels, it will be the users' assessment of perceived interoperability of networked systems about which we will be most concerned. We can assume that the User Task level may be an intersection of concepts related to interoperability and concepts related to usability.

There is work to be done since in this dynamic environment, evaluation strategies and methods continually need to evolve to address the critical issues of interoperability in its many guises. The proposed multi-level framework for interoperability will inform a rigorous testbed to be established at the Texas Center for Digital Knowledge. The testbed initially will allow the investigation of kinds of interoperability and methods for assessing semantic interoperability within the context of Z39.50 implementations and library catalogs. We anticipate, however, new insights about interoperability issues that may have broader utility in evaluation strategies for the networked environment. There is, however, a pragmatic aspect to interoperability that must be addressed, and that is facing up to the cost of solving interoperability deficiencies. Yet, without an understanding of what can be considered acceptable levels of interoperability for different users groups, there can be little in the way of reasoned discussion on the cost effectiveness of various solutions to improve interoperability.

ACKNOWLEDGMENTS

The author is grateful to several colleagues who read earlier drafts of this chapter and suggested improvements, in particular, Clifford Lynch and Teresa Lepchenske.

ABOUT THE AUTHOR

William E. Moen, Ph.D., (http://www.unt.edu/wmoen) is an assistant professor in the School of Library and Information Sciences, and a Research Fellow in the Texas Center for Digital Knowledge, University of North Texas. In recent years Moen focused his attention on problems and issues concerning Z39.50 interoperability and assisted in the development of Z39.50 profiles for library applications (the Bath Profile and the Z Texas Profile). He currently serves as chair of a National Information Standards Organization committee developing a national Z39.50 profile for library applications. He teaches courses and conducts research on information organization, metadata, networked information discovery and retrieval, information policy, and technical standards.

E-mail: wemoen@unt.edu

REFERENCES

Abbas, June; Antonelli, Monika; Gilman, Mark; Hight, Pamiela; Hoski, Valli; Kearns, Jodi; Lepchenske, Teresa; Peet, Martha; Pullin, Mike; and Stults, Amy. (1999). An Overview of Z39.50, supplemented by a case study of implementing the ZebraServer under the Linux operating system. Denton, TX: School of Library and Information Sciences, University of North Texas. From http://www.unt.edu/wmoen/Z3950/GIZMO/contents. htm

Bath Profile Group. (2000, June). The Bath profile: An international Z39.50 specification for library applications and resource discovery, Release 1.1. An internationally registered profile. From http://www.nlc-bnc.ca/bath/bath-e.htm

Blue Angel Technologies, Inc. (1998, May). An evaluation of Z39.50 within the SILO project. Chester, PA: Blue Angel Technologies, Inc. From http://www.silo.lib.ia.us/bluang.html.

Coyle, Karen. (2000, March). The virtual union catalog: A comparative study. DLib Magazine, 6(3). From http://www.dlib.org/dlib/march00/coyle/03coyle.html.

Hinnebusch, Mark. (1998, August). Report to the CIC on the state of Z39.50 within the consortium. Champaign, IL: Committee on Institutional Cooperation. From http://ntx2.cso.uiuc.edu/cic/cli/z39-50report.htm.

Lunau, Carrol. (2000, March). The Bath profile: What is it and why should I care? Ottawa, Canada: National Library of Canada. From http://www.nlc-bnc.ca/bath/prof.pdf.

Lunau, Carrol. (1998, June). Virtual Canadian union catalogue pilot project: Final report. Ottawa: National Library of Canada. From http://www.nlc-bnc.ca/resource/vcuc/vcfinrep.pdf.

Lunau, Carrol. (1997, September). Bib-1 attributes supported by selected vendor servers. Ottawa: National Library of Canada. From http://www.nlc-bnc.ca/resource/vcuc/ebib-1.pdf.

Lynch, Clifford. (1993, March) Interoperability: The standards challenge for the 1990s. Wilson Library Bulletin, 67(7), 38–42.

Lynch, Clifford and Garcia-Molina, Hector. (1995). Interoperability, scaling, and the digital libraries research agenda: A report on the May 18-19, 1995 IITA digital libraries workshop. (U.S. Government's Information Infrastructure Technology and Applications [IITA] Working Group, Reston, Virginia). From http://www-diglib.stanford.edu/diglib/pub/reports/iita-dlw/.

Miller, Paul. (2000, June). Interoperability: What is it and why should I want it? Ariadne 24. From http://www.ariadne.ac.uk/issue24/interoperability/intro.html.

Moen, William E. (2000). Interoperability for information access: Technical standards and policy considerations. The Journal of Academic Librarianship, 26(2), 129–132.

Moen, William E. (1998a). Texas Z: The Texas Z39.50 requirements and specifications project. A discussion paper. Prepared for the Texas State Library and Archives Commission. From http://www.unt.edu/wmoen/Z3950/ TexasZDPAug98.htm.

Moen, William E. (1998b, winter). The Z Texas project: Implements Z39.50 to improve statewide access to library catalogs and other online resources. Texas Library Journal, 7(4). From http://www.txla.org/pubs/tlj74_4/moen.html.

Moen, William E. (1995). A guide to the ANSI/NISO Z39.50 protocol: Information retrieval in the information infrastructure. Bethesda, MD: NISO Press. From http://www.cni.org/pub/NISO/docs/Z39.50-brochure.

Moen, William E. and Lepchenske, Teresa. (2000, May). Z39.50: Selected list of resources. Denton, TX: School of Library and Information Sciences, University of North Texas. From http://www.unt.edu/wmoen/Z3950/BasicZReferences.htm.

National Information Standards Organization. (1995). Information retrieval (Z39.50): Application service definition and protocol specification (ANSI/NISO Z39.50-1995). Bethesda, MD: NISO Press. From http://lcweb.loc.gov/z3950/agency/document.html.

Payette, Sandra; Blanchi Christophe; Lagoze, Carl; and Overly, Edward A. (1999, May). Interoperability for digital objects and repositories. D-Lib Magazine, 5(5). From http://www.dlib.org/dlib/may99/payette/05payette.html.

Piscitello, David M. and Chapin, A. Lyman. (1993). Open systems networking: TCP/IP and OSI. Reading, MA: Addison–Wesley.

Preston, Cecilia M. and Lynch, Clifford A. (1994). Interoperability and conformance issues in the development and implementation of the government information locator service (GILS). In William E. Moen and Charles R. McClure, The Government Information Locator Service (GILS): Expanding Research and Development on the ANSI/NISO Z39.50 Information Retrieval Standard, Final Report. Syracuse, NY: School of Information Studies, Syracuse University.

Texas Z39.50 Implementors Group. (1999, April). Z Texas profile: A Z39.50 profile for library systems applications in Texas, Release 1.0. From http://www.tsl.state.tx.us/ld/projects/z3950/TZIGProfile99Apr20.htm.

Williams, Joan Frye. (1998, May). Linked systems study update and proposed technology infrastructure for the library of California. Sacramento, CA: Information Technology Consultant. From http://ferguson.library.ca.gov:80/loc/telecom/t_studies/index.cfm.

Williams, Joan Frye. (1999, November). A study of linked systems with recommendations for the future of the CLSA statewide data base. Sacramento, CA: Information Technology Planning, Management + Marketing. From http://ferguson.library.ca.gov:80/lds/linksys.pdf.

Chapter 6

Choosing Measures to Evaluate Networked Information Resources and Services: Selected Issues

Joe Ryan
Charles R. McClure
John Carlo Bertot

ABSTRACT

Information managers find developing measures to evaluate their organization's network-based information services increasingly important. This research considers two questions related to the process information managers' employ to choose these network measures: What are the key elements of a strategy adopted when choosing network measures? What are key issues faced when adopting such a strategy?

INTRODUCTION

Information managers find the development of measures to evaluate their organization's network-based information resources and services increasingly important. The measures developed may be

- quantitative elements, such as statistics;
- ratios of such statistics like performance measures;
- qualitative measures, such as interview or open-ended survey questions; or
- some combination of the above.

Networked information resources and services may include an information resource, such as a database, or a service, such a virtual help desk, provided via a network, such as a local area network, intranet, or the Internet. The phase network measures will be used throughout this chapter to mean quantitative or qualitative measures developed to evaluate networked information resources and services.

This work addresses two research questions related to the process information managers' employ to choose measures to evaluate an organization's network-based information resources and services:

1. What are the key elements of a strategy adopted when choosing network measures?
2. What key issues do information managers consider when choosing network measures?

The research suggests that successful information managers embrace a strategy and consider key issues *prior* to adopting a network measure and implementing data collection, analysis and use procedures.

Briefly discussed are the research methodology used for the statistics, measures, and strategies presented in this chapter and the general context information managers face when choosing measures. The study team identifies key elements of a strategy used by successful information managers when developing network measures. Then the researchers describe and analyze the range of issues information managers may need to consider when developing network measures.

BACKGROUND

The research presented here summarizes one component of a recently completed study, *Developing National Public Library and Statewide Network Electronic Performance Measures and Statistics*. The study was sponsored by the United States Institute for Museum and Library Services [Research Grant #LL 80102] and the state libraries of Delaware, Maryland, Michigan, North Carolina, Pennsylvania, and Utah. For further information on this study, see the project Web site: http://www.ii.fsu.edu. Portions of this chapter appear in Bertot, McClure, and Ryan (2001).

The study team used a multi-method approach summarized in Table 6.1. Data collection techniques included site visits, case studies, individual and focus group interviews, paper and electronic surveys, document content analysis, critical path analysis, and participant observation. The researchers followed standard guidelines and practice and have extensive experience with each of the techniques chosen. The present paper does not review the literature to any great degree, although relevant sources are mentioned where appropriate.

Table 6.1: Study Approach Summary of Data Collection Activities

Data Collection Activities	Summary
Convened an advisory committee that assisted the researchers throughout the course of the study.	The advisory committee members are leading national experts on library measurement in general and network measures specifically. The committee's purpose was to advise the study team on all aspects of the research. This was accomplished using periodic group meetings, e-mail, and telephone interviews.
Interviewed and surveyed state librarians and relevant senior information managers from the six participating state libraries in the study.	The study asked participants to identify key issues when they developed network measures. In addition, study participants were asked to comment on an evolving set of proposed network measures. The participants' comments identified additional issues when developing network measures. The researchers prepared and distributed a report summarizing the findings from this phase of the study and obtained additional feedback.
Interviewed and surveyed directors and relevant information managers from twelve public libraries drawn from the six participating states.	The libraries were active in the development of network-based information resources and services and in several cases had developed network measures locally. Key issues were identified using an approach similar to that used with State Library personnel.
Interviewed and surveyed the Federal State Cooperative System (FSCS) coordinators on several occasions.	FSCS is a collaborative public library data collection system that involves the National Center for Education Statistics (NCES), the National Commission on Libraries and Information Science (NCLIS), and the 50 U.S. states and District of Columbia. FSCS coordinates public library data collection efforts at the local, state, and national levels. The members of the FSCS have a substantial interest in developing state and national public library network measures. Coordinators were asked to identify key issues when they developed network measures and to comment on an evolving set of proposed network measures. The participants' comments identified additional issues of concern to information managers developing network measures.
Developed the study team's own set of proposed network measures.	The results of this effort are presented in Bertot, McClure, and Ryan (2001). Direct participation in the development of network measures provided deepened insight into the challenges information managers' face.
Conducted a field test of the proposed measures with a six public libraries from the six participating states. Interviewed field test participants by telephone and via e-mail.	The comments on the proposed measures and the process of implementing them in local settings by field test participants proved useful in identifying and describing the key issues information managers' face.

The general approach employed by the study team was an iterative learning strategy in which individual data collection events and their analysis were sequenced such that findings from one activity were incorporated into subsequent data collection and analysis events. Periodic summaries of study findings and analysis were shared with study participants to cross check factual accuracy, completeness, and agreement on interpretation and to elicit further comment. This iterative learning approach allowed the study team to modify, adapt, and refine its data collection and analysis activities as the study team learned.

The authors offer a word of caution on the study results presented next. The study team includes here only those issues reported to it on numerous occasions via more than one of the data collection techniques employed. But the study methodology was exploratory, the topic remains volatile, and the study participants were public library information managers (rather than information managers of all types). Thus, the results offered here are suggestive rather than prescriptive.

FINDINGS AND ISSUES

Key Factors Influencing Network Measure Development

Table 6.2 summarizes the key contextual factors that influence network measure development as identified by information managers participating in the study.

Information managers want accurate, credible, and valid data but that does not mean that an estimate is not good enough.

Table 6.2: Key Factors that Influence Network Measure Development

Continuous change in IT means continuous change in measures of IT based services	The IT that supports network-based information resources and services continues to change and fosters an environment of continual change. Each time an organization introduces new IT, older measures must be reconsidered or new measures introduced. This in turn requires time and resources to enable governing boards, managers, staff, and users to understand the new IT, its use, its fit, and its value. These stakeholder learning activities must precede decisions on what to measure, how to measure, determining who knows how to measure (and has time), and at what cost?
Reasonable measures, of limited life span, are acceptable	The pace of new IT introduction into the organization make the identification of useful measures, even with a utility of three to five years, difficult. The desire for data of the highest quality and upholding standards to obtain such data may be stifling the production of needed data, data of any reasonable quality at all, to inform the decisions on networked information services that information managers need to make today.
Limited resources to commit to measurement	Most organizations do not have the resources to commit, the staff with the necessary methodological knowledge base, or the staff with the necessary motivation, to sustain the methodological rigor necessary to achieve results at the highest confidence levels.
Complex environment fosters paralysis and skepticism	Information managers often view their environment as chaotic, or at least so complex as to defy easy attempts to rationalize it. This view has at least two consequences for network measure development: a form of managerial paralysis, a reluctance to measure in the first place, or, a healthy skepticism toward any approach that promises to fully, completely, and accurately describe or order a complex environment.

Key Elements of a Strategy for Network Measure Development

Successful information managers interviewed by the study team identified several common elements in their strategy to develop and deploy network measures in the context of continual change, reduced expectations, limited resources, and complexity. Table 6.3 identifies these elements.

Information managers perceived potential sources of error as issues to resolve, or at least address, *prior* to adopting the measure and proceeding with data collection, analysis or use. Table 6.4 summarizes the key recurring issues

Table 6.3: Elements of a Strategy for Successfully Developing Network Measures

Recognize when data are "good enough"	Successful information managers recognize that it is unlikely that they will develop or find network measures that fully, completely, and accurately describe or order the complex environment of networked information resources and services. Instead, these managers look for data that are good enough, accept estimates, work with incomplete data where necessary, acknowledge the limited life span of even good measures, welcome samples, and devote extra effort to understanding the limits of the data collected. As one savvy manager summarized, "Network measure results do not have to be true to be useful."
Develop a process for iterative reduction of error	Successful information managers combine a willingness to accept data that are "good enough" with an iterative effort to reduce network measures' potential error. As Katzer, et al. (1998, 4th ed., p. 8) suggest, "the researcher's job is first, to identify, and then remove or reduce, sources of potential error so that findings can be trusted." These evaluators develop new measures with a process in place for iterative detection, public report, and correction of errors and limits rather than seek the perfect measure the first time.
Identify potential error across a measure's life cycle	Experienced evaluators examine a proposed measure's entire life cycle for sources of error *prior* to adopting the measure and the start of data collection. They step through each phase of the measure's life cycle: selection, data collection, data analysis, reporting, and use. Are there barriers or obstacles at any point to successful local implementation? Managers who identify potential error early may have greater opportunity to reduce error or to reject the measure before incurring unnecessary collection, analysis and use costs.
Involve key stakeholders early in measure development	Information managers noted that it was easy to make the mistake of selecting a network measure in isolation from the people and processes necessary to implement it. A significant element in developing a successful network measure is early involvement of staff and stakeholders in each stage of the process and in addressing key issues like those mentioned in Table 6.4.

that information managers identified. The presentation of these issues is in measurement life cycle order, from selection, to data collection, data analysis

Table 6.4: Worksheet for Identifying Potential Isssues When Choosing a Network Measure

Name of Proposed Measure:	
Questions to ask	**Comments**
General Concerns	
What are the measure's potential sources of error?	
What obstacles exist to the measure's implementation over its life cycle?	
How can you involve key stakeholders in network measure development?	
Selection Issues	
Are you measuring something just because you can?	
What are the measure's potential uses?	
What is the potential for misuse?	
Should you measure capacity, use, efficiency, impact, or outcome?	
What comparisons does the measure allow?	
Can the definition be made clearer?	
Is the measure fair?	
Data Collection Issues	
Can data be collected from all relevant sources?	
Will partners supply needed data?	
Are new data collection techniques required?	
Are there confidentiality and privacy concerns?	
How can the burden of data collection be balanced or reduced?	
What preparation and instruction will be needed to collect the data?	
Data Analysis and Use Issues	
Can new data be used with existing internal and external data?	
How should the results of new measure be presented and to whom?	
What instruction will be needed to analyze and use the proposed measure?	
Does the cost of collection, analysis and use exceed the benefit?	

and use. A barrier to adoption may present itself at any point in a measure's life. Careful early planning can eliminate many obstacles. Considering the proposed measure's life cycle also increases the information managers' abilities to assess the measure's worth when compared to the labor necessary to obtain and use the results.

Selection Issues

Are you measuring something just because you can?

The list of selection issues begins with a simple, provocative, question: Are you measuring something simply because you can? The study team noted an increase in this tendency when information managers proposed the use of automated measurement software, such as log analysis. Evaluators, faced with the new or unknown, noted the compulsion to accept certain measures because they *might* be nice to know. Experienced managers noted, however, that each new measure has a cost and time component and increases the burden on the staff that must collect, analyze and interpret the results. In addition, if the results from a new measure are meaningless, all measurement activities become tarnished.

What are the measure's potential uses?

Effective information managers determine a network measure's potential uses when choosing the measure rather than when its results are available. A potential use can be the intended effect on key stakeholders of a measure's data or its analysis that results in certain actions based on assumptions that you believe the stakeholders' will make. For example, results from the *number of virtual visits* measure are very positive. The systems administrator (stakeholder) may be provoked (intended effect) to (the action of) adding necessary Web server capacity if (assumption) the connection between increased use and increased need for server capacity is clear and other more compelling demands for system resources are not made. Or consider the case of not reporting a measure's results to those who collected the data. Those who collected the data (stakeholders) might be provoked (intended effect) to resist collecting data in the future (resulting action) because (they assume that) management believes that their effort does not matter.

Table 6.5: Worksheet for Assessing a Network Measure's Potential Uses

Measure:					
	Stakeholder	Intended Effect	Resulting Action	Assumption(s)	Preparation Needed
If positive result					
If negative result					
If positive result					
If negative result					

Table 6.5 offers a worksheet to assess a network measure's potential uses. Note that a network measure's results may be positive or negative and both results should be assessed for each stakeholder. Key stakeholders might include those who will collect the data, senior management, local governing boards and funding authorities, peer organizations, local opinion leaders, and the media. Another way to identify key stakeholders is to ask who are the most important audiences that should hear the results of a proposed measure.

Table 6.6 presents a selection of possible intended effects. The best way to assess stakeholders' actions and assumptions may simply be to ask the stakeholder. Identifying and expressing in writing key stakeholder assumptions regarding an action may reveal that a proposed network measure does not really address the assumption that the stakeholder is actually making. In this case, the measure should be rejected or modified. In other cases, additional preparation may be needed to make clear the link between a measure's results and the stakeholders' assumptions. One common preparation needed is to educate key stakeholders about the meaning of a network measure well in advance of presenting the measure's results.

Table 6.6: Selected Examples of Network Measures Intended Effects

Intended Effect	Description and Discussion
Provoke	Perhaps the most common purpose for a measure is to cause organizational change. But these changes need to be assessed carefully. A careful assessment of the proposed network measure and the situation it addresses may be necessary before accepting or rejecting a proposed measure's ability to provoke.
Clarify	Another common use is to better understand a situation in advance of decision making.
Test Compliance	Measures can be used to test compliance with various internal and external standards, regulations, and laws.
Sanction	Measure results can supply evidence used to sanction or punish.
Reward	Measure results can provide support for rewarding positive staff activity. Information managers were concerned with unintended uses of a measure's data to reward. For example, given a limited budget how will you reward newly empowered staff with a new quantitative way of demonstrating their worth?
Distract	Measure results may be used to distract or misdirect stakeholder attention from one organizational activity to another.
Delay	One of the oldest techniques for delaying a decision or doing nothing is to demand more data. This technique can be especially successful if, after the data are obtained, they are found to be ***unreliable***.

Does the measure's results contribute to a solution of a local problem or might the results unnecessarily provoke, distract, or prolong the search for a solution? Or, does the information manager intend to provoke, distract, or prolong? Reconsider or drop the proposed network measure if the measure's potential use does not connect with your intended uses and that of key local stakeholders. Identify potential uses, and the stakeholder preparation needed, before selecting a proposed network measure.

What is the potential for misuse?

After considering a network measure's potential uses, an evaluator should also ask what is the potential for misuse? Measures of services that are new or poorly understood and that must scale across many departments, organizations, governmental units, and serve multiple purposes among diverse communities

Table 6.7: Selected Measure Types

Measure Type	Definition	Example
Capacity measure	A capacity measure is an input measure that describes the ability of an organization to make use of a networked information resource or deliver a networked information service.	Examples include the number of Internet workstations or the maximum speed of public access Internet workstations.
Use measure	A use measure is an output measure that describes the utilization of the information resource or service. A common approach is to measure the *extensiveness* of a resource or service. That is, how much of a service does a network provide.	Examples include the number of public access Internet workstation users or the number of electronic reference transactions or number of visits to an organization's Web site.
Efficiency measure	An efficiency measure relates resources used to service provided. As efficiency measure may relate a capacity measure to a use, impact or outcome, measure.	Examples include cost per virtual visit or average daily use per public access Internet workstation.
Impact measure	An impact measure is a further extension of an output measure that describes the effects of an information resource or service's use on some other activity or situation.	Examples include increased revenue attributed to a company's e-commerce Web site, the number employed or the number of newly literate readers as a result of the library's networked information services.
Outcome measure	An outcome or *effectiveness* measure is explicitly tied to the organization's (or unit's) goals, objectives and planning process unlike measures of input, use, and impact that do not necessarily depend on the organization's explicit objectives and planning. A good outcome measure provides data that tells a information manager if a specific unit or organizational objective has been achieved.	An example would be the average weekly number of hours a Web service is available given an organizational mandate to serve its customers 24 hours a day, seven days a week.

have an increased potential for misuse or misinterpretation. The intended use and intended audience for a measure may not be an unintended audience's use. A careful early assessment may avoid later pitfalls and improve the presentation and use of a proposed measure by advanced planning. Begin by identifying one way each proposed measure could be used to damage the organization or information unit and who might use the measure in this fashion.

Should you measure capacity, use, efficiency, impact, or outcome?

When considering an area of the information unit's operations or services, it may be useful to ask which would be most helpful: a measure of capacity, use, efficiency, impact, or outcome? This question used to be reduced to should one use a measure of input or output? Table 6.7 summarizes the differences between these types of measures.

What comparisons does the measure allow?

A principal interest when using any measure is for comparison either across time or to compare oneself with one's peers. Network measures may also need to be comparable across organizations of different type as well. Longitudinal data, looking at the results from the same measure over time, are useful to benchmark trends and as a check for unusual spikes or bad data. But the rapidly changing nature of contemporary information technology has a substantial impact on the life span of many network measures. For example, it may not make sense to begin to track the number of modems an organization owns today when it is likely that direct network connections will be the norm within the next five years. A good run of longitudinal data may only be three to five years given the rapidly changing information technology environment.

Peer comparisons with neighbors or with organizations that share some similar characteristics are one of the most popular uses of the existing measures of information resources and services. For an example of a comparison of local libraries with out-of-state peers, see Loessner and Fanjoy (1996a, 1996b). But comparisons can be a blessing or a curse. Field test participants told the study team of comparisons that led to divisiveness and ill will, of frustration when nothing was done or could be done to raise the standard of the lower tier organizations, and extensive time wasting when an unprepared media or public misinterpreted the comparison. Peer comparisons are powerful tools but must be thoughtfully constructed and communicated.

There is great interest in network measures that can be used by organizations of different types for a variety of reasons:

- Some data must be obtained from vendors who serve multi-type organizations not just one market. Vendors may find it cost effective to develop a single measure to serve multiple markets.
- Organizations (e.g., libraries that license databases) increasingly participate in multi-type consortia and other networks. A measure's collection and use may require a common, shared definition among all of the organizations participating regardless of type.
- Adding data together from different types of organizations will be necessary in some cases. For example, a state library might need to aggregate the data from a single network measure across all library types when seeking to renew state funding for licensed databases available to libraries within the state.
- The problem a network measure addresses may be faced in organizations of different type and comparisons may be fruitful.
- Co-development of network measures with different types of organizations, networks, consortia, and vendors will be the norm, if it is not already. New measures will need to be applicable to different types of organizations.

Summarizing, these questions should be carefully considered: What comparisons do you want to make with the proposed measure? What is worth benchmarking when three to five years of potential longitudinal tracking may be a good run? Are your likely partners participating in the development of the measure? If your peers are not participating, is it worthwhile to participate? Do you have a plan for when the comparison is in your favor and when it is not?

Can the definition be made clearer?

Information managers noted that a good definition consists of a clear statement of meaning, a set of explicit data collection procedures, with a helpful example or two, that has been pre-tested by a sample of professionals who are likely to want to collect and use the measure's data. Common errors identified by information managers include the following:

- Thinking that a label, like hits, is a sufficient substitute for a statement of meaning, procedures, examples, and pre-test.
- Failure to include any procedures in a definition or not making procedures explicit.
- Neglecting to give an example or failure to give an example that addresses common mis-perceptions.
- A definition in which label, statement of meaning, and examples do not seem to describing the same thing.
- Failing to pre-test, failing to allow time to pre-test, or using your friends as pre-testers.
- A definition that fails to take account of a measure's many audiences across its life cycle and across the levels of an organization. For example, does the definition have the same unambiguous

Table 6.8: Qualities of Good Definitions

Quality	Discussion
Essential	Does the measure extract what really matters, what the information manager or key stakeholders really want to know about the measure's subject? Can you do better?
Reliable	The definition should be unambiguous to those collecting data so that it can be collected reliably. A reliable measure is one where everyone counts the same thing, the same way, every time. Line information managers, in particular, asked for clear definitions that included examples where possible.
Valid	Does the measure in fact measure what it intends to measure. There is the intent of the measure's constructors and the intent perceived by those who will use the measure's results to make decisions. Information managers need to assess the local agreement on this second type of intent early. Is there clear agreement among key local stakeholders about how the results (good or bad) will be used to make or support local decisions?
Communicable	The definition should be easily understood and communicated to its intended audiences. The study team delayed recommending several very useful, but highly technical, measures because they could not be easily communicated. The organization's systems unit easily understood the definitions but none of the other key decision makers did.
Useful for decision making	Does the measure yield unambiguous results leading to a preferred action. If a definition is unclear or subject to a range of interpretation, decision making becomes more difficult.

meaning to the information manager that selects the measure, the data collector, and the funder using the measure's results?

Good definitions should contribute to achieving the qualities summarized in Table 6.8 for all their intended audiences.

Pre-test the measure's proposed definition with those who will collect the data and the audiences who will need to understand it. Is a lengthy explanation of what the measure means or its significance necessary? If so, it may be necessary to drop or delay the use of the measure until an education effort is undertaken.

Is the measure fair?

Measuring can call attention, can suggest importance, and can enable easier or more confident administration. Not measuring ignores and neglects, suggests a lack of importance, and makes decision making in the area less precise and easy. Does the proposed network measure (or a cluster of related measures) give inordinate attention to one operational area, one resource, or one service? Are other areas of the organization's operations, network resources, or services covered with equal or commensurate measurement attention? Does this measure contribute to an appropriate balance between measurement of network and non-network information resources and services in the organization?

There are consequences to measuring some things and not measuring or being unable to measure others. For example, one senior administrator interviewed applauded the proposed new measures of electronic public services (found in Bertot, McClure, and Ryan, 2001) saying, "Finally we will begin to have equivalent quantitative evidence of what goes on in the public service area as we have had for some time in technical services." She went on to add that now maybe information managers can feel more confident that they are treating both sectors of the information unit equally.

What gets measured is limited due to the effort demanded of an organization's staff, operations, and use. Adequately, equitably, and fairly measuring all the information unit's operational areas, resources, and services is the challenge highlighted here.

Data Collection Issues

Can data be collected from all relevant sources?

An organization may face a wide array of potential sources of data when developing data collection strategies for a specific network measure. Two common cases are summarized briefly here to illustrate the point: collecting data across a range of hardware and software platforms and obtaining comparable financial data on network information resources and services. Collecting data for certain network measures from a wide array of potential sources within one organization or across comparable organizations may be difficult or impossible.

For example, consider the collection of data on uses of public access Internet workstations just within one organization. There might be different generations of equipment with different operating systems, with different application and data collection software, networks, and configurations. Imagine the range of incompatible hardware, software, networks, and configurations, not just in one unit but across an organization or not just in one organization but across all participating organizations collecting data on a new network measure. These incompatibilities and differences create a substantial challenge for the collection of the *same data* across all units and organizations using similar (but different) technology in various configurations. Producing exact data quickly devolves to reducing estimate error. Developing a data collection strategy for a newly proposed measure may make the actual collection of data for a newly adopted measure possible.

A second case involves collecting financial data on network resources and services. The study team attempted for a number of years to devise a means of collecting useful financial information on public libraries' network services (See for example, Bertot, McClure, and Fletcher, 1997; McClure, Bertot, and Beachboard, 1995). But the study team found it difficult to collect uniform data from all of the potential sources.

For example, consider the case where researchers try to determine comparable costs for running a Web site? One organization has a paid staff running its own Web server. Another organization has a volunteer running the site on another government agency's server along with a group of other Web sites (and who is unwilling to disaggregate costs). In another case, a local Internet Service Provider (ISP) maintains another organization's Web site on the ISP's own server for free? Determining costs and then comparing actual costs of one organization to another meaningfully may present an insurmountable challenge at present because there is no agreement on how to collect this data from all sources in a uniform manner.

Participating information managers found it useful to ask the relevant staff five questions before adopting a proposed network measure:

- Do they understand the various issues involved?
- Can they identify all of the various sources of data related to the proposed measure?
- Can they develop strategies to collect the data from the range of sources involved?
- Can they collect the data uniformly?
- What is their best estimate of time and cost to collect all the data?

Early discussions and lead time with relevant technical staff can reduce data collection problems later.

Avoid the "My Technology, My Outlook" syndrome: An organization's local facility, its local technology infrastructure, and its local use of that technology can lead to a local view of network statistics. That is, information managers may base their need for networked information services statistics on their local facility's use of and involvement with networked information services. As such, it is often difficult for individual units or organizations to see the need for certain statistics and performance measures that do not *directly reflect* their local facility's current implementation and use of various network services and resources.

Will partners supply needed data?

Partnerships, both formal (i.e., contractual) and informal, are a way of life for public and private organizations. But partnerships can create problems when trying to collect data for a new network measure particularly when the technology, network, or databases are not owned by the organization seeking data. Perhaps the most obvious case involves libraries and states that are engaged in substantial licensing agreements for Internet-based database access with vendors (e.g., OCLC, Ebsco, UMI, Gale/IAC). Another common case can occur when an organization tries to obtain data that is collected by an ISP who may be another unit of local government or a private commercial firm.

Does the proposed measure require data owned by someone else or whose ownership needs to be negotiated? Are the data offered by an organization's partner a valid indicator of what it purports to measure? Are the offered data comparable with available data from peer comparative organizations? Can the data be obtained by using the definition and procedures required, when the data is needed, and at a reasonable cost? If the partner cannot provide trustworthy data on time and at an affordable cost, the organization may not be able to use the network measure.

Are new data collection techniques necessary?

A new network measure may require evaluators to consider the benefits and/or necessity of using new data collection techniques. Table 6.9 presents a sample of data collection techniques currently used to evaluate network-based resources and services. The use of multiple data collection techniques may allow the evaluator to cross-check the results and increase credibility and reliability.

In some cases, it may make sense to rely on carefully developed samples rather than 100 percent population responses to promote timely and responsive measures. In other cases, sequencing data collection, in which a question is not asked annually but every two or three years, may be appropriate to reduce local data collection burden. Table 6.10, based on McClure and Lopata (1996) offers some basic criteria to consider when selecting an appropriate technique.

The automation of aspects of the data collection and analysis processes holds great promise and threat for measurement of networked information services. The promise is that one day measures of networked information services will be

Table 6.9: Selected Network Measure Data Collection Methodologies

Qualitative Technique	Function/Purpose
Case Study	**Function**: In-depth exploration of selected communities and target audiences in those communities, use of and involvement with the network resources and services. **Purpose**: Gain an in-depth understanding of key stakeholders' views and how they interact. Use findings to inform quantitative data collection activities such as mail and electronic surveys.
Content Analysis	**Function**: Gather and examine various documentation and reports. **Purpose**: Review historical development, evolution of network-related activities, and future directions.
Policy Analysis	**Function**: Systematic review of policy instruments (e.g., legislation, regulations, standard operating procedures, governance documents) to assess scope, formation, implementation, execution, and impact of network policies. **Purpose**: Use findings to develop context of network activities, identify key governance issues, and develop recommendations for future network policy development.
Critical Path Analysis	**Function**: In-depth exploration of user-based interactions with project-related components (e.g., training, workstation use, and searching). **Purpose**: Use findings to uncover specific instance issues. Particularly appropriate for in-depth analysis of training and use issues.
Focus Groups	**Function**: Explore identified key issue areas of network content, services, management, and performance. **Purpose**: Better define and deepen appreciation of the views of key stakeholders regarding key issues. Use findings to inform quantitative data collection activities.
Interviews	**Function**: In-depth exploration of network content, services, management and performance with key project administrators and users. **Purpose**: Assess the relationship between network components and future educational use and development of network resources. Use findings to inform quantitative data collection activities such as mail and electronic surveys.
Quantitative Technique	**Function/Purpose**
In-house, Mail, or Electronic Surveys	**Function**: Further explore identified key issue areas of network content, services, management, and performance with broader project population. **Purpose**: Test findings from qualitative data collection activities with broader network population.
Automated Technique	**Function/Purpose**
Pop-up Surveys	**Function**: Web-based surveys triggered by access to a particular portion of a Web site. **Purpose**: Focused exploration of a section of Web site.
Network Traffic Measures	**Function**: Collect network/terminal traffic use statistics such as users, user access points, information and service content use, and network server and router load. **Purpose**: Provides sense of network load, capacity, and what services are used with what frequency.
Web Log File Analysis	**Function**: Measure Web-based services by the analysis of Web server log files. **Purpose**: Provides user profiles including locations from which users access services, server traffic, type of technology users have, and errors encountered.

collected and reported automatically and unobtrusively rather than through overt data collection efforts on the part of the organization. Already spreadsheet software is in common, productive use in the collection and analysis of data. See Bertot, McClure and Ryan (2001) for examples of data collection and analysis software of potential use. The threat is that organizations will wait until automatic data collection is perfected before collecting the data they need today to better manage networked information services.

Table 6.10: Basic Criteria When Selecting an Appropriate Data Collection Technique

Criteria	Brief Discussion
Can the method provide appropriate data?	If you want to find out why users of an organization's Web page spend their time in certain ways, interviews may be more appropriate than using log analysis software. If you want to find out how much time users spend on various activities, activity log analysis software may be more appropriate.
Time needed for collection and analysis	For example, interview transcripts might take more time to analyze than log files.
Instruction needed to collect and analyze	Both staff and users may need to learn a new technique.
Degree of user involvement	The greater the user involvement the greater the likely time commitment or inconvenience required of users.
Commitment required of data collectors	The quality of the data collected may depend of the commitment of the data collectors.
Degree to which the data is representative	Interviews with a few selected users may not represent the range of views of the entire community, etc.
Cost of collection and analysis	Costs may include costs of staff, consultants to do data entry or analysis, and costs to users who may collect data for the researchers. See Table 6.11.

The *Let the software do it* argument runs rampant among organizations considering new measures of networked information services. However, software analysis and monitoring of network activities may be best characterized as being in a pioneering phase. Many information managers' awareness and familiarity with data collection and analysis software is minimal. There is limited capacity to develop (or apply) tailored software solutions within individual organizations and the profession as a whole. Indeed, finding available technical staff that can install and operate off-the-shelf solutions may be difficult.

When considering a new measure of networked information services, are new data collection techniques used and are they appropriate?

Are there confidentiality and privacy concerns?

Many of the new networked information services offered by an organization simultaneously increase the opportunity for independent learning and use while reducing information manager's awareness of what exactly the independent user does. This has several unintended consequences:

- Information managers are less prepared to meet their users' needs because they are less certain what they are
- Information managers are less certain of how to allocate resources among costly networked information services because they are unsure how their users value them
- Information managers are feeling greater compulsion to monitor clients' use and their potential ability to do so is far greater with networked information services

Yet historically, many information managers have resisted collecting private or confidential data if for no other reason than to do so would inhibit the independent learning and use that organizations may seek to encourage.

Several questions regarding confidentiality may be worth addressing when considering a potential new measure. Would the methods used to collect data for the proposed measure violate users' privacy or confidentiality? What do users deserve to know about the proposed measure's data collection and use? What choices should users have about participating in the process, about the use of the data, about the impact of resulting decisions? How unobtrusive should data gathering be, and when does unobtrusive become secretive? Field test information managers already report that many of their users are very sensitive to being monitored when they use networked information services. Does the organization have a written policy on privacy and confidentiality? Does the proposed measure cause the organization to reconsider historic written or unwritten agreements on user privacy and confidentiality? If so, are the results worth it?

How can the burden of data collection be balanced or reduced?

A key issue for many of the managers interviewed was reducing staff data collection burden. A potential network measure's payoff must be clear to those who plan, to those who collect data, and to those who decide. For example, placing an excessive data collection burden on staff fosters "uncommitted record keepers." The result is, "The more statistics you ask me to collect, the more I'll make them up." Is the need for, and use of the proposed measure clear to those who will collect the data? Could better procedures reduce the burden of data collection? Can incentives be found for data collection staff to ease the burden of collection? Collecting data that are, or appear to be, never used for decision making discourages collecting such data the next time.

What preparation and instruction is necessary to collect the data?

Does the staff that will be asked to collect data for the proposed measure, have the ability to do so? What preparation and instruction will be needed to collect the data? Information managers and system directors expressed concern that staff may not be able to

- engage in rigorous data collection activities that require staff time and effort;
- support data collection activities with staff and resources;
- develop expertise in networked information service data collection activities;
- install and operate data collection and analysis software programs;
- collect any data other than that generated by system activity logs.

Essentially, the primary source of data collection—the staff who will collect the data—may not have the ability, resources, or expertise to engage in a network measure's data collection activities. Consider the abilities of the staff to collect the data when examining a proposed measure. It is often the organization or unit that is least able to collect the data that stands to benefit most from the concrete evidence the data provide to decision makers and potential funders.

Managers note that collecting network measure data will require lead time, preparation, and staff instruction to be successful. There are a number of instruction topics that may need attention:

- Identification of the range and diversity of technology that generate useful data relevant to a measure of networked information services
- Presentation of the notion that at least for the near term estimates, samples, and the lack of long-term longitudinal network data may be the norm
- Introduction to new data collection techniques and how they may be applied to collecting network measures relevant to the local setting
- Discussion of the impact of partnerships on collecting network data
- Presentation of strategies that can be used to overcome negative results
- Improvement of staff and information manager knowledge of the strengths, weaknesses, and practical uses of existing software used to monitor network use
- Discussion of the utility of the data collected by staff (who uses it and how). Where possible, connections need to be made between the network data collected and the resulting benefits to the organization

Any set of network measures will require a "roll-out" period that adequately educates and prepares organizations to collect the required data. Key roll-out activities include instruction in the need for the data and how to collect the data properly, a dry run to pretest forms and procedures, discussion with data collectors about what was learned, and revision of forms and procedures. What type of lead-time preparation and what type of instruction will staff need to collect the network measure's data effectively and efficiently?

Data Analysis and Use Issues

Can new data be combined with existing internal and external data?

Study participants note the need to consider whether data from new network measures can be combined with existing internal or external data to produce new measures and data at reduced cost. Three instances are common: composite measures, performance measures, and measures that use internal and external data. Additional examples of composite and performance measures for public library use can be found in Bertot, McClure, and Ryan (2001).

Composite measures combine data from measures together. Data from new network measures may be combined or data from new and existing measures combined. For example, *# Virtual visits excluding in-library use* can be combined with physical attendance at the library to form the composite measure: *Total library visits*. The advantage of composite measures is that the resulting composite numbers may represent more fully what organizations do. For example, the composite measure, total library visits, would show the increased library visits not indicated by the traditional physical attendance at the library statistic alone.

Performance measures relate data from one measure in proportion to another in a ratio. For example, the *Number of public access Internet workstation users* can be considered in proportion to the *Number of public access Internet workstations* (by division) to form the performance measure *Average annual use per workstation*. The advantage of a performance measure is that it may clarify, reveal, or highlight previously ignored information service activity. One of the field test information managers used the average annual use per workstation data to determine where to place additional, newly purchased workstations.

A third common use is to combine or relate internally produced data, like a new network measure's data, with externally produced data. For example, current data from the U.S. Census department indicate that there are 1,000 households in the community. The local newspaper reports that a private marketing firm has found that half the households in the community have Internet access. Thus using both statistics, 500 households have Internet access. A local non-profit using results from the recently adopted measure *Number of virtual visits excluding internal use* knows there was 80,000 visits last year. The organization might make the following statement. The average household with Internet access in the community visited the library 160 times using the Internet last year (i.e., 80,000 vists divided by the 500 households connected to the Internet). The use of internal and external data together can enrich data analysis and enhance the presentation of an organization or unit's contribution to its relevant audiences.

But there is a risk to consider when using composite or performance measures or measures that mix internal and external data. Perhaps the most important question to ask about these measures relate to credibility. Do you or key local stakeholders think you are combining or relating apples and oranges? If so, the credibility of the composite or performance measure is challenged and its utility may be reduced. Is it possible to combine the proposed measure with others to form credible, useful measures?

What instruction will be needed to analyze and use the proposed measure?

Information managers along with key stakeholders will need assistance in analyzing and interpreting the results generated by a new network measure. For example, instruction may be necessary to

- analyze a new measure's results, particularly if new analysis software is used;
- interpret the results. Are the results good or bad? What do the results mean for the unit or organization; and
- develop new, local, ways to meaningfully and persuasively present the data.

Local governing boards, senior managers, key opinion makers and the media may need instruction to increase the benefits from a new measure as well as to limit negative impacts. Information managers should expect to invest in instruction efforts with the introduction of any new measure. Who requires, what type of instruction, in order to better use the proposed new measure?

Does the cost of collection, analysis and use exceed the benefit?

Table 6.11 summarizes suggestions made by information managers for estimating costs and benefits for a proposed network measure. There are likely to be other costs and benefits more relevant to the local situation. Start-up costs and benefits may be different than those that reoccur.

CONCLUSIONS AND RECOMMENDATIONS

The preceding pages report results from research considering two questions related to the process information managers' employ to choose network measures: What are the key elements of the strategy adopted? What are key issues faced? The section draws conclusions, makes recommendations, and suggests the need for future research.

Choose a Strategy and Address Key Issues Prior to Adopting a Network Measure

Information managers must choose network measures in a context of continual change, complexity, reduced expectations as to a measure's utility, and with limited resources to commit to evaluation, as summarized in Table 6.2. This paper suggests a strategy information managers might use when choosing network measures, summarized in Table 6.3:

- Recognition of when data are good enough;
- Development of a process for iterative reduction of error;

Table 6.11: Estimating Costs and Benefits of Proposed Measure Worksheet

Proposed measure:			
Costs	**Assign $$ amount** (Comment if cannot)	**Benefits**	**Assign $$ amount** (Comment if cannot)
Administrative (to select and coordinate data collection, analysis, and use)		**Understanding** (Clearer description and comparison leads to problem solving and new goals and objectives)	
Staff (Time and salary to collect analyze and use data)		**Justification, Reward, Sanction** (Results justify actions)	
Technology (e.g., costs to purchase install and use measurement software.)		**Resource Allocation** (data enable better decisions)	
Instruction (Staff instruction in data collection, analysis, and use. Stakeholder instruction in using results.)		**Quality** (data enable tangible improvement in services)	
Materials (for forms, reports, press releases, etc.)		**Savings** (data enable the organization to save money)	
Intangibles (staff burden, negative publicity, disruption of services, etc.)		**Improved Image** (results improve image among key stakeholders)	
Other?		**Other?**	
Total		**Total**	

- Identification of potential error across a measure's life cycle; and
- Involvement of key stakeholders early in measure development.

Table 6.4 identifies issues information managers should consider when choosing a network measure. The study team recommends that information managers embrace a strategy like the one used by study participants and consider the key issues identified here *prior* to adopting a network measure and implementing data collection, analysis, and use.

Want to Improve Measurement, Reduce Staff Burden

Most study participants placed the issue of the reduction of staff burden very high on their priority list. Reducing staff burden requires a variety of approaches. The study team recommends information managers consider some of the following:

- Reduce the number of non-network measures used with the minimum goal of dropping one existing measure for every new network measure added.

- Improve management of data collection by giving staff clear instructions that prioritizes what they are to do, when and why. For further discussion see chapter five of Bertot, McClure, and Ryan (2001).
- Provide instruction in measurement to staff. Educators should be prepared to provide instruction to present and future information professionals in this area.
- Monitor the potential for future use of software to measure network services.

Motivated staff that know what to do, how to do it, and why increases the likelihood of good data collection and use.

Determine Network Measure Uses and Prepare Key Stakeholders

Successful managers know a network measure's uses (and misuses) prior to adopting the measure and have plans in place to prepare key stakeholders. Key opinion leaders and senior managers may be unprepared to use data effectively from new network measures in their decision-making process. The study team recommends that information managers conduct an early assessment of potential network measure uses (see Table 6.5) and the need for instruction of key stakeholders. Then, information managers should develop a plan to educate these key participants.

Evaluation Matters, Develop the Market

Information managers are now placing a priority on the need for evaluative data to manage and to justify funding for network services. Yet the evaluation component of commercial network-based information resource and service products remains generally underdeveloped, where it exists at all. Contract language should explicitly address both the purchaser's and vendor's need for evaluative data to support managerial decision making and funding. Suppliers of networked information and services should recognize the financial opportunity now available to supply evaluation solutions to their customers.

Need for Additional Research

Information managers need better measures now, yet the development of useful network measures is, in many respects, still in its infancy. Relevant industry, university, and government groups need to focus attention and resources in this area of increasing importance. There are several areas related to the process of choosing network measures requiring additional research:

- Explore different settings: The present research focused on public library information managers. How do information managers in other settings choose network measures?

- Bridge the theory-practice gap: Information managers rarely mention the concerns voiced by measurement experts, and vice versa. Yet both groups raise important issues. There is need for work that contributes to starting a dialogue. The potential payoff is great with results that are credible and useful.
- Develop Information Technology (IT) that measures IT-based services: There is need for better software to automatically measure network-based resources and services in meaningful ways. There may well be a need for software that assists information managers to choose network measures based on the present research as well as future efforts.
- Develop better solutions to the specific measurement choice issues raised here: The present research identifies a range of issues information managers should consider when choosing network measures. There is a need for identifying formal processes to assist managers when addressing these issues. For example, can a formal process be derived to improve a manager's ability to identify all relevant uses (and misuses) of a proposed network measure?

Additional research will assist information managers who are finding that developing network measures is increasingly important.

ENHANCING THE SUCCESS OF NETWORK MEASURES

Information managers find developing measures to evaluate their organization's network-based information resources and services increasingly important. The present research focused on how successful information managers, in this case public librarians, choose effective measures of network-based information resources and services. One key is the adoption of a strategy that enables managers to effectively address a range of issues across a proposed measure's life cycle before it is chosen. The present research benefits from a partnership that focused the attention of both measurement experts and successful information managers on research questions of mutual interest. Future research efforts in this area should consider such partnerships essential.

ABOUT THE AUTHORS

Joe Ryan was Project Coordinator for the IMLS funded study National Public Library and Statewide Network Electronic Performance Measures and Statistics. He is the co-author of Performance Measures for Public Library Networked Services (2000). Ryan is Director of Ryan Information Management, 1049 Ackerman Avenue, Syracuse, NY 13210. For additional information about him see http://Web.syr.edu/~jryan/index.html.

E-mail: jryan@mailbox.syr.edu

Charles R. McClure is the Francis Eppes Professor of Information Studies and Director of the Information Use Management and Policy Institute at Florida State University http://www.ii.fsu.edu. McClure has written extensively on topics related to planning and evaluation of information services, information resources management and Federal Information Policy. He is the co-author of *Public Libraries and the Internet 2000* funded and published by the National Commission on Libraries and Information Science and is currently completing a study funded by the U.S. Energy Information Administration, the Government Printing Office, and the Defense Technical Information Center to produce performance measures that assess Federal Web sites. McClure is also President of Information Management Consulting Services, Inc. Additional information about McClure can be found at http://slis-two.lis.fsu.edu/~cmcclure.

E-mail: cmcclure@lis.fsu.edu

John Carlo Bertot is Associate Professor in the School of Information Studies and Associate Director of the Information Use Management and Policy Institute at Florida State University http://www.ii.fsu.edu. Bertot was the co-principal investigator for the National Leadership Grant funded by the Institute of Museum and Library Services (IMLS) to develop national public library statistics and performance measures for the networked environment that made this manual possible. This effort led to the book *Statistics and Performance Measures for Public Library Networked Services*, published by the American Library Association. At present, Bertot is co-principal investigator for an IMLS National Leadership Grant to develop a national model for collecting public library network statistics and performance measures, as well as an Association of Research Libraries (ARL) project to develop measurement tools for networked services and resources in ARL libraries. Most recently, Bertot co-authored the *Public Libraries and the Internet 2000* study supported by the National Commission on Libraries and Information Science (see http://www.nclis.gov). Bertot continues to work with public and other libraries to develop, plan, and evaluate network-based services through a variety of projects. He is also the President of Bertot Information Consultant Services, Inc. Additional information on Bertot is available at http://slis-two.lis.fsu.edu/~jcbertot.

E-mail: jcbertot@elis.fsu.edu

REFERENCES

Bertot, J. C.; McClure, C. R.; and Fletcher, P. D. (1997). The 1997 national survey of public libraries and the Internet: Final report. Washington, DC: American Library Association, Washington Office for Information Technology Policy.

Bertot, J. C.; McClure, C. R.; and Ryan, J. (2001). Statistics and performance measures for public library networked services. Chicago: American Library Association.

International Standards Organization (ISO) (2000). ISO/CD 2789 Information and documentation—International library statistics. Stockholm, Sweden: Swedish General Standards Institute.

Katzer, J.; Cook, K. H.; and Crouch, W. W. (1998). Evaluating information: A guide for users of social science research (4th ed.). Boston: McGraw-Hill.

Loessner, G. A. and Fanjoy, E. H. (1996a). Improving public libraries in Delaware: An analysis of county-level public library systems (2nd ed.). Newark, DE: University of Delaware, College of Urban Affairs and Public Policy, Delaware Public Administration Institute.

Loessner, G. A. and Fanjoy, E. H. (1996b). Excellence in public libraries: A program to achieve better information and learning opportunities for Delawareans. Newark, DE: University of Delaware, College of Urban Affairs and Public Policy, Delaware Public Administration Institute.

McClure, C. R.; Bertot, J. C.; and Beachboard, J. C. (1995). Internet costs and cost models for public libraries. Washington, DC: National Commission on Libraries and Information Science.

McClure, C. R., and Lopata, C. L. (1996). Assessing the academic networked environment: Strategies and options. Washington, DC: Coalition for Networked Information.

Chapter 7

Using Electronic Surveys to Evaluate Networked Resources: From Idea to Implementation

Dr. Jonathan Lazar
Dr. Jennifer Preece

ABSTRACT

Increasingly, information resources are being made available through the World Wide Web. It is important to evaluate these networked resources to ensure that they are meeting the needs of the users. One of the most popular techniques to evaluate a networked resource is the use of electronic surveys. There are a number of important issues to consider when developing electronic surveys. One of the most challenging issues is how to develop a sampling method for use with an electronic survey. Without adequate attention to sampling, the response to an electronic survey might be biased and might not accurately represent the population of interest. This chapter will discuss the challenges of sampling techniques with electronic surveys, and offer case studies and solutions to this tricky issue of sampling. Other considerations in developing electronic surveys, such as technical and usability problems, will also be addressed.

INTRODUCTION

In recent years, local, state, and federal governments, as well as universities, organizations, and companies have begun to make many resources available through the Internet. Many examples exist. The Library of Congress provides information on bills, laws, and congressional actions through THOMAS (http://thomas.loc.gov). State libraries have created networks such as SAILOR (http://sailor.lib.md.us) and DelAWARE (http://www.lib.de.us) that provide access to library catalogs, article databases, and act as directories of state-wide resources. There are also metropolitan-area examples, such as the Seattle Community Network (http://www.scn.org) and CapAccess for Washington, DC (http://www.capaccess.org). Museums such as the Smithsonian Institution (http://www.si.edu) and the Franklin Institute (http://www.fi.edu) have resources available online.

Despite the increasing availability of these resources, users still have difficulty locating them and obtaining the information that they need from the Web sites. Since developing these resources is expensive, it is important to find out if these resources are being used, and if not, why they are being underutilized. Log analysis is very useful in determining which resources have been used, and how often those resources are requested, but log analysis only offers data on WHAT resources have been used. Log analysis can not offer any data on WHY the resources have been used. To determine why resources are or are not being used, communication with users is necessary. One way of obtaining this information is by sampling the population of users and potential users. Information from users could provide valuable answers about the value of the content presented and any usability problems that might exist. Information from potential users could reveal problems with Internet access, attitudes towards online information, and awareness of the existence of resources.

What tools could one use to access the population of users and potential users of networked resources, and learn more about why these resources are or are not being used? Among the tools that have been used to evaluate these resources are surveys, interviews, and focus groups. While "traditional" paper surveys can be used, electronic surveys are beginning to become more prevalent in evaluation. An electronic survey is similar in form to the traditional paper survey, the only difference being that the survey is in electronic form, and respondents answer the survey questions electronically. However, electronic surveys raise many questions. How does one design an electronic survey? Should the electronic survey be implemented as an e-mailed survey or a Web-based survey? How does one get a representative sample in cyberspace? How does one identify the survey respondents? How does one reach people who are potential users of a networked resource but do not currently have access to the network? These are all issues that are important for establishing the reliability of the electronic survey, but yet, many evaluations do not address these issues. This chapter will address the process of designing and implementing an electronic survey for an evaluation study, with specific attention paid to usability, sampling methods, and reaching out to potential users of networked resources.

ADVANTAGES OF ELECTRONIC SURVEYS

Electronic surveys can be implemented using either e-mail or the Web (Lazar and Preece, 1999). There are many advantages to using electronic surveys instead of paper surveys. By using electronic surveys, researchers can receive survey responses more quickly than with paper surveys (Lazar and Preece, 1999). Electronic surveys can eliminate the large copying and postage expenses of paper surveys (Lazar and Preece, 1999). It still may be necessary to send postal mail reminding people to respond to the Web-based survey (Bertot and McClure, 1996a; Bertot and McClure, 1998). It may be possible to configure electronic survey responses to directly enter the responses into a spreadsheet or database program (Bertot and McClure, 1998; Lazar and Preece, 1999). By doing this, errors upon data entry may be eliminated (Lazar and Preece, 1999). Electronic surveys can also be modified very easily.

Web-based surveys offer some advantages as compared to e-mailed surveys. Electronic mail surveys require that users have an e-mail account; Web-based surveys do not require that users have an e-mail account. Web-based surveys can also be used at the same time that users are actually accessing the networked resource. Web-based surveys can be implemented as "pop-up screens" to users. Web-based surveys can provide assistance to the user, in the form of images, help screens, and hyperlinks, none of which can be implemented with e-mail (Lazar and Preece, 1999). E-mail survey respondents can easily alter the survey instrument; this is not a problem in Web-based surveys (Witmer, Colman and Katzman, 1999). One advantage of using e-mailed surveys (as opposed to Web-based surveys) is that an e-mailed survey may provide more identification of the survey respondent, though the user's e-mail address. The nature of the population of interest may affect the decision to use an e-mailed survey instead of a Web-based survey. For instance, if there is a well-defined population and corresponding e-mail addresses available (such as in a professional organization), it may make more sense to utilize an e-mailed survey.

Advantages of Electronic Surveys:

- Responses can be received quickly
- Copying and postage costs can be eliminated
- Responses can be automatically recorded in a database, eliminating data entry errors

Disadvantages of Electronic Surveys:

- Can be hard to identify survey respondents
- Can be hard to ensure a representative sample

SAMPLING TECHNIQUES

There is one main disadvantage to using electronic surveys (both Web-based and via e-mail). With traditional paper surveys, procedures for selecting a sample are well-established (Fowler, 1993; Marshall and Rossman, 1995; Oppenheim, 1992). These sampling procedures are necessary to make true population estimates. Without these sampling procedures, the survey responses received might be biased and might not represent the true population. How does one select a sample using electronic surveys? Some different approaches to this problem are beginning to appear. The approaches chosen for a specific survey may be influenced by whether the population of users is well-defined.

POPULATIONS THAT ARE WELL-DEFINED

Federal, state, and local government networks, library networks, and educational networks usually offer a great deal of information to the general public, via the Internet. Many of these networks also offer communication tools to users, including listservers, newsgroups, and bulletin boards. In some of these resource networks, users are required to subscribe, or register, or login to use these resources. In these type of networks, the population of users is well-defined. Even without communication tools (such as listservers and bulletin boards), some networked resources may require users to log in to access specific database resources. For instance, resource usage might be limited to citizens of a certain state (such as Delaware), students at a certain university, or employees of a certain organization. These resources might be accessed via an organizational intranet, to which users are required to log in (Lazar and Preece, 1999). Online communities are a type of networked resource, where the focus is on the communication between users (Lazar and Preece, 1998). In many of these online communities, users must register once to become a "member of the community" and then log in with their user name every time that they want to use the resources. With other networked resources, some of these resources (such as access to full-text databases) might require users to login because of site license requirements (such as university students who must log in to access a citation database called UNCOVER).

In the cases where user registration/login is required, there will be a wealth of information about the user population, including the number of users, usually the e-mail address, and possibly some other demographic information. In all of these situations, the population of users will be well-defined, and will automatically be known, through the network transaction logs. With a well-defined population, traditional random sampling techniques can be modified, and used with electronic surveys to make true population estimates.

Examples of Studies Done on Well-Defined Populations:

Anderson and Gansneder conducted an evaluation of the Cleveland Freenet using electronic surveys (Anderson and Gansneder, 1995). The Cleveland Freenet provides communication tools such as bulletin boards and electronic mail, as well as databases (Anderson and Gansneder, 1995). Users are required to log in every time they want to access the Cleveland Freenet. To develop the sample in their study, Anderson and Gansneder examined a log file containing all of the logins in a two-week period. They then selected a random sample of 600 users, using SPSS (Anderson and Gansneder, 1995). The 600 randomly selected users received e-mailed information about the survey. The same sampling methodology was used by Anderson and Harris in a study of the Texas Educational Network (TENET) (Anderson and Harris, 1997).

In both the Cleveland Freenet and the Texas Educational Network, users were required to log in to access the networked resources. Therefore, a database of user information already existed. The researchers selected a random sample of registered, active users. This same methodology can be applied to any well-defined population of users, where the users must log in to utilize resources. Random samples can be drawn from databases of registered users. The population can be further segmented before the sample is drawn, to only include users who logged in within the previous two weeks (as in the Cleveland study), users who accessed specific tools or resources, or any other distinction. After the sample is drawn, when the *selected* users log in, they can be notified of the existence and importance of the survey. A Web-based survey can appear on the screen, and the users can be either asked or required to fill out a Web-based survey before moving forward to access the requested resources. If researchers are using an e-mailed survey, a message can appear upon login, bringing the users' attention to the e-mailed survey.

The AskERIC service recently did an evaluation study using electronic surveys. (See http://ericir.syr.edu/Qa/survey00summ.html for more detailed info.) AskERIC provides educational research information to educators around the world, through an Internet-based question and answer service. When users request information through AskERIC, they must provide their e-mail address. AskERIC recorded that 443 people used the AskERIC service in a one-month period at the beginning of the year 2000. One-third of that user population was randomly selected to take part in the evaluation study, and those selected received e-mails with a copy of the survey, as well as the option of filling out a Web-based copy of the survey.

Shaw and Davis conducted a study of technology usage in members of the Modern Language Association (Shaw and Davis, 1996). The Modern Language Association (MLA) is a well-defined population. There is a complete list of MLA members available. Shaw and Davis drew two different random samples: one sample was drawn from all members of the MLA ("general sample"), and the other sample was drawn from all members of the MLA who had listed an e-mail address ("e-mail sample") (Shaw and Davis, 1996). Those selected in the general sample received a paper survey in the mail. Those selected in the e-mail sample received an identical survey, sent via e-mail. Responses from the general sample and e-mail sample were compared (Shaw and Davis, 1996).

POPULATIONS THAT ARE NOT WELL-DEFINED

In some networked information resources, the population of users is not well-defined. In these networks, there are usually no communication tools. Users are not required to register, or log in, or be a part of a specific organization, or meet any requirements (such as citizenship of a certain state). The target audience for the resources is generally broad. In these network resources, there is no way to know the nature of the true population of users and make reliable population estimates (Lazar and Preece, 1999). However, that doesn't mean that researchers cannot learn more about the effectiveness of the networked resources.

Researchers can aim for a random sampling of usage (not users), which may mean that certain users are over-represented. For example, every fifth access of a specific Web page might cause a pop-up Web-based survey to appear on their screen. This is the type of methodology being used by a number of businesses on their Web sites. However, the limitation with this methodology is that the users who access a resource most often will also be the ones to receive a pop-up Web-based survey on their screen most often. To lessen the effects, a statement might be put on the survey, saying "If you have previously responded to this survey, please do not respond again." This approach is not currently feasible with e-mailed surveys.

Another technique is to aim for a diverse response (Lazar and Preece, 1999). Although this will not result in true population estimates (since the exact population of the users is not known), researchers can still learn more about the population of interest by getting a diverse response (Lazar and Preece, 1999).

A number of techniques can be used to ensure a diverse response:

1. The first technique is to include demographic questions on the survey (Lazar and Preece, 1999). Surveys can include questions about age, computer experience, and gender (Lazar and Preece, 1999). When analyzing the data, researchers can examine these demographic data to determine whether their responses were diverse. This is especially helpful if a limited amount of baseline data are available about the general population of interest. For instance, if the survey responses are only from men, but the general population of Internet users is known to include a large percentage of women (Pitkow and Kehoe, 1996), then this would mean that the response might be

very biased in the gender area, and the response would therefore not be representative of the true population of interest. On the other hand, if a population of interest is known to be mostly male, then the demographic information can be used to determine whether the survey responses were representative of that population (Lazar, Tsao, and Preece, 1999). This approach is feasible with both Web-based and e-mailed surveys.

2. The second technique is to examine the domains from which the electronic survey was sent. With Web-based surveys, this means examining Web site logs. These logs will provide information about the domains from which the Web-based survey was accessed (Bertot, McClure, Moen and Rubin, 1997). The amount of information given in the domain name will vary (Stout, 1997). In the best cases, a domain name will identify a specific user who is responding to the survey (Stout, 1997). At a minimum, the domain name may assist in determining if survey respondents represent geographic or organizational diversity (Bertot, McClure, Moen, and Rubin, 1997; Lazar, Tsao, and Preece, 1999). With e-mailed surveys, researchers can examine the e-mail addresses that the surveys were sent from. This will provide not only organizational information but, in most cases, identify the specific user who responded to the survey.
3. The third technique is to enforce response diversity. It is possible to set up the Web server to only accept one survey per Internet Protocol (IP) address (Harper, Slaughter, and Norman, 1997). This would ensure that the same person was not repeatedly responding to the survey from the same network location. This would not, however, stop someone from accessing the same survey from different network locations. This approach is feasible only with Web-based surveys.

The extreme example of a population that is not well-defined is the population of Internet users. Georgia Tech has implemented WWW User Surveys (http://www.gvu.gatech.edu/user_surveys) for a number of years, to learn more about the population of Web users. The primary data collection tool for this research study is the Web-based survey. The major drawback of the methodology is that, since there is no central repository listing all Web users, drawing a true random sample is nearly impossible. Georgia Tech therefore aims for as diverse a response as possible. Georgia Tech aims towards the goal of a diverse response by advertising the existence of their survey (see "Informing the Survey Respondents" later in this chapter) in very diverse locations. The survey is advertised on different Internet newsgroups, listservers, general-interest Web sites (such as CNN, Yahoo!, Excite, etc.), and on banners ads that are rotated through advertising networks. The hope is that a diverse audience would see these advertisements and respond to the survey. In addition, to increase the response rate, random cash prizes were awarded. The WWW User Survey is one of the largest studies that uses the Web-based survey as a primary data collection tool. Aiming for a diverse response, their survey methodology seems to work well for their purposes.

Another issue in populations that are not well-defined is the validity of responses. Can the survey responses be considered valid if the respondents are not from a well-known population?

Although it is impossible to guarantee that all survey responses are honest and accurate, this is no different in paper or in electronic surveys. Someone can provide dishonest answers on an electronic survey as easily as he or she can on a paper survey. In general, users tend to be more honest in their interactions in cyberspace. In many healthcare-related communities, people feel more comfortable, and are more honest, when communicating over the computer, as compared to face-to-face communication (Preece, 1999). Fowler also indicates that people may feel more comfortable revealing personal information through a computer (Fowler, 1993). Recent experimental research by Sussman and Sproull also indicates that people are more honest when using computer-mediated communication rather than face-to-face communication (Sussman and Sproull, 1999).

The notable exception to the assumption of trust is in networked resources where the whole purpose of the resource is deceive others and act out fantasies (Turkle, 1995). In these types of resources, sometimes called "virtual worlds," multi-user dimensions (MUDs), or multi-user dimension object-oriented technologies (MOOs), the whole purpose of the interaction is to "make things up" by creating virtual worlds (Curtis, 1997). Obviously, in these types of networked resources, the responses given to electronic surveys would be questionable. However, these virtual worlds do not compose a large percentage of networked resources.

DESIGNING AN ELECTRONIC SURVEY

Once a sampling method is chosen, the next step is to design the survey. Before considering how to technically implement an electronic survey, it is important to design the survey instrument on paper (Lazar and Preece, 1999). What questions need to be asked? Paper surveys must have questions that are clear and unambiguous (Oppenheim, 1992). An electronic survey is no different (Lazar and Preece, 1999). The survey respondent should not be confused as to what the survey is asking them. If a standard, validated survey is already in use, it may be a good source for well-designed questions. A popular type of question to use in an electronic survey is a Likert scale (Lazar, Tsao, and Preece, 1999; Williams, Rice, and Rogers, 1988). Once the survey questions are written, they should be pre-tested (also called a pilot study) to ensure clarity (Oppenheim, 1992; Preece, et al., 1994; Shneiderman, 1998).

This pre-testing of survey questions should be done with people who come from a similar background as those who are expected to respond to the survey (Lazar and Preece, 1999).

Once the survey instrument is designed on paper, it should then be turned into an electronic survey. There are two types of electronic surveys: e-mailed surveys and Web-based surveys. To implement an e-mailed survey, the survey can either be sent as part of an e-mail message text, or it can be sent as a file attachment (in a format such as WordPerfect or MS-Word). Sending an e-mail attachment allows for more control over formatting and type styles than sending the survey in the e-mail message text, but in most cases, the differences are minimal. Implementing an e-mailed survey is easier than implementing a Web-based survey. To implement a Web-based survey, it is necessary to have a Web server that has a dedicated connection to the Internet. To design the Web page for the survey instrument, a software package can be used (Schmidt, 1997b), or HTML code for forms can be written (Niederst, 1999). Schmidt (1997a) does an excellent job of describing the hardware and software requirements for a Web-based survey, which are beyond the scope of this chapter (Schmidt, 1997a).

Once the electronic version of the survey has been created, usability testing should then be done with a small number of users. Usability testing focuses on the interface and whether it is easy to use, whereas pre-testing of survey questions checks on whether the questions are written clearly. Usability testing is necessary to ensure that people are able to interact with the electronic survey without any confusion. Any anomalies discovered during usability testing should be resolved. Lazar and Preece (1999) describe heuristics for usability testing that are specific to Web-based surveys. Other resources describe usability testing in detail (Nielsen, 1992; Nielsen, 1994; Preece, 1990; Preece, et al., 1994; Shneiderman, 1998). When the electronic survey instrument has been designed and thoroughly tested, the next step is to inform the population of interest of the existence of the survey (Lazar and Preece, 1999).

Creating and Implementing an Electronic Survey:

1. Choose a target population and sampling method
2. Create the survey questions on paper
3. Pre-test the survey questions
4. Turn the survey instrument into an electronic survey
5. Perform usability testing on the electronic survey
6. Inform the target population about the existence of the survey

INFORMING THE SURVEY RESPONDENTS

It is obviously important to try and maximize the response rate to the survey (Fowler, 1993). The approach to this will differ based on whether the survey is e-mailed or Web-based. In most cases of using e-mailed surveys, the survey will be sent directly to the respondent. It may be useful to send an e-mail message before the actual survey instrument is sent, notifying the respondent that the survey instrument will arrive in their mailbox in a short amount of time. For a Web-based survey, researchers can inform the population of interest by posting an announcement to a newsgroup, bulletin board or listserver that relates to the population of interest (Schmidt, 1997a). Such a message should include the purpose of the survey, the Uniform Resource Locator (URL) of the survey, and who should respond (Swoboda, Muhlberger, Weitkunat and Schneeweib, 1997). If the users must log in to get access to the networked resources, the users can be informed of the survey when beginning their session. If e-mail addresses for users are available, then e-mail reminders should be sent to the users, reminding them to respond to the Web-based survey. Another suggestion is to include a description of the researchers and their qualifications, so that the potential respondents will not simply write off the survey announcement as spam or other junk mail (Hewson, Laurent, and Vogel, 1996). During the period of study, it may be useful to remind the population to participate in the study, either electronically, or through more traditional means (Bertot and McClure, 1996a; Fowler, 1993; Walsh, et al., 1992).

These previously discussed techniques can be used to encourage a higher response rate. However, the user might be asked to participate in a large number of surveys, and there are probably many other activities vying for the attention of the user. Therefore, many users may not respond to the survey. One question that is often asked is, "What response rate is acceptable?" This depends on the purpose of the survey. If the purpose of the survey is to make statistical population estimates, for policy purposes, then a high response rate is obviously needed. However, for evaluation purposes, a large response rate is not necessarily needed. The purpose of an evaluation is to learn more about why users are or are not using the resources made available on the Web. Therefore, statistical estimates are not necessary. Instead, it is important that the response is representative, i.e., that all important user groups have been represented in the survey responses. In addition, for the reasons discussed in a later section, using only electronic surveys for evaluation is inadequate, even with a high survey response rate. For evaluating networked resources, the multi-method approach is encouraged, where electronic surveys are used as part of an "evaluation toolbox," along with log analysis, focus groups, and paper surveys. All of these methods combine for a more complete evaluation.

USING ELECTRONIC SURVEYS IN CONJUNCTION WITH OTHER DATA COLLECTION METHODS

Network Access

It is important to note that electronic surveys will only be able to provide access to those who are already using the networked resource in question. The drawback in using exclusively electronic surveys is that it is possible only to reach users who are currently using the resources. For instance, it would be impossible to use electronic surveys to reach users who registered, but have not logged in within the last six months. It would also be impractical to use electronic surveys to reach potential users of certain networked resources. These are people who might possibly be interested in the networked resource. For instance, Catholic school teachers might be interested in the resources available at the National Catholic Educational Association (NCEA) at http://www.ncea.org. However, some Catholic School teachers might not even know about the existence of these resources. Electronic surveys could not reach the population of potential users.

Another important factor to consider is economic status (Bikson and Panis, 1997; Civille, 1996). Internet connectivity levels are related to wealth. People with lower household incomes are less likely to have access to computer networks (Bikson and Panis, 1997). Therefore, electronic surveys might be an inappropriate tool for learning more about issues related to poverty (Lazar and Preece, 1999).

If researchers want to know more about why users AREN'T using a networked resource, it is important to go to the population of people who are potential users of the network resource but have not chosen to use it. Numerous techniques exist to reach these populations.

Paper Surveys

In general, the methodology used in conjunction with paper surveys has been to send paper surveys to a population known to include both users and non-users of the networked resource. For instance, in evaluating the Blacksburg Electronic Village (BEV), an online community based on the town of Blacksburg, Virginia, researchers sent paper surveys to the citizens of Blacksburg. By doing this, the researchers were able to access the entire population of Blacksburg, which was known to consist of many users of BEV. By sending surveys to the citizens of Blacksburg, researchers could access not only users of BEV but also potential users who were not currently using BEV (Patterson, 1997).

Blacksburg, Virginia is a rare example of a well-networked town with a high level of data on connectivity levels. In other circumstances, it may be necessary to create a sample which would be known to include both users and non-users of a networked resource. In a study of e-mail usage in a corporation, Kraut and Attewell took two different samples from the corporation's records (Kraut and Attewell, 1997). The first sample was a random sample of employees selected from the corporate phone book (Kraut and Attewell, 1997). These people might or might not use e-mail. The second sample was a random sample of employees selected from the records of employees who used their e-mail accounts in 1991 (Kraut and Attewell, 1997). All of those selected received a paper survey in the mail (Kraut and Attewell, 1997).

Combining Paper and Electronic Surveys

It is possible to use a combination of paper and electronic surveys to access a population (Lazar and Preece, 1999). To ensure validity, both of these surveys must be alike. This hybrid approach might be used for two reasons:

1. *There is little data available on the demographics of the population, and therefore, the goal is to get a very diverse response.* In a study of an online community for people who play an academic sport called Quiz Bowl, researchers used a combination of Web-based and paper surveys (Lazar, Tsao, and Preece, 1999). There was no demographic information on the population of interest, but it was known that there were some people who took part in the online community but not the face-to-face meetings, some people who took part in the face-to-face meetings but not the online community, and some people who took part in both (Lazar, Tsao, and Preece, 1999). The paper surveys were distributed at face-to-face gatherings of community members in the Northeastern United States. The Web-based surveys were received from users all over the country. By using Web-based surveys, the researchers received a more geographically diverse response, and they were able to access users who only used the networked resources but did not come to the face-to-face meetings. By also using paper surveys, the researchers were able to gain access to people who were potential users of the networked resources, but 1) did not know about the existence of the networked resources, 2) knew about the networked resources but had chosen not to use them, or 3) had at one time used the networked resources but no longer used the resources.
2. *To increase the response rate by making it easy for networked respondents to respond, without limiting responses from non-networked respondents.* The 1998 Survey of Library Outlet Internet Connectivity used an interesting methodological approach (Bertot and McClure, 1998). The goal of this study was to find out about Internet connectivity levels and service provisions in library branches across the United States. Obviously, if the survey was conducted exclusively through electronic

> surveys, there would be a limited response (if any) from libraries who did not have Internet access. In this study, the researchers sent out paper letters to library branches selected in the sample, informing them that they were selected for response in the study (Bertot and McClure, 1998). The letter informed the libraries that they had two choices for responding: They could send back the paper survey in the self-addressed stamped envelope, or they could access the Web-based survey and respond electronically. Each selected library had a respondent ID number. The respondent ID number was included on the paper survey and in the informational letter. For respondents who used the Web-based survey, they were required to input their respondent ID number on the Web-based survey (they could also search for their respondent ID online). This way, all survey responses (paper and Web-based) were identified, so that the researchers could make accurate population estimates. For respondents who didn't have Internet access, the survey appeared to be just like any other traditional paper survey. For respondents who did have Internet access, they could save time by going online to fill out the survey.

A 1996 study by Shaw and Davis also used a combination of electronic and paper surveys (Shaw and Davis, 1996). Shaw and Davis did a study of technology usage in members of the MLA, a well-defined population (Shaw and Davis, 1996). Shaw and Davis drew two different random samples: one sample was drawn from all members of the MLA (*general sample*), and the other sample was drawn from all members of the MLA who had listed an e-mail address (*e-mail sample*) (Shaw and Davis, 1996). Those selected in the general sample received a paper survey in the mail. Those selected in the e-mail sample received an identical survey, sent via e-mail. Obviously, if only e-mail surveys were used, it would be impossible to get a representative response of MLA members about technology usage since those who responded to an e-mailed survey were likely to be people who were comfortable using technology. That would not necessarily be representative of the population of MLA members as a whole.

Recently, one of the largest data collection efforts, the 2000 U.S. Census, gave the option of collecting Census forms on-line. Americans who received the short form (five out of every six forms sent) had the option of filling out the census form on the Web (Cohn, 2000). To ensure appropriate sampling, each census form had an ID number, and to fill out the census form online, the respondent needed to enter their ID number (Cohn, 2000). After performing this action once, no more census forms (electronic or paper) were accepted from that ID number. This technique ensures an exact count of Web-based responses, with no duplicates.

Focus Groups

Another way to access people who are potential users of a networked resource but are not using that resource is to utilize traditional information gathering techniques such as focus groups or interviews (Krueger, 1994). These techniques have been used in evaluating state library networks such as SAILOR (Bertot and McClure, 1996b), DelAWARE (Bertot, McClure and Lazar, 1998), and Online at PA (McClure and Bertot, 1997). By talking face-to-face with potential users and actual users, it is possible to learn more about why users do or do not use a networked resource. This type of information gathering environment tends to be less structured and offer less control for the researcher, so to gather information effectively using these techniques, it is necessary to have an experienced focus group moderator (McClure and Bertot, 1997).

DATA ANALYSIS

Once survey responses start coming in, it is important to carefully manage the survey responses. In an electronic survey, respondents frequently send in MORE than one survey. This is usually accidental. For instance, respondents do not recall if they sent the e-mail survey, or respondents may click the "SEND" button too many times on the Web-based survey. By examining the e-mail address that an e-mailed survey was sent from, it is usually possible to determine whether a survey was sent twice by accident. The researcher can always send an e-mail message to the survey respondent for clarification. For a Web-based survey, it is important to track the IP addresses and time sent of the incoming surveys (Note: this can also be done after the fact by examining the Web site logs [Stout, 1997].) If more than one survey was sent from the same IP address within a short amount of time, it might be useful to examine the actual responses to the survey questions. If the survey was filled out with the same responses and sent from the same location in a short amount of time, chances are that the respondent only meant to respond once but was confused or was having technical problems. It is also possible to require respondents to a Web-based survey to provide their e-mail address, or provide a password or ID number, which would identify who the survey response came from. This technique could be used to validate survey responses.

SUMMARY

There are many advantages to using electronic surveys, especially Web-based surveys. However, in the networked environment, it is more complicated to develop and implement a quality survey. Aside from usability and technical issues, one of the largest obstacles to a successful electronic survey is a good sampling methodology. Examples of current approaches to sampling have been presented. It is important to address the issue of sampling with electronic surveys, to ensure that the survey results are valid. A number of research areas need to be expanded upon to create a full base of research literature for evaluating networked resources using electronic surveys. Standard approaches for sampling, such as those that exist for use with traditional paper surveys, need to be developed for use in the networked environment. Research needs to examine the usability of electronic surveys, focusing on issues such as survey length, text layout, and graphics. The different types of electronic surveys (e-mail in text, e-mail as an attachment, Web-based, pop-up Web-based imposed on screen) should be compared to determine whether one type of electronic survey encourages more responses. Research on the trustworthiness of electronic surveys should continue, because it will encourage the skeptical that electronic surveys are valid research instruments which can provide useful data for evaluation.

ABOUT THE AUTHORS

Dr. Jonathan Lazar is an Assistant Professor in the Department of Computer and Information Sciences at Towson University. Dr. Lazar has a number of research publications focusing on human-computer interaction issues in the Internet environment. Specifically, Dr. Lazar is interested in user error, user training, user-centered design, Web-based surveys, and Web usability. Dr. Lazar is the author of the book, *User-Centered Web Development*, published by Jones and Bartlett Publishers.

E-mail address: jlazar@towson.edu

Dr. Jenny Preece is a Professor and Chair of the Department of Information Systems at the University of Maryland Baltimore County. Dr. Preece's most recent book, *Online Communities: Designing Usability, Supporting Sociability* is published by John Wiley and Sons. She is also author of a number of other books including the leading text in human-computer interaction, and numerous other publications.

E-mail address: preece@umbc.edu

REFERENCES

Anderson, S. and Gansneder, B. (1995). Using electronic mail surveys and computer-monitored data for studying computer-mediated communication systems. Social Science Computer Review, 13(1), 33–46.

Anderson, S. and Harris, J. (1997). Factors associated with amount of use and benefits obtained by users of a state-wide educational telecomputing network. Educational Technology Research and Development, 45(1), 19–50.

Bertot, J. and McClure, C. (1996a). Electronic surveys: Methodological implications for using the World Wide Web to collect survey data. Proceedings of the 59th Annual Meeting of the American Society for Information Science, 173–185.

Bertot, J. and McClure, C. (1996b). SAILOR Network Assessment: Final Report Compendium. Baltimore, MD: Division of Library Development and Services, Maryland State Department of Education.

Bertot, J. and McClure, C. (1998). 1998 National Survey of Public Library Outlet Internet Connectivity. Washington, DC: American Library Association Office of Information Technology Policy.

Bertot, J.; McClure, C.; and Lazar, J. (1998). The DelAWARE Evaluation Project: Site Visit Report. Dover, DE: Delaware Division of Libraries.

Bertot, J.; McClure, C.; Moen, W.; and Rubin, J. (1997). Web usage statistics: Measurement issues and analytical techniques. Government Information Quarterly, 14(4), 373–395.

Bikson, T. and Panis, C. (1997). Computers and connectivity: Current trends. In Kiesler, S. (Ed.) Culture of the Internet (pp. 407–430). Mahwah, NJ: Lawrence Erlbaum Associates.

Civille, R. (1996). The Internet and the poor. In Kahin, B. and Keller, J. (Eds.) Public Access to the Internet (pp. 175–207). Cambridge, MA: MIT Press.

Cohn, D. (2000). Census goes online but gets few hits. The Washington Post, March 4, 2000.

Curtis, P. (1997). Mudding: Social phenomena in text-based virtual realities. In S. Kiesler (Ed.), Culture of the Internet (pp. 121–142). Mahwah, NJ: Lawrence Erlbaum Associates.

Fowler, F. (1993). Survey Research Methods. (2nd ed.). Newbury Park, CA: Sage Publications.

Harper, B.; Slaughter, L.; and Norman, K. (1997). Questionnaire Administration via the WWW: A Validation and Reliability Study for a User Satisfaction Questionnaire. Proceedings of the WebNet97: International Conference on the WWW, Internet and Intranet [on CD-ROM].

Hewson, C.; Laurent, D.; and Vogel, C. (1996). Proper methodologies for psychological and sociological studies conducted via the Internet. Behavior Research Methods, Instruments, and Computers, 28(2), 186–191.

Kraut, R. and Attewell, P. (1997). Media use in a global corporation: Electronic mail and organizational knowledge. In Kiesler, S. (Ed.) Culture of the Internet (pp. 323–341). Mahwah, NJ: Lawrence Erlbaum Associates.

Krueger, R. (1994). Focus Groups: A practical guide for applied research. Thousand Oaks, CA: Sage Publications.

Lazar, J. and Preece, J. (1998). Classification schema for online communities. Proceedings of the 1998 Association for Information Systems Americas Conference, 84–86.

Lazar, J. and Preece, J. (1999). Designing and Implementing Web-Based Surveys. Journal of Computer Information Systems, 39(4), 63–67.

Lazar, J.; Tsao, R.; and Preece, J. (1999). One Foot in Cyberspace and the Other on the Ground: A Case Study of Analysis and Design Issues in a Hybrid Virtual and Physical Community. WebNet Journal: Internet Technologies, Applications, and Issues, 1(3), 49–57.

Marshall, C. and Rossman, G. (1995). Designing Qualitative Research. (2nd ed.). Thousand Oaks, CA: Sage Publications.

McClure, C. and Bertot, J. (1997). Evaluation of the Online at PA Libraries Project: Public Access to the Internet Through Public Libraries. Harrisburg, PA: Pennsylvania Department of Education, Office of Commonwealth Libraries.

Niederst, J. (1999). Web Design in a Nutshell. Sebastopol, CA: O'Reilly and Associates.

Nielsen, J. (1992). Finding Usability Problems Through Heuristic Evaluation. Proceedings of the CHI 92: Human Factors in Computing Systems, 373–380.

Nielsen, J. (1994). Usability Engineering. Boston, MA: Academic Press.

Oppenheim, A. (1992). Questionnaire Design, Interviewing, and Attitude Measurement. London: Pinter Publishers.

Patterson, S. (1997). Evaluating the Blacksburg electronic village. In Cohill, A., and Kavanaugh, K. (Ed.) Community networks: Lessons from Blacksburg, Virginia (pp. 55–71). Boston, MA: Artech House.

Pitkow, J. and Kehoe, C. (1996). Emerging trends in the WWW population. Communications of the ACM, 39(6), 106–110.

Preece, J. (1990). A Guide to Usability. Milton Keynes, England: The Open University.

Preece, J. (1999). Empathic communities: Balancing emotional and factual communication. Interacting with Computers, The Interdisciplinary Journal of Human-Computer Interaction, 12 (1): 63–77.

Preece, J.; Rogers, Y.; Sharp, H.; Benyon, D.; Holland, S.; and Carey, T. (1994). Human-Computer Interaction. Wokingham, England: Addison Wesley Publishing.

Schmidt, W. (1997a). World Wide Web survey research: Benefits, potential problems, and solutions. Behavior Research Methods, Instruments, and Computers, 29(2), 274–279.

Schmidt, W. (1997b). World Wide Web survey research made easy with the www survey assistant. Behavior Research Methods, Instruments, and Computers, 29(2), 303–304.

Shaw, D. and Davis, C. (1996). The modern language association: Electronic and paper surveys of computer-based tool use. Journal of the American Society for Information Science, 47(12), 932–940.

Shneiderman, B. (1998). Designing the User Interface: Strategies for Effective Human-Computer Interaction. (3rd ed.). Reading, MA: Addison-Wesley.

Stout, R. (1997). Web Site Stats. Berkeley, CA: Osborne McGraw Hill.

Sussman, S. and Sproull, L. (1999). Straight talk: Delivering bad news through electronic communication. Information Systems Research, 10(2), 150–166.

Swoboda, W.; Muhlberger, N.; Weitkunat, R.; and Schneeweib, S. (1997). Internet surveys by direct mailing. Social Science Computer Review, 15(3), 242–255.

Turkle, S. (1995). Life on the Screen: Identity in the Age of the Internet. New York, NY: Simon and Schuster.

Walsh, J.; Kiesler, S.; Sproull, L.; and Hesse, B. (1992). Self-selected and randomly selected respondents in a computer network survey. Public Opinion Quarterly, 56(2), 241–244.

Williams, F.; Rice, R.; and Rogers, E. (1988). Research Methods and the New Media. New York, NY: The Free Press.

Witmer, D.; Colman, R.; and Katzman, S. (1999). From paper-and-pencil to screen-and-keyboard: Toward a methodology for survey research on the Internet. In Jones, S. (Ed.) Doing internet research: Critical issues and methods for examining the net (pp. 145–161). Thousand Oaks, CA: Sage Publications.

Chapter 8

User-Centered Evaluation and Its Connection to Design

Carol A. Hert

ABSTRACT

As the theme of this volume is evaluation of networked services, readers do not need to be convinced that evaluation is a critical activity in planning and making decisions associated with the provision of networked services. This chapter has as its focus user-centered evaluation. The chapter has several goals:

- It provides a conceptualization of user-centered evaluation in the context of networked information resources and services.
- It categorizes and describes the wide variety of user-centered metrics and data collection methods.
- Finally, it articulates a mechanism by which findings from user-centered evaluation can inform design.

The intent of the chapter is to provide an overview of user-centered evaluation (both theory and practice) that enables evaluators to appropriately employ such evaluation techniques and to use evaluation results to provide guidance to system designers.

TAKING USERS INTO ACCOUNT IN EVALUATIONS

Over the last 15 years, information systems researchers have begun to make a shift towards a focus on system users (and non-users) and their perceptions, cognitions and actions, which has variously been called a *user perspective*, a *user-oriented approach*, a *user-centric approach*, etc. An *Annual Review of Information Science and Technology* chapter by Dervin and Nilan (1986) stands out as a classic in articulating this shift. The user-centered approach is in contrast to a *system-oriented* approach where research focuses on aspects of system operations such as how to improve processing algorithms, transmit messages via the network, etc.

The user-centered approach is not monolithic; instead, it might be viewed as a continuum. At one end of the continuum of user-centeredness is an attempt to understand the phenomenon of interest (as defined by the researchers) from the viewpoint or perspective of the user. At the continuum's other end (which might be termed constructivist), a researcher would enable users to define the phenomenon of interest themselves.[1]

In an evaluation context, at the lower boundary of the user-centered approach (where user behavior is studied, but the researcher is still the expert), we would expect to see an evaluation that employs metrics that capture aspects of that behavior on the system. The evaluator would still define the system/service to be evaluated, the evaluation context, what dimensions of the user experience should be evaluated, and the data collection and analysis approaches and metrics. At the other end (the constructivist end) of the continuum, the stakeholders jointly define the phenomenon to be evaluated (with the potential to not examine the system at all), and often, the approaches to be used in the evaluation. The "evaluator" becomes a facilitator enabling the stakeholders to articulate their vision and direction. Thus, an evaluator might approach the situation first by polling the stakeholders for ideas about what should be evaluated (working for a consensus), how to evaluate it, and for identification of other stakeholders. Somewhere in between these two extremes might be placed "participatory design" in which a variety of techniques are used to solicit user input and evaluations throughout a design process. Authors such as Bawden (1990), Dalrymple (1991), and McClure (1994) are useful guides for general strategies in user-centered evaluation. Patton (1990; 1997) and Guba and Lincoln (1989) are the first sources to consult for the constructivist approaches to evaluation.

Constructivist approaches may be difficult to execute due to lack of understanding or buy-in from the stakeholders, and the power structure within a setting may work against the equal partnership the approach requires. Serafeimidis and Smithson (1996) and O'Neill (1995) provide good examples of constructivist evaluation in action and some of the potential pitfalls. While often difficult to execute, constructivist evaluation approaches should be considered in the context of networked services evaluation. There is increasing recognition that one must understand technology within its social and/or organizational contexts (Kling, Rosenbaum, and Hert, 1998) and that flexible technology is used flexibly. This flexibility reduces the ability for an external evaluator to preset the evaluation frame and he or she needs to rely on stakeholder perspectives of their work worlds in order to achieve the goals of evaluation.

Defining Users

How do we define users? For the purposes of this chapter, the term "users" refers to those people for whom the system/resource is designed or for whom the system facilitates tasks ("end-users"). While not the focus of this chapter, other stakeholders such as managers of resources, potential end-users, system designers, vendors, etc., might also be important to consider in evaluations. As a case in point, imagine a situation in which an end-user wants functionality or resources in a system that the agency providing the service cannot afford. An evaluation that considers only end-users has the potential to find the system lacking; one that includes other stakeholders might instead suggest that a balance among competing interests be found. So while the chapter considers only end-users, it is critical that evaluators be aware of the other potential stakeholders to include in evaluations and incorporate their perspectives into evaluation design.

The methods for data collection, analysis, and translation into design decisions described in this chapter are likely to be useful for a variety of stakeholders; what will be different is the conceptualization or theory behind the phenomenon being studied. Some of the other chapters in this volume provide additional perspectives on how to incorporate those stakeholders in evaluations.

CONCEPTUAL FRAMES FOR THE PHENOMENON TO BE EVALUATED

Having an evaluation perspective that places users in the central position is a necessary but not sufficient requirement for conducting user-centered evaluations. It still leaves open the aspects that need to be evaluated, how one gathers data, etc. Evaluators are fortunate in that several conceptualizations of user behavior with information systems are available (and to some extent have been empirically validated). This section of the chapter provides an overview of two conceptualizations of user behavior with networked resources and services that provide the basis for the metrics and methods discussed in later sections.

A conceptual frame will suggest appropriate methods for data gathering and analysis, metrics of evaluation, and how to connect evaluations to design. Two conceptual frames (somewhat overlapping) are discussed here. These conceptual frames are useful for resources/services/systems that support user information seeking. Such systems have been the dominant type in the first several years of networked resource availability. Recently, systems to support purchasing behavior of users (either consumers or businesses) have proliferated. Conceptual models to frame their evaluations would be driven by theories and concepts from marketing, consumer behavior, etc. This chapter does not include these models; however, once an appropriate conceptual frame is identified, many of the data collection methods and mechanisms to connect findings to design discussed here will generally be applicable.

Interaction as a Conceptual Frame

The vast majority of networked resources exist as real-time, interactive systems. That suggests that we must conceptualize the phenomenon as interactive. An extensive literature in information science and human-computer interaction (HCI) considers the nature of interaction and how to support it[2] and a wide variety of models exists for expressing the nature of the interaction. Increasingly there has been the recognition that both systems and users are changing over time, and thus users and systems need to continue to learn (and be evaluated).

Imagine a user going to a system he or she has never used. The user might have some general knowledge of systems of this type but needs to interact with the system to flesh that knowledge out with the specifics of the particular system. He or she might read the documentation (not likely) or experiment. For an optimal interaction, the user needs to be able to learn from the experimentation or be provided with learning tools (Shneiderman, 2000) in order to increase his or her likelihood of a satisfactory outcome. Finally, when the interaction is terminated, along with hopefully having achieved desired results, the user should also have gained some system knowledge useful the next time he or she uses the system.

From an evaluation perspective, the above model of interaction suggests a variety of specific aspects that could be evaluated. There are obvious user-centered criteria[3] for a successful interaction. The user

- is the partner that terminates an interaction;
- terminates the interaction because he or she has reached the desired goal and/or is satisfied;
- gains knowledge of aspects of the system that will improve the next interaction; and
- receives feedback and confirmation throughout the interaction about the validity of his or her knowledge of the system.

The user criteria can then be operationalized via specific metrics and data collection strategies. For example, one might record how frequently the user terminates a session versus a system-side termination (having decided on what constitutes an acceptable level of system-side terminations), assess user satisfaction, calculate the relevance of results (for a bibliographic search), assess user knowledge of the system via questionnaires or tests, etc.

Additionally, this model of interaction suggests that users change, may not return to the system or that new users will arrive. This dynamism indicates that evaluations might need to include the perspectives of new users, ongoing users, users that no longer use the system, etc.

Information Seeking and Use as a Conceptual Frame

There is an extensive literature associated with information seeking (summarized every several years in chapters in the *Annual Review of Information Science and Technology* entitled "Information Needs and Uses"). At the risk of over-summarizing, this literature indicates the following:

- Users experience gaps, anomalous states of knowledge which lead them to seek information. (Not all gaps lead to information seeking.)
- Users come to an information seeking process with information needs, as well as affective needs and a repertoire of behaviors.
- Information seeking is situational, contextual; each person is in a unique place in his or her life.
- Information seeking related to a given problem may extend over several information seeking episodes.

As with the conceptual frame of interaction, this frame helps an evaluator specify foci for an evaluation.

An optimal information seeking experience for a user would:

- allow resolution of a user's information need;
- enable a user to exploit (or compensate for) his/her affective needs and behaviors; and
- enable the user to retain and use information about previous searches.

These goals suggest evaluation of the extent to which user goals are met, which might include measuring satisfaction or relevance of results. One might also investigate the impact of user expectations, uncertainties and confusions on the accomplishment of goals.

These evaluation objectives probably seem less clear-cut than those posited above for interaction. This is due to the situational nature of information seeking processes. In most situations, an evaluator would first need to determine user information needs, uncertainties, etc., prior to development of evaluation objectives. In many evaluation situations, an evaluator might target most common information needs or tasks for a particular user community to manage the situational aspect of information seeking.

EVALUATION METRICS

If one accepts the two conceptual frames outlined above as legitimate in the context of networked information, then one can draw on a wide range of specific metrics to be used in conjunction with them. A huge number of user-oriented measures have been suggested and used in system and service evaluation. They can be broken down into two general classes: those in which users' perceptions and attitudes take precedence and those associated with user-system interaction. Metrics from both sets may be useful at all points on the user-centeredness continuum. This section reports on the most commonly used from both classes and Harter and Hert (1997) is a good source for an extensive list with associated discussion and references.

User Perceptions and Attitudes

Metrics that measure user perceptions and attitudes generally start with user assessments of a system/service/resource or components thereof but the metrics tend not to assess the system explicitly that contributes to those user assessments. For example, a user might be asked to indicate his or her satisfaction with a resource, but the evaluator does not investigate how the resource contributed to that satisfaction, whether other resources might have been equally satisfying, etc. The general rationale behind these metrics is that a system is successful if a user's score on a scale measuring the perception is maximized (or minimized in some cases).

Probably the most commonly employed metric of this class is *satisfaction*. It is intuitively understandable to both evaluators and users and a number of validated scales and questionnaires exists (e.g., Baroudi, Olson, and Ives, 1986; Doll and Torkzadeh, 1988; and Chin, Diehl, and Norman, 1987). There is some concern about satisfaction as a metric however. There is evidence that users are often satisfied without actually accomplishing tasks (discussed by Applegate [1993]). Other researchers point out that user satisfaction may not be clearly related to design features or actual use of a system. Thus, while satisfaction may be readily measured, it may not provide a good tool by which to make design recommendations.

Other metrics of user preceptions and attitudes include:

- Utility (Cooper, 1976)
- Value (Taylor, 1986)
- Helpfulness (Beghtol, 1989)
- Benefits (Dalrymple and Zweizig, 1992)
- Frustration (Dalrymple and Zweizig, 1992)
- Self-efficacy (Nahl, 1996)

The first four of these (utility, value, helpfulness, and benefits) are all defined similarly, being measures that attempt to capture the extent to which the system (or results of a system such as documents) provide value to a user. Self-efficacy is the extent to which a user feels in control of the experience and frustration takes its common sense definition.[4] (These variables are most often measured via Likert scale questionnaires though none have been validated to the extent that satisfaction metrics have.)

These measures of user perceptions and feelings share a common disadvantage in usage for system design. Without additional information, none provide insight into what aspects of a system led to the perception or feeling. To use in system design contexts, it is likely that an evaluator might first assess several dimensions of a system using one of the metrics (such as satisfaction), then gather more detailed information from users on those components with which they were less satisfied.

User-System Interaction Metrics

The second class of metrics are those that assess the interaction. These tend to assess the extent to which a system has minimized or maximized some aspect of the user's experience. Most of these are derived from human-computer interaction and usability testing and studies. Usability (of a system) may be defined as "the extent to which the information technology affords (or is deemed capable of affording) an effective and satisfying interaction to the intended users, performing the intended tasks within the intended environment at an acceptable cost" (Sweeney, Maguire, and Shackel, 1993, p. 690). This definition leads to the specification of measures for efficiency, effectiveness, and satisfaction.

An important component to stress from the above definition, in terms of its implications for metric use, is that usability is assessed for "intended users ... intended tasks within the intended environment." This contextuality results in the need to operationalize the three general evaluation metrics specifically for a given context. Approaches often used include measuring errors (effectiveness),[5] and time to complete tasks (efficiency). In a Web environment, number of clicks and pages navigated also have been heavily used.

An evaluator will need to understand the aspects of system operation and the tasks it supports in order to specify appropriate measures. The usability community had its beginnings in procedural systems (such as word processing systems) rather than information systems of the sort discussed here so that usability measures are often insufficiently articulated for this evaluation context. More metrics are being developed for use in usability evaluations of information resources and services and one can expect that growth to continue. At this point, an evaluator is often left to search for previous evaluations with similar goals to determine what metrics others have used. *The Handbook of Human-Computer Interaction* (1997) is also a good starting place for metric identification and development.

Unlike the perceptual measures presented in the previous section, the choice of a user-system interaction metric constrains design recommendations to some extent. Counting the number of clicks, for example, suggests that reducing (or increasing) the number of clicks should be the goal of design. How to accomplish that goal still would need to be determined and it is likely that data would need to be collected about why the users performed in particular ways. (See information in the next section about verbal protocols for further information.)

DATA COLLECTION STRATEGIES

An extensive range of strategies is available for collecting user-centered data. Given this extensiveness, it will not be possible to provide sufficient detail on each to enable a reader to execute them; however, the recommended citations to relevant texts and a study which employed the method should provide some guidance. Table 8.1 provides a brief summary of these methods.

The collection of user-centered data takes three general approaches. One can collect artifacts of user behavior, interview people, or observe people.[6] Artifacts of user behavior include examination of transaction logs (for Web pages and search engines), comments and e-mails sent via the system (or by snail mail, telephone, etc.), results of searches (such as Web pages printed off), etc. Interview strategies could include real-time interactions, online questionnaires, etc. Observations might take place as a person used a system or resource or in other contexts. Each method has its pros and cons to consider.

Collecting and Examining Artifacts

As one might imagine, collecting and examining artifacts represent largely unobtrusive approaches to data collection. While an evaluator is probably ethically bound to inform users that data are being collected, the user doesn't necessarily have to change his or her behavior to accommodate the data collection process. A separate chapter in this volume discusses transaction log analyses so their utility won't be belabored here. A word concerning search engine logs may be useful since they provide a unique view of user terminology and search errors which researchers have not fully exploited.

Search Engine Logs

Search engine logs record the searches input by users and often the number of hits (though not the actual hits themselves). They are often analyzed to determine the most frequent searches but perhaps even more interesting is that one can analyze them to determine typical errors in semantic or syntactic search construction (and thus provide appropriate help) or to examine the terminology employed in the expression of concepts. In a recent study, Haas and Hert (Haas and Hert, 2000; Hert, 1999) mapped user terminology from search engine logs to the terminology employed by the agency sponsoring a Web site to determine the extent of overlap in those terminologies. This information enabled the researchers to specify times when vocabulary enhancement might be employed by the agency.

Table 8.1: Summary of General Approaches to Data Collection

General Approach	General Method	Description	Analysis Techniques	Representative Study
Collection of Artifacts		Unobtrusive but cannot understand user rationales for actions: may not represent all users		
	Transaction logs (see related chapter)	Good for general picture of usage and trends in usage	A variety depending on log structure and content	Hert, et al. (1999)
	E-mail messages and comments	Used to examine user questions, complaints, problems	Content Analysis (Holsti, 1969; Krippendorf, 1980)	Hert and Marchionini, (1997)
Interviews, Question-naires, Surveys		Excellent for capturing user perceptions and attitudes; may not give good picture of actual behaviors; may be difficult to identify and access users	Tabulation and statistical analysis of results, content analysis of open ended questions (Fowler, 1988; Babbie, 1990; 1998)	Bertot and McClure (1996)
	Focus groups	Used in early stages of design to gather impressions, not a good method for validating or generalizing, often used as a preliminary information gathering tool	Content analysis, some tabulation (Krueger, 1994)	Hert and Marchionini (1997)
	Critical incident technique	An interview strategy in which a user is asked to focus on an incident that was crucial, particularly memorable to the phenomenon being studied, it overcomes some of the problems with surveys as users tend to be more reliable in reporting critical incidents; however you will not get a generalized picture of usage	Tabulation and statistical analysis with content analysis of open-ended answers	
	Timeline Interviews	A form of interviewing in which respondents report on events and information usage, feelings, etc. during each event; used to capture processes	Tabulation, with statistical analysis if appropriate, content analysis of open-ended answers	Miwa (2000)
Observational Strategies		Excellent for capturing user behavior; hard to generalize as it is difficult to observe large numbers of users		
	Usability studies and tests	These terms cover a broad spectrum of methods but in general, respondents think aloud while performing action on a system. Actions may be researcher-defined tasks or free choice on part of respondent	Tabulation of usability metrics, statistical analysis, content analysis or other qualitative techniques such as constant comparative technique (Glaser and Strauss, 1967)	Marchionini and Crane, (1994); Hert, Jacob, and Dawson (2000)
	Observations in other contexts	Useful for understanding user behavior more broadly than just as it is manifested on a given system, however time to observe may be significantly more than with other techniques		Nardi and O'Day (1999)

E-mail messages and other commentary

E-mails and other commentary also provide an unobtrusive way to understand users and their questions and concerns. Unlike logging methods, however, the population of users is self-selected and does not represent the full spectrum of users of a system. Often one will get a preponderance of *complainers* or *praisers*, neither of which is representative. Another challenge in using e-mail messages is categorizing them in useful ways. Generally, there will be too many to "eyeball" and get a sense of; instead one should perform a content analysis. Content analysis is a technique for systematically capturing and categorizing data from free-text materials. This entails development of a coding scheme that states rules for identification of the particular categories of responses. Several useful texts by Holsti (1969) and Krippendorf (1980) present this process. Hert and Marchionini (1997) provide details of coding schemes used in a Web site evaluation.

All of the artifact-based approaches are also limited in two ways that may be important to an evaluation. The first is that one must infer the rationale for user actions as the user his or herself in not available to ask. These inferences are difficult to make without substantive knowledge of users and their behavior and it is difficult to assess the extent to which evaluator inferences map to user rationales without explicitly confirming them with a user. In addition, one can only gather information on actual users; what if non-users or potential users also matter? These methods cannot help an evaluator understand how to support or design for people who do not currently use the system. Some of the other methods discussed below do.

Interviews and Questionnaires

Interviews and questionnaires are the second class of user-centered data collection methods. Textbooks by Babbie (1990; 1998) and Fowler (1988) provide detailed guidance in choosing particular interview strategies, designing questions, etc. Interviews are an excellent vehicle for capturing data on attitudes and perceptions but are less useful for capturing actual behaviors. If one wants to know what someone actually does, observing that person will provide more valid data that asking the person to report on what he or she did. Often we are unable to remember with any accuracy. Imagine a user attempting to tell an evaluator what he or she did the last time surfing the Internet. Most likely he or she will only be able to report the most general of information; a search engine used, a Web site visited but not details of action. However, interviews are excellent for the evaluation of user satisfaction, ease of use, and other important attitudinal aspects.

In some situations, interviews might be the only mechanism available. Networked resource users are often remote and difficult to observe because they are geographically distributed or one doesn't know when they will use a resource. In such situations, one may have to rely on interviews or surveys. In it critical in these situation to ask only those questions for which one can reasonably expect valid answers.

Interviews and surveys also require some mechanism for getting them to a user. This is a major issue in using the approach in the networked environment where it is often exceedingly difficult to identify individual users. Survey forms on a Web site (even if they pop up randomly) are subject to self-selection problems (Who responds? Do they respond more than once?) and probably will not provide a representative picture of users. If an evaluator has access to user IDs, one may be able to target surveys to random users. Background information on who can get user IDs on the system, whether people can have multiple IDs, whether a user ID represents multiple users, and whether some IDs are never used is necessary to create a sample frame that is efficient.

Observational Strategies

Observational strategies might also be employed. Observational strategies are particularly useful when one wants to link behaviors to rationales for behaviors. This is accomplished via a technique called *think-aloud* or *verbal* protocols. Essentially, the evaluator asks the respondent to think-aloud as he or she is using a system saying anything that occurs to him or her. Verbal protocols are widely used in usability studies to pinpoint which features of a system cause problems. Verbal protocols during observations are generally combined with observations of other aspects of an interaction. In most cases, the evaluator would videotape or record the actions of the respondent and using time-stamps, in order to synchronize the actions with the think-aloud protocols. Metrics from usability studies (such as number of clicks, pages viewed, time to complete task) can be used to analyze the data. There is some concern that asking people to think aloud while executing tasks changes their behavior; however there do not appear to be alternative mechanisms to elicit respondent reasoning.

Observations might also occur in settings in which the system is not the central focus. Systems constrain user behavior, thus if one wishes to understand user behavior more generally, one may want to find other settings in which users are doing tasks similar to those they would execute on the system. For information seeking tasks, a very logical option is to observe users in libraries and bookstores. In one study where the author was interested in understanding how to provide help for users, the research team observed users interacting with intermediaries in libraries and other settings to identify the value-added services provided (Hert, 1998).

Naturally, it is possible to combine techniques from all three of these general approaches. In fact, it is likely that stronger findings will result. For example, in one study (Hert, et al., 1999) the researchers conducted a usability test of a Web site in which users reported that they didn't notice the navigation buttons at the top of the screen. This finding was confirmed via a transaction log analysis that indicated that the navigation buttons were not frequently used.

CONNECTING EVALUATION RESULTS TO DESIGN

The goal of this chapter is to provide a connection between user-centered evaluation processes and system design. Two rationales underlie this goal. The first is that system design is a planning process with a set of critical decisions to be made. Evaluation is an integral part of any planning process and provides a systematic way to collect and analyze data in support of decision making. The second rationale is captured in a quote by Rasmussen, Pejtersen, and Goodstein: "evaluation should be a dynamic process; that is, a continuing design refinement throughout the design process itself" (1994, p. 211). Allen (1996) reiterates the close connection of design and evaluation pointing out that a summative evaluation, done at the end of a design process, is limited by the quality of the base system. "If the base system is not carefully crafted, incremental improvements may be incapable of transforming it into a usable, functioning information system" (Allen, 1996, p. 291).

How do we transform evaluation results into design decisions? There are two aspects:

- A carefully designed evaluation process
- Understanding the chain of logic from the conceptualization through the evaluation to design options

The carefully designed evaluation process is one in which the evaluator has articulated a conceptual frame for the evaluation, chosen metrics appropriate for that frame, specified criteria for action based on the values of the metrics, and collected and analyzed data appropriately. This first aspect is not unique to user-centered evaluation or design—in any research design the goal is to conduct research in such a way that techniques yield valid data that answer the research questions.

The second aspect is specific to the transformation discussed here. This chapter has been structured as follows: conceptualizations of the phenomena of interest (e.g., interaction, information seeking), metrics and data collection options, and finally design. The author argues that in order to provide guidance to designers, an evaluator must be clear on the logic that connects these three areas, target his or her study appropriately, and indicate to a designer what design guidance is indicated by the study at hand. User studies associated with design can be placed within the hierarchy indicated in Figure 8.1.

At the highest level (and furthest removed from design specifics) are studies that clarify the "meta-themes" and ask questions such as:

- How can this phenomenon be conceptualized?
- What behaviors, cognitions, feelings do users have as they use this system/resource and how might these be categorized?

User studies at this level are distant from specific design recommendations. They are important in that they point to aspects to be investigated in the next level. Returning to the conceptualization that started this chapter (interaction) as an example, design guidance at this level consists of suggesting that feedback should be incorporated, strategies/tools to help users should be available, etc. Evaluation studies of this type tend to be time-consuming as the researcher cannot constrain the investigation in any great extent. All aspects

Level	Evaluation Goal	Related Design Guidelines	Strength of Connection
Highest	Establish appropriate conceptual frames	General aspects that design should support	Connection between evaluation findings and specific design requirements weak
Middle	Investigate aspects relevant to conceptual frames	Indicate nature and content of aspects of design	Connection strong enough to indicate basic functionality of aspect of design but not its implementation
Lowest	Test alternative design approaches	Choice among alternative designs possible	Strong connection

Figure 8.1: Connecting Levels for Evaluation and Design Guidelines

of a project may take a great deal of time and thus a study of this sort is not appropriate if designers need quick input.

At the second level indicated on Figure 8.1, an evaluator has determined (through previous empirical work, literature review, etc.) which conceptualization will drive research efforts and explores aspects of that conceptualization. Following through the interaction example, an evaluator might ask questions such as

- What do users need/want to learn?
- What types of feedback improve their searching?

Answers to these questions provide more detail to designers, however the actual mechanisms by which an answer is implemented cannot be specified. These studies will be less time-consuming than those of the highest level though data are still likely to be rather freeform and require analysis strategies such as content analysis.

At the lowest level, a designer uses his or her expertise and suggests approaches for implementing the design guidelines from the higher levels. Several alternatives might be mocked up. At this point, an evaluator would test among the alternative designs. In the interaction example, it might be decided that information about how to use the system, interpret its results, etc., could be provided either via mouse-overs or through linked pages. An evaluator would be asking questions such as

- Which alternative is most satisfactory to users?
- Which alternative improves user performance on a post-interaction knowledge test?
- Which alternative improves interaction outcomes?

There is a very specific connection between evaluation and design at this level. These studies provide information that will enable a designer to make specific choices and are likely to be the fastest type study to construct and execute.

A one considers the range of options available for evaluation studies, it is clear that an ongoing dialog with designers is critical. Since designers operate on short time scales, they will tend to push for fast turnarounds on evaluation work. While they may request or expect a study at the lowest level, it is critical that an evaluator engage in a dialogue where it becomes clear what the goal of a given evaluation should be. If a higher-level study is necessary to provide conceptual guidance, for example, a designer needs to be aware of the time, cost, and type of findings that would likely result. Working throughout a design process enables an evaluator to provide services at all the levels indicated in Figure 8.1, at optimal times for the findings to be incorporated into design.

CONCLUSION

A number of key issue areas remain to be investigated within the domain of user-centered evaluation of networked resources. Evaluators need to do the following:

- Develop metrics that are explicitly derived from theoretical conceptualizations. User-centered metrics are, by their nature, intimately connected to the phenomenon of interest, thus are not easily portable. In the context of networked resources, we are only beginning to see attempts to develop metrics that reflect the phenomenon. (See Heard [1999] as an example.) Metrics connected to the phenomenon will be more intuitively understandable by evaluators, designers, and other stakeholders.
- Acquire more knowledge of constructivist approaches. Constructivist methods have a place in evaluations of technology of all sorts particularly when the technologies enable individual users the freedom to shape the tool and their use of it. There is currently a limited understanding of the theoretical underpinnings of these methods and how to incorporate them into evaluation. Evaluators will need a rich understanding both to use the methods as well as to articulate their value to designers.
- Educate the design community about the potential of various kinds of user studies. The design community will continue to be driven by fast turnaround projects. It is critical that the user-centered evaluation community does not oversell its services in this pressured environment. If one does a high level study as indicated in Figure 8.1 of this chapter, one must also be responsible for not reasoning beyond what the findings can support. Ongoing educational efforts that

articulate what user-centered evaluations entail in terms of costs, time, etc., and what they can deliver is critical to bridging the gap between evaluation and design.

- Work simultaneously on the three levels of the evaluation-design connection. While designers want fast-turnaround, it also critical that the user-centered research community keep itself focussed on the value it can add at all levels of design. As much as possible, if the community can work at all levels of the hierarchy the more value it can provide. A logical division might be for academic researchers to tackle more theoretical aspects while in-house evaluators perform more time-sensitive research.

This chapter's objective was to provide an orienting perspective on how one conducts user-centered evaluations in networked environments. These environments have some unique aspects—users are geographically dispersed and often hard to identify, and the environments are complex. But they share many characteristics of other environments in which a user-centered focus is appropriate. Orienting theoretical frameworks—such as interaction and information seeking and use, and a wide range of appropriate methods and metrics—make it possible to rigorously evaluate aspects of these environments in support of design decisions.

ENDNOTES

1. This general approach goes by several names: constructivist, naturalistic, qualitative, and interpretivist. There are distinctions that may be made among the terms though for the purposes of this discussion we can consider them as synonyms.
2. A good starting point for understanding the human-computer interaction (HCI)-field would be *The Handbook of Human-Computer Interaction* (1997).
3. There are also criteria relevant to the system's side of the interaction not considered here.
4. In the Dalrymple and Zweizig article (1992), frustration is a construct, which combines more specific concepts.
5. Wildemuth and Moore (1995) suggest that missed opportunities might also be a useful measure, one that suggests that the user does not make errors but instead misses some approach, activity, etc. that might be more efficient or effective than the one employed.
6. Typically in the research methods world, we talk about experimental, quasi-experimental, and field studies, surveys, or naturalistic studies. This categorization is not used here; readers are reminded that along with the choice of data collection approach, one simultaneously makes choices about the study design.

ABOUT THE AUTHOR

Dr. Carol A. Hert is on the faculty of the School of Information Studies at Syracuse University and a 2000-2001 Senior Research Fellow at the United States Bureau of Labor Statistics. Her research concerns how people seek and use information on information systems and on the Web with the goal of using this understanding to support design activities. Most recently, she has been investigating these themes in the context of statistical Web sites. She has extensive evaluation experience and has been a consultant to the United States Department of Education, the United States Bureau of Labor Statistics, the Federal Interagency Task Force on Statistics, Onondaga County (NY), and Syracuse University Library. She currently has funded research projects through the National Science Foundation and the American Statistical Association. She is the author of numerous research articles and the book, *Understanding Information Retrieval Interactions: Theoretical and Practical Implications*. Greenwich, CT: Ablex Publishing Corp. 1997.

E-mail address: Cahert@syr.edu

REFERENCES

Allen, B. L. (1996). Information Tasks: Towards a User-Centered Approach to Information Systems. San Diego, CA: Academic Press.

Applegate, R. (1993). Models of user satisfaction: Understanding false positives. RQ 32(4): 525–539.

Babbie, E. (1998). Practice of Social Research, 8th ed. Belmont, CA: Wadsworth.

Babbie, E. (1990). Survey Research Methods, 2nd ed. Belmont, CA: Wadsworth.

Baroudi, J. J.; Olson, M. H.; and Ives, B. (1986). An Empirical study of the impact of user involvement on system usage and information satisfaction. Communications of the ACM 29(3): 232–238.

Bawden, D. (1990). User-oriented Evaluation of Information Systems and Services. Brookfield, VT: Gower Publishing Co.

Beghtol, C. (1989). Retrieval effectiveness: Theory for an experimental methodology measuring user-perceived value of search outcome. Libri 39: 18–35.

Bertot, J. C. and McClure, C. R. (1996). Electronic surveys: Methodological implications for using the world-wide-Web to collect survey data. In Global Complexity: Proceedings of the ASIS 1996 Annual Meeting. Medford, NJ: Information Today, pp. 173–185.

Chin, J. P.; Diehl, V. A.; and Norman, K. (1987). Development of an instrument measuring user satisfaction of the human-computer interface. Proceedings of the Computer Human Interface '88 Meeting. New York: Association for Computing Machinery, pp. 213–218.

Cooper, W. S. (1976). The Paradoxical role of unexamined documents in the evaluation of retrieval effectiveness. Information Processing and Management 12(5): 367–375.

Dalrymple, P. W. (1991). User-centered evaluation of information retrieval. In Allen, B. L. (Ed.) Evaluation of Public Services and Public Services Personnel. Urbana-Champaign, IL: University of Illinois, pp. 85–102.

Dalrymple, P. W. and Zweizig, D. L. (1992). Users' experience of information retrieval systems: An Exploration of the relationship between search experience and affective measures. Library and Information Science Research 14(2): 167–181.

Dervin, B. and Nilan, M. (1986). Information needs and uses. Annual Review of Information Science and Technology 21: 3–33.

Doll, W. J. and Torkzadeh, G. (1988). The Measurement of end-user computing satisfaction. MIS Quarterly 12(2): 258–274.

Fowler, F. J. (1988) Survey Research Methods, rev. ed. Newbury Park, CA: Sage Publications.

Glaser, B. G. and Strauss, A. L. (1967). The Discovery of Grounded Theory: Strategies for Qualitative Research. Hawthorne, NY: Aldine de Gruyter.

Guba, E. G. and Lincoln, Y. S. (1989). Fourth Generation Evaluation. Newbury Park, CA: Sage Publications.

Haas, S. and Hert, C. A. (2000). Terminology Development And Organization In Multi-Community Environments: The Case Of Statistical Information. To be published in the Proceedings of the 2000 American Society for Information Science SIGCR Meeting, Nov. 2000.

Handbook of Human-Computer Interaction, 2nd ed. (1997). Martin G. Helander; Landauer, Thomas K.; and Prabhu, Prasad V. (Eds.) Amsterdam: Elsevier.

Harter, S. P. and Hert, C. A. (1997). Evaluation of information retrieval systems: Approaches, issues and methods. Annual Review of Information Science and Technology 32: 3–94.

Hert, C. A. (1999). Federal Statistical Web site Users And Their Tasks: Investigations Of Avenues To Facilitate Access: Final Report to the United States Bureau of Labor Statistics. From http://istWeb.syr.edu/~hert/BLSphase3.PDF.

Hert, C. A. (1998). FedStats Users and Their Tasks: Providing Support and Learning Tools: Final Report to the United States Bureau of Labor Statistics. From http://istWeb.syr.edu/~hert/BLSphase2.html.

Hert, C. A. and Marchionini, G. (1997). Seeking Statistical Information in Federal Web sites: Users, Tasks, Strategies, and Design Recommendations: Final Report to the Bureau of Labor Statistics. From http://ils.unc.edu/~march/blsreport/mainbls.html.

Hert, C. A.; Eschenfelder, K. R.; McClure, C. R.; Rubin, J.; Taffet, M. D.; Abend, E. J.; and Pimental, D. M. (1999). Evaluation of Selected Web sites at the U.S. Department of Education: Increasing Access to Web-Based Resources: Final Report to the U.S. Department of Education. From http://iis.syr.edu/Webeval/index.html.

Hert, C. A.; Jacob, E.; and Dawson, P. (2000). A Usability assessment of online indexing structures the networked environment. To be published in Journal of the American Society for Information Science 51(11) 971–988.

Holsti, O. R. (1969). Content Analysis for the Social Sciences and the Humanities. Reading, MA: Addison-Wesley.

Kling, R.; Rosenbaum, H.; and Hert, C. A. (1998). Social Informatics in Information Science: An Introduction. Journal of the American Society for Information Science 49(12): 1047–1052.

Krippendorf, K. (1980). Content Analysis: An Introduction to its Methodology. Beverly Hills, CA: Sage Publications.

Krueger, R. A. (1994). Focus Groups: A Practical Guide for Applied Research, 2nd ed. Newbury Park, CA: Sage Publications.

Marchionini, G. and Crane, G. (1994). Evaluating hypermedia and learning: Methods and results from the Perseus Project. ACM Transactions on Information Systems 12(1): 5–34.

McClure, C. R. (1994). User-based data collection techniques and strategies for evaluating networked information services. Library Trends 42(4):591–607.

Miwa, M. (2000). Use of Human Intermediation in Information Problem Solving: A User's Perspective. Unpublished doctoral dissertation. Syracuse University: Syracuse, NY.

Nahl, D. (1996). Affective monitoring of Internet learners: Perceived self-efficacy and success. Proceedings of the Annual Meeting of the American Society for Information Science 33: 100–109.

Nardi, B. A. and O'Day, V. L. (1999) Information Ecologies: Using Technology With Heart. Cambridge, MA: MIT Press.

O'Neill, T. (1995). Implementation frailties of Guba and Lincoln's Fourth Generation Evaluation theory. Studies in Educational Evaluation 21: 5–21.

Patton, M. Q. (1990) Qualitative Evaluation and Research Methods, 2nd ed. Newbury Park, CA: Sage Publications.

Patton, M. Q. (1997). Utilization-focused Evaluation: The New Century Text, 3rd ed. Thousand Oaks, CA: Sage Publications.

Rasmussen, J.; Pejtersen, A. M.; and Goodstein, L. P. (1994). Cognitive Systems Engineering. New York, NY: Wiley.

Shneiderman, B. (2000). Universal usability. Communications of the ACM 43(5): 85–91.

Serefeimidis, V. and Smithson, S. (1996). The Management of change for information systems evaluation practice: Experience from a case study. International Journal of Information Management 16(3): 205–217.

Sweeney, M.; Maguire, M.; and Shackel, B. (1993). Evaluating user-machine interaction: A Framework. International Journal of Man-Machine Studies 38: 689–711.

Taylor, R. S. (1986). Value-added Processes in Information Systems. Norwood, NJ: Ablex.

Wildemuth, B. M. and Moore, M. E. (1995). End-user search behaviors and their relationship to search effectiveness. Bulletin of the Medical Library Association 83(3): 294–304.

Chapter 9

Digital Reference Services in Public and Academic Libraries

Joseph Janes

ABSTRACT

A national sample of public libraries' Web sites was examined in March 2000 to determine the extent, nature and aspects of digital reference services in public libraries. Services found (in approximately 13 percent of libraries) were analyzed by size of library, placement within Web site, technological sophistication, policy statements, and descriptive names.

INTRODUCTION AND REVIEW OF RELEVANT LITERATURE

Digital reference continues to be an area of much activity and interest in the library world. Many libraries are experimenting with the use of Internet technologies to answer questions from patrons, and articles continue to appear in the professional literature describing experiments, services, experiences, questions, and concerns.

In the last two years, for example, articles have appeared which describe individual services (Reger 1998), the need for more aggressive digital services (Lipow 1999), the future of the mission of reference in a technologically dynamic world (Baker, Pelster, and McHugh, 1998), the impact of technology in the reference world (Rose, Stoklosa, and Gray, 1998; Lawrence and Ross, 1999; and Sager 1999) and ideas and guidelines for the development of services (Sloan 1999, Foster 1999, and Wasik 1999).

These articles are intended as representative of the emerging literature of digital reference and a comprehensive review is beyond our scope. The common issues and themes one finds in this literature largely relate to questions about the future and role of reference (and, for that matter, libraries and librarianship in general) in a rapidly changing, highly networked world. Probably the central question is how reference will evolve, assuming it survives, and how it will be different from what we now know as reference. Issues such as how to conduct interviews, how to answer questions, appropriate uses of technology, and administration and resource allocation are often discussed. Of particular concern is the need for training staff to prepare them for escalating expectations of users. The primary underlying theme here is a reaffirmation (rarely challenged or systematically examined) of the importance of human mediation and service between people and information resources, and a reexamination of the basic principles of "reference" work in the light of the emerging information world.

Very little has been done to help understand the extent to which these services are being developed and what they are like. The study reported here is a replication of the method of Janes, Carter, and Memmott's first study of digital reference services in academic libraries (1999). That study looked at the Web sites of 150 academic libraries in the United States to find out how many offered digital reference services and important characteristics of those services, including whether the service was pointed to from the library's main Web page, how users could submit questions, and service policies.

The present study used nearly identical methods to examine digital reference services in United States public libraries. Our objectives were to understand the current nature of digital reference services in public libraries and from our results make observations and recommendations for the further development of such services. We had seven research questions:

- What percentage of U.S. public libraries is offering digital reference services?
- How many of those services are pointed to from their libraries' home Web pages?
- What names are used to describe those services?
- What methods of submitting questions are provided?
- Does the service point to a Frequently Asked Question (FAQ) list or collections of previously answered questions?
- What policies are stated by and about these services?
- How many services use technological barriers to authenticate users?

As libraries plan, develop, and refine digital reference services, their decisions are often made in a vacuum. Important questions about service policies, use of technologies, resource allocation, publicity and presentation, training and so on are better informed with a fuller picture of the ways in which other libraries are providing digital reference services. This is particularly true in the highly dynamic information world we now live in, with an increasing number of options for people to ask questions and receive answers. In addition, our findings will help the profession better understand how professional practice is changing in the reference arena.

We will present our findings and compare them to those of the preceding study of academic library digital reference services throughout.

METHODOLOGY

Sample

Our population of interest was public libraries in the United States. Since the distribution of public libraries by size of population served is so dramatically skewed, with a great many libraries serving very small communities, we chose to limit our focus to libraries serving at least 10,000 people and which employ at least one full-time equivalent (FTE) librarian. This gave us a population of 3,325 libraries (from the 8,946 in the 1996 survey of public libraries conducted by the National Center for Education Statistics) from which to draw our sample. We chose to draw a sample of 352 libraries, which yields a ±5 percent confidence interval at the 95 percent level.

Since this population is still highly skewed, we chose to draw a weighted sample stratified by service population. Table 9.1 shows the sampling scheme we used.

Table 9.1: Sampling Scheme

Group	Populations Served	%iles	Population Size	Sample Size	% of Population in Sample
1	10,000–28,245	0–50	1663	88	5.3%
2	28,245–58,890	50–75	831	88	10.6%
3	58,890–136,847	75–90	499	88	17.6%
4	136,847+	90–100	332	88	26.5%
TOTAL			3325	352	10.6%

Based on the findings of the academic library study, it seemed likely that the larger libraries would be more likely to have services. Therefore, to be able to study characteristics of services, it would be best to have many to examine. This led to the decision to weight the sample towards libraries serving larger communities.

Method

The investigation was carried out during March 2000. Four investigators, graduate students, and professionals, searched for the Web sites of the 352 libraries in the sample, using a variety of methods: lists of public libraries with Web sites as maintained by state libraries, other directories such as LibWeb, as well as searching with search engines.

When a library Web site was found, the investigators determined whether or not the library offered a digital reference service. We defined a "digital reference service" thus: a mechanism by which people can submit their reference questions and have them answered by a library staff member through some electronic means (e-mail, chat, Web forms, etc.), not in person or over the phone. For libraries with branches, only the main library's Web page was examined. If investigators could not identify a digital reference service within five minutes, they stopped searching, under the presumption that if experienced Web users and information professionals couldn't find a service in that period of time, neither could a patron.

Once a service was identified, the investigators filled out a Web-based questionnaire. This questionnaire is almost identical to the one used in the academic library study, with only one or two minor changes in wording, and with the addition of one option. Several libraries examined in the pretest phase had generic e-mail addresses or Web forms, which could be used to send messages to the library, but they were not specifically labeled as "reference" or "ask us a question." These were separately coded in Question 5.

Several measures were taken to help ensure the reliability of the data. Two of the investigators had been part of the previous academic library study and thus had experience in data collection; the other two were trained and assisted by their experienced colleagues and the principal investigator. The instrument was pretested prior to the main study by all investigators and difficulties and inconsistencies were resolved. Each investigator examined roughly one-quarter of the sample of libraries, divided by state to make searching for library Web sites more efficient and easier. The data collected by each of the investigators were also compared, and no significant differences between their results were found.

As with the academic library study, we made no attempt to contact the libraries involved. We examined these services as a potential patron would, as presented on the Web. As such, we had no access to policy decisions or rationales, how services are staffed, resources available, processes the libraries use,

Table 9.2: Web Sites Found

Group	Web Sites	Sample Size	%	Population Size	Estimated # of Web Sites
1	68	88	77.3%	1663	1,285.0
2	74	88	84.1%	831	698.8
3	67	88	76.1%	499	379.9
4	84	88	95.5%	332	316.9
					2,680.7

volume of questions received, and so on. Some of these may be inferred from information we did find, but these are inferences only.

RESULTS

Of the 352 libraries in the sample, we were able to find Web sites for 293 of them. Based on our weighted sample, we were able to estimate that approximately 80.6 percent of public libraries had Web sites during the study period, with the largest libraries more likely than smaller ones. (See Table 9.2 for details.)

Of those, 64 offered digital reference services, 131 had generic e-mail addresses or Web forms, and 159 had neither. Taking weighting into account, we estimate that 427 public libraries were offering digital reference services in March of 2000, approximately 12.8 percent of all public libraries in our population of interest. See Table 9.3 for details. *We are thus 95 percent confident that the true proportion of public libraries within our population of interest that offer digital reference services is between 7.8 and 17.8 percent.* This figure is dramatically lower than for the academic libraries previously studied, 44.7 percent of which offered digital reference services in May of 1999.

Such a difference raises a question of validity, and leads one to ask whether it is feasible or intuitive that the proportion of public libraries offering digital reference could be less than a third than that of academic libraries. Given the number of public libraries with Web sites (or, perhaps more saliently, the number without them), and the relatively greater access most academic libraries have to technology and technological expertise on their campuses, this result is perhaps not overly surprising. Further, we have found the same pattern in

Table 9.3: Digital Reference Services Found

Group	Services	Sample Size	%	Population Size	Estimated # of Services
1	6	88	6.8%	1663	113.4
2	13	88	14.8%	831	122.8
3	11	88	12.5%	499	62.4
4	34	88	38.6%	332	128.3
					426.8

both settings: the larger the institution (or community), the more likely they will be offering digital reference.

Due to the small numbers involved, for most of the succeeding discussion, we will examine the libraries in two categories: the largest libraries (group 4, serving populations of at least 135,000 people) and the smaller ones (all others), although where possible and reasonable, we will look at smaller groups.

Where Services Exist

As Table 9.3 indicates, approximately half of the services we found were in the largest libraries, serving communities of at least 135,000 people. Further analysis of the 1996 Department of Education survey data reveals that libraries with services also employed more librarians (median of 13.8 compared to three for libraries without services), had higher annual circulation rates (median of 864,000 per year compared to 260,000) and more reference transactions per year (median of 84,000 compared to 30,000). This mirrors the academic library pattern and demonstrates that resources are an important factor—though by no means the only one—in determining whether a library has mounted a digital reference service.

We developed a rough geographical picture of where services are located by examining the first digit of libraries' ZIP codes. The results are presented in Table 9.4.

There are interesting differences here. Rates of services range from a high of 26.5 percent in the far west to a low of 8.6 percent in the south central region, but no general pattern emerges from initial observations.

Table 9.4: Digital Reference Services by Region

Region	States	# with Services	Sample Size	%
9	AK, CA, HI, OR, WA	9	34	26.5%
3	AL, FL, GA, MS, TN	11	47	23.4%
4	IN, KY, MI, OH	10	43	23.3%
5	IA, MN, MT, ND, SD, WI	4	20	20.0%
6	IL, KS, MO, NE	7	37	18.9%
2	DC, MD, NC, SC, VA, WV	6	37	16.2%
0	CT, ME, MA, NH, NJ, RI, VT	6	37	16.2%
8	AZ, CO, ID, NV, NM, UT, WY	3	20	15.0%
1	DE, NY, PA	5	40	12.5%
7	AR, LA, OK, TX	3	35	8.6%

What Services Are Like

The remaining questions referred only to libraries that offered digital library services, so the following analysis pertains only to those 64 services. Table 9.5 shows the data for the questions on characteristics of those services.

Link from Home Page, FAQs, Technological Barriers

A little over half, 37 of the 64, of the libraries' services were directly linked from the home page of their Web site, nearly the same proportion as for academic libraries. Conversely, nearly half did not, making it more difficult to know about and locate the service. We are unable to say definitively why this is the case, although analysis below of the statements made on the forms regarding policies, especially on time to answer, may give us a partial picture. It is interesting to note that the largest libraries (those in group 4) are as likely to be directly linked as smaller ones (those in all other groups).

A series of inferential (t and x^2) tests were performed to look for patterns among services that share characteristics. These are intended as exploratory techniques only, and should be read and interpreted that way. This analysis showed very little in this case; only one test even approached significance: Libraries with services linked from their home pages are somewhat more likely

Table 9.5: Characteristics of Services

Characteristic	Group 1	Group 2	Group 3	Group 4	Total	Total %	Small Publics	Large Publics	Academic (1999)
Total number of services	6	13	11	34	**64**				
Direct link from home page	3	5	9	19	**36**	56%	57%	56%	49%
Point to FAQ	0	1	0	8	**9**	14%	3%	24%	4%
Technological barrier	1	2	2	19	**24**	38%	17%	56%	27%
Submit via e-mail	3	9	9	13	**34**	53%	70%	38%	42%
Submit via simple Web form	4	3	4	13	**24**	38%	37%	38%	55%
Submit via detailed Web form	0	2	0	14	**16**	25%	7%	41%	10%
Policy on type of users	1	2	1	6	**10**	16%	13%	18%	55%
Policy on type of questions answered	3	2	3	21	**29**	45%	27%	62%	55%
Policy on time to answer questions	4	4	3	21	**32**	50%	37%	62%	60%
Other policy	3	1	2	9	**15**	23%	20%	26%	6%

to have a detailed Web form for submitting questions ($p = .081$, $C = .213$),[1] but all other analyses were unremarkable.

Very few, only nine, services pointed to a list of FAQs or collection of previously answered questions. (Only three of the 67 academic libraries had such links.) All but one of these are in the largest libraries. Of those nine, two are strictly procedural, answering questions about the library, policies, procedures, etc. Both had a great many questions (20 or more), and were single pages with anchor tags to answers.

Four of the nine had *real* reference questions; one was an eclectic list of ten pathfinders on science, consumer issues, job searching, the Supreme Court, and so on. One was an archive of seasonally interesting Web pages (resources for Martin Luther King Day, holidays, Women's History Month, the *Titanic*). The other two could be described as Frequently Asked Reference Question pages; one with six, the other with 24 questions, both with characteristic public library reference questions, and lots of links to resources.

The other three were hybrid policy and reference question pages; one was largely procedural with about five reference questions, and the other two had a substantial policy focus and a handful of reference questions with few external links.

This seems to imply that these pages are not seen as necessary, although they are quite common in many kinds of Web-based ask-an-expert services and other venues, an interesting distinction.

Somewhat more than a third of services had some sort of technological barrier, usually requiring or requesting a library bar code number (although sometimes ZIP code or phone number). These barriers were rarely insurmountable; in the academic library study, there were libraries whose services could not be completely examined because they were inaccessible without passwords or other authentication. Here they tended to be statements informing users that questions would only be answered if valid bar code or phone numbers were provided. The largest libraries were more likely to have such provisions (about half of them, only one in six of the smaller ones). This would seem to reflect the general public library orientation of openness of service, but it also might suggest these services get few questions or do not have the technology or expertise to build technological barriers.

Exploratory inferential testing shows that services with technological barriers are less likely to take questions via e-mail (C = .272), more likely to use a detailed form (C = .286), more likely to have a policy on the kind of users they will serve (C = .278).

Ways of Taking Questions

As public libraries serve larger communities, they are more likely to use detailed Web forms and less likely to use e-mail as ways for patrons to submit digital reference questions. 70 percent of the smaller libraries use e-mail (largely mailto links from Web pages), about a third use simple Web forms (asking only for name, e-mail address and question), and only two of 30 uses a detailed Web form. Conversely, among the largest libraries, the proportions are much more evenly distributed—about four in 10 use each method. In both cases, some libraries use both e-mail and some kind of Web form. Simple Web forms were the most prevalent method among the academic libraries, with a few detailed Web forms and many e-mail addresses, but this may be a case where the technological development of the intervening year made a difference. Once again, we see the correlation between size of library and the technological sophistication of its service.

The libraries which use the detailed forms, the most sophisticated method for taking questions, are more likely to have a direct link to the service from the home page (C = .213), more likely to point to an FAQ page (C = .274), more likely to have a technological barrier (C = .286), and more likely to have a policy on the kinds of users they will serve (C = .241).

These forms ask for a wide variety of kinds of information; a list of the most common appears in Figure 9.1.

There is nothing overly surprising here; these are the kinds of information either needed to get an answer back to the user or to help in understanding the question. It is interesting, however, that so many of the questions here are functional rather than content-oriented. These services are more likely to ask for a phone or fax number or address than for sources consulted, intended use

where do you live/address (11)
phone number (10)
date by which you need an answer (7)
grade/level/age (7)
what have you searched already (6)
subject area of request (4)
is question factual or research (3)
have you used this service before (3)
fax number (3)
how will you use the information (2)
is question for a school assignment (2)
best way to contact you (2)
where did you hear about this (TV/radio) (2)
library branch (2)
country of residence (2)
keywords
retype your e-mail address for confirmation
company/institution
are you a state resident
school district number
adult/youth
date of question
do you regularly use the library

Figure 9.1: Information Requested on Digital Reference Forms

of the information, what the user already knows, etc., which are usually seen as important parts of the reference interview. To be sure, the libraries will then have direct access to the user via phone or fax to refine their understanding of the question, but this may reveal something about the way in which these libraries perceive this kind of service as opposed to in-person or phone service.

Other interesting features of these forms: two, upon requesting an e-mail address, immediately gave advice on how to get a free e-mail account (from hotmail or similar services), two (and only two) stressed the confidentiality of the service, and two forms were perfectly identical, other than the name of the library at the top of the page. One form said that their service was "best used for questions ... staff can research and answer without further input from you."

In addition, three other related forms were found. One was to request a check of the stacks for an item to be shipped to a local branch, one was to ask a question about the local community or government (the regular form was blocked to users without a valid bar code number), and the third advertised a research support service, an opportunity for one-on-one, in-person, free work with an Information Specialist. The form asked for the goal of the session, comments and restrictions on the search and the best time for an appointment. This service was listed as experimental for a three-month test period.

Policies on Questions, Questioners, Time to Answer

We looked at three kinds of policies, as stated on libraries' Web pages: on types of questions they will answer, on kinds of people they will serve, and on the turnaround time for answers. Other kinds of policies were noted as observed.

Ten services, about one in six overall, listed policies on the kinds of users they would serve; this compares to about 55 percent of academic libraries. There was no difference between large and small libraries on these policies. In all cases, these were geographic restrictions, usually by residence in the library's service area, or by holding a library card. One library will answer questions "as long as we can reach you at a local telephone number," another, in New England, will answer questions for all state residents. Most said that they would answer questions for others if they were about the local area or community, one added that they would respond if questions were about "some unique resource of the library." These libraries were more likely to use a detailed Web form (C = .241). Again, we see the public library orientation; they'll serve anybody who comes in the door, up to a point, but are keenly aware of who their community and funders are.

About a quarter of smaller libraries, and more than half of large libraries, had policies about the kinds of questions they would answer; 55 percent of academic library services had such policies. These public libraries were more likely to use e-mail to take questions (C = .297), more likely to have a policy on users (C = .287), and to point to an FAQ list (C = .334).

Of these 29 libraries, 23 said that their services would answer brief, factual questions, 11 said they would suggest sources for more involved or in-depth questions, and 11 also said that such involved research questions would receive better service if the patron came to the library in person (including four which would suggest sources). Seven said they would answer questions about the local area, five declined to answer genealogy questions, three declined to answer questions on medical, legal or tax matters, and one would answer questions about their local holdings.

In addition, one library advertised both a special genealogy service and a fee-based research service, one said they would spend up to 20 minutes researching questions, and said "[p]lease feel free to ask a question you might ask at the reference desk of any public library." Another said they would answer neither lengthy research questions nor trivia questions. One library had an extensive page of guidelines for their service, advising patrons to be specific, and they would make collect long-distance calls outside their service area and would mail or fax photocopies or printouts for a fee.

The tone of most of these policies was not stern; they tended to be phrased as advice or information to potential patrons about the nature and limitations of the services. Some were more officious, but the majority was of the help-us-to-help-you variety.

Slightly more, about half, of all services had policies on turnaround time for answers. Again, larger libraries were more likely to have such policies (more than half) than smaller ones (slightly more than a third); 60 percentof academic libraries had time statements or policies. These public libraries were also likely to have policies on the types of questions they will answer (C = .378).

It is difficult to easily summarize or quantify statements about these policies; most provided ranges of time (24–72 hours, for example) within which a response would be sent. The accompanying Figures 9.2 and 9.3 attempt to characterize the pattern of times described graphically for the smaller and larger libraries respectively. When a range was described, the mark was made at its midpoint, so a range of 24–48 hours was represented as 1½ days.

Among the smaller libraries, most indicated responses within one or two days (often *working days* or *business days*), with one indicating a response in "up to five days." Among the larger libraries, there were a number in the one- to two-day range but with another large group around four days. Many services also specified that weekends or holidays were different, and that requests received then would be dealt with as if received on the next business or working day, which would extend the time to receive a response.

The most striking aspect of these statements on turnaround time is the language in which these time estimates were couched. Of the 32 statements, only 10 were definitive, stating that patrons "would" or eould "expect" to receive

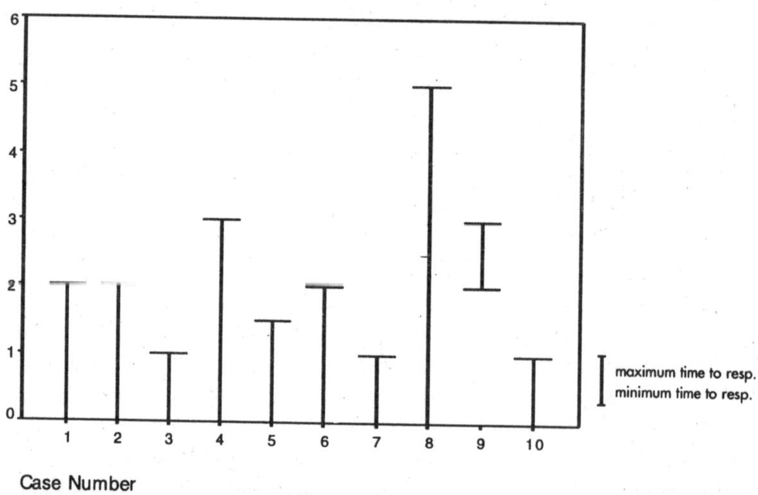

Figure 9.2: Turnaround Time Policies, Smaller Libraries

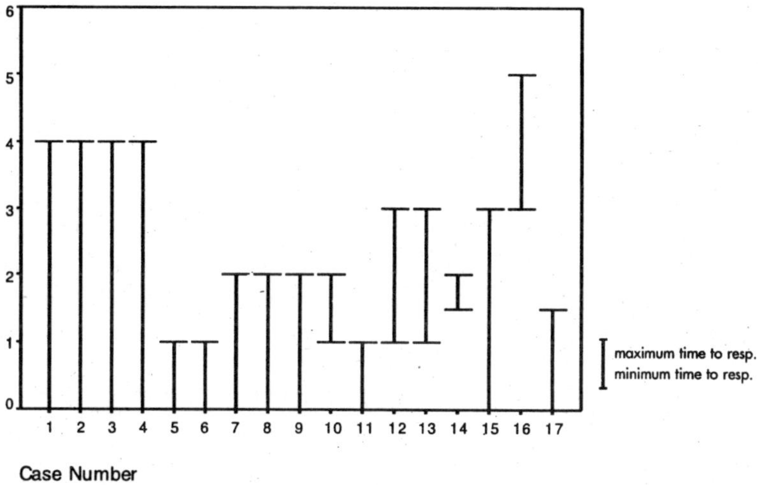

Figure 9.3: Turnaround Time Policies, Largest Libraries

answers within a certain time period. Another 20 used much less specific words, such as "our goal is to ...," "most questions will be answered ...," "usually," "generally," "try," "strive," "should receive," and "we will attempt." To be sure, this language likely reflects the experimental or novel aspects of these services, but one wonders the impact these words, accompanying such long time periods compared to what one might expect on the phone or at the reference desk in the library, might have on potential patrons and their confidence in using these services. In addition, of these 32 libraries, 13 indicated that calling the library would provide quicker response times and include a phone number to call; a further seven include a phone number on the form.

A few of these time policy statements stand out. One said that the "goal is to answer all questions in three to five business days. However, please understand that reference staff will answer questions by patrons in the library first, telephone questions second, and e-mail question as time permits." A few said things such as "depending on the difficulty/depth of your question, you may expect an answer or status report with one to three days." The most definitive said, "look for your answer within 24 hours, maybe sooner."

A number of other policies were found. Some have already been mentioned (confidentiality policies, alternate services for different kinds of questions), but in addition, two described their digital reference service hours, one specified that "Reference Question" must appear in the subject line of an e-mail message, and another that the Web form must be completely filled out to receive a response.

Service Names

Perhaps the most intriguing aspect of the analysis of these services is the names used to describe them. Anecdotal evidence and observation prior to this study indicated that a wide variety of names were used to describe digital reference services; our analysis has borne this out.

Looking at the Web pages that contain the forms, directions, or e-mail addresses to be used to send questions, we find that the 62 services used a total of 28 different titles at the top of those pages. The largest number (13) said "Ask a Librarian;" an additional two said "Ask the Librarian." In addition, six pages said "E-mail Reference" and three said "Reference Questions." No other name was used more than twice. The complete list can be found in Figure 9.4.

The most frequently used word among these names is "ask," with 27 uses, followed by "reference" with 23, "librarians" with 17, and "question" with 13, so none of these appears on a majority of pages. The use of the word "reference" indicates some connection with traditional reference services, either for librarians or for potential users of the service. Several pages (13) use words that refer directly to technology ("electronic," "e-mail," "online," and "cyber"). Three used the word "desk," referring again to a traditional technology. Only two use the words "information" or "service" or "request."

In most cases, other Web pages pointed to these pages. The names on those links are also of interest, since they form the path by which potential users find out about and get to the services. In some cases, the service page is pointed to directly from the library's home page; in others, there is an intermediate page. Figure 9.5 shows the names used on home pages when there is another link to be followed; Figure 9.6 shows the names used on links users click to get to the service page.

Three aspects of these lists are most striking. First, as we saw before, is the diversity of names used, in this case, to lead potential users to these services. Of the 25 services which required two clicks to get there, there are 18 different names used on home pages to direct people, ranging from obvious ones such as "Reference" and "Library Services" to the more obscure "Feedback" and "Using the Library." Similarly, there are 29 distinct names on links one click away.

In both cases, jargon is evident. It's possible that casual library users would know what "reference" means, but links such as "Information Search Service," "Virtual Reference Room," "Other Services," and "Adult Services" might well confuse even patrons familiar with libraries, let alone people who don't use libraries as a rule.

Finally, and perhaps most disturbingly, is the inconsistency within services. We identified 17 services where the name at the top of the page where the service is described is substantially *different* from the name on the link users must click to get there. And 12 of the 62 services used three different names. In

Ask a Librarian	13
E-Mail Reference	6
Reference Questions	3
Ask a Reference Librarian	2
Ask a Reference Question	2
Ask the Librarian	2
Ask Us a Question	2
Electronic Reference	2
Ask a Question	1
Ask a Question Online	1
Ask a Quick Question	1
Ask Adult Services	1
Ask Our Reference Staff a Challenging Question	1
Ask the Library	1
Contact Us	1
CyberReference	1
Electronic Reference Request	1
E-mail Us!	1
Got a Question?	1
infoNow e-mail Information Service	1
Information Line	1
Need an Answer?	1
Online Reference Desk	1
Question Form	1
Questions?	1
Reference Desk	1
Reference Question Request Form	1
Reference Service Fees	1
Write to the Reference Desk	1
misc pages with mailto links	7

Figure 9.4: Names on Service Forms

these cases, users must follow paths such as these to get to the library's digital reference service:

- Research/Ask a Question/Electronic Reference Form
- Library Services/Ask a Librarian/Reference Question Request Form
- Reference Desk/Information Search Service/Ask the Library
- Quick Answers!/Electronic Reference and Information/Ask a Librarian!
- Online Databases and Virtual Reference Room/Virtual Reference Room/Ask a Reference Question

Reference	4
Reference Services	3
Library Services	2
Research	2
About Your Library/ask-a-librarian	1
Ask Us - E-mail Reference	1
CyberReference	1
Feedback	1
HPL interactive	1
Info Center/Ask a Librarian	1
New Stuff/Information Services	1
Online Databases and Virtual Reference Room	1
Quick Answers!	1
Reference and Adult Services	1
Reference Desk	1
Services	1
Using the Library	1
Using Your Library	1

Figure 9.5: Names on Library Home Pages

To be sure, many of these are at least broadly indicative of where people are to go, but it cannot be the case that such inconsistency and use of jargon *helps* people to find where to go to ask a question. Links with text such as "To ask a reference question, click here" or "Ask Our Reference Staff a Challenging Question!" or even "Ask a Librarian" seem much clearer and more obvious, especially to inexperienced or new library users.

DISCUSSION, CONCLUSIONS, RECOMMENDATIONS

To summarize, we have found a much smaller proportion of public libraries are offering digital reference services than academic libraries, although we can estimate that the total number is over 400. Over one-third of the largest libraries have digital reference services; about one in 10 of smaller libraries do. They tend to have fewer policy statements than academic libraries and those policies are more prevalent in the larger libraries. Larger libraries are also more likely to use detailed Web forms to take reference questions, have FAQ pages, and to request authenticating information.

A word on our method and its limitations. The data collection method we have developed is quick and relatively painless, is easy to replicate, and yields essential data. But it leaves us with many questions and much we don't know. Without actually talking to librarians, we don't know what decisions they made and why, how many questions they get, what those questions are like, who asks them, how long it really takes to answer, and so on. This deeper analysis can now go on based on our initial findings. It is true, though, that

Ask a Librarian	13
Ask a Question	4
Adult Services	2
Ask the Librarian	2
E-Mail Reference	2
Reference	2
Adult Resources	1
Answers!HPL	1
Ask for Information	1
Ask Reference	1
Ask the Reference Center	1
Ask Us	1
Ask Us a Question	1
Ask Us a Question Online!	1
AskUs@GRPL	1
Basic Reference Links	1
CyberReference	1
Electronic Reference and Information	1
E-mail Quick Reference	1
E-Mail Reference Help	1
Information Search Service	1
Information Services	1
Interactive Reference	1
Need an Answer?	1
Other Services	1
Reference Desk	1
Reference Service Fees	1
To ask a reference question, click here	1
Virtual Reference Room	1
Ask a Question Online	0
Ask a Quick Question	0
Ask a Reference Librarian	0
Ask a Reference Question	0
Ask Adult Services	0
Ask Our Reference Staff a Challenging Question	0
Ask the Library	0
Contact Us	0
Electronic Reference	0
Electronic Reference Request	0
E-mail Us!	0
Got a Question?	0
infoNow e-mail Information Service	0
Information Line	0
Online Reference Desk	0
Question Form	0
Questions?	0
Reference Question Request Form	0
Reference Questions	0
Write to the Reference Desk	0

Figure 9.6: Names on Links to Service Forms

these data are important in their own right, as it reflects how these services present themselves and what potential users really see, and it will be interesting to see how our findings change over time.

In general, then, we find that more sophisticated services—those with FAQs, authentication questions, more policies—are in the larger libraries, with the best indication being the use of a detailed Web form for question intake.

And yet let us consider the smaller libraries for a moment. Although the proportion of smaller libraries with services is much lower, and those services are more likely to use the simpler technology of e-mail and have fewer policies, it is to their credit that they are trying digital reference services at all. Without intending to be patronizing, given the limited financial, information and staff resources of smaller public libraries, it is remarkable that many of them are experimenting with these new ways of serving their communities.

In particular, consider the smallest libraries. Our group 1, libraries serving communities of 10,000 to 28,000 people, represents half of our population of libraries, and stands for the several thousand even smaller libraries that we did not include in our sample. We found only six services among the 88 we examined, a rate of only 6.8 percent, but this implies that over 100 such libraries are taking and answering digital reference questions.

Three of those six services are linked directly from their libraries' home pages, the same rate as libraries overall. Three use e-mail and four simple Web forms to take questions. Four of them specify a turnaround time, ranging from one to three business days; a substantial number of larger libraries suggest significantly longer times. In general, the names they give their services are simple and traditional (e.g., Ask a Librarian, Ask a Reference Question, E-Mail Reference Questions, Reference Desk), and are relatively consistent and free of jargon.

In some ways, it might be easier for these smaller libraries to experiment with and implement services. Although they have fewer staff, there is also less bureaucracy involved, and it could be as simple as adding a mailto tag to the library's home page. The only apparent distinguishing characteristics between the services of the smaller libraries are the number of policies and their level of technological sophistication—perhaps as technology becomes even more prevalent and affordable, smaller libraries' services will outperform their larger colleagues.

Examination of the names of services, policy statements and language describing the services leaves one with the impression that in general, these libraries are trying to be helpful, trying to provide a useful service to their patrons, but that jargon and tradition get in the way. To be sure, the traditions of library reference service, intended to help members of the community to use the resources of the library to their fullest extent to satisfy their information and entertainment needs, are worthy of extension into the digital environment, and many libraries are doing precisely that.

But some of the ways in which they are doing it are open to discussion at best. Slightly more than half of the services are hidden from users on the library's home page. Statements on the amount of time people can expect to wait for responses are evasive and in many cases the times are very long, longer by orders of magnitude than one would expect if visiting the library in person or calling on the phone. Furthermore, the names and links used to get people to the services can be confusing.

More than once, in e-mail list discussions or conversations, we have heard librarians say that people aren't using digital reference services. Perhaps we now know some of the reasons why.

Based on our findings, we offer the following recommendations for those currently offering, planning or considering a digital reference service:

- Be out there. In both studies, we found that half of the libraries didn't link their service from the front page, the rough equivalent of hiding the reference desk or not listing its phone number. Concern about being overwhelmed is understandable in a new domain, but it's difficult to know what demand for your service is like if people don't know it exists.
- Tell the truth about time. The wide and long potential ranges for receiving answers compare quite unfavorably with potential questioners' experience with in-person or phone reference, where responses generally take minutes, not days. Answers here will likely take longer, but many of these ranges appear to be overly broad to cover worst cases. An honest statement ("We'll probably get back to you in a day or so, but it might take longer if your question is really difficult.") would inspire more confidence.
- Think really hard about the questions you'll be best at. Paradoxically, many services encourage only quick, ready-reference type questions and say that it might take up to three days to get an answer. It might be that digital reference is best suited for broader questions, those best served by pointers and resources. This is complicated the thin nature of the reference interview, but a more detailed form and a more penetrating analysis of the best uses of a digital reference service might prove quite fruitful.

This is a new area of practice in librarianship, or perhaps more correctly, a new way of looking at an old area. As Ryan (1996) has pointed out, reference librarians have been very quick over the years to adopt new technologies to assist in their work. Correspondence, telephone, and teletype services have all been developed in the last century, and each new technology is seen as an opportunity, but in each case limitations and policies are quickly adopted to make those services manageable and to fit them in with existing services. Digital reference is apparently following the same pattern, not surprisingly, and libraries and librarians are certainly learning much about how to use the networked environment to its best advantage for reference.

But one is left to wonder how much time they will have to learn those lessons. The most salient difference between the advent of the networked environment is the rise of both commercial and non-commercial services, often called Ask an Expert services, which are offering to answer questions either in specific subject areas or across all areas. Many of these employ experts, but some are effectively simple bulletin board systems, allowing anyone to post a question, and anyone to answer, regardless of background or training. Add automated services such as Ask Jeeves to the mix, and you see a much more populated, accessible, and competitive market for question-answering than libraries have ever before seen. The services those libraries offer must take account not only of the available technologies and the traditions of librarianship but also this context and environment if they are to provide the best services to their users and communities.

ACKNOWLEDGMENTS

The author wishes to thank Chrystie Hill, Alex Rolfe, Patricia Memmott and Gretchen Almy for their invaluable assistance in the conduct of this study.

This study was funded by a grant from the Library of Congress Collaborative Digital Reference Service.

ENDNOTE

1. C here is the Pearson contingency coefficient, a measure of association used with two nominal-level variables and sometimes used as a follow-up to the chi-square test of independence. For the situations we are examining, it has a maximal value of .707 and a minimal value of 0; a C of .213 would be considered a low-to-moderate association.

ABOUT THE AUTHOR

Joseph Janes is Assistant Professor and Coordinator of the MLIS Program at The Information School of the University of Washington, Box 352930, Seattle WA 98195-2930. His research interests are on mediation in the networked digital environment, specifically the development and evolving professional practice of digital reference.

E-mail: jwj@u.washington.edu

REFERENCES

Baker, B.; Pelster, N.; and McHugh, W. (1998). Refinding reference: carrying the reference mission into the libraries of the 21st century. In LaGuardia, C. and Mitchell, B. A. (Eds.), Finding common ground: creating the library of the future without diminishing the library of the past (pp. 99–110). New York, NY: Neal-Schuman.

Foster, J. (1999, March/April). Web reference: a virtual reality. Public Libraries, 38, 94–95.

Janes, J.; Carter, D. S.; and Memmott, P. (1999). Digital reference services in academic libraries. Reference and User Services Quarterly 39: 145–150.

Lawrence, J. and Ross, M. (1999, May). Internet reference: boon or bane? American Libraries, 30, 74–76.

Lipow, A. (1999, August). "In your face" reference service. Library Journal, 124, 50-52.

Reger, N. K. (1998). Redefining reference services: transitioning at one public library. Reference and User Services Quarterly 38: 73–75.

Rose, P. M.; Stoklosa, K.; and Gray, S. A. (1998). A focus group approach to assessing technostress at the reference desk. Reference and User Services Quarterly 37: 311–317.

Ryan, S. (1996). Reference service for the Internet community: a case study of the Internet Public Library Reference Division. Library and Information Science Research 18: 241–259.

Sager, D. (1999, January/February). John Henry versus the computer. Public Libraries 38: 21–25.

Sloan, B. (1998). Electronic reference services: some suggested guidelines. Reference and User Services Quarterly 38: 77–81.

Wasik, J. M. (1999). Building and maintaining digital reference services. Syracuse, NY: ERIC Clearinghouse on Information and Technology.

Chapter 10

Introduction to Log Analysis Techniques: Methods for Evaluating Networked Services

Jeffrey H. Rubin

INTRODUCTION: WHY LOG ANALYSIS?

Using any mainstream Web server and high-end log analysis software, Web administrators can extract far more information about a digital user than about a user who enters a bricks and mortar storefront. Despite this, few organizations use data gathered through log analysis as an integral part of their ongoing Internet strategy. Unfortunately, it is common for organizations to invest thousands of dollars in top-notch log analysis software, only to create basic reports showing hits, page views, and visits.

This chapter reviews the type of data that can be extracted from Web server log files and the types of analysis that Web administrators can perform. In addition, this chapter offers a technical overview of cookies and discusses how they relate to the privacy of Internet users.

Log analysis can be used for two separate organizational functions: Information Technology (IT) and marketing. Web administrators are more concerned with page layout, errors, path analysis, and browser summaries, while marketers will be more interested in advertising analysis, user demographics, and search engine analysis. For example, marketers should be able to exact keywords or phrases users search for using external search engines.

Web sites that implement cookies are capable of tracking, storing, and reporting on more information about individual users than ever before. Tying this information to an existing organizational database (i.e., customer database), one can customize a Web site based on a user's preferences and begin to offer one-to-one marketing.

There is an ever growing need to collect, analyze, store, and manage information that users provide to a Web site. Decisions must be made regarding

- the method for collecting users' information;
- how this information is to be analyzed;
- where and for how long the information is stored;
- who will have access to this information; and
- who will manage this entire process.

While little has been written on log analysis, below are two resources that show specific examples on how log analysis can be used to manage Web sites

1. Evaluation of Selected Web sites at the U.S. Department of Education: (http://iis.syr.edu/Webeval/), by Carol Hert, Kristen Eshenfelder, and Charles McClure. A part of this study focused on collecting and analyzing log data from the Department of Education. Recommendations were made as how the Department could better use log analysis to improve access to their Web site.
2. Web Site Stats, By: Rick Stout is a more technical description of log data and analysis. While this book gives an overview of log data, quite a bit has changed since this book was published.

ANALYZING TRADITIONAL VERSUS VIRTUAL VISITORS

What does Wal-Mart know about customers who walk into a Wal-Mart store? The company does not know where the customers came from (do the customers live in the U.S. or some other country). They do not know what brought the customers to Wal-Mart (did the customers see an ad in the paper, were they referred by a friend, were they driving by?). They do not know any details about their customers (age, sex, buying habits). They do not have statistics on what aisles the customers walked down and which ones they skipped. They do not know what items the customers picked up (perhaps to read directions or look at the price) and placed back on the shelf. They do not know what problems or frustrations the customers had when they were at the store (i.e., was an item out of stock?). Finally, if the customers pay by cash, they are completely anonymous to Wal-Mart. All Wal-Mart knows is that it sold certain items on a given day.

If a customer visits www.walmart.com, the transaction is infinitely more descriptive. Immediately Wal-Mart knows where the customer is from (within the United States, outside the United States, and perhaps even the city and state). In many cases, Wal-Mart will know what (Web site) brought the customer. Wal-Mart will know if the customer typed in www.walmart.com or if the site was accessed via a mouse click from another Web site. Perhaps the customer came through a search engine; if so, Wal-Mart will know which search engine and the keywords or search string used. Wal-Mart will know each item the customer clicked on and can determine how much time the customer spent browsing the Web site. In addition, Wal-Mart will know what errors the customer received while browsing the Web site (e.g., Error 404—file not found). Finally, with the current lack of anonymous e-payment mechanisms in the United States, Wal-Mart can determine the customers' name, sex, age, and buying habits (using credit card records).

TYPES OF DATA IN LOG FILES

This section explains the significance of data in a standard log file. Applications of this data and what a Web administrator can learn, are explained in the subsequent sections.

Log files are text files that every Web server is capable of producing. Every time a client (e.g., Web browser) accesses a Web server (e.g., Web site) the client passes several pieces of data to the Web server. Example 10.1 is a single line of a standard log file. There are 12 pieces of data in the log file, each separated by a space.

Example 10.1: Tide11.microsoft.com jhrubin [17/Nov/1999:02:57:07 -400] "GET /text/logs.html HTTP/1.0" 200 2326 http://www.links.com/yoursite/ Mozilla/4.0 (Compatible; MSIE 4.0; Windows 95)

1. Domain name or Internet Protocol (IP) address: (Tide11.microsoft.com) This is the domain name or IP address of the visitor's computer (in this log file a domain name is used). Web servers can be configured to either log IP addresses or domain names, however, performance can suffer Domain Name System (DNS) lookups must occur. DNS lookups occur when a Web server has to translate an IP address to a domain name. Thus, Web administrators should configure Web servers to track IP addresses and utilize log analysis software to perform DNS lookups.
2. User Authentication: (jhrubin) If a user logs into a Web site using the Web server's built in authentication then the Web server captures the username in this field. Once a user logs on to a Web site, that visitor's username is tracked throughout the entire visit, giving a complete record of what pages the user has viewed. It is important here to differentiate between Web server authentication and database authentication. Most sites have moved away from Web server authentication and track usernames and passwords in a database; visitor's information stored in the database does not appear in the Web server log file.

3. Date and Time: (17/Nov/2000:02:57:07) This is the date and time of the visitor's request. It is important to note that this is time on the server's system, not the client's.
4. Greenwich Mean Time: (-400) This is the server GMT not the visitors GMT. In the above example, the Web server is minus four hours from the GMT. Web administrators that have multiple servers located in different time zones use this field to combine log files and run one set of reports.
5. Method of Request: (GET) This is the method by which the Web browser (client) communicates with the Web server. The three most commonly found methods are GET, POST, and HEAD:

   GET: The client requests a file from the server

   POST: The client fills out a form and the form data is posted back to the server

   HEAD: Primarily used by intelligent agents (i.e., search engine robots) to retrieve metadata
6. Path and file requested: (/text/logs.html) This is the path and file that the client requested from the server. Note that the Web server does not log the domain name (since all requests are to one Web server).
7. Protocol and version of the protocol: (HTTP/1.0) This field will either show HyperText Transfer Protocol (HTTP) version 1.0 or HTTP version 1.1. HTTP 1.1 is a newer better performing protocol, however in order to take advantage of the performance both the Web server and client must support 1.1.
8. Status Code: (200) This will be one of several status codes that range from 200-500:

   200: success; file was successfully transferred

   300: referral; the browser requested one file, but was referred to another

   400: client error (e.g., 404: file not found)

   500: server error (e.g., A user fills out a form and receives a server error)
9. Bytes Transferred: (2326) This is the number of bytes that transferred from the Web server to the client.
10. Referral: (http://www.links.com/yoursite/) If there were no referral, this field would be blank (or ""). In this example, the Web administrator can determine the referring domain and the specific page that is making linking to their site. In addition, referrals can also show Web administrators the phrase that visitors searched for within external search engines. For example the following referral shows a

user who searched for analytical task writing about power and tyranny poems, using the AltaVista search engine. http://www.altavista.com/cgibin/query?q=analytical+task+writing+about+power+%26+tyranny+poemsandkl=XXandpg=qandTranslate=on

11. Browser and Version: Mozilla/4.0 (Compatible; MSIE 4.0) This field details the client's browser and version of the browser. If this field only displayed one piece of information (e.g., Mozilla/4.0), then it would mean the visitors' browser was Netscape 4.0 (Netscape named their Web browser Mozilla). However, if the first part of this field is followed by parenthesis then the Web administrator needs to read inside the parenthesis. In this example, the user's browser was Microsoft Internet Explorer 4.0.
12. Operating System: (Windows 95) This field details the client's operating system.

ANALYSIS OF LOG DATA

Commercial log analysis software is available to help organizations analyze their Web server(s) log data. This section focuses on some of the analysis that can be performed and how this information can help an organization manage their Web site(s).

Table 10.1: Traffic Analysis

Hits	Entire Site (Successful)	362,338
	Average Per Day	181,169
	Home Page	7,464
Page Views	Page Views (Impressions)	226,493
	Average Per Day	113,277
Visitor Sessions (visits)	Visitor Sessions	22,029
	Average Per Day	11,014
	Average Visitor Session Length	00:17:30
	International Visitor Sessions	11.18%
	Visitor Sessions of Unknown Origin	20.86%
	Visitor Sessions from United States	67.95%
Visitors	Unique Visitors	14,556
	Visitors Who Visited Once	12,172
	Visitors Who Visited More Than Once	2,384

Table 10.2: Visitors by Number of Visits

Number of Visits	Number of Visitors	% of Total Unique Visitors
1 visit	12172	83.62
2 visits	1302	8.94
3 visits	415	2.85
4 visits	173	1.18
5 visits	83	0.57
6 visits	54	0.37
7 visits	47	0.32
8 visits	34	0.23
9 visits	19	0.13
10 or more visits	257	1.76

Metrics Terminology

Various terms are used in different context to measure Web site traffic:

- Hit: Any file requested from a Web server. If a given Web page has eight images, each request for this page yields nine hits (one for each image and one for the html document file).
- Page view: Any document requested from a Web site regardless of related objects. If a user requests three documents from a Web site, each document containing five images, then the user would generate 19 hits, but only three page views. (Page view's a.k.a. is impression.)
- Visit: One user's interaction with a Web site, based on a unique IP

Table 10.3: Top Geographic Regions

	Geographic Regions	Visitor Sessions
1	North America	15,281
2	Region Unspecified	4,596
3	Western Europe	735
4	Asia	474
5	Australia	367
6	Pacific Islands	145
7	Middle East	134
8	South America	83
9	Northern Europe	76
10	Eastern Europe	48
11	Sub-Saharan Africa	44
12	North Africa	28
13	Caribbean Islands	11
14	Region Not Known	6
15	Central America	1
Total		**22,029**

address within a specific timeframe. In practice, 30 minutes of inactivity from a specific IP address marks the end of a given visit.

- Visitor: The number of unique IP addresses (or cookies) that visited a Web site during a reporting period (i.e., day or week). A user that goes to cnn.com once a day for five from the same IP address) would have visited the site five times, but be recorded as a single visitor.

All the following tables are examples from actual Web sites using WebTrends log analyzer (a leader in log analysis software). Table 10.1 shows some of the raw information that can be analyzed using hits, page views, visits,

Table 10.4: Top Entry Pages

	File	% of Total	Visitor Sessions
1	**Welcome to AskERIC** http://www.askeric.org/	20.06	4,104
2	**Search the ERIC Database** http://www.askeric.org/Eric/	14.24	2,915
3	**AskERIC Lesson Plans** http://www.askeric.org/Virtual/Lessons/	8.32	1,703
4	http://www.askeric.org/plWeb-cgi/fastWeb	5.48	1,123
5	http://www.askeric.org/cgi-bin/ericdbquery2.pl	3.02	618
6	**AskERIC Lesson Plans: Mathematics** http://www.askeric.org/Virtual/Lessons/Mathematics/	1.53	313
7	**Newton's Apple Index** http://www.askeric.org/Projects/Newton/	1.46	299
8	**AskERIC Virtual Library** http://www.askeric.org/Virtual/	1.26	258
9	**AskERIC Lesson Plans: Language Arts** http://www.askeric.org/Virtual/Lessons/Lang_arts/	1.25	257
10	http://www.askeric.org/cgi-bin/imagemap/virtual	0.99	204

and visitors. Included in this Table is the Average Visitor Session Length that helps determine how long a visitor spends at a Web site.

Table 10.2 gives a breakdown of the number of times a user visited a Web site. This helps determine usage patterns and is most reliable when based on cookies and not on IP addresses. Most IP addresses are dynamic, therefore several users could have the same IP address within the same day or week.

Geographical Analysis

Based on the domain name (i.e., syr.edu), it is possible to generate several geographical reports. Table 10.3 analyzes the top geographical regions of customers that visited a Web site. This information can then be further broken down into most frequent visits from countries, states, and cities. This report

Table 10.5: Top Exit Pages

	Pages	% of Total	Visitor Sessions
1	http://www.askeric.org/plWeb-cgi/fastWeb	21.75	4,451
2	**Welcome to AskERIC** http://www.askeric.org/	7.16	1,465
3	**Search the ERIC Database** http://www.askeric.org/Eric/	6.19	1,268
4	**AskERIC Lesson Plans** http://www.askeric.org/Virtual/Lessons/	3.05	625
5	http://www.askeric.org/plWeb-cgi/obtain.pl	2.85	585
6	http://www.askeric.org/cgi-bin/imagemap/virtual	1.46	299
7	**AskERIC Virtual Library** http://www.askeric.org/Virtual/	1.09	223
8	**Search AskERIC** http://www.askeric.org/Search/	1.07	220
9	**Newton's Apple Index** http://www.askeric.org/Projects/Newton/	0.98	202
10	**ERIC Resources** http://www.askeric.org/Virtual/ERIC_resources/	0.77	158

information is obtained by performing WHOIS queries on the domain names that visit the Web site. A WHOIS query asks an Internet registrar (i.e., Network Solutions) what organziation a domain name is registered to. For example, a WHOIS query on syr.edu would show the domain name as registered to Syracuse University, in Syracuse, NY, USA. Often visitors appear to originate from the city, state, and country where their Internet Service Provider's (ISP) domain name is registered (e.g., America Online). This information is misleading as this may not be the visitors actual geograhpic location.

Entry Page Analysis

As Web sites grow in size, it is important to determine on what page visitors enter a site. This type of analysis is helpful if an organization wants to highlight a new section of their Web site. Table 10.4 shows that the most common entry

Table 10.6: Client (Browser) Errors

Error	Hits	% of Failed Hits
404 Page or File Not Found	2,889	96.58
401 Unauthorized Access	79	2.64
403 Forbidden Access	9	0.30
000 Incomplete / Undefined	11	0.36
400 Bad Request	3	0.10
Total	**2,991**	**100.00**

page for this site is the home page. Although this is true for many Web sites, Table 10.4 also shows that approximately 80 percent of visitors enter the Web site on something other than the homepage. Therefore, this organization may choose to highlight new content or services of their Web site on more than the home page.

Table 10.7: Page Not Found (404) Errors

Target URL and Referrer	Hits	% of 404 Hits
/Virtual/Lessons/Java/morelike/pgemsBeanInfo.class (no referrer)	73	2.52
/search/ (no referrer)	6	0.2
/favicon.ico (no referrer)	497	17.2
/virtual/lessons/ (no referrer)	42	1.45
/Virtual/Lessons/Lang_arts/Reading/alexander.gif http://ericir.syr.edu/Virtual/Lessons/Lang_arts/Reading/RDG0032.html	39	1.34
/About/Cow/cownet.html http://www.nucleus.com/~jbird/links.htm	3	0.1
/Discovery/w11.html (no referrer)	3	0.1
/Virtual/InfoGuides/Alphabetical_List_of_InfoGuides/homeschooling12_96.html (no referrer)	2	0.06
/rdm/incoming?type=status-request (no referrer)	2	0.06
/Discovery/ http://www.ebso.com.tr/Turkce/Medya/tv/Amerika/usa.htm	1	0.03
/Virtual/InfoGuides/I/ (no referrer)	1	0.03

Exit Page Analysis

While some visitors find the information they are looking for and leave a Web site, Table 10.5 shows a high percentage of users who left the AskERIC Web site on specific pages. After analyzing Table 10.5, Web administrators may find a broken link, a graphic takes too long to load, the content is too long, or perhaps a search request was taking too long. Whatever the case, pages that frequently occur as user exit points may be potential areas. Web administrators should consider the reasons for the user leaving and adjust accordingly.

Table 10.8: Top Referring URLs

	URL	Visitor Sessions
1	No Referrer	5,028
2	http://www.accesseric.org/searchdb/dbTable.html	553
3	http://ericir.syr.edu/Virtual/Lessons/	369
4	http://ericir.syr.edu/Eric/	365
5	http://askeric.org/Eric/	225
6	http://ericir.syr.edu/	198
7	http://ericir.syr.edu/plWeb-cgi/fastWeb?search	145
8	[unknown origin]	141
9	http://dir.yahoo.com/Education/K_12/Teaching/Lesson_Plans/	131
10	http://askeric.org/Search/	110
11	bookmarks	92
12	http://ericir.syr.edu/Virtual/Lessons/Lang_arts/index.html	89
13	http://dir.yahoo.com/Government/U_S__Government/Executive_Branch/Departments_and_Agencies/Department_of_Education/Office_of_Educational_Research_and_Improvement__OERI_/National_Library_of_Education/ERIC/	82
14	http://ericir.syr.edu/Virtual/Lessons/new2.html	76
15	http://search.yahoo.com/bin/search?p=lesson+plans	72
16	http://ericir.syr.edu/Virtual/Lessons/Social_St/index.html	66
17	http://www.indiana.edu/~eric_rec/bks/lmenu.html	60

Table 10.9: Top Search Engines with Search Phrases Detail

Engines	Phrases	Phrases Found	% of Total
Yahoo	lesson plans	142	6.39
	ask eric	75	3.37
	askeric	58	2.61
	Chinese calendar	20	0.9
AltaVista	lesson plans	22	0.99
	askeric	12	0.54
	photosynthesis	11	0.49
	bread	10	0.45
Google	eric	43	1.93
	eric database	11	0.49
	askeric	8	0.36
AOL NetFind	askeric	62	2.79
	kindergarten lesson plans	28	1.26
	lesson plans	15	0.67
Excite	eric	21	0.94
	ask eric	10	0.45
	askeric	7	0.31

Table 10.10: Most Used Browsers

	Browser	Hits	% of Total Hits	Visitor Sessions
1	Microsoft Internet Explorer	173,839	48.19	13,766
2	Netscape	113,494	31.46	6,413

Table 10.11: Microsoft Explorer Browsers

	Browser	Hits	% of Total Hits	Visitor Sessions
1	Explorer 5.x	119,031	68.47	9,723
2	Explorer 4.x	49,337	28.38	3,463
3	Explorer 3.x	4,858	2.79	392
4	Explorer 2.x	613	0.35	188
Total For Browsers Above		**173,839**	**100**	**13,766**

Client Errors

The most common client error is "Error 404—File Not Found." This error can occur when a user types in an incorrect Uniform Resource Locator (URL), if the requested page moved, or the document has been deleted from a Web server. Analyzing 404 errors can help Web administrators determine if the errors are coming from internal or external links. Table 10.6 shows the number of different client errors that occurred, while Table 10.7 shows where specific 404 errors are occurring.

Referral Information

Referral information is useful for viewing who is linking to a Web site. There are internal and external referrals. Internal referrals occur when a visitor clicks from one page in the site to another page in the site (the first page refers the user to the second page). External referrals occur when a visitor is on a Web site and follows a link that refers to a separate Web site. Table 10.8 shows examples of both internal and external referrals. A "No Referrer" occurs when a user types in a URL into their browser.

External Search Engine Analysis

Analyzing search engine queries can help Web administrators determine the efficacy of their metadata. Table 10.9 shows a breakdown of the major search engines and the phrases most commonly searched to find AskERIC. Additional analysis can be performed to determine top keywords or phrases, regardless of the search engine used.

Browser Analysis

Determining what browsers most visitors use can help Web administrators determine when to implement specific technologies. Table 10.10 shows the breakdown between Netscape and Internet Explorer visitors. Table 10.11 breaks this down further by showing the specific breakdown of MS Internet Explorer visitors (the same type of analysis can be done for Netscape browsers).

COOKIES AS LOG FILE ENHANCEMENTS

Until 1995 the English language had only one meaning for the word cookie. In today's technologically rich environment, cookie takes on a whole new meaning. A cookie is a piece of textual data that a Web server places on a client's system. Many users are not aware that such textual data is being stored on their systems, and those that do know are typically unaware of the purpose behind cookies.

Web sites may claim that cookies are used only to better the user experience; however, many of these same sites use cookies to track a user's every move and ultimately to provide personal information to global organizations.

Technical Details

There are several specifications which control both the cookie string that is passed between servers and clients (part of the HTTP protocol), and the cookie file that is maintained by Web browsers (e.g., Netscape Navigator or MS Internet Explorer). Cookies are passed in the header of an HTML file and can contain up to six variables (listed and described below). The easiest way to view these variables is to enable the Web browser option to alert users before accepting cookies. Six of the variables are listed here:

1. Name: Any unique character string assigned by a specific Web site, so long as it does not match other cookie names given by the same Web site.
2. Value: Used to store a piece of data (e.g., visitor's name or IP address).
3. Expiration date: The date put here greatly depends on the use of the cookie. For example, shopping carts tend to have short-lived cookies (session cookies), while cookies used for site customization may not expire for several years (persistent cookies).
4. Valid path: Specifies which URL the implemented cookie can use. For example, if one wanted a cookie to be used throughout the entire Web site, the path could be set to "/" to signify the root directory. However, if one wanted to set a cookie that could only be used within a specific sub-directory of a Web site, then the path could be set to /directoryname/.

5. Valid domain: If the domain value is set, it shows what domains can read and write to the cookie. For example, if an organization had two Web servers within their domain (server1.test.com and server2.test.com), and the organization wanted both servers to be able to use the same cookie, administrators could specify both domains within this setting.
6. Secure connection: Specifies if the cookie transferred over a secure connection. Normally this option is set to false, however, there may be times when the Web site issuing the cookie can only be used under a secure connection (e.g., if the cookie is storing credit card or other personal information).

Setting and storing cookies

Regardless of what domain sends a cookie, there are rules that specify the total size of an individual cookie and the maximum number of cookies that one domain can issue. A single domain can issue no more than 20 cookies to a given client. It is possible for said domain to issue additional cookies, but once a client attempts to accept the twenty-first cookie from the same domain, the browser will delete the last used cookie issued from that domain. In addition, most browsers can only store 300 total cookies. Just as in the single domain example above, when Netscape Navigator receives its 301st cookie, the last used cookie (from any domain) is deleted. This point helps ensure that the cookie file stored on the client's hard drive will never take up a substantial amount of space.

Use of Cookies in Log Analysis

Cookies were introduced to define an individual user better. If every computer in the world had static IP addresses, then cookies may have never been created. However, dynamic IP addresses are used for dial-up users and organizations across the world to help solve the problem of issuing static IP addresses.

To demonstrate how this works, let us say that user A lives in Syracuse, New York, and dials up to AOL (his or her ISP) from 12:00 p.m.–12:30 p.m. As soon as user A connects to AOL, his or her computer is issued an IP address (e.g., 152.163.189.130). While user A is on the Web, he or she visits cnn.com. As soon as user A logs off, his or her IP address is returned to the pool of dynamic IP addresses available to AOL users.

User B who also lives in Syracuse logs on to AOL at 12:31 p.m. and is issued the IP address 152.163.189.130, the one recently freed upon user A's log off. User B also visits CNN's Web site to get the latest news and then logs off AOL around 1:00 in the afternoon. Anyone analyzing the CNN log files would have little way of knowing that user A and B were two different visitors. The same outcome could take place if two users shared the same public terminal.

Customization/Personalization

One difference between a user subscribing to the print version of The New York Times versus subscribing to nytimes.com is customized content. For example, nytimes.com customizes his or her site based on user preferences. This information is stored in a database, and the user is issued a cookie that specifically matches him or her to the database based on a unique identifier (possibly storing a username/password allowing the user to quickly log in). This type of customization using cookies use allows the user to come back to nytimes.com (from the same computer), and get his or her personalized news—without having to log in to the site.

Online ordering

The Web consists of thousands of Web sites that use cookies for online shopping. Netgrocer.com is one example that uses cookies to remember what users have in their virtual grocery cart. At anytime, users can click a "view cart" icon and display the contents of their cart.

Targeted Advertising

If users look in the "cookies.txt" file (if using Netscape navigator) on their hard drive, they would likely notice Web sites listed that they had never visited. Most likely these cookies were set by advertisements. Many Web sites hire companies (e.g., such as DoubleClick) to deploy and track advertisements.

DoubleClick issues cookies for many Web sites that stores which advertisement visitors have seen. If a particular user goes to another Web site that employs DoubleClick, chances are the user will not see the same advertisement twice.

Privacy Issues Surrounding Cookies

There are few privacy concerns for organizations that use log data and cookies for internal use. However, organizations that share this information with third parties, specifically advertisers, have created quite a stir in the industry. Keith Reagan (in an e-commerce Times article titled TRUSTe Stung by Own Privacy Gaffe, August 25, 2000 at http://www.ecommercetimes.com/news/articles2000/000825-3.shtml) explains how TrustE, considered by many Internet users as the king of privacy, allegedly violated their own privacy policy by using a third-party software program.

While privacy continues to be a major concern for Internet users, the issue recently reached new heights. Linda Rosencrance, in an August 1, 2000, Computer World article "Sharing of personal data by Web sites sparks new privacy controversy." at http://www.computerworld.com/cwi/story/0,1199,NAV47_STO47902,00.html, talks about several companies including Toys 'R Us that allegedly are violating their privacy policies by sharing log data with third parties. However, in this case the third-party was Coremetrics, Inc., who specializes in log analysis. Toys 'R Us responded by explaining that it has specific contracts with Coremetrics to ensure the privacy of the data.

ISSUES/RECOMMENDATIONS

Outlined below are several people and process, and technology issues/considerations that organizations must address if they plan to manage an effective Web environment:

1. Planning for log analysis: Organizations need to decide what goals/objectives they want to achieve by analyzing their log files. It is not realistic nor necessary for an organization to run every report available to them. In addition, log analysis software can take a long time to run comprehensive reports on large log files (files over a gigabyte in size). An organization must plan their technical infrastructure to ensure that log analysis software will run on isolated systems and that reports will be distributed to the appropriate parties.
2. Managing the analysis process: Unless organizations take a proactive approach to log analysis, log files will merely waste storage space on the Web server. For larger organizations it is becoming an accepted practice to implement distributed log analysis, where different departments can view customized reports for their portion of the Web site. However, having the IT department install log analysis software and run weekly reports is not enough. Individual departments must be trained on how to read and act upon the reports that are generated.
3. Policy: Organizations should ensure that they have a privacy policy that details the personal information they collect about their customers. In addition, the privacy policy should indicate how the organization plans to use/share this information. It is effortless for an organization to create its privacy policy using a free privacy policy generator (e.g., TrustE at http://www.truste.org/wizard/). While these generators do a decent job in outlining the issues surrounding organizations privacy policies, it is important for an organization to modify the generated statement to fit their business.
4. Moving forward: Log analysis can only be as useful as the investment a company makes in it. While some organizations hire outside consultants to analyze log data, others are creating new positions that specifically deal with electronic data analysis. The future lies in some form of data mining, where an organization will compare log data with customer profiles or similar types of information. This will

make it possible to track individual users across a Web site and make decisions based on groups of people (approaching the goal of one-to-one marketing).

Today most organizations are analyzing log files daily or weekly. However, as e-commerce becomes the major focus of many organizations, e-managers will use log data to track user behavior in real time. Organizations will be able to make instant decisions based on the effectiveness of advertising campaigns or current online promotions.

ABOUT THE AUTHOR

Jeffrey Rubin is president of Internet Consulting Services and an Instructor at the Syracuse University School of Information Studies. He is passionate about teaching both in the classroom and in the boardroom. Rubin's company has consulted for Lucent, Ericsson, Sony Music, and IEEE.

Jeffrey H. Rubin
4-206 Center for Science and Technology
Syracuse, NY 13244
E-mail: jhrubin@internetconsult.com

Chapter 11

Policy Analysis and Networked Information: "There Are Eight Million Stories ..."

Philip Doty

The science on which we have depended has missed all the squiggly bits, and, unfortunately, it is the squiggly bits that matter. (Thompson, 1997, p. 208)

ABSTRACT

Policy analysis is a very useful means for understanding important elements of networked information services. Using such policy concerns as universal access, the digital divide, and the "first mile," the chapter explores how it is that policy analysis can inform the evaluation of networked digital technologies. After outlining traditional and alternative approaches to policy analysis, the discussion identifies how we can use the narrative and rhetorical aspects of policy analysis to understand the value and frame conflicts that characterize the evaluation of situated uses of information technologies. We can also gain insight into users' construction of meaning around and using such technologies. Information policy analysis in particular broadens and deepens our understanding of networked information, the design of such systems, their deployment, and their evaluation.

INTRODUCTION

The study of public policy is contentious and inherently controversial. Among the reasons are disagreements about what public policy is, how to define important terms and concepts, how to do policy analysis, and what role policy analysis should play in the development, implementation, and evaluation of public policy. Further, like other social sciences, the epistemological ground under policy analysis has been radically shifted in the past several decades with the growth of postmodernist, qualitative, and critical approaches to the study of identity and social life. Despite these difficulties, however, policy analysis provides a number of contributions to the evaluation of networked information services through its structuring of problems, forecasting, recommendation, monitoring, evaluation, and communication with decision makers and other stakeholders (Dunn, 1994; Majchrzak, 1984; Roe, 1994). This chapter will provide a brief introduction to the "classical" approach to policy analysis, alternative approaches, and how it is that the combination of the classical and alternative perspectives provides us with useful tools for networked information service evaluation. One of the particular strengths of policy analysis is its ability to reframe conflicts through the uncovering of implicit assumptions and values that underlie policy conflicts. What the discussion will lead us to is an increasingly user-centered, narratively sensitive, qualitative, and holistic approach to doing policy analysis that reflects the complexity of social life and the role of networked information in it. It is in this way that policy analysis makes a unique contribution to the evaluation of networked information services.

THE NATURE OF POLICY ANALYSIS

The history of policy studies generally and policy analysis in particular is both short and long (Dunn, 1994, pp. 31–60 and Nagel, 1994a, *passim*, 1994b, and 1994d). The history is long insofar as public life and the actions and effects of government have been studied in the Western tradition for at least 3,000 years. At the same time, however, policy studies as a formally recognized discipline is the result of the work of Harold Lasswell and others immediately after World War II. Schools of public policy are more recent, dating from the early 1970s. Lasswell's classic work (1951) identified seven characteristics of policy studies: it must be interdisciplinary, empirical, geared toward fundamental problems, theoretically complex, applied, normative, and prescriptive (McCool, 1995).

Like all other disciplines, policy studies has conflicting schools of thought as well as disagreements about what it is and what it purports to do. A brief look at policy studies is merited here because it allows us to contextualize and ground subsequent discussions of what policy analysis is; a fuller exploration of the history and nature of policy studies generally is beyond the scope of this chapter. Elements of consensus, however, are that policy studies can no longer be subsumed into political science as it once was; the dominant conceptual framework is disjointed incrementalism as developed in the work of Charles Lindblom, Aaron Wildavsky, and others; policy studies is normative; and policy studies, especially policy analysis, are intended to be pragmatic and to offer actionable recommendations.

Theodoulou (1995a) demonstrates how studying public policy is made difficult by the diversity of theoretical problems in the field and further by the conflict among terms, concepts, and frameworks for studying policy. Bobrow and Dryzek go so far as to characterize the study of public policy as a "babel of tongues in which participants talk past rather than to one another" (1987, p.4).

So, what is policy analysis? For Dye (1995, pp. 5–6), a political scientist, policy analysis involves answering the question: "What can we learn about public policy?" To address that question, the analyst must: describe public policy, building an empirical basis for understanding policy; investigate the causes of public policy; and identify and investigate the consequences of public policy. Dye's approach is traditional insofar as it springs from a political science perspective and tends to underplay major concerns of more critical policy scholars identified below.

Majchrzak (1984) shares Dye's orientation. Although she marks a dichotomy between policy research and policy analysis, most policy analysts do not accept this dichotomy, choosing instead to emphasize the multi-disciplinary nature of policy analysis that includes intellectual as well as practical, political elements. Majchrzak's book has other characteristics, however, that make it of considerable value. She emphasizes that policy research (her term; I would use *policy analysis*) combines science, art, and craft; involves the study of complex social phenomena that often appear irrational; and must be timely and responsive to the constraints faced by policy makers. It is this pragmatic, action orientation that underlies her understanding of policy analysis. Majchrzak takes great care to help her readers avoid a purely technicist orientation, urging them to use an *empirico-inductive* approach that adapts elements of grounded theory and contextualizes policy conflicts and approaches to addressing them.

Jones (1984) offers a paradigmatic description of the policy process and its component parts: problem identification, problem formulation, program legitimization, program budgeting, program implementation, program evaluation, and problem resolution/program termination. He is careful to remind us that these are stages in the policy process, not steps followed in linear or lockstep fashion. Many of the stages are in play at any one time, and the process has a number of feedback loops and unpredictabilities. This model for understanding the policy process is a nearly universal element in the traditional approach to policy analysis, e.g., Dunn (1994), Majchrzak (1984), Roe (1994), and Theodoulou (1995b).

One of the most cogent discussions of both the classical and alternative paradigms in policy analysis is in Dunn (1994). His primary working definition of policy analysis is as an applied discipline in social science that uses multiple research methods, in the context of public argumentation and debate, to generate, evaluate, and communicate knowledge that is policy-relevant. Dunn's major argument is that policy analysis is "a series of *intellectual* activities carried out within a process comprised of activities that are essentially *political*," and this is the policy-making process (p. 15; emphasis in the original).

The multiple methods of inquiry used by the policy analyst are used to provide guidance about three kinds of questions as identified in Table 11.1: Values whose achievement will determine if a problem has been adequately addressed; "Facts" whose presence may limit or support the attainment of values; and Actions whose adoption may result in the attainment of values.

Unlike other social sciences, policy analysis is prescriptive, offering recommendations to policy makers and others. Thus, the utilization of the policy-relevant knowledge that the analyst creates, evaluates, and communicates is important, and Dunn explores methods of and obstacles to utilization of the policy analysts' work.

Dunn identifies three major kinds of policy problems, described in Table 11.2. These characteristics are particularly important to Dunn since he sees the structuring of problems as the essence of policy analysis. The evaluation of networked information provides a useful example. One of the particularly volatile conflicts in network policy at all levels of government is whether it is good public policy to impose a charge on telecommunications carriers in order to support universal access programs that rely on discounted telecommunications rates for K-12 schools, public libraries, public higher education, and telemedicine providers. While the national e-rate initiative has had mixed results at

Table 11.1: Three Approaches to Policy Analysis

Approach	Primary question	Type of information
Empirical	Does it exist? (*facts*)	Descriptive or predictive
Valuative	Of what worth is it? (*values*)	Valuative
Normative	What should be done? (*action*)	Prescriptive

best, initiatives such as the Texas Telecommunications Infrastructure Fund (TIF) have been more successful.

Among the conflicts involved is whether incumbent telephone companies should bear the greatest weight of this "subsidy," or if actors such as cable television (CATV) and small Internet Service Providers (ISPs) should contribute as well. Plainly this conflict is, in Dunn's terms, an ill-structured problem, as is

Table 11.2: Structure of Policy Problems

STRUCTURE OF PROBLEM			
ELEMENT	**Well-structured**	**Moderately structured**	**Ill-structured**
Decision maker(s)	One or a few	One or a few	Many
Alternatives	Limited	Limited	Unlimited
Values	Consensus	Consensus	Conflict
Outcomes	Certainty or risk	Uncertainty	Unknown
Probabilities	Calculable	Incalculable	Incalculable

usually the case with important public conflicts. The conflict among stakeholders' values is fundamental and apparently irreconcilable, as are their presumptions about whether such universal access programs should exist and what criteria should be used to evaluate them. First, Dunn's template can help the analyst identify important elements of the conflict beyond the simple assertions of self-interest that characterize many policy conflicts: "We (the telcos) should pay less, they (CATV providers) should pay just as we do" or "We (ISPs) are innovative, small businesses, why shouldn't the rich incumbent telcos pay after having had nearly a century's worth of monopoly, tax incentives, and political influence?" Further, using techniques such as ethnomethodology described below, policy analysis can elicit these stakeholders' presumptions and values and create an intellectual structure that helps us to see where, if anywhere, we can take action to achieve the goals of such programs. One of the most basic of these values is that the private sector should determine much of telecommunications policy. As discussed below, Aufderheide (1999), Dervin (1989), and Strover (2000) posit that we can peel back the skin of many policy conflicts and question whether the public interest is, in fact, supported by such universal access and e-rate programs if all they do is make more members of the public into consumers of homogenized, sensationalist entertainment that characterize net-based and offline media.

Dunn's typology gives rise to another perspective on this same policy conflict: the deconstruction of the concept of the digital divide (Nicholas, 2000). The concept ordinarily centers on the provision of "access," however defined. What it leaves unanswered, of course, are a number of very important questions. What is useful access? What specific functionalities, both upstream and downstream, does useful access demand? How can we ensure access? What is the role of local service providers? What barriers to access exist beyond the usual research categories of income, class, and geographic location? What does effective use mean? What a methodologically self-reflective policy analysis can do is help address these questions in the context of formal and informal means of creating and implementing policy. Given the constitutive nature of problem formulation, the nature and place of policy problems in policy analysis deserves closer examination.

The Problematic of Policy Problems

The status of problems in policy analysis is of special interest because evaluation of policy alternatives and courses of action depends upon attitudes toward the concept of problems. For Schön (1983 and 1993), Dunn (1994), and others, problem setting is the most important of the professional analyst's responsibilities. Schön (1993) focuses on the ability of policy metaphors to make the implicit explicit. Thus, the policy analyst must be aware of several elements of policy conflicts. First is the fact that metaphors, examples of SEEING-AS, encapsulate our perspectives on the world and offer certain possibilities for action while delimiting others. Second, the role of the social scientist, including the policy analyst, is to account for the meanings of those perspectives. This point recalls Carey (1988) who notes that the researcher must make sense of the senses that people make of the world as well as Bruner's (1990) description of us as persons who bring our lives into being through the telling of stories. Third, what appear to be intractable policy problems often are, in fact, dilemmas or conundra that result from problem-framing conflicts based in conflicting metaphors of the problematic situation (the term "problematic situation" stems from Dewey, 1939). Last, developing new (policy) metaphors for framing these problematic situations can generate new perspectives that may lead to more successful, cooperative understandings and actions on the part of policy makers, citizens, other stakeholders, and analysts.

Schön explicitly explores the concept of the generative metaphor that makes the tacit metaphors, frames, and frame conflicts explicit. With a new metaphor, one attends to new things, renaming, reordering, regrouping them and putting them into a temporal sequence—seeing even the old anew. Thus, the analyst does not *solve problems*. Rather, she constructs new insights into the conflict by laying bare the way that the previous problem was constructed.

The analyst performs this task by dissolving what appears to be obvious, by reading the metaphors constructing policy conflicts as literary texts, and by recording and analyzing the stories we tell about what we call social problems. The analyst helps stakeholders in a conflict as well as analysts to see the frame conflicts in play and to avoid them, to the extent possible, through helping to create new frames. These new frames are not simply compromises between existing perspectives. They are new insights, new perspectives generated from the self-conscious analysis of the meta-conflicts that social problems are symptoms of—that is, the value conflicts and contention among visions of the good life, citizenship, and the just society that underlie seemingly irresolvable social problems (Majone, 1989). Schön's examples of the paintbrush as pump and the slum as natural community can help us understand what generative metaphors are and how they work in the policy context. This approach is plainly not a panacea for the limitations of other forms of analysis, but it serves as a useful complement to other approaches.

A useful example of a generative metaphor in the context of networked information services is the first mile (Strover, 2000). What this trope does is turn the provider-centric, system-centric image of the last mile on its head without ignoring the need for certain system characteristics and without emphasizing the user at the expense of the telecommunications provider. Instead of looking from the service provider's perspective, the first mile looks from the citizen's home outward. As discussed in Dervin (1989), the user occupies the center of initiatives for networked information provision without the moral scolding that so many user-based images and concepts imply. The first mile becomes a metanarrative, a mediating story that transcends the often simplistic dichotomy drawn between the user as customer and the user as creator (Roe, 1994; see the next section).

Further, the first mile overcomes the labyrinth of incumbent set-asides, cost structures, regulations, and telephone company dominance that e-rate and universal service or access programs find themselves in. The analyst can use such a metanarrative to break the bonds imposed by too-close adherence to the usual models and metaphors (Mitchell, 1994) and reflect on the ideology of the so-called Information Age. The first mile poses questions that matter to users: How can we have electrical outlets and net ports close to each other in 100-year-old buildings? Who can help me learn what I can do with a net connection? What other local organizations and actors, besides schools and libraries, should be local nodes and contributors to the net? (p. 152). Successful generative metaphors like the first mile, or other evocative public policy tropes such as Putnam's bowling alone, are powerful linguistic tools. They alert us to new ways of seeing and to the way that metaphors determine what we regard as possible. The first mile can also serve as a catalyst to help us consider the substantive issue areas surrounding networked information services such as freedom of association, free speech, unreasonable search and seizure, copyright, and privacy in different ways. In this way, we can generate alternative readings of the challenges and opportunities of networked information.

Narrative Policy Analysis

The most comprehensive look at the role of stories in policy analysis is in Roe (1994). Roe describes and uses techniques from literary analysis, especially those developed in the past few decades, to help illuminate policy making and conflicts. The goals of doing so are to emphasize the constitutive role that policy narratives play in public policy and to demonstrate the value of analyzing narrative for reframing increasingly irresolvable policy problems so that more conventional policy analytical approaches such as statistics, law, and public management can better address them.

For him, evocation of the facts is insufficient to resolve many policy dilemmas: "Sometimes what we are left to deal with are not the facts—that is why there is a controversy—but the different stories people tell as a way of articulating and making sense of the uncertainties and complexities that matter to them" (p. ix). This point recalls Weick (1995) and his concepts of retrospective sensemaking, the radical link between identity and narrative (also see Wenger, 1998, pp. 143–221), and the emphasis in sensemaking on coherence, plausibility, and reasonableness, not accuracy.

Some policy conflicts are characterized, *per* Roe (1994), by intractable conflicts among competing narratives. How can we make social decisions when faced with such deep uncertainty, complexity, and polarization? Policy narratives are "stories (scenarios and arguments) which underwrite and stabilize the assumptions for policy making in situations that persist with many unknowns, a high degree of interdependence, and little, if any, agreement" (p. 34). In other words, policy narratives are strategies for making meaning in situations characterized as policy dilemmas (Schön, 1993) or ill-structured policy problems (Dunn, 1994). There are other forms of policy narratives besides stories, e.g., what Roe calls counterstories, nonstories, and metanarratives. Analysis based on policy narratives can move us to abandon the search for consensus and ground for compromise, turning to a metanarrative that changes polarization into another story altogether that is more responsive to policy intervention.

What makes narrative policy analysis useful, as well as complex, is its adoption of literary strategies to address the uncertainty and conflicting interpretations that characterize many policy conflicts. Roe gives several specific examples throughout his book, including conflict about the disposition of Native Americans' remains currently in museums, water salinity and toxicity, and animal rights, that clarify how literary theory can contribute to policy analysis.

Perhaps the most valuable part of the work is Appendix A (pp. 155–162) that describes and demonstrates methods for narrative policy analysis. A narrative policy analysis has four basic steps, taking essentially a case study approach:

1. Beginning with the conventional definition of stories, the analyst identifies those policy narratives of high uncertainty that emerge from in-depth interviews with major actors and stakeholders in the controversy.
2. The analyst must then identify other narratives about the conflict that adopt other definitions than those in the predominant

narratives or are nonstories or counterstories.

3. The third step is the comparison of these sets of narratives to generate a metanarrative that springs from how the narratives differ, using content analysis (although Roe does not use the term) and the generation of frequency distributions.
4. After the metanarrative has been generated, the goal is to determine "if and how the metanarrative recasts the problem" so that more traditional policy analysis tools can be used (p. 156).

The metanarrative is characterized by its ability to establish and fix assumptions for decision making that recognizes and uses uncertainty, complexity, and polarization, not ignores it. It is these common assumptions that serve as the catalyst for political opponents to act together even while their stories, nonstories, and counterstories fundamentally diverge. Acceptance of intractability contrasts narrative policy analysis with other approaches that aim for consensus and closure.

Essential to the workings of narrative policy analysis in Roe's conception are four elements of Michael Riffaterre's model for analyzing texts, e.g., in *Text Production* (1983). While those elements are beyond the focus of the discussion here, it is worthwhile to note that Riffaterre's and Roe's perspective evokes two fundamentally important concepts in social analysis: Peirce's concept of the indexical (Suchman, pp. 58ff [1987] and Weick, 1995, pp. 51–53) and Polanyi's tacit knowledge (1966's *The Tacit Dimension*). These two concepts emphasize the largely unarticulated and locally situated workarounds, implications, and significances that determine meaning in particular communities of practice.

Policy Narratives about Networked Information

There are a large number of current narratives about networked information services. The first narrative to mention is one that has characterized American life and its political *mythos* since the birth of the Republic: the narrative of economic, political, and cultural unity based on technology and communication (Carey, 1988). This tenet of the American secular faith is explored in the work of Leo Marx, David Noble, and others, but its main tenet is that technology is somehow believed to be able to "solve" persistent social problems. Carey even goes so far as to say that contemporary intellectuals often consider "revolutionary potential in the latest technological gadgets that are pictured as a force *outside* history and politics" (p. 137; emphasis in the original). This narrative of the technologically induced social utopia is a strong theme in much of what we read and hear; more importantly, however, is its appearance in the psyches of those of us brought up to believe in it. This tendency to see all things technologic as redemptive is mirrored by a smaller but not insignificant body of thought that see technological change as the catalyst for the destruction of human dignity and civilization (Kling, 1996).

Table 11.3 illustrates some of the many stories and counterstories that networked information services have been characterized by. The intention of the table is not to be exhaustive; instead, the table is illustrative of common narratives. The table is also not a claim that x is one alternative in a dichotomy, and y is another; rather, the elements can be combined and recombined in many different ways.

As is clear, constituting networked information services along one or more of these axes entails what might become intractable conundra, even though, in many circumstances, the ends of the axes are not mutually exclusive. Therefore, it makes good analytic and political sense to evoke Schön (1993), Roe (1994), Carey (1988), and other commentators who take narrative and rhetoric as the essence of the policy analytic process.

Rist (1994) and Nardi and O'Day (1999) remind us that local, situated, naturalistic perspectives, ones that policy analysis can contribute to, offer a "third way." For example, such perspectives provide an alternative to the absolutist nature of utopian and dystopian discourse. They provide a specific, grounded focus for understanding information technologies and the communities that adopt and adapt them. Similarly, and just as importantly, policy analysis can help us overcome the paralysis that the abstractions of large-scale utopian/dystopian arguments engender. Instead, we can think how we can *act* in particular, localized communities. The ability of policy analysis to identify frame and value conflicts and to offer alternative courses of action are especially important here.

In addition to Schön (1993) and Roe (1994), other useful sources for exploring the constitutive role of narratives in policy conflicts, analysis, and making include: Anderson (1987), Carey (1988), Klamer (1987), Nelson (1987), Schram and Neisser (1997), Scott (1998), Shapiro (1987, 1988, and 1992), and Weick (1995). What these and similar sources do is sensitize us to the constitutive role of the stories we tell in the policy problems we construct for ourselves as well as demonstrate how seemingly irreconcilable value positions can be resources for analysis, not simply frustrations to it.

A CLOSER LOOK AT ALTERNATIVE APPROACHES TO POLICY ANALYSIS

There is a large and growing body of literature that is critical of the prevailing practice and theory of policy studies and of policy analysis. This section will touch upon some of these critiques and their implications for the evaluation of networked information services.

As with the other social sciences, policy analysis is caught in a maelstrom that questions its nature, purposes, epistemological assumptions, outcomes, criteria for judgment, and so on. One of the most important critiques is of the "rationality project" as a whole (White, 1994). Briefly put, the rationality project aimed to use reason and analysis to intervene in public affairs, to rationalize its outcomes and professionalize its study, taking a path that many critical policy theorists regard as "analycentric" (e.g., Dunn, 1994, pp. 48–50). The prevailing mode of policy analysis has three major assumptions that the critical approaches decry; these assumptions are summarized in Table 11.4.

The alternative approach emphasizes that professional analysts must be more overtly political, moving beyond so-called rational analysis' instrumentality to a

Table 11.3: Illustrative Policy Narratives, Stories, and Counterstories

The information superhighway	vs.	the network community
Networks as tools for creating culture		networks as the means to transmit information
Government as guarantor of equity		government as aggregator of markets for the private sector
The network community		the information ecology
Individuals and groups as customers		individuals and groups as citizens
Strong privacy		necessity of open and traceable communication
User as passive consumer of media images		user as active creator and contributor to public discourse
Protection of intellectual property users and creators		Protection of intellectual property rights owners
Education		e-commerce
Downstream bias		upstream focus
Democratic action		police surveillance
Delivery of government services		facilitation of identity formation and discursive equality
Digital utopia		digital dystopia

Table 11.4: Worldviews in Collision—Dominant and Critical Perspectives in Policy Analysis

	Epistemology	Data, norms, and values	Role of theory
Classical view	Positivism that assumes an "objective world"	A value-free empiricism that emphasizes individuals' rational preferences and an economistic foundation	Can be overcome through analysis
Critical view	Post-positivism that asserts that the objective reality assumed by positivism cannot be known independently	An empiricism that claims that the value conflicts that policy analysis gives rise to must be part of policy debates	Informs and permeates analysis

more participatory project that involves ordinary citizens more broadly and includes reflection about political values. While the classical view has many strengths, e.g., its emphasis on results and recognition of the motives for individual behavior, this approach has been consistently criticized for excessive technicism and an unfounded faith in expertise, as well as its basic assumptions of individual and institutional rationality (de Leon, 1994; Mosco, 1996).

White emphasizes that policy analysis investigates the construction of meaning, that is, analysis must embrace the important policy debates that different policy definitions and knowledge assumptions give rise to as its primary resource. The critical approach asserts that one of the primary responsibilities of policy analysis is to demonstrate how different policy values, intentions, meanings, interpretations, and stories are in collision—to offer alternative ways of understanding the conflicts, and to "expose underlying norms to critical examination" (White, 1994, p. 862, citing Robert Reich's *The Power of Public Ideas*, 1988). The analyst cannot claim to be a so-called neutral observer, removed from the complicated value conflicts around her. The analyst, aware of her own values and perspectives, must help to generate and communicate alternative perspectives on public conflicts. This recognition, however, does not ignore "the facts." Instead, it accepts that all factual assertions are based on theories that assume and support some values and not others.

Dror (1994) provides one of the most comprehensive of alternative approaches to policy analysis. He suggests an advanced policy sciences that values heuristics, policy reflection, and reasoning and deliberation rather than calculation. Dror describes how policy worlds are constructs, not unquestionable reflections of reality. This point is underscored by other, alternative approaches to policy analysis, notably Dunn (1994, pp. 138–140) and his admonition, noted above, that the analyst does not begin with clearly articulated, well-defined problems. Instead, she begins with a sense of stress in the polity that leads to a problem definition, which "like atoms or cells, are conceptual constructs" (p. 140; also see Kaplan, 1964, and Schön, 1983). The digital divide and universal access discussed briefly above help illustrate this point.

Another important part of alternative approaches is the increased involvement of other actors in the process of policy analysis and policy making beyond the traditional *troika* of policy maker, analyst, and lobbyist. Such involvement stems from critical theorists' assertion that power is concentrated in the hands of the few with political and social influence. For example, Lindblom and Woodhouse (1993) demonstrate how the supposed marketplace of ideas has been stunted by the lack of political equity and inability of many to be part of the policy conversation. They warn us that expert analysis, while essential to policy making, cannot substitute for widespread political interaction and participation in policy making. De Leon (1993 and 1994), based on the work of Habermas, are good examples of work that aims to make the policy sciences more responsive to the values and concerns of ordinary citizens, to what Lindblom and Cohen, in *Usable Knowledge* (1979), call citizens' "ordinary knowledge." To do so, the policy sciences must overcome their economistic and behavioristic orientation and the technocratic elements of the state to which the policy sciences have been primary contributors (Mosco, 1996).

Thompson (1997), Scott (1998), Majone (1989), de Leon (1994), Dobuzinskis (1992), White (1994), and Mosco (1996) attribute the policy sciences' spotty success generally to a number of factors. Social conflicts and their contexts are inherently complex. Policy analysis displays an over-reliance on (Newtonian, mechanistic) instrumental rationality, especially positivism and the tenets of neoclassical economics, with a concomitant supposed facts/values dichotomy and the resultant denigration of policy analysis as argument. Similarly, there is a very strong influence of public choice theory, with its emphasis on (rational) economic analysis, and the overemphasis on private self-interest at the expense of the public interest "because it [public choice theory] starts with the view that people are, above all else, pursuers of private self-interest" (Mosco, 1996, p. 253). In addition to this "methodological and substantive individualism" (p. 262), policy analysts display a technocratic and often undemocratic orientation and valorization of expertise that excludes most forms of reflection about political values. Like all social analysts, policy analysts have significant limitations they are unwilling to recognize. Policy analysis also canonizes markets and hierarchies as the only important institutional forms. As might be expected from the earlier items in the list, policy analysis neglects the complex roles of power and class in policy development, implementation, and evaluation, stemming from the field's individualistic biases and the tone of capitalist triumphalism that infects it. In light of these burdens, de Leon and other critical policy analysts calls for a return to

Lasswell's original vision of the policy sciences that affirm human dignity and the processes of democracy, by being explicitly normative.

The methods de Leon explores in both papers are post-positivist and based on critical theory and participative policy analysis (PPA). PPA tries to establish an environment in which all interested parties have equal footing—to identify conflicts, characterize them, explore alternatives, propose courses of action, evaluate outcomes, and terminate as well as start programs. While he recognizes the limitations of participative policy analysis, especially its plausibility and conceptual foundations, de Leon provides some explicit advice about how to make such an approach to policy analysis work:

- Choose citizens randomly from affected groups to be part of a policy panel to address a particular policy issue
- Prepare background and policy papers, briefings, and memoranda for the panel with the same high level of quality as those meant to serve decision makers
- Provide staff support for logistical, research, political, and other kinds of questions that the panel members develop
- Model discursive procedures for discussion, writing, position papers, and the like
- Sensitize the participants to conditions of power and dependence through the use of critical theory as feasible.

To accomplish such tasks, the policy analyst must be an expert facilitator of discussion; a catalyst of citizens' learning as well as that of policy makers; an expert in survey, ethnographic, and other research methods; and an astute political actor. A brief look at the discussion of privacy as property can help illustrate how participatory policy analysis can work and contribute to our understanding of networked information services.

PPA: Why Privacy Is Not Property

Because of the growing concerns among the American public about privacy, especially online, and the increased value of information about persons, a number of assertions have been made that privacy should be protected as property. These assertions have been made by those who wish to give privacy greater protection (e.g., Branscomb, 1994), those who wish to support the growth of ecommerce (e.g., Laudon, 1996), and those who deny the need for any right to privacy and any need for its protection (e.g., Thomson, 1984 and 1990). Further, the Congress has given greater impetus to this movement through the use of property interest language in bills such as the Consumer Privacy Protection Act (S. 2606 of the Second Session of the 104th Congress), introduced by Senator Hollings in May 2000. The temptation to use intellectual property rights, in particular, to address online privacy conflicts has been quite strong (National Research Council, 2000, p. 238).

Such a choice, however, would be disastrous for a number of reasons (Doty, forthcoming). First, the goals of intellectual property protection to create and distribute knowledge are quite divergent from the protection of privacy, and this divergence would compromise both privacy and intellectual property protection. Second, and more important, reducing privacy to simply another form of property misses many of privacy's essential contributions to identity, autonomy, social relationships, and protection of the self and its intimates. Third, privacy is often an attribute of groups, not just individuals, and the property and market schemes suggested to protect privacy cannot adequately address shared privacy interests. Fourth, privacy would simply be added to the list of consumer goods to be bought and sold without regard to its moral status. Last, the kinds of property contracts that advocates of privacy as property suggest ignore the marked inequities that exist between individuals and small groups of individuals on the one hand and powerful, hegemonic institutions such as the government and large commercial enterprises on the other.

Participative policy analysis can help citizens and their advocates to avoid the knee-jerk reaction of searching for privacy protection under any property regime, including intellectual property, simply because they feel that there is no other effective means to protect privacy online. Analysts can identify important inequities in social and political power that make the invocation of property interests a bad choice for privacy protection and bring this analysis to PPA panels and other citizens' groups, as well as decision makers. A major difficulty is our inability to determine the implications of "selling" our privacy, especially in the long term. Even this brief discussion demonstrates the kind of policy analysis that can contribute to our understanding and evaluation of networked information services.

POLICY RESEARCH METHODS AND NETWORKED INFORMATION

The classical and alternative perspectives on policy analysis give rise to an increasingly complex study of public policy. This complexity begins with a closer examination of the epistemological and methodological bases of the field. Dewey (1939) is the classical source of what we might call the logic of inquiry, expanded in Lasswell (1951) and Kaplan (1964). This is the traditional understanding that the policy analyst must apply the canons of scientific research to achieve greater understanding of social life and, thereby, to use that understanding to help policy makers make "better" policy. In contrast to the logic of inquiry, Nelson, Megill, and McCloskey (1987, pp. 4–5) posit the rhetoric of inquiry that joins politics, public participation, and rhetoric into the policy analysis that Lasswell, and Dewey before him, imagined.

Among the policy analyst's primary methods of research in the rhetoric of inquiry is ethnography, quite literally letting the people speak. This approach builds upon the democratic goals of policy analysis as laid out by Lasswell 50 years ago and resurrected by alternative analysts in the past two decades. The people included in ethnographically based policy analysis range from the ordinary citizen to the interest group representative to the career civil servant to the political appointee. Such catholicity in choice of informants provides the thick, rich description necessary to understand the causes as well as the symptoms of policy issues; insight into the frame and value conflicts that analysis seeks to make explicit and to articulate; demonstration of responsiveness to the complexity and unpredictability of social conflict; and greater buy-in into the course of subsequent action. Ethnomethodology, increasingly used by policy researchers of all kinds, helps move us from the extremes of grand theory and "ideographic micro-studies" (Dror, quoted in McCool, 1995, p. 394). Further, ethnography transcends, in de Leon's words, the Eastonian black box (Easton, 1965) that obsession with systems theory and mechanistic models often leaves us in and complements other techniques in de Leon's participatory policy analysis.

Suchman (1987, pp. 50 and 57) describes essential elements of action, social practices, and the construction of meaning that reveals:

> What traditional behavioral sciences take to be cognitive phenomena have an essential relationship to a publicly available, collaboratively organized world of artifacts and actions, and ... the significance of artifacts and actions, and the methods by which their significance is conveyed, have an essential relationship to their particular, concrete circumstances. ... [Ethnomethodology lets us see that] our everyday social practices render the world publicly available and mutually intelligible. The methodology of interest to ethnomethodologists ... is ... that deployed by members of the society in coming to know, and making sense out of, the everyday world of talk and action.

Thus, policy analysts must provide insight to these relationships, between the cognitive and the social, and the social and specific, localized situations. It is here that the "scientific" truth of an ethnomethodologically based, user-responsive policy analysis of networked information services lies.

Rigorously performed ethnographic research, whether in the naturalistic, grounded theory, critical theory, constructivist, or other qualitative approaches, helps to break the stranglehold of technicist dictates and sub-governments or iron triangles, the combination of mission agencies in the executive branch, oversight and appropriating committees in the legislative branch, and the lobbying, interest groups that coalesce around policy issues and programs. Ethnomethodology also helps the analyst make more of the issue networks of which s/he is a part (Heclo, 1995) and play the catalytic role of the policy entrepreneur (Majone, 1989).

Perhaps the most important element of a rhetorical/narrative perspective is its emphasis on the frame conflicts that underlie many intractable policy issues. Carey (1988) provides us some insight into one of the most fractious of conflicts in communication studies: communication as transmission or as ritual (see the discussion of Dervin and her critique of this view and its links to traditional categories of users). The transmission view is characterized by the following beliefs:

- Electronic media, despite evidence to the contrary, continue the pre-existing conceptual link of transport and communication
- Communication is the creation of information that exists in things and outside of any relationship
- Messages impart this information
- The true state of persons is the radical individualism of traditional political theory and economics.

The ritual view, on the other hand, emphasizes that communication:

- maintains society in and through time and is not interested in simple reach through space
- represents and maintains shared beliefs and shared culture as it is created, modified, and transformed
- provides confirmation of, not information about, underlying social relations and social groups

According to the more complete and phenomenologically consistent, "ritual" understanding, the social science researcher must grasp the meanings people put into their words and behavior, make the meanings explicit, and judge/evaluate them (p. 59). This conflict in conceiving communication is valuable because it clarifies how policy analysis can view the use of communication media, especially networked information services, as ritual and constitutive of culture and identity. This contrast is between the narratives of networks as community and networks as conduits for fostering e-commerce. Policy analysis, then, must understand how communication media create the communities and social reality that they are also used to describe. Individuals, groups, and the highly localized and contingent nature of their use of digital communication, not transport characteristics such as simplistic concepts like universal access or the last mile as discussed above, must be the focus of policy analysts who want to understand and evaluate networked information services. Listening to users talk about community formation and maintenance can tell us why network technologies matter, if at all, and what those technologies must be like and how they must be deployed and supported to facilitate users' social, work, and rhetorical practices.

Critics of the classical approach to policy analysis such as Mosco, Dunn, Majone, White, and Dobuzinskis identify many of the manifold strengths of the traditional approach to policy analysis. These strengths include an understanding of the state as constitutive of social life, an interest in all of social reality, the commitment to using knowledge of social life to transform it, a growing engagement with normative and value questions, and the power of Occam's Razor. Critics of the traditional approach such as de Leon, Roe, Dror, and others consistently emphasize that their goal is not the abandonment of the "scientific perspective," but rather its expansion to include contingency, localized meaning, qualitative and critical methods, and the importance of the individual's situation and perspective. Good policy analysis, then, combines these strengths with the strengths of alternative approaches so that analysis is increasingly syncretistic in its methods, its sources of data, its kinds of data, its analytic techniques, and its perspectives. Traditional strengths combine with awareness of the argumentative, rhetorical nature of policy analysis, while maintaining the policy sciences' commitment to methodological rigor to effect real change in society. The policy analyst must successfully combine the quantitative and qualitative, the predictive and contingent. It is in the marriage of the classical and traditional that policy analysis becomes better able to combine the theoretic and the practical and to provide the best advice to policy makers and citizens.

Summary

We are seeing the birth of a richer and more complex policy analysis—one that is more catholic in its methods, more self-conscious, more sensitive to narrative and values, more ethnographically sophisticated, and more aware of the limitations of all of its methodological resources. McCool (1995) reassures us that the growing number of hard questions about methods and concepts in policy analysis is a sign of disciplinary maturity, not a sign of disciplinary weakness; it shows a recognition of the profound complexity and uncertainty that define social life. What policy analysis makes of its methodological resources in order to understand and evaluate networked information services is what we turn to now.

POLICY ANALYSIS AND EVALUATING NETWORKED INFORMATION SERVICES

There are many reasons for using policy analysis to evaluate networked information services. Among the most important is the fact that much of Information Technology (IT) research, as well as many leading networked information programs and initiatives, are sponsored by government, especially the U.S. federal government. The military origins of networked technologies, functions, and institutions is an especially important public element of the story of networked information services (Abbate, 1999; Edwards, 1996; Flamm, 1988). Further, government is among the primary users of networked information services, both those provided by others and by various levels of government itself; this role is also linked to governmental IT procurement programs that amount to billions of dollars *per annum*. Government sometimes plays the role of a proactive standards setter for hardware, software, and communication protocols. Of wider interest is the fact that evolving networked information technologies and services have emergent implications for access to information in an open society that relies upon the private sector to satisfy most information demands.

Of equal value, however, is the ability of policy analysis to illuminate conflicts beyond those related to public policy. For instance, institutions of higher education, businesses, non-profits, and other organizations can all benefit from the techniques of policy analysis. The structuring of problems, monitoring of outcomes, and the articulation of conflicting frames of reference are of particular importance in such non-governmental venues.

Among the specific contributions that policy analysis can make to the evaluation of networked information services springs from the structure of the policy issue paper, one of the most important products of the policy analyst. Dunn (1994, Appendix 1, pp. 423–431) gives a very useful summary of the most common elements of the issue paper. These elements and illustrative criteria for evaluation of them are in Table 11.5. Among the strengths of this structure is that it can help (1) provide guidance in the formulation and articulation of policy conflicts, (2) identify component parts of the conflicts, (3) make explicit underlying values and assumptions, and (4) offer some alternative methods of understanding that may, in fact, provide a "third way" beyond the ordinary dichotomies in which we think and tend to cast political issues.

Policy analysis can serve as an important antidote to technological determinism that often characterizes both informal and analytic discussions of computer networks. Further, a methodologically diverse and context-sensitive policy analysis can move us beyond the pure reactivity of media deregulation and the inevitable conflict about visions of government that discussions of regulation and deregulation evoke in American politics. Similarly, policy analysis can also help us focus on important policy actors outside of government and outside of the market-driven decisions of private sector actors. None of this is to say that technological change, discussion of regulation and deregulation, and governmental and private sector actors are not important—quite the contrary. What policy analysis can help us do, however, is help us attend to other things, actors, perspectives, and values that matter as well. For example, ethnographically based policy analysis can help us move beyond the simple human-machine dichotomy (Nardi and O'Day, 1999, p. 30) that characterizes an overwhelming mass of research to a wider perspective that considers value conflicts, social relationships, historical trends, and important stakeholders and the power relationships among them.

Dunn (1994) has particular value for using policy analysis as a lens for considering networked information services. First, it is clear that policy *problems* associated with networked information are messy, complex, and ill-structured, with virtually unlimited alternatives and radical conflict among values and

Table 11.5: Elements of the Policy Issue Paper

Element	Examples of Evaluative Criteria
Executive summary	Are recommendations highlighted?
Background of the problem or dilemma	Are all important terms clearly defined?
Description of the problem situation	Are all appropriate dimensions described?
Outcomes of earlier efforts to address the problem	Are prior efforts clearly assessed?
Scope and severity of the problem	
Assessment of past policy efforts	Why is the problematic situation important?
Significance of the problem situation	What are the major assumptions and questions to be considered?
Need for analysis	
Problem statement	
	Is the problematic situation clearly stated?
Definition of the problem	Are all major stakeholders identified and prioritized?
Major stakeholders	
Goals and objectives	Is the approach to analysis clearly specified?
Measures of effectiveness	Are goals and objectives clearly specified?
Potential "solutions"	Are major value conflicts identified and described?
Policy alternatives	
Description of alternatives	Are alternatives compared in terms of costs and effectiveness?
Comparison of future outcome	
Externalities	Are alternatives systematically compared in terms of political feasibility?
Constraints and political feasibility	
Policy recommendations	
Criteria for recommending alternatives	Are all relevant criteria clearly specified?
Descriptions of preferred alternative(s)	Is a strategy for implementation clearly specified?
Outline of implementation strategy	
Limitations and possible unanticipated outcomes	Are there adequate provisions for monitoring and evaluating policies, particularly unintended consequences?
References	
Appendices	

visions. Thus, the problem-solving model is either not equal to the task of giving us substantial insight into conflicts about networked information or is simply inappropriate. A further useful concept in Dunn is that of multiple advocacy. The analyst is clearly advocative according to this model but is involved in a systematic comparison and critical assessment of many potential courses of action, not adamantly and blindly attached to any single position at all costs.

Brown and Duguid (1991), using the work of Lave and Wenger among others, provide us further insight into some important elements of communities that shed light on networked information and policy analysis. They remind us that communities are not canonical or clearly bounded, and emerge from members' activity rather than being formed to complete a task. This characterization is especially important to our understanding of online communities.

Evaluation Techniques

This section of the chapter will focus on a number of particular ways that policy analysis can contribute to the evaluation of networked information services. Dunn (1994) has a chapter devoted to policy analysis and evaluation (pp. 403–422), and he identifies three important outcomes of policy analytic evaluation: to provide information about policy performance; to help identify, clarify, and critique the values that underlie the selection of goals and objectives; and to lead to the application of other policy analytic techniques such as problem structuring and recommendation. Evaluation in policy analysis is characterized by its explicit focus on values, its recognition of the interdependence of "facts" and values, its retrospective and prospective foci, and the role that values play as both means (extrinsic to the achievement of another goal) and ends (intrinsic and valuable unto themselves). For example, the development of job-related skills using and focusing on networked information can be regarded as both intrinsic, valuable in and of itself, and extrinsic, because it leads to other valuable ends such as greater social equity, increased economic productivity, enhanced self-image, and greater diversity in the workforce.

For Dunn, the criteria for evaluating the performance of policy choices are the same six as those that inform the creation of policy action alternatives: effectiveness, efficiency, adequacy, equity, responsiveness, and appropriateness. Each of these, in turn, is operationalized by answering a particular question (pp. 282 and 405). For effectiveness, closely tied to technical rationality, has a valued outcome been realized? How does one know? Using what criteria or metrics? For efficiency, equivalent to economic rationality, to what extent have resources been called upon to achieve some valued outcome? For adequacy, which cannot be completely determined by any one measure or criterion, to what extent does the realization of some desired outcome resolve the policy problematic? For equity, justice, or fairness, are both costs and benefits distributed equitably across different stakeholder groups? This criterion is especially complex since equity and welfare are notoriously complex to measure and there are fiercely competing conceptions of what is just and what is not, e.g., should we maximize individual welfare, protect minimum welfare, maximize net welfare, or maximize redistributive welfare (p. 287)? Again, no one metric is sufficient to gauge whether the criterion of equity has been achieved. With regard to responsiveness, do the policy outcomes satisfy the needs, developing preferences, or values of a particular group or groups? A policy outcome may satisfy all of the other evaluative criteria but may still not respond to the specific needs of the group(s) that are supposed to benefit from the policy. For appropriateness, necessarily a situation-specific criterion, are the desired outcomes worthwhile and valuable? What makes such a judgment especially difficult is that, by definition, appropriateness is intended to transcend other criteria (p. 289).

The reader can see how such criteria might be invoked in evaluating networked information services. A brief example will illustrate the power of Dunn's approach using the evaluative criteria of effectiveness and responsiveness. As discussed elsewhere in this chapter, how well are universal access, e-rate, and related programs working? Using Dunn's criteria, we can see that such programs have rarely achieved their goals, or, if they have, it is generally only the goal of the grossest sort of net connectivity. Further, we can see that the programs are hamstrung by the lack of clearly articulated goals and the lack of integration of the programs with the actual behavior and needs of their intended beneficiaries. In fact, as discussed elsewhere in this chapter, such universal access programs have too often devolved into debates about allocating the costs of such programs rather than concern with achieving their social goals. With regard to responsiveness, such universal access programs have focused on net connectivity, telecommunication rates, equipment purchases, and software. All of these are essential to the success of such programs, but they are necessary, not sufficient. The success of these programs has been severely limited by the lack of commitment of adequate resources to identifying users' and potential users' needs, communication patterns, social relations, and communities of practice. Further, important elements such as program evaluation, training, consulting, and sustainability have too often been ignored or only summarily addressed.

Majchrzak (1984) provides a useful reminder that there is no single, comprehensive, canonical method for doing the technical analysis and evaluation of policy research (policy analysis). Like Dunn and others, she provides a useful discussion of a number of techniques for understanding policy dilemmas. These include focused synthesis, which integrates literature review with discussions with stakeholders and issue experts, personal past experience of the analyst, unpublished documents, and so on. Other important techniques are secondary analysis, and its cousin, meta-analysis; field experiments, especially useful in determining the origins of a social conflict; what she calls qualitative methods; large- and small-scale surveys; case studies for their in-depth, holistic, and naturalistic strengths; and cost-benefit and cost-effectiveness analyses, despite the great difficulty in quantifying the benefits of most policy outcomes. She provides an especially useful discussion of the nature and effects of the political power structure in analyzing and evaluating policy outcomes, focusing on four characteristics of stakeholders (p. 79):

- Identification of key stakeholders affected by a particular recommendation
- Stakeholders' support or opposition to a recommendation
- Power position of stakeholders relative to the key decision makers for the issue
- Support of key decision makers for implementation of recommendations, given the power and the opinions of stakeholders.

The evaluation of networked information services, whether the policies evaluated are public, private, or some combination of the two, can plainly benefit from such focused power analyses, especially in determining the actual ability of stakeholder groups to influence the development, deployment, and evaluation of networked technologies and services.

Nagel (1988, pp. 255–259, and 1994c) and Majone (1989, pp. 167–183) provide further sophisticated discussion of evaluation research and policy studies that lie beyond the scope of this chapter. Many commentators, e.g., de Leon (1993), Dror (1994), Dunn (1994), and Majchrzak (1984), hold that one of the most important responsibilities of the policy analyst is the appropriate presentation of policy analyses to various stakeholder groups and policy makers. Especially vital is the ability to make policy analysis accessible to the nonexpert while avoiding oversimplification of policy issues. As policy analysis pursues its participatory and democratic project, being able to present complex analyses of networked information issues to ordinary citizens, business people, educators, and more will grow increasingly important. Without such professional but accessible presentations, the overall evaluation of networked information services will be incomplete and without sufficient grounding.

Focusing on Users

It is plain that policy analysis must be more explicitly based on methodological self-reflection, ethnographic methods, inclusion of a wider range of affected parties in policy study and deliberation, concern with narratives and frame conflicts, and values. The most important element specifically tied to networked information is the adoption of user-based research methods. At the same time, however, there are two important elements of such a research program that must be considered briefly.

The first is the need for a critical approach to users' narratives. A researcher must evaluate them, while recalling that users know best what their motives and experiences are. Rigorous ethnomethodologists constantly use other sources besides respondents' narratives to gather and evaluate evidence. That rule does not disappear in ethnographic policy analysis. Of special concern are the following:

- The need to recall that all persons are experts at retrospective sense-making. We use outcomes to "explain" how it is we approached a particular set of circumstances. Clearly, organizational and other forms of research have demonstrated that the emergence of meaning makes plans, and the evocation of plans in explaining outcomes, suspect (Brown and Duguid, 1991; Suchman, 1987; Weick, 1995). For example, researchers must interrogate respondents' assertions that the co-evolution of networked technologies and local workarounds and work practices were all deliberate and planned. Some were, and some were not—identifying which were planned and which were not and how they are alike and different gives us greater insight into the situated effects of technologies and what criteria should be used to evaluate them.
- Methodological self-consciousness that reminds us that analysts, like other persons, see what they expect to see; thus, the need for triangulation about data collection methods, kinds and sources of data, and modes of analysis, as well as the generation of alternative explanations.
- The expectancy effect (where respondents try to provide what they think the researcher wants to hear) and the social desirability effect (where respondents misrepresent their behavior in order to appear that they are adhering to social mores).

This awareness of the limits of narrative and ethnomethodology do not mean that we can summarily dismiss users' perspectives, as researchers have in times past, as "merely" self-reports. Instead, it reminds us to be methodologically diverse and self-conscious.

The second caveat to keep in mind springs from the work of Brenda Dervin. Certainly, policy analysis built on a holistic, user-based perspective is vital to the success of the analysis of information services, but we need to remember that users, like policy narratives and policy problems, are constructs (see Scott, 1998, on abstract citizens). Dervin (1989) provides us with several useful insights into the limitations of the ways in which we ordinarily construe users and the ill effects of those limitations. This and related work, especially that related to communities of practice (Wenger, 1998), provides us with a foundation on which to build a more complex and sophisticated representation of users that can further the project of using policy analysis to evaluate networked information services and to achieve democratic goals.

Dervin's strongest critique of traditional categories of users is that most analysts treat these categories as if they actually existed. These traditional categories and some of their sub-categories are listed in Table 11.6, focusing on her description of individual characteristics while leaving out her discussion of groups and nations.

Table 11.6: Traditional Categories of Users

Criteria	Characteristics of individuals
Demography	Marital status, age, race, ethnicity, gender, education
Personality/psychology	Cognitive characteristics and styles, apprehensions
Communication literacies	Reading, computer, interpersonal
Access to technology	Computers, telephones, television
Role in communication	Source, receiver, seller, consumer
Location of transaction	Home, work, leisure center, library
Observer-defined purpose of system	Informative, entertaining, instrumental, cultural, political, economic

What we as analysts fail to do is recognize how such categories are our own inventions, the results of our training and assumptions about other persons. For Dervin, such assumptions tend to (1) defend the *status quo*, especially through the Matthew Effect whereby the rich get richer, (2) rest upon the utility of these categories for marketing, (3) push sub-groups into cultural homogenization, and (4) legitimate existing power relationships and inequities without recognizing those effects. The foundation of such assumptions is the transmission view of communication discussed earlier by Carey (1988)—the belief that communication is transmission of the thing called information. Instead we can adopt a view that communication, including that using computer networks, is the mutual construction of meaning and community.

Dervin then presents an alternative vision of how we can use our understandings of users to inform the development of information systems that support users' own concerns, summarizing alternative categories of users in Table 11.7.

The particular research value of these alternative categories is that they more closely match what users do in constructing groups and meanings, more

Table 11.7: Alternative Categories of Users

Criteria	Characteristics of individuals
Actor's situation	Nature of barrier to communication, complexity, power
Gaps in sense making	Questions asked, understandings missed, anomalies faced
Actor-defined purpose	To get ideas, find direction, get support, be happy, be heard
Information-using strategy	Browsing, formatting, grouping, highlighting, interpreting
Information values (Taylor, 1986)	Timeliness, depth, breadth, touchability
Information traits (MacMullin and Taylor, 1984)	Quantitative/qualitative, single point/options, case study/census

completely support the democratic project, enrich models for policy making, and can be measured in specific circumstances. Thus, while the categories seem too general or dynamic to some, they can be clearly and usefully identified in situated behaviors. Dervin spends the last few pages of her paper exploring how the alternative categories affect our understanding and ability to generate alternatives for action with regard to three major information policy areas: deregulation of media, privatization of governmental information services and products, and the vertical and horizontal integration of communication businesses. This discussion is informed by the alternative categories that are communication-based, situated in particular times and places, and relevant to the actors in communication themselves.

More specifically, policy analysis can use these alternative categories of users to unearth the assumptions that users, policy makers, technology vendors, networked information service providers, and other stakeholders hold. For example, what does universal access mean using the alternative categories? What insights do we gain on the effects the 1996 Telecommunications Act (PL 104-104) has had on media hegemony, media mergers, and vertical and horizontal integration of media firms? Where is the public interest in such legislation (Aufderheide, 1999)? As Dervin notes, redesign of information systems seems unnecessary if we adhere to the traditional categories; redesign becomes visible and imperative, however, when we focus on the new categories (p. 222). A context-sensitive, naturalistic policy analysis makes us see networked information services as important raw material for making meaning, for making community, *not simply* for aggregating markets and satisfying existing consumers' demands. In addition, networked information systems can be judged on how well they have helped users to succeed using the alternative categories. Using strategies such as recommender systems, the generation of user-based Frequently Asked Questions (FAQs) and responses, and the like, earlier users can help support newer users. Further, they can help the newer users and others see to what extent specific networked information systems and services support a sophisticated user-based perspective.

Some Linguistic Obstacles to Policy Analysis and its Utilization

While it should be clear that policy analysis is a difficult task to do well, there are a number of ordinary linguistic usages beyond that of "problem" that make it more difficult still. Chief among these are the common-sense uses of important terms in the study of public life, e.g., policy. In ordinary speech, such uses, of course, are not at all problematic. As part of the context in which policy analysis is done and used and as part of the stuff from which policy analysis is made, however, common parlance tends to obscure the careful use of the terms in the field and to compromise our understanding of public life. Policy analysis can help sensitize us to our linguistic habits and, thereby, achieve a fuller understanding of the various roles of networked information services.

Policy analysis is both political and rhetorical, combining intellectual work with awareness of the political context in which it is done. Policy analysis makes recommendations and evaluations, i.e., makes rhetorical assertions, that attempt to change not just describe their political environment. The policy analyst is (1) part of and trying to understand and affect a political context (political) and (2) a rhetor, a speaker trying to aggregate, inform, and influence an audience (rhetorical). Fischer and Forester (1993, p. 7; Majone, 1989) discuss the "argumentative turn" in policy analysis, the "context-specific character of analytical practices—the ways the symbolism of their language matters, the ways the consideration of their audience matters, the ways they construct problems before solving them." Dobuzinskis (1992) emphasizes that rhetoric and policy analysis are inseparable, especially since the analyst, like other persons, constructs and regenerates the real in the process of analyzing and arguing about it. While these aspects of policy analysis may appear obvious, it is useful here to talk explicitly about them. These two terms, like others (e.g., mythological, theoretical, and ideological), bear an uneasy burden. The political and the rhetorical are of the utmost importance in understanding what policy analysis is and how it can contribute to the evaluation of networked information services, but they are commonly used unreflectively, pejoratively, and dismissively in common parlance and in many analytic frameworks. This kind of dismissal is so common that it has become almost transparent or is considered so engrained that nothing can

Table 11.8: Commonsensical Linguistic Traps

Term	Common, pejorative meanings	More "technical" meanings
Political	Subject to undue influence, messy, unpredictable	linked to formal and informal methods for identifying and resolving conflict among members of communities
Rhetorical	Deceptive, manipulative, decorative	emphasizes and examines how language can be clear and convincing and how language forms and maintains social groups

come from its examination. Looking more closely at these linguistic problems, as in Table 11.8, bears some useful fruit.

What is the Value of the Political?

We commonly use the term "political" to imply that a process or outcome was less than fair, that it ignored credible and convincing evidence to the contrary, and that it unfairly overlooked competence and ability while favoring personal and social acquaintance. "Oh, that decision was only political," or "Well, you know how political the entire question was," or "The conflict became so politicized that it was impossible to resolve." Such uses of "political" are code that evokes and are based on many sources, three of which will be briefly discussed.

The first source is the traditional American mistrust of government, and the second is the related fashionably cynical dismissal of government as ineffectual and contrary to citizens' interests common in American social life since at least the early 1970s. While the Watergate scandal, disaffection with the war in Vietnam, and the "Reagan Revolution" are the purported causes of this dismissal, its roots also lie in a desire to appear sophisticated and anything other than naïve. The final cause to mention here is the belief that what my political allies have is reason, competence, and indisputable fact on our side, while all my political opponents have is unfair social influence. Thus, the pejorative use of the term "political" reinforces the increasing tendency to demonize one's political opponents (Glendon, 1991). While this tendency has always characterized American political life, it appears much more common now. The negative effects of dismissing the "merely political" are acute, and the term needs rehabilitation, especially, so that we can recognize the communal aspects of networked information services and their community-building potential.

A useful example of the ill effects of these assumptions centers on some of the arcane rules governing extended area service (EAS) programs (Nicholas, 2000). Texas, like other states, has a number of programs to expand access to plain old telephone service (POTS), advanced telephony, and Internet services. EAS is a Texas program targeted specifically to rural areas and aims to expand a telephone customer's local calling scope, which is the range of telephone exchanges outside the home exchange that can be reached for the price of a local call (pp. 93–94). One of the five characteristics of EAS programs illustrates the danger of dismissing the political: determination of community of interest (COI).

COI defines linked geographical regions that exhibit one-way or two-way dependence, especially for education, government services, work, and medical treatment. Texans must formally establish a COI for the Texas Public Utility Commission if they want local phone rates to apply to telephone exchanges between 22 and 50 air miles from the home exchange. Presence of an ISP in a neighboring exchange is generally considered adequate proof of a community of interest.

The major policy obstacle to achieving the politically valuable goal of extended area service are exemptions granted to telephone carriers if: they have fewer than 10,000 lines in Texas; the company is a telephone cooperative; there is no digital switch available; local calling is already available; or one of the proposed exchanges is in a major Texas metropolitan area (Nicholas, 2000, p. 107). Since many rural customers in Texas rely on telephone carriers who qualify under one or more of these exemptions, such customers either forego Internet use or pay substantial long-distance telecommunications charges. Although EAS can help create demand for Internet services, regulatory exemptions meant especially to protect rural telephone cooperatives paradoxically deny rural customers even the illusion of equity of access to networked information services. Similarly, these exemptions make it very difficult for rural ISPs to prosper.

Policy makers, major news media, and, especially, ordinary citizens are perplexed and overwhelmed by such arcane and apparently self-contradictory situations. Even state regulatory administrators have often characterized these kinds of situations as "natural outcomes" of a political process dominated by incumbent telephone companies that also tries to protect rural cooperatives. Thus, we are led to believe that these "merely political" situations are beyond the ability of most persons to understand much less change. Plainly, policy analysis can give us important resources to identify such situations, connect such regulatory arcana to ill effects on citizens, clarify the competing goods at issue (e.g., expanded net access in rural areas and protection of rural telephone cooperatives), and identify alternative modes of thinking about such conflicts. Telecommunications policy analysis, for example, clearly demonstrates how telecommunications service areas are daunting admixtures of telephone exchanges, carrier service areas, wire centers, counties, school districts, local governmental entities, LATAs (Local Access and Transport Areas), ISPs, communities, and businesses. It is the nature of carrier territories as both commercial and political boundaries (Nicholas, 2000, p. 215) that demands the use of policy analytic techniques. Dismissing the "merely political" precludes any such insight.

What is the Value of the Rhetorical?

The term "rhetoric" exhibits a similar problematic: "Mass media commentators often use [rhetoric] to mean 'hot air' or 'lies'" (Campbell, 1996, p. 3) or make easy contrasts between rhetoric and rationality, rhetoric and "truth." We use or hear expressions such as "That was only a rhetorical exercise," that is, it was simply a means for doing nothing but talking; "I was tired of her rhetoric," that is, the speaker was only posing instead of "really communicating;" or "It was rhetorical, all style and no substance." This common-sense and dismissive attitude of the rhetorical, like our attitude toward the political, springs from a number of sources. Among the most important are the contested nature of rhetoric in Western thought. While Aristotle's *On Rhetoric* is commonly seen as the first major scholarly work on rhetoric, his teacher Plato successfully denigrated the sophists and their reliance on public, persuasive acts (Burke, 1969; Hobart and Schiffman, 1998; Nelson, et al., 1987). Indeed, Plato's literal abhorrence of rhetoric stemmed from its lack of absolute moorings for knowledge and its lack of "a final referential language" (Lanham, 1993, p. 146). Plato and others in the Western tradition looking for absolute knowledge or some absolute ground on which to build knowledge (the business that most philosophers, scientists, and scholars have said they were in) won the battle for our hearts and minds. For us, knowledge is ordinarily affiliated with words such as "certainty," "proof," "universal," "permanence," and "unassailable." Thus, rhetoric's assertion of the localized, temporal, and contingent seems somewhat foreign and not trustworthy, despite rhetoric's millennia-long tradition in the West.

A second source of our dismissive attitude toward the rhetorical is a related epistemology: naive empiricism that eschews a more integrated, realist epistemology that recognizes the real is "made up of both what we see and how we explain what we see" (Mosco, 1996, p. 2; and see Burke, 1969; Lanham, 1993). A third obstacle to our fuller embrace of the rhetorical is discomfort with the concept of multiple social roles of individuals. Rhetoric, as a practice and as the study of that practice, informs us how communication allows the rhetor to adopt multiple *personae*, voices, and perspectives, especially to adopt a public role or roles not coincident with the private self. As Lanham (1993, p. 219) notes: "We have in America always resisted a formal public self and society: that represented the kind of European insincerity America meant to escape." The fourth source to note here is our contemporary aversion to the serious study of rhetoric because of our identification of persuasion with political propaganda, subliminal suggestion, and the worst excesses of advertising, especially in political campaigns. This aversion is particularly grounded in our horror of modern warfare, modern right-wing and left-wing totalitarian states, and the dystopias built on political propaganda such as those in Orwell's *1984* and Huxley's *Brave New World*. Thus, we tend to ignore the strengths of rhetoric in social etiquette, courtship, education, the sermon, and community formation, definition, and maintenance (Burke, 1969; Carey, 1988).

Policy Analysis: Uniting the Political and Rhetorical

Nelson (1987, p. 215) is a good example of research that describes the special tie that has always existed between politics and rhetoric. In fact, he notes that the first meaning of political science was what we now recognize as the discipline of rhetoric—the concentrated study of speech, persuasion, symbols, symbolic exchanges, deception, metaphors, and mutual influence among persons (Campbell, 1996; Dobuzinskis, 1992). The political is rhetorical at its heart, and, therefore, policy analysis is as well. Since the 1950s, interest in rhetoric as a discipline has experienced a rebirth (Nelson, et al., 1987), and that rebirth reminds us that policy analysis is intended explicitly to be persuasive. Somewhat ironically, according to some interpretations of the classical paradigm of the field, policy analysis aspires to be persuasive by *not* taking an advocacy position. As discussed above, policy analysis is advocative and rhetorical even as it claims not to be, demonstrating Burke's assertion that "a rhetorical motive is often present where it is not usually recognized, or thought to belong" (1969, xiii).

This point shows how this linguistic discussion is much more than an aside. Instead, it is central to considering the question of how policy analysis can inform the evaluation of networked information services. A contextualized understanding of the political and the rhetorical aspects of policy analysis reveals to us important characteristics of networked information services. For example, how one communicates is partially constitutive of the communication and its effects on the audience, enabling us to go beyond the simplistic content/conduit distinction and the limited view of computer networks as only information distribution mechanisms (Carey, 1988; Dervin, 1989; Hobart and Schiffman, 1998, Part III; Lanham, 1993; Nicholas 2000).

Further, we can recognize the role of the audience as creative, engaged, collaborative with the rhetor in the communication act (Campbell, 1996). The networked communicator aggregates and characterizes an audience, thereby forming and reaffirming social ties. Networked services that undermine these rhetorical, communal functions are seriously flawed. The policy analyst and evaluator is also a rhetor who tells a story, a narrative that seeks to explain, legitimate, and "acts as a symbolic means of inducing cooperation" in persons who, by their nature, respond to symbols (Burke, 1969, p. 43; see also Eco,

1979). The analyst wants to form her audience's attitudes and move her audience to act, not just policy makers but fellow citizens as well.

In addition, rhetorical and political perspectives point us to community as an essential component in networked information services, both as a pre-condition and an outcome of such services. As widely recognized, any perspective on computer networks that does not include an understanding of community as central to digital life is incomplete. Even more seriously, such a perspective leaves us with only individual, atomistic actors, driven by self-absorption. A more complete understanding of networked information services springs from the recognition that rhetoric is not simply the study of persuasion; it aims to constitute an audience, a community that shares perspective(s), values, and commitment to communal action. This aspect of the rhetorical builds upon and contributes to our understanding of politics as the art of living together, of forming and maintaining community, often in the face of conflict among perspectives.

CONCLUSION

Policies imply theories (Rist, 1994, p. 550, citing Pressman and Wildavsky's *Implementation*, [1984]): e.g., theories of causality, social action, identity, social relations, social conflicts, and relations between the state and other institutions. Policy analysis that combines traditional and alternative methods offers the greatest promise of rigorous, effective, and holistic research about information policies and their implicit theories. Further, this combination makes it much more likely that policy analysis can achieve its two major goals of informing the creation of social policy and the support of participatory democratic initiatives. Like Lévi-Strauss' *bricoleur*, post-positivist policy analysts must improvise, using the resources at hand, especially stories/counterstories, meanings, and frame conflicts. As Suchman (1987, p. 183) notes, policy analysts as social scientists must make constructive use of trouble, gaps, breakdowns, and misunderstandings, one of the greatest contributions of Heidegger to contemporary social science (Winograd and Flores, 1987, pp. 36–37 and 68–69). Using language reminiscent of Dervin and other communication and information science researchers, Suchman calls for a fundamental change in research perspective so that (p. 179):

> [T]he contingence of action on a complex world of objects, artifacts, and other actors, located in space and time, is no longer treated as an extraneous problem with which the individual actor must contend, but rather is sees as the essential resource that makes knowledge possible and gives action its sense.

Thus, this mode of research is inductive, naturalistic, and holistic, and it recognizes that meaning is neither predetermined (as in mechanistic models) nor entirely random. Steinberger (1995) echoes this series of assumptions and methods in discussing meaning making and policy analysis. He emphasizes that ambiguity and conflict in policy meanings are not defects in comprehension, rather they are significant and unavoidable characteristics of public policy. Thus, our inability to define "the" meaning of policy is a constitutive, evocative element of analysis, not simply an obstacle. Policies have different meanings for different participants in the policy process, and such meanings are ambiguous and manipulable, not self-evident (p. 223).

Since the technical change related to networked information is complex, unpredictable, and emergent, we need to go beyond the mechanistic models of neoclassical economics and the tradition of technological assessment that assume that the market and technical expertise, respectively, can guide technology, its evolution, its "effects," and its uses. So we are left with the question of how to evaluate technical developments. What Thompson (1997) suggests is the reduction of technical inflexibility, not increased insistence on predictability of socio-technical systems. We need to grow beyond our unfounded belief in the rationalizing, standardizing "empirical or hegemonic planning mentality that excludes the necessary role of local knowledge and know-how" (Scott, 1998, p. 6). Policy analysis generally must overcome this misplaced belief in ratiocination, while still holding to the rigor and strength of its traditional rationality project. Winograd and Flores (1987, pp. 164–174) provide useful insight into how using Heidegger's and others' work on breakdowns and problems can lead us to important understandings of sophisticated information systems. What is especially important is that trouble helps us to examine our preconceptions about out projects and the premises on which we operate. Thus, certain kinds of trouble, or self-conscious rhetorical examination of frame conflicts, provide important opportunities for learning about networked information.

Policy analysis must continue its evolution to a more ethnomethodologically informed, rhetorically self-conscious, frame-sensitive, and narratively formed discipline. As it does so, it will grow more valuable to the understanding of networked information services and making them better. Information policy analysis, in particular, must be more value-critical, methodologically rigorous and self-conscious, post-positivist, and more attentive to similar themes in policy studies generally (Browne 1997a and 1997b; Rowlands, 1996). More specifically, policy analytic evaluation of networked information products and services can combine commitment by the analyst to a user perspective and commitment to open and responsive policy making.

One of the most fundamental of critiques of the dominant positivist model of policy analysis is the accusation that policy research is only peripheral to policy making, that it has been used only to support or undermine a position reached through other means (de Leon, 1993). Certainly, there are multiple and conflicting influences beyond policy analysis on the making of a political decision, and policy analysis has considerable weaknesses. Policy analysis, however, must be able to play a role in policy making if it is to maintain any credibility as an academic discipline and any claim to affirming dignity, democracy, and citizens' values. A particularly damning critique is noted in Dunn (1994, p. 56, citing Laurence Tribe as well as others). Because of the political influence that policy analysis seeks to have and the intellectually and social conservatism of many analyses:

> Policy analysis ... has been characterized as a conservative and superficial kind of social science which fails to pose radical questions about basic social values and institutions and neglects policy alternatives that depart significantly from existing practices. Under such conditions it is understandable that professional policy analysts may be used as instruments of everyday politics.

Such an accusation stems in part from the predominance in policy analysis of disjointed incrementalism, interest group pluralism, limited rationality, a naïve belief in the marketplace of ideas, and narrow views of what is politically feasible. It also explains the insistence of alternative policy analysts that policy research must include examining goals, questioning how policies can reach chosen goals rather than taking policies as givens, being more sensitive to values, and looking at outcomes critically and from multiple perspectives (Nagel, 1988). White (1994), Majchrzak (1984), Majone (1989), and Dunn (1994) also insist on the role of the policy analyst as the catalyst for revealing the value conflicts that underlie policy issues. Thus, policy analysis is successful if it is able to help us further understand the complexity of policy issues, especially to demonstrate the frame conflicts that contextualize such issues.

A particular point of interest for evaluating networked information is policy analysis' ambivalent attitude toward the state as the "vexed institution that is the ground of both our freedoms and our unfreedoms" (Scott, 1998, p. 345). Among other things, policy analysis can remind us that we cannot dismiss the state and other important institutions, nor can we accede to their demands. Better still, policy analysis can provide us with specific political, rhetorical, and conceptual strategies to maximize the value of our social institutions while limiting the oppressive damage they do. Perhaps that is one of the greatest contribution that policy analysis can make to the conversation about networked information. Recognition of the constitutive role of the stories we tell, the metaphors we use, and the policy problems we create shows us how value conflicts are tools for the policy analyst. Such conflicts are not frustrations to analysis; they are catalysts for it and its raw material. If nothing else, the evaluation of networked information services exhibits such fundamental value conflicts.

At the heart of both networked information technologies and policy analysis is the creation of meaning in communities. Thus, policy analysis must take its place among the several disciplines that contribute to the evaluation of networked information services. These disciplines, like the policy analysis described in this chapter, put their research emphasis on (1) the user of networked technologies grounded in a social setting; (2) the naturalistic investigation of technologies' situated uses, meanings, and related practices; and (3) the achievement of democratic, participatory design and social relations. The policy analytic activities of problem structuring, forecasting, making recommendations, monitoring policy outcomes, evaluating alternative courses of action, and communicating with stakeholders beyond decision makers can make important and unique contributions to such evaluation. The identification of stakeholders and the value conflicts that characterize networked information are among its chief contributions.

Ethnographic, narratively-sensitive, and historically-responsive policy analysis gives us the "on-the-ground" perspective demanded for addressing the challenges and possibilities of networked information. The complexity of policy problems related to networked information and the concomitant responsibility of policy analysts demand no less.

ABOUT THE AUTHOR

Philip Doty is an Associate Professor at the Graduate School of Library and Information Science at the University of Texas at Austin, which he joined in 1992. He is also an Associate Director of the Telecommunications and Information Policy Institute at the University, a multi-disciplinary center for the study of information and telecommunications policy and the advising of public decision makers in Texas and elsewhere. His research and teaching focus on Federal information policy, copyright, privacy, computer networks, research methods, and cultural aspects of information technologies. He has done research sponsored by a number of Federal and state entities and can be reached at the Graduate School of Library and Information Science, SZB 564, University of Texas at Austin, Austin, TX 78712-1276.

E-mail: pdoty@gslis.utexas.edu

REFERENCES

Abbate, Janet. (1999). Inventing the Internet. Cambridge, MA: MIT Press.

Anderson, Charles W. (1987). The Human sciences and the liberal polity in rhetorical relationship. In Nelson, John S., Megill, Allan, and McCloskey, Donald N. (Eds.) The Rhetoric of the Human Sciences: Language and Argument in Scholarship and Public Affairs (pp. 341–362). Madison, WI: University of Wisconsin Press.

Aufderheide, Patricia. (1999). Communications Policy and the Public Interest. New York: Guilford Press.

Bobrow, Davis, and Dryzek, John. (1987). Policy Analysis by Design. Pittsburgh, PA: University of Pittsburgh Press.

Branscomb, Anne Wells. (1994). Who Owns Information? From Privacy to Public Access. New York: BasicBooks.

Brown, John Seely and Duguid, Paul. (1991). Organizational learning and communities-of-practice: Toward a unified view of working, learning, and innovation. Organization Science, 2(1): 40–57.

Browne, Mairéad. (1997a). The field of information policy: 1. Fundamental concepts. Journal of Information Science, 23(4): 261–275.

Browne, Mairéad. (1997b). The field of information policy: 2. Redefining the boundaries and methodologies. Journal of Information Science, 23(5): 339–351.

Bruner, Jerome S. (1990). Acts of Meaning. Cambridge, MA: Harvard University Press.

Burke, Kenneth. (1969). A Rhetoric of Motives. Berkeley, CA: University of California Press. (Originally published 1950)

Campbell, Karlyn Kohrs. (1996). The Rhetorical Act, 2nd ed. Belmont, CA: Wadsworth Publishing.

Carey, James W. (1988). Communication as Culture: Essays on Media and Society. Boston: Unwin Hyman.

de Leon, Peter. (1993). Democracy and the policy sciences: Aspirations and operations. Policy Studies Journal, 22(21): 200–212.

de Leon, Peter. (1994). Reinventing the policy sciences: Three steps back to the future. Policy Sciences, 27(1): 77–95.

Dervin, Brenda. (1989). Users as research inventions: How research categories perpetuate inequities. Journal of Communication, 39(3): 216–232.

Dewey, John. (1927). The Public and its Problems. New York: Henry Holt and Co.

Dewey, John. (1939). Intelligence in the Modern World: John Dewey's Philosophy. Edited and with an introduction by Joseph Ratner. New York: Modern Library.

Dobuzinskis, Laurent. (1992). Modernist and postmodernist metaphors of the policy process: Control and stability vs. chaos and reflexive understanding. Policy Sciences, 25(4): 355–380.

Doty, Philip. (2001, forthcoming). Digital privacy: Towards a new politics and discursive practice. In Williams, Martha (Ed.) Annual Review of Information Science and Technology. Medford, NJ: Information Today.

Dror, Yehezkel. (1994). Basic concepts in advanced policy sciences. In Nagel, Stuart S.(Ed.) Encyclopedia of Policy Studies, 2nd ed., revised and expanded) (pp. 1–30). New York: Marcel Dekker.

Dunn, William N. (1994). Public Policy Analysis: An Introduction, 2nd ed. Englewood Cliffs, NJ: Prentice-Hall.

Dye, Thomas R. (1995). Understanding Public Policy, 8th ed. Englewood Cliffs, NJ: Prentice-Hall.

Easton, David. (1965). A Framework for Political Analysis. Chicago: University of Chicago Press.

Eco, Umberto. (1979). The Role of the Reader: Explorations in the Semiotics of Texts. Bloomington, IN: Indiana University Press.

Edwards, Paul N. (1996). The Closed World: Computers and the Politics of Discourse in Cold War America. Cambridge, MA: MIT Press.

Fischer, Frank and Forester, John. (Eds.), The Argumentative Turn in Policy Analysis and Planning. Durham, NC: Duke University Press.

Flamm, Kenneth. (1988). Creating the Computer: Government, Industry and High Technology. Washington, DC: Brookings Institution.

Glendon, Mary Ann. (1991). Rights Talk: The Impoverishment of Political Discourse. New York: The Free Press.

Heclo, Hugh. (1995). Issue networks and the executive establishment. In McCool, Daniel C. (Ed.) Public Policy Theories, Models, and Concepts: An anthology (pp. 262–287). Englewood Cliffs, NJ: Prentice-Hall. (Originally published 1978)

Hobart, Michael E. and Schiffman, Zachary S. (1998). Information Ages: Literacy, Numeracy, and the Computer Revolution. Baltimore, MD: The Johns Hopkins University Press.

Jones, Charles O. (1984). An Introduction to the Study of Public Policy, 3rd ed. Monterey, CA: Brooks/Cole.

Kaplan, Abraham. (1964). The Conduct of Inquiry: Methodology for Behavioral Science. New York: Harper and Row.

Klamer, Arjo. (1987). As if economists and their subjects were rational. In Nelson, John S., Megill, Allan, and McCloskey, Donald N. (Eds.) The Rhetoric of the Human Sciences: Language and Argument in Scholarship and Public Affairs (pp. 163–183). Madison, WI: University of Wisconsin Press.

Kling, Rob. (1996). Hopes and horrors: Technological utopianism and anti-utopicanism in narratives of computerization. In Kling, Rob (Ed.) Computerization and Controversy: Value Conflicts and Social Choices. 2nd ed, (pp. 40–58). San Diego, CA: Academic Press.

Lanham, Richard A. (1993). The Electronic Word: Democracy, Technology, and the Arts. Chicago: University of Chicago Press.

Lasswell, Harold. (1951). The policy orientation. In Lernet, Daniel and Lasswell, Harold (Eds.) The Policy Sciences (pp. 3–15). Stanford, CA: Stanford University Press.

Laudon, Kenneth C. (1996). Markets and privacy. Communications of the ACM, 39(9): 92–104.

Lindblom, Charles E. and Woodhouse, Edward J. (1993). The Policy-making Process, 3rd ed. Englewood Cliffs, NJ: Prentice-Hall.

MacMullin, Susan, and Taylor, Robert. (1984). Problem dimensions and information traits. The Information Society, 3(1): 91–111.

Majchrzak, Ann. (1984). Methods for Policy Research. Newbury Park, CA: Sage Publications.

Majone, Giandomenico. (1989). Evidence, Argument, and Persuasion in the Policy Process. New Haven, CT: Yale University Press.

McCool, Daniel C. (Ed.) (1995). Public Policy Theories, Models, and Concepts: An Anthology. Englewood Cliffs, NJ: Prentice-Hall.

Mitchell, W. J. T. (1994). Picture Theory: Essays on Verbal and Visual Representation. Chicago: University of Chicago Press.

Mosco, Vincent. (1996). The Political Economy of Communication: Rethinking and Renewal. Thousand Oaks, CA: Sage Publications.

Nagel, Stuart S. (1988). Policy Studies: Integration and Evaluation. New York: Praeger.

Nagel, Stuart S. (Ed.) (1994a). Encyclopedia of Policy Studies, 2nd ed., revised and expanded. New York: Marcel Dekker.

Nagel, Stuart S. (1994b). Introduction to the first edition. In Nagel, Stuart S. (Ed.) Encyclopedia of Policy Studies, 2nd ed., revised and expanded (pp. xi–xviii). New York: Marcel Dekker.

Nagel, Stuart S. (1994c). Systematic policy evaluation. In Nagel, Stuart S. (Ed.) Encyclopedia of Policy Studies, 2nd ed., revised and expanded (pp. 31–48). New York: Marcel Dekker.

Nagel, Stuart S. (1994d). Epilog: Projecting trends in public policy. In Nagel, Stuart S. (Ed.) Encyclopedia of Policy Studies, 2nd ed., revised and expanded (pp. 879–913). New York: Marcel Dekker.

Nardi, Bonnie A., and O'Day, Vicki L. (1999). Information Ecologies: Using Technology with Heart. Cambridge, MA: MIT Press.

National Research Council. Committee on Intellectual Property Rights in the Emerging Information Infrastructure. (2000). The digital dilemma: Intellectual property in the Information Age. Washington, DC: National Academy Press.

Nelson, John S. (1987). Stories of science and politics: Some rhetorics of political research. In Nelson, John S., Megill, Allan, and McCloskey, Donald N. (Eds.) The Rhetoric of the Human Sciences: Language and Argument in Scholarship and Public Affairs (pp. 198–220). Madison, WI: University of Wisconsin Press.

Nelson, John S.; Megill, Allan; and McCloskey, Donald N. (1987). Rhetoric of inquiry. In Nelson, John S., Megill, Allan, and McCloskey, Donald N. (Eds.) The Rhetoric of the Human Sciences: Language and Argument in Scholarship and Public Affairs (pp. 3–18). Madison, WI: University of Wisconsin Press.

Nicholas, Kyle. (2000). Digital Arroyos and Imaginary Fences: Assessing the Impact of Public Policy, Communication Technologies, and Commercial Investment on Internet Access in Rural Texas. Unpublished doctoral dissertation. Austin, TX: University of Texas at Austin.

Rist, Ray C. (1994). Influencing the policy process with qualitative research. In Denzin, Norman K. and Lincoln, Yvonna S. (Eds.) Handbook of Qualitative Research (pp. 545–557). Thousand Oaks, CA: Sage Publications.

Roe, Emery. (1994). Narrative Policy Analysis: Theory and Practice. Durham, NC: Duke University Press.

Rowlands, Ian. (1996). Understanding information policy: Concepts, frameworks and research tools. Journal of Information Science, 22(1): 13-25.

Schön, Donald A. (1983). The Reflective Practitioner. New York: BasicBooks.

Schön, Donald A. (1993). Generative metaphor: A perspective on problem-setting in social policy. In Andrew Ortony (Ed.), Metaphor and Thought, 2nd ed. (pp. 137–163). Cambridge, UK: Cambridge University Press.

Schram, Sanford F., and Neisser, Philip T. (1997). Tales of the State: Narrative in Contemporary U.S. Politics and Public Policy. Lanham, MD: Rowman and Littlefield.

Scott, James C. (1998). Seeing like a State: How Certain Schemes to Improve the Human Condition Have Failed. New Haven, CT: Yale University Press.

Shapiro, Michael J. (1987). The rhetoric of social science: The political responsibilities of the scholar. In Nelson, John S., Megill, Allan, and McCloskey, Donald N. (Eds.) The Rhetoric of the Human Sciences: Language and Argument in Scholarship and Public Affairs (pp. 363–380). Madison, WI: University of Wisconsin Press.

Shapiro, Michael J. (1988). The Politics of Representation: Writing Practices in Biography, Photography, and Policy Analysis. Madison, WI: University of Wisconsin Press.

Shapiro, Michael J. (1992). Reading the Postmodern Polity: Political Theory as Textual Practice. Minneapolis, MN: University of Minnesota Press.

Steinberger, Peter J. (1995). Typologies of public policy: Meaning construction and the policy process. In McCool, Daniel C. (Ed.) Public Policy Theories, Models, and Concepts An Anthology (pp. 220–233). Englewood Cliffs, NJ: Prentice-Hall. (Originally published 1980)

Strover, Sharon, (2000). The first mile. The Information Society, 16(2): 151–154.

Suchman, Lucy A. (1987). Plans and Situated Actions: The Problem of Human-Machine Communication. Cambridge, UK: Cambridge University Press.

Taylor, Robert S. (1986). Value-Added Processes in Information Systems. Norwood, NJ: Ablex.

Theodoulou, Stella Z. (1995a). The contemporary language of public policy: A starting point. In Theodoulou, Stella Z. and Cahn, Matthew A. (Eds.) Public Policy: The Essential Readings (pp. 1–9). Englewood Cliffs, NJ: Prentice-Hall.

Theodoulou, Stella Z. (1995b). How public policy is made. In Theodoulou, Stella Z. and Cahn, Matthew A. (Eds.), Public Policy: The Essential Readings (pp. 86–96). Englewood Cliffs, NJ: Prentice-Hall.

Theodoulou, Stella Z and Cahn, Matthew A. (Eds.) (1995). Public Policy: The Essential Readings. Englewood Cliffs, NJ: Prentice-Hall.

Thomson, Judith Jarvis. (1984). The right to privacy. In Ferdinand David Schoeman (Ed.) Philosophical Dimensions of Privacy: An Anthology (pp. 272–289). Cambridge, UK: Cambridge University Press. (Originally published 1975)

Thomson, Judith Jarvis. (1990). The Realm of Rights. Cambridge, MA: Harvard University Press.

Thompson, Michael. (1997). Rewriting the precepts of policy analysis. In Ellis, Richard J. and Thompson, Michael (Eds.), Culture Matters: Essays in Honor of Aaron Wildavsky (pp. 203–216). Boulder, CO: Westview Press.

Weick, Karl E. (1995). Sensemaking in Organizations. Thousand Oaks, CA: Sage Publications.

Wenger, Étienne. (1998). Communities of Practice: Learning, Meaning, and Identity. Cambridge, UK: Cambridge University Press.

White, Louise G. (1994). Values, ethics, and standards in policy analysis. In Nagel, Stuart S. (Ed.) Encyclopedia of Policy Studies 2nd ed. revised and expanded (pp. 857–878). New York: Marcel Dekker.

Winograd, Terry, and Flores, Fernando. (1987). Understanding Computers and Cognition: A New Foundation for Design. Reading, MA: Addison-Wesley.

Chapter 12

Using U.S. Information Policies to Evaluate Federal Web Sites

Charles R. McClure
J. Timothy Sprehe

ABSTRACT

This chapter demonstrates the importance of identifying and describing the U.S. information policy system as a basis for assessing federal Web sites. The quality of a federal Web site depends, in part, on the degree to which the Web site complies with existing policy. There is a large and significant amount of information policy that affects federal Web site development and operations. These policies are identified and described. The chapter suggests that identifying and describing the information policy environment is a key component for evaluating federal Web sites.

INTRODUCTION

Federal information policies establish the legal and procedural framework in which government information and services are made available to the public. "An information policy instrument is a written law, guideline, regulation, or other official statement that describes how information will be collected, managed, protected, accessed, disseminated, and used" (McClure 1999, 307). The information policy system of the U.S. federal government has a significant impact on agency Web site development and management.

Because of the complexity of this policy system there has been no systematic description of the policies that can be used to evaluate the degree to which agencies comply with specific policy instruments affecting the development of their Web sites. Without such a description it is impossible to assess the degree to which agencies comply with the policies since many federal Webmasters are unfamiliar with the extent to which these policies exist. Thus, identifying and describing the information policy system that affects federal Web sites is an essential first step in determining the degree to which the agencies are in compliance with the policies.

The purpose of this chapter is to offer an overview that describes the policy instruments that affect federal Web site development and management. This description suggests that there is significant complexity in this information policy system. In addition, the chapter suggests the importance of descriptive policy assessment in the overall process of evaluating networked information services and resources. As such, the chapter builds upon the techniques and approaches outlined for descriptive policy analysis by McClure, Moen, and Bertot (1999).

While specific references to the Internet or the World Wide Web may not appear in a given policy instrument, this does not necessarily mean the policy has no application to federal Web sites. These instruments are directed toward federal government procedures and operations in the context of federal information and/or Information Technology (IT), and thus would apply to federal Web sites unless special rules require otherwise.

This listing is not comprehensive but rather offers a general sense of the range of existing federal policies that should be considered in the development, management, and evaluation of Web sites. Where possible, citations to Web-based sources of information regarding a particular policy are provided,[1] as are selected excerpts of the policy that may be of interest to federal Web designers, managers, and evaluators.

The selection of policies could be extended much more broadly. For example, the chapter does not include the area of electronic commerce. Federal agencies do use their Web sites for selling goods and services, and electronic buying of goods and services is a major thrust in the Federal procurement community. Readers who wish to explore the area of federal e-commerce are referred to http://www.e-commerce.gov.

A number of methods can be used to identify policy instruments related to a particular topic such as federal Web site development and management. As in the case here, emphasis was placed on policy instruments developed since 1990 to provide a limited scope. Traditional bibliographic database searching via a number of appropriate databases was employed by knowledgeable information professionals. The authors also queried key informants and policymakers in various federal agencies as to policy instruments affecting Web sites. They were also asked to identify other individuals who might have additional information regarding such policy instruments—who were then queried by the authors. Finally, draft versions of this descriptive assessment were reviewed by knowledgeable individuals to determine if additional policy instruments had been overlooked.

The policy instruments are organized in a schematic outline, moving from general government policy to general information policy and then to specific information policies. Within each heading occurs a listing of statutory policies and implementing policy guidance. It is within this context that federal agencies develop and manage their Web sites for providing government information and services, which must also meet the agencies' mission statements, objectives, and goals. Any evaluation of federal Web sites must take into consideration the information policy environment that affects the development and management of these Web sites.

Federal information policy and agency Web site development occur in a dynamic environment. Technological changes impacting on established information policies or creation of new ones occur rapidly, but federal agencies often must adjust their operations almost immediately. Policy tends to follow technology and practice. Sometimes the lag between policy and practice can be great, so that agencies must craft their own policies to rationalize practices before Congress enacts new laws.

I. GENERAL GOVERNMENT POLICY

A. Government Performance and Results: Performance Plans and Measures

1. **STATUTE: Government Performance and Results Act of 1993. (Public Law 103-62).** Available at http://thomas.loc.gov/cgi-bin/bdquery/ z?d103:SN00020: | TOM:bss/d103query.html

Application to Federal Information Technology and Web Management:

The Government Performance and Results Act of 1993 (GPRA) is intended to help reduce waste and inefficiency in federal programs and federal agency operations. It is also designed to assist Congress and the Executive in their oversight, legislative, and administrative tasks related to authorizing, appropriating, and implementing federal services. GPRA mandates the adoption of a strategic and annual planning process, which is tied to budget and authorization cycles and will be based on established and measurable performance indicators for every program. Although this act was made law prior to the expansion and wide public use of the Internet, particularly the Web, the mandate for the development of performance indicators tied to annual budgeting and strategic planning applies to services offered in an electronic environment. Performance indicators for federal Web sites consist of measures that permit an agency to demonstrate whether its Web sites are or are not meeting the performance goals set forth for the sites. Performance measures could include things such as log transaction files and impact measurements.

Excerpt of Original Text from Policy Instrument:

Section 3. Strategic Planning

Chapter 3 of title 5, United States Code, is amended by adding after section 305 the following new section:

Sec. 306. Strategic plans

(a) No later than September 30, 1997, the head of each agency shall submit to the Director of the Office of Management and Budget and to the Congress a strategic plan for program activities. Such plan shall contain—

* * *

(3) a description of how the goals and objectives are to be achieved, including a description of the operational processes, skills and technology, and the human, capital, information, and other resources required to meet those goals and objectives;

* * *

(6) a description of the program evaluations used in establishing or revising general goals and objectives, with a schedule for future program evaluations.

* * *

Section 4. Annual Performance Plans and Reports

* * *

(b) PERFORMANCE PLANS AND REPORTS—Chapter 11 of title 31, United States Code, is amended by adding after section 1114 the following new sections:

Sec. 1115. Performance plans

(a) In carrying out the provisions of section 1105(a)(29), the Director of the Office of Management and Budget shall require each agency to prepare an annual performance plan covering each program activity set forth in the budget of such agency. Such plan shall—

(1) establish performance goals to define the level of performance to be achieved by a program activity;

(2) express such goals in an objective, quantifiable, and measurable form unless authorized to be in an alternative form under subsection (b);

(3) briefly describe the operational processes, skills and technology, and the human, capital, information, or other resources required to meet the performance goals;

(4) establish performance indicators to be used in measuring or assessing the relevant outputs, service levels, and outcomes of each program activity;

(5) provide a basis for comparing actual program results with the established performance goals; and

(6) describe the means to be used to verify and validate measured values.

2. **IMPLEMENTING GUIDANCE: OMB Circular No. A-11, Part II, Preparation and Submission of Strategic Plans, Annual Performance Plans, and Annual Program Performance Reports** Available at http://www.whitehouse.gov/omb/circulars/a11/99toc.html

Application to Federal Information Technology and Web Management:

OMB Circular No. A-11, issued annually, instructs federal agencies how they are to submit their budget requests for two years hence; that is, in fiscal year (FY) 2000 agencies submit budget requests for FY 2002. Part II was added to Circular A-11 after the passage of the Government Performance and Results Act. It sets forth detailed procedural guidance for formulating the agencies' annual performance plans and describes what agencies are to include in their annual program performance report. Included in Part II is the requirement for program performance goals and the enumeration of the performance measures agencies will use to assess their relative success or failure in achieving performance goals. Part II is the basic federal policy guidance regarding performance measures in general, as applied to all Executive Branch programs, and has applicability to federal Web sites.

B. **Customer Service Standards: Setting Customer Service Standards. (Executive Order 12862). 1993.** Available at http://www.pub.whitehouse.gov/uri-res/I2R?urn:pdi://oma.eop.gov.us/1993/9/14/3.text.2

Application to Federal Information Technology and Web Management:

Although this Executive Order does not specifically address Customer Service Standards in an electronic environment, federal agency Web site development teams still need to identify their customers, their customers' needs, and set standards and benchmarks.

Excerpt of Original Text from Policy Instrument:

Sec. 1. Customer Service Standards.
* * *

All executive departments and agencies (hereinafter referred to collectively as "agency" or "agencies") that provide significant services directly to the public shall provide those services in a manner that seeks to meet the customer service standard established herein and shall take the following actions:

- identify the customers who are, or should be, served by the agency;
- survey customers to determine the kind and quality of services they want and their level of satisfaction with existing services;
- post service standards and measure results against them;
- benchmark customer service performance against the best in business;
- survey front-line employees on barriers to, and ideas for, matching the best in business;
- provide customers with choices in both the sources of service and the means of delivery;
- make information, services, and complaint systems easily accessible; and
- provide means to address customer complaints.

Provisions of the Executive Order also require agencies to have a "Customer Service Plan," to develop assessment techniques to gauge the success of the plans, and to report on the degree to which the plan is being accomplished.

C. Accessible Electronic and Information Technology

Rehabilitation Act of 1973 (Pub. L. 93-112), section 508 (added by the Rehabilitation Act Amendments of 1986, Pub. L. 99–506, section 603(a), codified as amended at 29 U.S.C. § 794d). 1998. Available at http://frWebgate.access.gpo.gov/cgibin/getdoc.cgi?dbname=1994_uscode_suppl_4anddocid=29usc794d

Application to Federal Information Technology and Web Management:

Section 508 requires that federal agencies' electronic and information technology be accessible to people with disabilities, including employees and members of the public. It also establishes requirements for any electronic and information technology developed, maintained, procured, or used by the federal government. The Attorney General must determine and communicate what information is necessary from federal agencies to conduct evaluations of their current electronic and information technology systems' accessibility. Agencies must then evaluate the accessibility of their IT to individuals with disabilities. In addition, by February 7, 2000, the Architectural and Transportation Barriers Compliance Board is required to issue standards that define which electronic and information technology is covered and describe what is meant by "accessible technology" by setting forth technical and functional performance criteria. The deadline for issuing of the Standards has been extended to August 7, 2000. Federal agency Web site development teams can find additional information at the Center for IT Accommodation (CITA) to aid in their design of Web sites accessible to people with disabilities. CITA is available at http://www.itpolicy.gsa.gov/cita/index.htm.

Excerpt of Original Text from Policy Instrument:

(a) Requirements for Federal departments and agencies

(1) Accessibility

(A) Development, procurement, maintenance, or use of electronic and information technology

When developing, procuring, maintaining, or using electronic and information technology, each Federal department or agency, including the United States Postal Service, shall ensure, unless an undue burden would be imposed on the department or agency, that the electronic and information technology allows, regardless of the type of medium of the technology—

(i) individuals with disabilities who are Federal employees to have access to and use of information and data that is comparable to the access to and use of the information and data by Federal employees who are not individuals with disabilities; and

(ii) individuals with disabilities who are members of the public seeking information or services from a Federal department or agency to have access to and use of information and data that is comparable to the access to and use of the information and data by such members of the public who are not individuals with disabilities.

* * *

(c) Agency evaluations

Not later than six months after the date of enactment of the Rehabilitation Act Amendments of 1998, the head of each Federal department or agency shall evaluate the extent to which the electronic and information technology of the department or agency is accessible to and usable by individuals with disabilities described in subsection (a)(1), compared to the access to and use of the technology by individuals described in such subsection who are not individuals with disabilities, and submit a report containing the evaluation to the Attorney General.

D. President's Memorandum on Electronic Government. December 17,1999. Available at http://www.pub.whitehouse.gov/uri-res/I2R?urn:pdi://oma.eop.gov.us/1999/12/20/5.text.1

Application to Federal Information Technology and Web Management:

President Clinton announced twelve actions that federal agencies can take in conjunction with private industry to provide American citizens with improved access to government services and information. The President desired federal agencies to provide standardized access to government information and services. People should be able to find needed government information without needing to know what agency is responsible for disseminating the information. People should also be confident that that their communication with government is secure and their privacy protected.

Excerpt of Original Text from Policy Instrument:

2. The heads of executive departments and agencies (agencies) shall, to the maximum extent possible, make available online,

by December 2000, the forms needed for the top 500 Government services used by the public. Under the Government Paperwork Elimination Act, where appropriate, by October 2003, transactions with the federal government should be available online for online processing of services. To achieve this goal, the Director of the Office of Management and Budget (OMB) shall oversee agency development of responsible strategies to make transactions available online.

4. The heads of agencies shall continue to build good privacy practices into their Web sites by posting privacy policies as directed by the Director of the Office of Management and Budget and by adopting and implementing information policies to protect children's information on Web sites that are directed at children.

5. The head of each agency shall permit greater access to its officials by creating a public electronic mail address through which citizens can contact the agency with questions, comments, or concerns. The heads of each agency shall also provide disability access on federal Web sites.

7. The Secretaries of Health and Human Services, Education, Veterans Affairs, and Agriculture, the Commissioner of Social Security, and the Director of the Federal Emergency Management Agency, working closely with other Federal agencies that provide benefit assistance to citizens, shall make a broad range of benefits and services available though private and secure electronic use of the Internet.

9. The heads of agencies shall develop a strategy for upgrading their respective agency's capacity for using the Internet to become more open, efficient, and responsive, and to more effectively carry out the agency's mission. At a minimum, this strategy should involve: (a) expanded training of federal employees, including employees with policy and senior management responsibility; (b) identification and adoption of "best practices" implemented by leading public and private sector organizations; (c) recognition for federal employees who suggest new and innovative agency applications of the Internet; (d) partnerships with the research community for experimentation with advanced applications; and (e) mechanisms for collecting input from the agency's stakeholders regarding agency use of the Internet.

II. FEDERAL INFORMATION POLICY

A. U.S. Information Infrastructure Task Force (IITF). 1993. *The National Information Infrastructure: Agenda for Action.*

Available at http://metalab.unc.edu/nii/toc.html.

Application to Federal Information Technology and Web Management:

This document has served as a blueprint for President Clinton's National Information Infrastructure Initiative. The document outlined the President's map for developing a National Information Infrastructure (NII) listing goals and the necessary actions to accomplish the goals. Goal nine called for an increase in access to government information and to improve government procurement. This goal called for federal agencies in conjunction with state and local governments to use the NII to expand the information available to the public, and make that information so it can be accessed easily and equitably.

Excerpt of Original Text from Policy Instrument:

9. Provide Access to Government Information and Improve Government Procurement

Thomas Jefferson said that information is the currency of democracy. Federal agencies are among the most prolific collectors and generators of information that is useful and valuable to citizens and business. Improvement of the nation's information infrastructure provides a tremendous opportunity to improve the delivery of government information to the taxpayers who paid for its collection; to provide it equitably, at a fair price, as efficiently as possible.

The federal government is improving every step of the process of information collection, manipulation, and dissemination. The Administration is funding research programs that will improve the software used for browsing, searching, describing, organizing, and managing information. But it is committed as well to applying those tools to the distribution of information that can be useful to the public in their various roles as teachers, researchers, businesspeople, consumers, etc.

Action: Improve the accessibility of government information. IITF working groups will carefully consider the problems associated with making government information broadly accessible to the public electronically. Additionally, several inter-agency efforts have been started to ensure that the right information is stored and available. Finally, to help the public find government information, an inter-agency project has been formed to develop a virtual card catalogue that will indicate the availability of government information in whatever form it takes.

Action: Enhance citizen access to government information. In June 1993, the OMB prescribed new polices pertaining to the acquisition, use, and distribution of government information by federal agencies. Among other things, the policies mandate that, in distributing information to the public, federal agencies should recoup only those costs associated with the dissemination of that information, not with its creation or collection. Moreover, a number of interagency efforts are under way to afford greater public access to government information. One project seeks to turn thousands of local and field offices of various federal agencies into Interactive Citizen Participation Centers, at which citizens can communicate with the public affairs departments of all federal agencies.

B. **Privacy and the National Information Infrastructure: Principles for Providing and Using Personal Information. Privacy Working Group. Information Policy Committee. Information Infrastructure Task Force. (June 6, 1995.)** Available at http://www.iitf.nist.gov/ipc/ipc/ ipc-pubs/niiprivprin_final.html.

Application to Federal Information Technology and Web Management:

The Privacy Working Group (PWG), part of the Information Infrastructure Task Force (IITF) was formed to develop guidelines or principles for providing and using personal information in the electronic environment or within the National Information Infrastructure (NII). Personal information refers to information such as identifying information, social security number, name, address, and phone number; financial records or statements; and health records. The principles were designed to provide guidelines to personal information users and personal information providers. These principles are not legally binding, and only serve to guide. In developing the standards, PWG generally followed international standards such as the OECD guidelines written in 1980.

Federal Web site developers and administrators need to be concerned with:

- *Acquisition Principle*: only collect and keep information that supports current or planned activities, and assess the impact on privacy in collecting, disclosing, or using a person's personal information.
- *Protection Principle*: use appropriate technical and managerial controls to protect the integrity, confidentiality, and quality of the personal information.
- *Notice Principle*: personal information providers should be informed by the Web site as to why information collection is occurring; how the information is to be used; what steps are taken to protect the information; consequences of providing or withholding information; any rights of redress; and what happens if information loses integrity, or is leaked.
- *Fairness principle*: Information should be used in the manner in which the user was told it would be used.
- *Education principle*: Information users should educate themselves and the public about how information privacy can be maintained.

C. Copyright Act

(a) **STATUTE: Digital Millennium Copyright Act. (Public Law 105-304, Title 1, Sec. 103(a), codified at 17 U.S.C. §§ 1201-1205). 1998.** Available at http://frWebgate.access.gpo.gov/cgi-bin/getdoc.cgi?dbname=1994_uscode_suppl_4anddocid=17usc1201.

Application to Federal Information Technology and Web Management:

This law amended Title 17 of the U.S. Code to implement the World Intellectual Property Organization Copyright Treaty and Performance and Phonograms Treaty. The Digital Millennium Copyright Act (DMCA) incorporated into Title 17 provisions preventing the circumvention of technological protections of works. The DMCA also added provisions prohibiting the removal or alteration of "copyright management information." As such, the DMCA tailors protection to holders of copyright in electronic media. It prohibits the circumvention of technological measures that control access to protected works and/or manufacturing or trafficking in technology designed to circumvent measures that control access to, or protect rights of copyright owners in, such works. The act provides exemptions for nonprofit libraries, archives, or educational institutions that gain access to a commercially exploited copyrighted work solely to make a good faith determination of whether to acquire such work, subject to certain restrictions; for purposes of achieving interoperability of computer programs; and for authorized investigative, protective, information security, or intelligence activities of the United States, a state, or political subdivision of a state.

(b) **IMPLEMENTING GUIDANCE:** The Copyright Office completed a statutorily mandated study on the Digital Millennium Copyright Act in December 1998. The study is available at http://www.loc.gov/copyright/legislation/dmca.pdf.

D. Rights of Access to Information

1. Freedom of Information

(a) **STATUTE: Freedom of Information Act. (Public Law 89-487, codified as amended, 5 U.S.C. § 552).** Available at http://frWebgate.access.gpo.gov/cgi-bin/getdoc.cgi?dbname=1994_uscode_suppl_4anddocid=5usc552.

Application to Federal Information Technology and Web Management:

The purpose of the *Freedom of Information Act* ("FOIA") is to allow public access to agency records, thereby promoting an informed citizenry. Unless exempted under section 552a, agency records are subject to proper request. The Electronic FOIA Amendments of 1996 (EFOIA) eliminated doubt that information stored on computers is a "record" within the definition of the statute. Because digital information, including information posted by a federal agency on its Web site, falls under the statutory definition of a record, federal agencies are responsible for providing information in this format just as they are for providing print materials.

Certain government bodies are exempted from the requirements of FOIA because they fall outside the definition of "agency" set forth in the statute, and the law contains nine exemptions for various classes of records. As noted in the section dealing with the Privacy Act, certain types of information are protected from public disclosure and consequently their disclosure is not required under FOIA. Each section is defined in terms of the other: records required under FOIA include everything not protected under the Privacy Act.

2. **STATUTE: Electronic Freedom of Information Act Amendments of 1996. (Public Law 104-231, amending 5 U.S.C. §552).** Available at http://frWebgate.access.gpo.gov/cgi-bin/getdoc.cgi?dbname=104_cong_public_lawsanddocid=f:publ231.104.pdf.

Application to Federal Information Technology and Web Management:

The EFOIA encourages government agencies to use new technology to enhance public access to agency records and information. The act amends the FOIA to define "record" to mean information in records maintained by an agency in any format. Agencies responding to a request for records also must make reasonable efforts to search for the records in electronic form or format.

All agencies are to make available electronically frequently requested records obtainable under FOIA and are to maintain an Electronic Reading Room. These Electronic Reading Rooms present special interest collections as well as "policy statements, administrative rulings and manuals, and other materials that affect members of the public." For a report on agency compliance see the OMB Watch study report at http://www.ombwatch.org/site/info/efoia99/efoiareport.html.

Excerpt of Original Text from Policy Instrument:

Section 3. Application of Requirements to Electronic Format Information

(f) For purposes of this section, the term—

(2) "record" and any other term used in this section in reference to information includes any information that would be an agency record subject to the requirements of this section when maintained by an agency in any format, including an electronic format.

Section 5. Honoring Form or Format Requests

(C) In responding under this paragraph to a request for records, an agency shall make reasonable efforts to search for the records in electronic form or format, except when such efforts would significantly interfere with the operation of the agency's automated information system.

3. **STATUTE: Privacy Act of 1974. (Public Law 93-579, Sec. 3, codified as amended at 5 U.S.C. § 552a).** Available at

http://fr Webgate.access.gpo.gov/cgibin/getdoc.cgi?dbname=1994_uscode_suppl_4anddocid=5usc552a.

Application to Federal Information Technology and Web Management:

Congress intended the Privacy Act to protect citizens against disclosure of their personal information unless required by the FOIA, section 552. Congress was especially concerned with the automation of information retrieval and technological advances in information storage when it enacted this legislation. The legislative history of the Privacy Act shows it contemplates the problem of individuals' increased personal exposure through the automation of government operations and development of computerized government systems.[2]

The Privacy Act describes the manner in which personal information of individuals can be disclosed by the government. No record containing personal information may be disclosed without the prior written consent of the individual to whom the information pertains. The act also requires agencies to allow individuals access to their records.

Excerpt of Original Text from Policy Instrument:

(b) Conditions of Disclosure.

No agency shall disclose any record which is contained in a system of records by any means of communication to any person, or to another agency, except pursuant to a written request by, or with the prior written consent of, the individual to whom the record pertains, unless disclosure of the record would be—

(e) Agency Requirements.

Each agency that maintains a system of records shall

(1) maintain in its records only such information about an individual as is relevant and necessary to accomplish a purpose of the agency required to be accomplished by statute or by executive order of the President;

(2) collect information to the greatest extent practicable directly from the subject individual when the information may result in adverse determinations about an individual's rights, benefits, and privileges under federal programs;

(3) inform each individual whom it asks to supply information, on the form which it uses to collect the information or on a separate form that can be retained by the individual.

(i) IMPLEMENTING GUIDANCE: Appendix I to OMB Circular No. A-130-Federal Agency Responsibilities for Maintaining Records About Individuals

"This Appendix describes agency responsibilities for implementing the reporting and publication requirements of the Privacy Act of 1974, 5 U.S.C. 552a, as amended (hereinafter "the Act"). It applies to all agencies subject to the Act. Note that this Appendix does not rescind other guidance OMB has issued to help agencies interpret the Privacy Act's provisions, e.g., Privacy Act Guidelines (40 FR 28949-28978, July 9, 1975), or Final Guidance for Conducting Matching Programs (54 FR at 25819, June 19, 1989)."

(ii) IMPLEMENTING GUIDANCE: Instructions on complying with President's Memorandum of May 14, 1998, "Privacy and Personal Information in Federal Records." Available at http://www.pub.whitehouse.gov/urires/I2R?urn:pdi://oma.eop.gov.us/1998/5/14/8.text.1.

Application to Federal Information Technology and Web Management:

In this Memorandum the President directed Federal agencies to review their current information practices and ensure that they are being conducted in accordance with the Privacy Act of 1974. The President also directed OMB to issue instructions to the agencies on how to conduct this review.

Excerpt of Original Text from Policy Instrument:

1. Designate a Senior Official for Privacy Policy

Each agency head should have already designated a senior official within the agency to assume primary responsibility for privacy policy, in accordance with the President's Memorandum. This individual will not necessarily be the same person who is responsible for implementation of the Privacy Act. For most Cabinet agencies, the appropriate official would probably be a policy official at the Assistant Secretary level, or equivalent, who in a position within the agency to consider privacy policy issues on a national level.

2. Review and Improve the Management of Privacy Act Systems of Records

Each agency shall conduct a thorough review of its systems of records, system of records notices, and routine uses in accordance with the criteria and guidance below. Because the President directed agencies to review systems of records, we have provided guidance on a subset of the Privacy Act's requirements that are particularly relevant to systems of records.

(iii) **IMPLEMENTING GUIDANCE: M-99-18. Director Jacob J. Lew's Memorandum for the Heads of Executive Departments and Agencies on Privacy Policies on Federal Web Sites. 1999.** Available at http://cio.gov/docs/Webprivl. htm.

Application to Federal Information Technology and Web Management:

This memo instructs departments and agencies to display their privacy policies on their Web sites, and to comply with various laws and regulations governing privacy policies, such as the Privacy Act, OMB Circular No. A-130, and Principles for Providing and Using Personal Information published by the Information Infrastructure Task Force on June 6, 1995. Federal agency Web developers must include a privacy statement on their departmental Web sites.

(iv) **IMPLEMENTING GUIDANCE: M-00-13, Director Jacob J. Lew's Memorandum for the Heads of Executive Departments and Agencies on Privacy Policies and Data Collection on Federal Web Sites, June 22, 2000.** Available at http://www.whitehouse.gov/OMB/memoranda/m00-13.html.

Application to Federal Information Technology and Web Management

"Particular privacy concerns may be raised when uses of Web technology can track the activities of users over time and across different Web sites. ... 'Cookies'—small bits of software that are placed on a Web user's hard drive—are a principal example of current Web technology that can be used this way ... Because of the unique laws and traditions about government access to citizens' personal information, the presumption should be that 'cookies' will not be used a federal Web sites. Under this new federal policy, 'cookies' should not be used at federal Web sites, or by contractors when operating Web sites on behalf of agencies, unless, in addition to clear and conspicuous notice, the following conditions are met: a compelling need to gather the data on the site; appropriate and publicly disclosed privacy safeguards for handling of information derived from 'cookies'; and personal approval by the head of the agency."

Also, "It is federal policy that all federal Web sites and contractors when operating on behalf of agencies shall comply with the standards set forth in the Children's Online Privacy Protection Act of 1998 with respect to the collection of personal information online at Web sites directed to children."

E. Paperwork Reduction Act

(a) **STATUTE: Paperwork Reduction Act of 1995. (Public Law 104-13, codified at 44 U.S.C. 3501 et seq.)** Available at P.L. 104-13: http://frWebgate.access.gpo.gov/cgi-bin/getdoc.cgi?dbname=104_cong_public_lawsanddocid=f:publ13.104.pdf.
44 U.S.C. 3501 at http://frWebgate.access.gpo.gov/cgi-bin/getdoc.cgi?dbname=1994_uscode_suppl_3anddocid=44usc3501.

Application to Federal Information Technology and Web Management:

The Paperwork Reduction Act (PRA) intends to minimize the paperwork burden for individuals, small businesses, educational and nonprofit institutions, federal contractors, state, local, and tribal governments, and other persons which results from the collection of information by or for the federal government. PRA is also designed to coordinate, integrate, and make uniform federal information resources management policies and practices in order to improve the efficiency of government programs. The 1995 amendments to the PRA added extensive agency responsibilities for information dissemination, responsibilities that are applicable to agency Web sites. Suggested implementation of this law in conjunction with the Government Performance and Results Act of 1993 and the Information Technology Management Reform Act of 1996 occurs in Executive Order 13011, Federal Information Technology. This implementation was followed up with another memorandum issued by the President on December 17, 1999, Memorandum on E-Government, to improve the interoperability of government agencies and the sharing of information resources.

Excerpt of Original Text from Policy Instrument:

Sec. 2. Coordination of Federal Information Policy.

Chapter 35 of title 44, United States Code, is amended to read as follows:

* * *

"Section 3504. Authority and Functions of Director

"(a)(1) The Director shall oversee the use of information resources to improve the efficiency and effectiveness of governmental operations to serve agency missions, including burden reduction and service delivery to the public. In performing such oversight, the Director shall—

"(A) develop, coordinate and oversee the implementation of federal information resources management policies, principles, standards, and guidelines; and

"(B) provide direction and oversee—

* * *

"(v) privacy, confidentiality, security, disclosure, and sharing of information; and

"(vi) the acquisition and use of information technology.

* * *

"Section 3506. Federal Agency Responsibilities

* * *

"(d) With respect to information dissemination, each agency shall—

"(1) ensure that the public has timely and equitable access to the agency's public information, including ensuring such access through—

"(A) encouraging a diversity of public and private sources for information based on government public information;

"(B) in cases in which the agency provides public information maintained in electronic format, providing timely and equitable access to the underlying data (in whole or in part); and

"(C) agency dissemination of public information in an efficient, effective, and economical manner;

"(2) regularly solicit and consider public input on the agency's information dissemination activities;

"(3) provide adequate notice when initiating, substantially modifying, or terminating significant information dissemination products;"

(b) IMPLEMENTING GUIDANCE: Office of Management and Budget (OMB), Circular A-130, Management of Federal Information Resources. 1996. (61 FR 6428.) Available at http://www.whitehouse.gov/OMB/circulars/a130/a130.html.

Application to Federal Information Technology and Web Management:

Circular A-130 provides uniform government-wide information resources management policies as required by the Paperwork Reduction Act of 1980 and as amended by the Paperwork Reduction Act of 1995 (44 U.S.C. 35). This policy instrument provides a framework for the development of an information management plan to aid federal agencies in the development of their Web sites.

Excerpt of Original Text from Policy Instrument:

8. Policy. a. Information Management Policy

1. Information Management Planning. Agencies shall plan in an integrated manner for managing information throughout its life cycle. Agencies shall:

(a) Consider, at each stage of the information life cycle, the effects of decisions and actions on other stages of the life cycle, particularly those concerning information dissemination

(e) Integrate planning for information systems with plans for resource allocation and use, including budgeting, acquisition, and use of information technology;

8. Policy. b. Information Systems and Information Technology Management

1. Evaluation and Performance Measurement.

Agencies shall promote the appropriate application of Federal information resources as follows:

(a) Seek opportunities to improve the effectiveness and efficiency of government programs through work process redesign and the judicious application of information technology;

(b) Prepare, and update as necessary throughout the information system life cycle, a benefit-cost analysis for each information system:

9. Assignment of Responsibilities. c. Department of Commerce. The Secretary of Commerce shall:

4. Conduct studies and evaluations concerning telecommunications technology, and concerning the improvement, expansion, testing, operation, and use of federal telecommunications systems and advise the Director, OMB, and appropriate agencies of the recommendations that result from such studies;

F. Clinger-Cohen Act

1. **STATUTE: Information Technology Management Reform Act of 1996. (Public Law 104-106, Division E). 1996. Amended by Public Law 104-208, Division A, Title I, Sec. 101(f) (Title VIII, Sec. 808(b), providing that this act (and the Federal Acquisition Reform Act of 1996 [Public Law 104-106, Division D]) may be cited as the "Clinger-Cohen Act of 1996."** Available at P.L. 104-106 http://frWebgate.access.gpo.gov/cgi-bin/getdoc.cgi?dbname=104_cong_public_lawsanddocid=f:publ106.104.pdf.

   P.L. 104-208 at http://frWebgate.access.gpo.gov/cgi-bin/getdoc.cgi?dbname=104_cong_public_lawsanddocid=f:publ208.104.pdf

Application to Federal Information Technology and Web Management:

The Clinger-Cohen Act is intended to address the management of IT in the Federal government. It is to accomplish this goal through a variety of methods, including the use of capital planning for IT acquisitions and investments, the establishment of Chief Information Officer (CIO) positions in federal departments and agencies, and the requirement of performance measurements of IT. The CIO, through IT, would also be responsible for making government more effective, efficient, and productive, and include the implementation of policies affecting Federal agency Web development. The CIO has agency responsibility for IT management and development and reports directly to the head of the agency. As regard performance measures, the Clinger-Cohen Act represents the specific application of the Government Performance and Results Act to the area of IT.

Excerpt of Original Text from Policy Instrument:

Section 5112. Capital Planning And Investment Control

(b) USE OF INFORMATION TECHNOLOGY IN FEDERAL PROGRAMS—The Director shall promote and be responsible for improving the acquisition, use, and disposal of IT by the federal government to improve the productivity, efficiency, and effectiveness of federal programs, including through dissemination of public information and the reduction of information collection burdens on the public

(f) USE OF BEST PRACTICES IN ACQUISITIONS—The Director shall encourage the heads of the executive agencies to develop and use the best practices in the acquisition of information technology.

Section 5113. Performance-Based and Results-Based Management

(a) IN GENERAL—The Director shall encourage the use of performance-based and results-based management in fulfilling the responsibilities assigned under section 3504(h), of title 44, United States Code.

(b) Evaluation of Agency Programs and Investments-

(1) REQUIREMENT—The Director shall evaluate the information resources management practices of the executive agencies with respect to the performance and results of the investments made by the executive agencies in information technology.

(2) DIRECTION FOR EXECUTIVE AGENCY ACTION—The Director shall issue to the head of each executive agency clear and concise direction that the head of such agency shall

(A) establish effective and efficient capital planning processes for selecting, managing, and evaluating the results of all of its major investments in information systems.

2. IMPLEMENTING GUIDANCE:

(a) Executive Order

Federal Information Technology. (Executive Order 13011.) 1996. Available at http://frWebgate.access.gpo.gov/cgi-bin/getdoc.cgi?dbname=1996_registeranddocid=fr19jy96-133.pdf.

Application to Federal Information Technology and Web Management:

This Executive Order links the Clinger-Cohen Act, the PRA, and the GPRA. It formalizes OMB's oversight of IT management and stresses the importance of performance-based planning and implementation of federal IT. Executive Order 13011 also creates the Chief Information Officer Council, the Government Information Technology Services Board, and the Information Technology Resources Board. Also falling under the domain of this executive order are the establishment of interagency support structures to share IT ideas, minimize duplication, and increase interoperability; and design technology procedures and standards. The order does not formally define the support structure. Federal Web site design under this executive order should be interoperable and standardized with other agencies. Web site design must also operate within the realm of the Clinger-Cohen Act, the PRA, and the GPRA. The CIO would be in charge of overseeing the design with ultimate control still resting with the OMB.

Excerpt of Original Text from Policy Instrument:

Section 1. Policy. It shall be the policy of the United States Government that executive agencies shall:
* * *

(b) refocus information technology management to support directly their strategic missions, implement an investment review process that drives budget formulation and execution for information systems, and rethink and restructure the way they perform their functions before investing in information technology to support that work;

(c) establish clear accountability for information resources management activities by creating agency Chief Information Officers (CIOs) with the visibility and management responsibilities necessary to advise the agency head on the design, development, and implementation of those information systems. These responsibilities include: (1) participating in the investment review process for information systems; (2) monitoring and evaluating the performance of those information systems on the basis of applicable performance measures; and, (3) as necessary, advising the agency head to modify or terminate those systems ....

Section 2. Responsibilities of Agency Heads. The head of each executive agency shall: (a) effectively use information technology to improve mission performance and service to the public;

(b) strengthen the quality of decisions about the employment of information resources to meet mission needs through integrated analysis, planning, budgeting, and evaluation processes, including:

* * *

(2) establishing mission-based performance measures for information systems investments, aligned with agency performance plans prepared pursuant to the Government Performance and Results Act of 1993 (Public Law 103-62) ....

(b) **OMB CIRCULAR: Proposed Revision of OMB Circular No. A-130, Management of Federal Information Resources, April 13, 2000.** Available at http://www.whitehouse.gov/omb/federeg/reva130.pdg.

Application to Federal Information Technology and Web Management:

In proposing to revise OMB Circular No. A-130, OMB announced that its primary reason for doing so was to implement provisions of the Clinger-Cohen Act. Agencies must develop annually an Information Resources Management Plan. The plan must include an annual performance plan as required by GPRA. This must include an accountability report, comparing actual performance with expected performance. Their benefit-cost analyses of information systems must include performance measures. In its capital planning process, each agency must institute performance measures that monitor actual performance as compared with expected results. They must also conduct evaluations of information systems and of information resource management processes.

G. Security

1. **STATUTE: Computer Security Act of 1987. (Public Law 100-235, codified in part as amended at 15 U.S.C. §§ 278g-3, 278g-4.) 1988.** Available at http://cio.doe.gov/ucsp/csa.htm.

Application to Federal Information Technology and Web Management:

The Computer Security Act of 1987 establishes in law for information technology the basic principle of security, namely, security commensurate with the risk and magnitude of the harm resulting from the loss, misuse, or unauthorized access to or modification of information. It also creates a means, through the National Institute of Standards and Technology (NIST), for establishing minimum acceptable security practices for federal computer systems without limiting the scope of security measures already planned or in use. The act requires each agency with a federal computer system to establish a plan for the security and privacy of sensitive information, and prescribes "cost effective" rather than "absolute" computer security. The NIST is responsible for developing standards and guidelines necessary for assuring the protection of sensitive information. Federal Web sites offer one more entry point through which security can be breached. Federal CIOs must utilize the most recent proven effective hardware and software to protect sensitive departmental information and computer systems.

Congress is currently considering H.R. 2413, the Computer Security Enhancement Act of 1999.

Available at http://frWebgate.access.gpo.gov/cgi-bin/getdoc.cgi?dbname=106_cong_billsanddocid=f:h2413ih.txt.pdf.

This bill would enhance the ability of NIST to improve computer security for nonclassified information on Federal computer systems. It would also promote the use of private sector security technology to protect federal computer systems. Rather than government driving security technology, private industry or the market would be responsible for developing security technology.

Excerpt of Original Text from Policy Instrument:

Section 3. Establishment of Computer Standards Program

The Act of March 3, 1901, (15 U.S.C. 271-278h), is amended—

* * *

(2) by redesignating section 20 as section 22, and by inserting after section 19 the following new sections: "SEC. 20. (a) The National Bureau of Standards shall—

* * *

"(3) have responsibility within the federal government for developing technical, management, physical, and administrative standards and guidelines for the cost-effective security and privacy of sensitive information in federal computer systems except [as specified in the law];

* * *

"(6) develop validation procedures for, and evaluate the effectiveness of, standards and guidelines developed pursuant to paragraphs (1), (2), and (3) of this subsection through research and liaison with other government and private agencies."

2. IMPLEMENTING GUIDANCE

(a) OMB Circular No. A-130, Appendix III, Security of Federal Automated Information Resources

Available at http://www.whitehouse.gov/OMB/circulars/a130/a130.html.

Application to Federal Information Technology and Web Management

"This Appendix establishes a minimum set of controls to be included in federal automated information security programs; assigns federal agency responsibilities for the security of automated information; and links agency automated information security programs and agency management control systems established in accordance with OMB Circular No. A-123. The Appendix revises procedures formerly contained in Appendix III to OMB Circular No. A-130 (50 FR 52730; December 24, 1985), and incorporates requirements of the Computer Security Act of 1987 (P.L. 100-235) and responsibilities assigned in applicable national security directives."

(b) **Presidential Decision Directive 63, "Protecting America's Critical Infrastructures."** Available at http://www.pub.whitehouse.gov/uri-res/I2R?urn:pdi://oma.eop.gov.us/1998/5/26/1.text.1.

Application to Federal Information Technology and Web Management:

This Presidential Directive built on the recommendations of the President's Commission on Critical Infrastructure Protection and sets a goal of a reliable, interconnected, and secure information system infrastructure by the year 2003, and significantly increased security to government systems by the year 2000, by: Immediately establishing a national center to warn of and respond to attacks. Ensuring the capability to protect critical infrastructures from intentional acts by 2003. PDD 63 addressed the cyber and physical infrastructure vulnerabilities of the federal government by requiring each department and agency to work to reduce its exposure to new threats. It set up a new structure to deal with this important challenge: a National Coordinator; the National Infrastructure Protection Center (NIPC); Information Sharing and Analysis Centers (ISACs); a National Infrastructure Assurance Council; and The Critical Infrastructure Assurance Office to provide support to the National Coordinator's work with government agencies and the private sector in developing a national plan. The applicability to agency Web sites is that PPD 63 is fundamental for Web site security and effectively requires that agencies have performance measures of Web site security.

H. Electronic Collection and Digital Signatures

1. **STATUTE: Government Paperwork Elimination Act. (Public Law 105-277, Division C, Title XVII, amending 44 U.S.C.) 1998.** Available at http://thomas.loc.gov/cgi-bin/bdquery/z?d105:HR04328: | TOM:/bss/d105query.html.

Application to Federal Information Technology and Web Management:

The Government Paperwork Elimination Act (GPEA) provides for federal agencies to give persons who are required to maintain, submit, or disclose information the option of doing so electronically, when practicable, by October 21, 2003. In addition, GPEA directs that electronic authentication (electronic signature) methods be used to verify the identity of the sender and the integrity of the electronic content. The Director of the OMB is required to develop procedures for the use and acceptance of electronic signatures by executive agencies and, in cooperation with the National Telecommunications and Information Administration (NTIA), to conduct and report to Congress an ongoing study of the use of electronic signatures on paperwork reduction and electronic commerce, individual privacy, and the security and authenticity of transactions.

Excerpt of Original Text from Policy Instrument:

Section 1. Policy

The Office of Management and Budget is directed to maintain compatibility with standards and technology for electronic signatures generally used in commerce and industry and by state governments and to ensure that electronic signatures are as reliable as is appropriate for the purpose in question ant that the electronic record keeping systems readily preserve the information submitted.

Section 2. Procedures

An agency's determination of which technology is appropriate for a given transaction must include a risk assessment, and an evaluation of targeted customer or user needs. Performing a risk assessment to evaluate electronic signature alternatives should not be viewed as an isolated activity or an end in itself. These agency risk assessments should draw from and feed into the interrelated requirements of the Paperwork Reduction Act, the Computer Security Act, the Government Performance and Results Act, the Clinger-Cohen Act, the Federal Managers Financial Integrity Act, and the Chief Financial Officers Act.

2. **IMPLEMENTING GUIDANCE: Implementation of the Government Paperwork Elimination Act. 1999.** Available at http://www.whitehouse.gov/omb/fedreg/gpea2.html.

Application to Federal Information Technology and Web Management:

The Government Paperwork Elimination Act provides for federal agencies, by October 21, 2003, to give persons who are required to maintain, submit, or disclose information the option of doing so electronically when practicable as a substitute for paper, and to use electronic authentication (electronic signature) methods to verify the identity of the sender and the integrity of electronic content. The Act specifically provides that electronic records and their related electronic signatures are not to be denied legal effect, validity, or enforceability merely because they are in electronic form. The OMB's implementation of the Act is in two parts. The first part sets forth the policies and procedures for implementing the Act, and requesting certain specific agencies to provide assistance in particular areas. The second part is intended to provide federal managers with practical implementation guidance.

Excerpt of Original Text from Policy Instrument:

Section 2. What GPEA procedures should agencies follow?

a. Accordingly, agencies should develop and implement plans, supported by an assessment of whether to use and accept documents in electronic form and to engage in electronic transactions. The assessment should weigh costs and benefits and involve an appropriate risk analysis, recognizing that low-risk information processes may need only minimal consideration, while high-risk processes may need extensive analysis.

c. The assessment should develop strategies to mitigate risks and maximize benefits in the context of available technologies, and the relative total costs and effects of implementing those technologies on the program being analyzed. The assessment also should be used to develop baselines and verifiable performance measures that track the agency's mission, strategic plans, and tactical goals, as required by the Clinger-Cohen Act.

d. In addition to serving as a guide for selecting the most appropriate technologies, the assessment of costs and benefits should be designed so that it can be used to generate a business case and verifiable return on investment to support agency decisions regarding overall programmatic direction, investment decisions, and budgetary priorities.

Section 3. How should agencies implement these policies and procedures?

a. To ensure a smooth and cost-effective transition to an electronic government that provides improved service to the public, each agency must:

(1) Develop a plan (including a schedule) by October, 2000 that provides for continued implementation, by the end of Fiscal Year 2003, of optional electronic maintenance, submission, or transaction of information when practicable as a substitute for paper, including through the use of electronic signatures when practicable. A copy of the plan should be provided to OMB.

(7) Consider the record keeping functionality of any systems that store electronic documents and electronic signatures, to ensure users have appropriate access to the information and can meet the agency's record keeping needs.

Section 2. Procedures

b. An agency's determination of which technology is appropriate for a given transaction must include a risk assessment, and an evaluation of targeted customer or user needs. Performing a risk assessment to evaluate electronic signature alternatives should not be viewed as an isolated activity or an end in itself. These agency risk assessments should draw from and feed into the interrelated requirements of the Paperwork Reduction Act, the Computer Security Act, the Government Performance and

Results Act, the Clinger-Cohen Act, the Federal Managers Financial Integrity Act, and the Chief Financial Officers Act.

Section 3. Agency Responsibilities

a. In order to ensure a smooth and cost-effective transition to a more electronic government providing improved service to the public, each agency shall:

1. Include in its strategic IT plans supporting program responsibilities (required under OMB Circular A-11) a summary of the agency's schedule to implement optional electronic maintenance, submission, or disclosure of information when practicable as a substitute for paper, including through the use of electronic signatures when practicable, by the end of Fiscal Year 2003. (Note: agencies need not revise their reports on Federal purchasing and payment already required by OMB M-99-02, but should include the automation of purchasing and payment functions in their schedule.)

I. FEDERAL RECORDS

1. **STATUTE: Federal Records Act, Title 44 U.S. Code, Chapter 31, Records Management by Federal Agencies.** Available from http://frWebgate.access.gpo.gov/cgi-bin/getdoc.cgi?dbname=1994_uscode_suppl_3anddocid=44usc3101.

"The head of each federal agency shall make and preserve records containing adequate and proper documentation of the organization, functions, policies, decisions, procedures, and essential transactions of the agency and designed to furnish the information necessary to protect the legal and financial rights of the government and of persons directly affected by the agency's activities."

2. **IMPLEMENTING GUIDANCE:**

a. **NARA Bulletin 98-02. 1998 [disposition of electronic records].** Available at http://www.nara.gov/records/policy/b9802.html.

Application to Federal Information Technology and Web Management:

NARA Bulletin 98-02 reminds federal agencies of their obligations under federal law, 36 CFR Part 1234, to provide adequate documentation of agency activities, and provides guidance to federal agencies in accomplishing this obligation. Agency CIO's are obligated to ensure that Web site records, Web pages, are adequately documented and preserved.

Excerpt of Original Text from Policy Instrument:

a. Agency heads are required by 44 U.S.C. 3101 to "make and preserve records containing adequate and proper documentation of the organization, functions, policies, decisions, procedures, and essential transactions of the agency. ..." NARA regulations at 36 CFR Part 1222 specify agency record keeping responsibilities, including standards for record keeping requirements. NARA regulations at 36 CFR Part 1234 Subpart C specify standards for managing the creation, use, preservation, and disposition of electronic records.

b. **NARA Bulletin 99-05. 1999. [Disposition of Electronic Records (NARA Bulletin 98-02)].** Available at http://www.nara.gov/records/policy/b9905.html.

Application to Federal Information Technology and Web Management:

NARA Bulletin 99-05 informs federal agencies that they should continue to follow NARA Bulletin 98-02, and reminds agency heads as to their responsibilities to maintain adequate documentation of records. Although not specifically stated, Web pages should be considered federal agency records, and subject to the same guidelines as print records.

c. **General Record Schedule 20 (GRS 20). 1995 version. [Electronic Records Workgroup.]** Available at http://ardor.nara.gov/grs/grs20.html.

Application to Federal Information Technology and Web Management:

General Records Schedule 20 (GRS 20) was first published in 1972 as an attempt to address record management for electronic materials. Since then GRS 20 has been rewritten five times with the latest version being in 1995. The 1995 version of GRS 20 has been through several actions in court, and may be revised again.

The 1995 version of GRS 20 addresses the topic of disposal for certain electronic records and the paper or microform records associated with them. If a department desires to dispose of electronic records, which are not covered by GRS 20, the department must file for authorization using SF 115s, Request for Records Disposition Authority. Web pages and documents associated with

Web pages may be federal records, and if so, their disposal should be regulated by NARA.

III. JUDICIAL OPINIONS

An enormous body of case law exists interpreting certain policy instruments affecting aspects of public access to government information, while other policy instruments have spawned no case law. The following materials illustrate *some* courts' approaches to fine-tuning statutory language, with their resulting potential effects on federal information technology management. A survey of all relevant case law is beyond the scope of this chapter.

A. Freedom of Information Act (FOIA)

The cases speak to courts' willingness to apply a liberal interpretation to statutes governing public access based on a perceived statutory intent to promote open government. Courts check this impulse where the duty to provide this information seems onerous for the agency or when the information bears slight resemblance to that identified in the statute.

Cases pertaining to:

Freedom of Information Act, Public Law 89-487, codified as amended at 5 U.S.C. § 552. Electronic Freedom of Information Act Amendments of 1996, Public Law 104-231, amending 5 U.S.C. §552.

1. Regulation promulgated by National Archives and Records Administration (GRS 20) authorizing disposal of electronic government records without distinguishing significant records for different treatment violated the Records Disposal Act and interfered with plaintiff's right, under EFOIA, to request electronic records. *Public Citizen v. Carlin*, 2 F. Supp 2d 1 (D.DC 1997); reversed by *Public Citizen v. Carlin*, 184 F.3d 900 (DC Cir. 1997) (agencies expected to develop their own Web site records management policies within existing NARA guidelines subject to NARA approval).

Available at http://www.cadc.uscourts.gov/common/opinions/199908/97-5356a.txt; certiorari denied by *Public Citizen v. Carlin*, 68 U.S.L.W. 3565, 2000 U.S. LEXIS 1744, 2000 WL 240442 (March 6, 2000).

2. Federal agencies are not required to provide records concerning software over which they lack "sufficient control"; software and technical documentation is protected by FOIA exemption for

trade secrets and commercial or financial information. *Gilmore v. U.S. Department of Energy*, 4 F. Supp. 2d 912, 153 A.L.R. Fed. 759 (N.D. Cal.1998).

3. Federal agencies requested to search "all records" must search relevant computer databases to comply with FOIA. *Mayock v. Immigration and Naturalization Service*, 714 F. Supp. 1558 (N.D. Cal. 1989).

4. Computer backup tapes of electronic messages are records within the meaning of FOIA. NARA must change its guidance to Federal agencies on record management. *Armstrong v. Executive Office of the President*, 877 F. Supp. 690 (D.DC 1995); reversed by *Armstrong v. Executive Office of the President*, 90 F.3d 553 (DC Cir. 1996); certiorari denied by *Armstrong v. Executive Office of the President*, 520 U.S. 1239 (1997).

Privacy Act of 1974, Public Law 93-579, Sec. 3, codified as amended at 5 U.S.C. § 552a.

1. Exemptions to FOIA under the Privacy Act of 1974 pertain to electronic records. *Manna v. United States Department of Justice*, 1994 WL 808070 (D.N.J. 1994).

B. The Copyright Act of 1976

Case law interpreting the Copyright Act of 1976 is similarly abundant and similarly limited as regards federal IT and electronic media. Aside from disallowing copyright protection for government work, 17 U.S.C. § 105, the statute does not directly address the interests and duties of the federal government in its provisions. The Digital Millennium Copyright Act amended the Copyright Act in 1998 to increase protection for authors of work in electronic media.

Individual Case Laws pertaining to:

Copyright law is governed by Title 17 of the U.S. code as amended by The Digital Millennium Copyright Act, Pub. L. 105–304, 112 Stat. 2860.

1. Compilations of facts are not protected by copyright under the "sweat-of-the-brow" doctrine. *Feist Publications v. Rural Telephone Service Co.*, 499 U.S. 340 (1991).

2. Holders of copyright may submit protected work to government agencies without fear of losing protection of copyright. *Practice Management Information Corporation v. American Medical*

Association, 121 F.3d 516 (9th Cir. 1997); *Veeck v. Southern Building Code Congress International, Inc.*, 49 F. Supp 2d 885, (E.D. Tex. 1999).

C. Electronic Records

Since the Iran-Contra scandal in the late 1980s, electronic records have been the subject of a series of federal court cases. The cases arose originally because the White House announced its intent to destroy the computer backup tapes containing the electronic mail that led to discovery of the Iran-Contra materials. Public interest groups sued to prohibit destruction on the grounds that the materials in question were federal records. In response to judicial opinions, the National Archives and Records Administration issued *General Records Schedule 20, Electronic Records* (see above). GRS-20 itself then became the subject of further litigation.

A seminal case in the series of litigation was *Public Citizen et al. v. John Carlin et al.*, U.S. District Court, October 22, 1997. In his opinion, Judge Paul Friedman voided GRS-20, stating that the Archivist of the United States had overstepped his authority in promulgating GRS-20 and arguing, among other things, that electronic records had unique value that was not captured with paper printouts. The U.S. Court of Appeals later overturned Friedman's opinion on August 6, 1999, and the Supreme Court denied *certiorari* on March 6, 2000.

The opinions cited above are available, together with additional legal resources, at http://www.nara.gov/records/grs20.

NEXT STEPS IN POLICY ANALYSIS

Figure 12.1 is a summary presentation of the federal policies affecting agency Web sites. For each topic the table shows the relevant statute, executive order, or other key document, plus implementing policy guidance, if any. The right-hand column summarizes the implications for Web sites. It is important to stress, however, that this summary table and the detail provided above in this chapter offers only a descriptive assessment of policy affecting federal Web sites.

The process of *identifying* which policy instruments affect federal Web site development is significant and time-consuming in itself. As suggested in this chapter, the extent and range of possible policy instruments that affect federal Web site development is significant. Nonetheless, the development and management of federal Web sites cannot be adequately assessed unless considered in the context of the federal information policy system. Despite a comprehensive

	Topic	Statute, Presidential Directive, or Other Document	Implementing Guidance	Web Site Implications
I. General Government Policy	A. Performance and Results	Government Performance and Results Act	OMB Circular A-11, Part II	Performance plans, goals, and measures for agency programs
	B. Customer Service	E.O. 12862, Setting Customer Service Standards	-	Identify customers, their needs, and set standards and benchmarks
	C. Accessible Information Technology	Rehabilitation Act, section 508	-	Information technology accessible to persons with disabilities
	D. Electronic Government	Pres. Memo on Electronic Government	-	Standardized access to and ease of finding government information, plus privacy and security
II. Federal Information Policy	A. National Information Infrastructure	NII Agenda for Action	-	Make govt. information more easily and equitably accessible
	B. Privacy and the NII	Principles for Providing and Using Personal Information	-	Guidelines to personal information users and providers
	C. Copyright	Digital Millennium Copyright Act	-	Protecting copyright in electronic media
	D. Rights of Access to Information	Freedom of Information Act	-	State FOIA procedures on Web sites
		Electronic Freedom of Information Act	-	Establish electronic reading room on Web sites
		Privacy Act	OMB Circular A-130, Appendix I	Handling of personal information
			Pres. Memo on Privacy and Personal Information in Federal Records	Review privacy policies and practices; update notices of systems of records
			M-99-18 on Privacy Policies on Federal Web sites	Display privacy policies on Web sites
			M-00-13 on Privacy Policies and Data Collection on Federal Web sites	Discouragement of and restrictions on use of "cookies" on Web sites; comply with COPPA
	E. Paperwork Reduction Act	Paperwork Reduction Act	OMB Circular A-130	Framework for agency information management plan, including information dissemination
	F. Clinger-Cohen Act	Information Technology Management Reform Act	E.O. 13011, Federal Information Technology	Web sites to be interoperable and standardized across government
			Proposed Revision of OMB Circular A-130, April 13, 2000	Mission based performance measures for information systems
	G. Security	Computer Security Act	OMB Circular A-130, Appendix III	Security controls for federal information systems
			PDD 63, Protecting America's Critical Infrastructures	Performance measures for Web site security
	H. Electronic Collection and Digital Signatures	Government Paperwork Elimination Act	OMB Notice: Implementation of the Government Paperwork Elimination Act	Increase and encourage electronic data collection and implement digital signatures
	I. Federal Records	Federal Records Act	General Records Schedule 20, Electronic Records, and various NARA Bulletins	Provide for management of records created on Web sites

Figure 12.1: Summary of Federal Policies Pertaining to Agency Web Sites

- Ambiguity
  - Can a reasonable outsidet infer what the policy is (briefly summarize the policy)?
  - Can the policy be interpreted in multiple ways, and if so, how?
  - What is the extent of length of the policy?
  - Are key terms carefully defined?
  - Does the policy contain examples or application to minimize confusion?
  - Does the policy cover one topic or multiple topics and are there clear links between the various topics?
- Contradictions
  - Do policies appear in the same document which contradict this particular policy?
  - Do policies appear in other government-wide document which contradict this particular policy?
  - Do policies appear in (internal) agency documents which contradict this particular policy?
  - Are there judicial decisions that contradict this particular policy?
- Duplication
  - Does the same policy or wording appear more than once within the same document?
  - Does the same policy or wording appear in other government-wide or agency documents?
- Gaps
  - Are there areas where additional guidance in how to interpret or implement the policy are needed?
  - Should more detail or explanation or justification be provided in the policy?
- Inconsistencies (grey areas that are not necessarily contradictions)
  - Are different directions for implementation of policies provided within a given document?
  - Are different directions for implementation of policiies provided across similar policy instruments?
  - Are responsibilities and roles of policymakers the same for similar policies across different policy instruments?
- Enforcement
  - Are there explicit statements as to how the policy will be enforced?
  - Are there explicit statements as to who or which agency will have oversight for agency compliance?
  - Are penalties for non-compliance made explicit?
- Possibility for Modification
  - Is there an explicit process for collecting user feedback (users both within and outside the agency)?
  - Are details provided on the process by which the policy can be modified, updated, rescinded, etc.?

Figure 12.2: Criteria for Assessing Information Policies

and systematic search process, it is possible that additional policy instruments affect federal Web site development and were not identified here. Moreover, this descriptive assessment of policy instruments is current as of January 2001 and is likely to require updating and revision in the near future.

Example policy areas that federal agencies need to consider in developing Web sites include information security, information privacy, information access, electronic records management, and intellectual property. Information security instruments concern risks to the ongoing operation of government computer systems, their integrity, and the protection of classified or confidential materials they contain. Information privacy instruments seek to protect personal information that may be collected from agency Web site users. Internet access policy instruments are concerned with ensuring the equitable access for U.S. citizens to electronic information contained on federal government Web sites. Electronic records management policy instruments concern issues regarding the creation, maintenance, use, and disposal of federal records. Intellectual property policy instruments include a wide variety of ownership rights in intangible products, such as copyrights, patents, trademarks, and trade secrets. In each of these policy areas there are a range of issues that will affect Web site development and management.

Yet to be done is an assessment of the policies described in this chapter. Figure 12.2 provides a summary of the criteria that might be used in making such an assessment. This figure offers a beginning set of criteria that can be used to assess the policies that are described in this chapter. The process for completing such an analysis include content analysis, side by side comparisons of the policies, and impact assessment resulting from the implementation of the policies. An example of the results of such an analysis can be found in Hert, Eschenfelder, and McClure (1999).

Thus, the first step of identifying and describing the relevant policies is crucial for the second step—analysis of the policies—is to occur. Clearly, both steps are extremely time-consuming and require significant skill and knowledge on the part of the policy analyst. In fact, such descriptive policy assessment is rarely done unless policy areas that are regularly codified in the *United States Code*. Nonetheless, an evaluation of the networked services provided by federal Web sites requires the type of descriptive policy assessment described in this chapter.

ENDNOTE

1. These URLs were current as of January 2001.
2. See Senator Ervin's speech on June 11, 1974: "It is a rare person who has escaped the quest of modern government for information. ...When this quite natural tendency of Government to acquire and keep and share information about citizens is enhanced by computer technology and when it is subjected to the unrestrained motives of countless political administrators, the resulting threat to individual privacy make it necessary for Congress to reaffirm the principle of limited, responsive Government on behalf of freedom." Senate Rpt. (of Government Operations Committee) No. 93-1183, page 6919; *Thomas v. U.S. Dept. of Energy*, 719 F3d 342 (1983).

ACKNOWLEDGMENTS

The authors wish to acknowledge the contributions to earlier drafts of this paper by Bruce Smith, Bruce Fraser, and Goldberry Burton of the Florida State University, School of Information Studies, Information Use Management and Policy.

ABOUT THE AUTHORS

Charles R. McClure's information is included in Chapter 6 in this book.

J. Timothy Sprehe is President of Sprehe Information Management Associates, Washington, DC. He previously served in the Office of Management and Budget, Office of Information Regulatory Affairs prior to establishing his own company. He has written extensively on topics related to electronic records management, privacy, security, and access to electronic government information. With Charles R. McClure, he was the Co-Principal Investigator in 2000 for the study *Developing Performance Measures for Federal Web sites*.

E-mail: jtsprehe@jtsprehe.com

REFERENCES

Hert, Carol A.; Eschenfelder, Kristin; and McClure, Charles R. (1999). Evaluation of Selected Web sites at the U.S. Department of Education: Increasing Access to Web-based Resources. Syracuse, NY: ERIC Clearinghouse on Information Services.

McClure, Charles R. (1999). Federal Information Policy, in Kent, Allen, ed. Encyclopedia of Library and Information Science, Vol. 65, Supp. 28. New York: Marcel Dekker p. 306.

McClure, Charles R.; Moen, William A.; and Bertot, John Carlo. Descriptive Assessment of Information Policy Initiatives: The Government Information Locator System (GILS) as Example. Journal of the American Society for Information Science, 50 (March, 1999): 313–330.

National Telecommunications and Information Infrastructure (NTIA). 1999. Falling Through the Net: Defining the Digital Divide. Available at http://www.ntia.doc.gov/ntiahome/fttn99/.

Chapter 13

Measurement and Evaluation in the Networked Information World

Clifford Lynch

ABSTRACT

This chapter, based on a keynote speech at the American Society for Information Science (ASIS) 1999 Midyear meeting, is a broad survey of the current state, use, misuse, and limitations of the evaluation and measurement of networked information systems, digital libraries and other electronic information resources; it also considers cultural and social behaviors that surround them. It proposes a variety of research problems and initiatives to advance evaluation and measurement, describes how work on evaluation needs to respond the changing environment, and concludes with a number of "grand challenge" problems facing the evaluation of libraries, education, and information use in the digital world.

INTRODUCTION

This chapter is loosely based on a keynote address delivered at the ASIS 1999 Midyear meeting in Pasadena California; while adding and updating some material, I have tried to keep the somewhat informal character of a keynote address. References are limited and, like the rest of the paper, intended to be more suggestive than comprehensive. In particular, I've tried to draw some connections to work that I know, or work that I've been involved in, rather than trying to do a systematic survey of the topics here.

It's flattering to be asked to provide my thoughts and opinions on measurement, evaluation, and analysis when I'm not an evaluation specialist; my background is much more that of a systems builder. While I've always been concerned with measurement as part of specifying, validating, managing and enhancing systems, and understanding what they are doing and how they are being used, my encounters with formal methodologies of evaluation have been more limited.

And, speaking as a system developer, I've often found the products of these evaluations to be of disappointingly limited use (for reasons I'll discuss later). More recently, I've become increasingly involved in policy and planning questions, where I'm finding the limitations on our ability to even measure, much less evaluate, many of the things we intuitively believe in—and are investing heavily to accomplish, based on these intuitions and beliefs—very troublesome. I'll speak to some of these issues as well. So, those readers who are specialists in evaluation might want to view this paper as a (hopefully) somewhat informed outsider's critique of past work and a wish list for future research.

I'll apologize in advance for what is a messy and perhaps intellectually uneasy aspect of this paper. In some places, I'm really addressing the role of evaluation and measurement within information science (very broadly defined, and encompassing the design and use of networked information delivery systems, and the operation of the networked information environment). In other parts, I'm really talking about evaluation and measurement in much broader, albeit still information-intensive contexts such as information technology and instructional technology in higher education. This is not purely an information science issue though information scientists unquestionably have to be key players in a multi-disciplinary collaboration to address the issue, just as they have to be key participants in the design of instructional technology systems or in applying information technology (IT) to support research, teaching and learning in the educational environment. But I hope that my comments in these areas will still be of real interest to information scientists.

Put another way, I have carefully avoided addressing the question of "What is the scope and subject of information science, and how does evaluation and measurement fit into information science?" Instead, I have taken a pragmatic view of issues involving evaluation and measurement from a very broad perspective that sometimes goes beyond the specific concerns of information science; these are the issues I wanted to address.

Let me offer a quick roadmap of what I intend to cover. I'll begin with some general comments about how and why we practice evaluation and measurement, with some emphasis on what we expect to learn from it and whether this makes sense. I'll then turn to how the scale, scope, and rate of change in the Internet and the broader networked information environment is changing the processes of evaluation, and creating new needs for pragmatic evaluation strategies. The next sections cover some areas where I believe that new approaches will be particularly fruitful, and some of the trailblazing work that is taking place in those areas. I'll cover new issues that are emerging with data availability for evaluation, benchmark evaluations in information science, models of interaction with retrieval systems and what these imply for evaluation and measurement. Then, I'll highlight some of the very interesting work going on in allied fields of simulation of societies, organizations and individual behaviors. In the final section of this talk, I propose a series of "grand challenge" evaluation problems dealing with intellectual property, the value of libraries, and the implications of information technology and networked information in education.

EVALUATING EVALUATION

I want to start with a rather abstract set of observations. We need to spend some time thinking critically about evaluation and when and how we practice it. We need an evaluation of evaluation, if you will.

There's a constant tension between system building and system evaluation, and the funding pendulum moves between one extreme and the other. Lately, we've settled on what I think is a poor compromise: fund system building, but insist that it includes an evaluation *component*. We might often be better served making grant funding available specifically for evaluation activities, quite separate from system building.

Measurement and evaluation are clearly important. Indeed, they've achieved perhaps too much unquestioned and uncritical support over the past few years. Most grants—particularly federal grants—seem to demand an evaluation component as part of every project, whether it makes any sense or not. In my view, if you are just trying to create an experimental service and get it up and running, evaluating it in any elaborate way may be simply unrealistic, and may not produce anything useful. Doing statistical analysis on a few questionnaires about the system is not likely to accomplish much if people haven't had any meaningful chance to use it (much less integrate it into their work) and it isn't stable because it's a rapidly evolving research project. We may learn more from careful analysis of well established, mature production systems.

The right thing to do may be to make an intuitive judgement after the prototype is running about whether it's even worth evaluating formally, and if so maybe a separate grant for that may be in order. Sometimes, most of the knowledge gained may be in technical issues involved in the system implementation, and it may not be necessary to do user studies or elaborate system evaluations. Indeed, sometimes we need to just bet on and reward vision and intuition and recognize that we'll need to invest in formal and systematic evaluation later if the vision proves valid. We must not rush to evaluation.

Evaluation is an intervention that requires resources and has real costs—including real opportunity costs. We don't need to establish an entitlement for evaluators as part of the overhead of every project. What we do need is a serious discussion of what sorts of measurement and evaluation makes sense at various stages of the life cycle of different kinds of systems, and what we can reasonably expect to learn from these efforts—if you will, an informed meta-analysis of the applicability and expected benefits of various kinds of evaluation programs. This itself is a challenge for evaluation.

In fact, we need to ask another broader, and harder question about when and in what contexts evaluation programs really make a difference, and about which ones count and which ones don't. Here, I'm thinking about evaluation broadly—not just after the fact evaluation, but a whole interactive process of understanding user needs and behavior, their interactions with a system under design and development. Ann Bishop, Nancy van House, and Barbara Buttenfield (in press) have edited a book which addresses what they call *socially grounded design*—design practices that incorporate intensive engagement of users as individuals and social groups in the design and development process—which I think will help to frame some of these issues. I think it's helpful to think about evaluation in this broad, action-oriented way.

Of course, not all evaluation activity leads to action—to system design and redesign. Some is appropriately concerned with broader understanding of social trends and implications. But we should know when we can reasonably expect actionable results from our evaluation work.

Finally, in so many other areas of information systems, information technology and information retrieval, the real world is changing much faster that the research questions—and particularly the accepted measurement and evaluation strategies, and research methodologies—central to academic inquiry in these fields. We have seen some particularly painful examples of this in academic information retrieval, with not only the Cranfield benchmark collections (Cleverdon, Mills, and Keen, 1966) but in fact the entire academic research canon of static, centralized databases. Relevance and recall measures remained sacred and unquestioned while massive changes swept real-world information access and retrieval, leaving academic researchers churning out rigorous and sometimes interesting but often irrelevant research.

I will have more to say about this later. But I want to highlight the larger point here: A much needed, regular and serious examination of evaluation methodologies and strategies is critical if information science is to remain relevant and connected to the real world of systems building and systems use. Such re-examination is likely to cause disruptive changes in research communities, which are often bound together by the adoption of common measures and evaluative criteria for their work.

MEASUREMENT, DATA COLLECTION, AND EVALUATION

We measure and collect data for a host of reasons. Some are operational (problem determination, customer service, and legal and accounting requirements); others are more technical but still have a strongly operational component (capacity planning, performance, and resource utilization of system components). Some are to support research and analysis, to help us understand how the system is being used, and how well it is accomplishing its objectives and serving its users. Of course, one of the problems is that the farther we move away from operationally oriented data the less confident we can be that we are collecting the right data since the uses to which that data is going to be put are open-ended and ill-defined.

Yet another part of data collection is to allow us to identify and understand change—how technical changes to the system may alter its performance or use or how changes in user community behavior take place over time. This is not done enough in the research world—either for experimental systems or for production systems—and it is not funded sufficiently, in my view. It's definitely not done enough in the world of production systems by the people who operate them; often, this is viewed as unnecessary research fluff rather than vital management data.

I'd like to see some funding shift from routine evaluation of experimental systems as part of their construction to deeper, longer term and more systematic evaluation and understanding of what's happening with operational systems. It is very likely more important to understand how the use of widely deployed and accepted systems is changing over time than it is to understand whether users feel good about new experimental systems. Because most of the important production systems are no longer constructed or operated by the research or higher education communities, access to data for such research is a major barrier. I'll return to this point later.

We also collect data from users as well as from systems, through techniques like interviews, questionnaires, and focus groups. It's often hard to collect this data, to get meaningful samples from appropriately diverse user populations, to be confident about its accuracy, and it is frequently very difficult to link this data in useful ways to related data collected from our systems. We collect data about society, marketplaces, economics, and large-scale behavior that is not directly connected to a specific system but rather to broad technological and informational developments.

Sometimes—though not nearly as often as we would like—we can define success criteria for systems and then define measurements that we can use to evaluate how well systems are meeting these criteria. As we look at bigger and more complex systems, as we both seek to build systems with transformative impact and recognize that our systems may have such transformative effects, and as we define success more in social or work product (economic efficiency, user empowerment, the amplification of human intellect and the enhancement of human creativity) terms than in terms of the systems themselves, it has become more and more difficult to develop these evaluation criteria in any kind of a rigorous or quantitative way, much less to determine what data to collect to measure progress.

Evaluation in information science asks questions about information retrieval algorithms, information systems, and the production, use and impacts of information and information systems on individuals, communities, and society. In some sense, evaluating algorithms is simple; it's a one-time analysis. Other forms of evaluation are much harder; systems evaluation has an iterative relationship with design and development and can even precede and form a basis for design. We've moved to a much broader view of evaluation, but our knowledge of how to measure hasn't kept pace.

There are a few things we know how to do, or at least many of us believe we know how to do. They have become enshrined as widely accepted research and evaluation methodologies in information science and information technology fields. While we have been cranking out evaluation research through the twin machines of user studies and relevance/recall computations, in a very narrow technical way, we have failed to address the hard problems that don't fall within these frameworks. (I believe there is also ample reason to question whether these frameworks are valid even in the areas where they are applied, and I'll examine that issue later.)

Our failures to develop good measurement, analysis and evaluation tools and methodologies in some of the areas that really matter—the big, complex systems with important social impact, technologies with broad cultural and societal implications—are becoming very visible, and the consequences of these failures are serious. Our libraries and our institutions of higher education are now at political risk due to our inability to provide them with useable tools for meaningful measurement and evaluation.

As a society, we are making critical, high-impact public policy in areas as diverse as the applications of technology to education or the connections among technology, intellectual property and the management and preservation of our cultural record based on very little meaningful data. Our schools and universities are making enormous investments in IT strategies based largely on belief and anecdote. Not only are we making these choices with little data, but we have few tools or measurements to understand the effects and outcomes of these choices (and consequently to try to correct for bad choices).

There is growing public demand for accountability, which cannot be addressed without strategies for measurement and evaluation. Today, this is perhaps most prominent in debates about the quality of K-12 education in America and the various proposals to improve the elementary and secondary education systems: Much of the debate is about how to measure and evaluate the quality of the education system, and the standards against which is should be measured and evaluated. Many people are reaching out to IT, network connections, digital libraries and other technologies as a panacea for the many problems in the K-12 system, and we are going to see a convergence between the debates about educational evaluation and the need to evaluate these technologies. There are many other examples, such as the proposals to improve and streamline government through the use of IT and digital information.

WHAT'S DIFFERENT NOW? INTERNET SCALE AND INTERNET TIME

With the proliferation of large-scale information systems and the use of the Internet (and other information technologies) by the general public, plus the availability of digital information and the systems to offer access to it, two new problems have emerged which are reshaping our approaches to evaluation and measurement. The first is the sheer scale and ubiquity of the systems in question, the volumes of use and the range of impacts.

Data management and computational problems show up everywhere as we try to analyze data from these systems. In the 1990s when I was at the University of California, the MELVYL information system[1] was generating on the order of a gigabyte a week of log files, and even basic data analysis required substantial computational resources; you can extrapolate from there to see the kind of technical challenge any real analysis, measurement and evaluation of the major Internet search engines presents.

Recently, some of the long-distance telephone companies have been looking at databases representing a day, or a week, of calling patterns for all of their customers to understand patterns of connectivity (size of calling cliques, for example). Basically, this boils down to some fairly basic graph theory operations. For this much data, getting computationally tractable algorithms to perform these operations are fundamental computer science research problems in their own right. (See the work of Joan Feigenbaum [2000] and her colleagues at Bell Labs in this area.) Similar issues show up at all levels of the networked information environment, from understanding basic packet flows through higher-level services. As two examples, look at the supercomputer-based vocabulary work that Bruce Schatz (1997) and his colleagues at UIUC are doing or at the various efforts to analyze the link structures within the Web, such as the efforts at Stanford and Cornell which led to search engines like Google.[2] See Brin (1998), Brin and Page (1998), Gibson, Kleinberg, and Raghaver (1998), and Chakrabarti, et al. (1999). I would speculate that one of the important roles for supercomputer centers, with their expertise in large-scale computation, large-scale data management, and data visualization may well be the collection and analysis of performance and usage data for other large-scale systems.

It's worth recognizing the emergence of a new culture here. For almost all *traditional* user studies or *traditional* evaluation of query processing algorithms that have been the heart of so much information science research over the past few decades, the data management and analysis are trivial compared to system studies. (One exception being the Census, which can be looked at from one perspective as a monster user study.) Analysis of system measurements is a serious computational science because of the scale factor. Large-scale computational measurement, analysis and evaluation of systems are the future, in my view. We need to get serious about embracing it, and about providing—and requiring—graduates of information science programs to learn to deal with it. Better tools for data management and analysis are also going to be an important issue here.

The second problem is rate of change. With systems changing "on Internet time" and user behavior changing in response to new systems and system changes almost as rapidly, old data quickly become incommensurate with new data. Long-term trend analysis becomes virtually impossible. User studies offer insights only into last year's systems because they take so long. Even worse, most user studies represent a snapshot, when what you really want is an understanding of the evolving *relationship* between system and user over a period of time, as the user learns about the system, the system learns about the user, and both the system and the user change.

PRAGMATIC MEASUREMENT, EVALUATION AND ANALYSIS

There's a tradition in information science that I think we need to examine critically with regard to user studies. Historically, it has been easy to grind out a paper (or a Ph.D. thesis) by doing a user study that consists of little more than administering a questionnaire or structured interview to a small group of people and then doing some analysis of the results; often it takes years to move from measurements to publication of the results here. The fundamental problem with this class of work is that it ignores the realities of rate of change and of scale. Speaking as a system designer, I can say that most of these are of little help, either as a source of insight or as a source of guidance in improving systems. (They can be helpful in identifying errors in system design, but there are quicker, less formal, and more expedient ways of getting the same information quickly and cheaply, e.g., focus groups, talking to users, examining system transaction logs.) Even if these studies can be tied to system-generated measurement data, the data are often so old it's impractical or uninteresting to try to use the results of the user study as a guide to further analysis of the system logs or measurement data by the time the user study is completed. So many of the studies are questionable because of the small size of the user sample, and the way the user sample was selected (i.e., people who would respond to the questions).

Similarly, I worry when I see studies that examine 100 or 200 queries captured from a log; the real world today is one of hundreds of thousands of queries per day (or more), and one in which properly designed software should be able to look at the real data, not tiny samples. And it should be able to run the analysis every day, and tell you something about patterns of change.

We need to develop a set of engineering approaches to evaluation and measurement, something that will provide not just a general evaluation or insights into use, but that will help system developers in a practical way as they try to improve their systems. Let me give a few examples of the kinds of things I'm concerned with here:

- It is not helpful to conduct a large-scale evaluation at considerable expense which concludes that the system you had operating last year is horrible: it gives users inaccurate or incomplete answers about 40 percent of the time, and 50 percent of the users think that it either "sucks" or "sucks a lot." There's really no obvious place for a system developer to go with an evaluation like this; it's almost more of a political statement (i.e., one conclusion is the system is hopeless, rip it out and replace it, or shut it down, and fire everybody involved). It's only when the study begins to tell why the results are wrong and what to do to fix it that it becomes useful.
- We know a lot about usability. Huge amounts of money have been spent on usability studies and usability testing, and we have at least some knowledge of processes that can be employed to improve the usability of a specific system, but we don't have any way to measure the usability of a system. (Actually, there are some commercial products and services that purport to do this; it's not clear that they've had any serious examination in the research world.) This is very weird. Given a system, we can analyze it and tell the developers how to make it better, but we can't compare the usability of one system to that of another in a quantifiable way. There are some interesting developments in this area in terms of checkups for usability. One of the things I have been very pleased to see lately is the work of the World Wide Web Consortium (W3C) Web Accessibility Initiative (2000) on accessibility of Web services for people with disabilities. This initiative has encouraged the development of diagnostic tools that help you to analyze a Web site and highlight problem areas. We need a lot more of these kinds of tools, which are not deeply system-specific. Note that work in this area is not easy and not without controversy: For a cautionary parallel, consider the various computer programs that allegedly check grammar and reading level of prose. These are certainly of dubious utility though they can produce results that are at least entertaining.
- Another interesting area of measurement, analysis, and evaluation that resists quantification or rigor is interoperability. At very low levels interoperability is pretty clear-cut (the plug does or does not

> fit in the socket); as we move up the food chain to higher-level services interoperability becomes a complex, multi-faceted, and subtle problem. Bill Moen (2000) has done some good work on this in the Z39.50 area. What's striking to me is that we not only don't have crisp definitions of interoperability (or maybe we have too many), but we have no way of measuring whether one system is more interoperable than another. We can look at interoperability problems on a case-by-case basis, and just as with usability we have a lot of experience that helps us to look for certain kinds of problems that may exist. But, we have no general theory. Though again we do have some tool approaches that have been developed, e.g., conformance testing suites.

In all of these cases, one of the questions we haven't asked enough, in my view, is "How can the evaluators help the system developers?" This is a high payoff area.

This is not, of course, to suggest that we should ignore deeper studies that try to understand social and cultural impacts of technology and networked information, bringing to bear insights from disciplines like anthropology, sociology, ethnography, and economics; those are also important. However, particularly in light of the problems of scale and rate of change, too much of the measurement and evaluation we are doing fails to be either pragmatic or deep.

ISSUES AND RESEARCH TOPICS IN MEASUREMENT AND EVALUATION

In the next part of this paper, I want to detail six important areas related either to the conduct of measurement and evaluation or key areas where measurement and evaluation are applied that I think need some serious attention and exploration. These six areas are the following:

- Data Collection
- Data Processing
- Information Retrieval as an Experimental Science
- Queries, Sessions, Relationships, and Users
- Cataloging, Metadata, and Information Retrieval
- Social and Behavioral Implications of Information and Information Systems

DATA COLLECTION

Without access to data, without measurements, we can't do research or analysis, much less evaluation. Data, analysis, and evaluation based on that data should guide the formulation of public policy and personal and organizational decision making. And I think we need to admit that we are flying blind. Most of the data we need to drive research and decision making has become private property. Too often today, we are doing research based on the data we can get access to rather than the data that defines important systems.

Let me just make a few points to underscore the severity and extent of this problem.

Many of you probably remember the wonderful graphics that were distributed as posters in the early 1990s showing traffic patterns across the NSFNet backbones (there was actually even a digital video rendering of how this ebbed and flowed over the course of a day).[3] You may also recall tables that show the amount of Internet traffic by protocol and, for example, reveal the explosive emergence of the World Wide Web over an amazingly short period (more precisely, the growth in data volumes for the Hypertext Transfer Protocol and the concomitant decline in predecessor protocols like Gopher).

At that time, NSF was underwriting one of the primary Internet backbones and also had significant policy control over the interchange points where the public and commercial backbones linked together within the Internet. As a result, networking researchers had tremendous access to data characterizing the traffic flows and dynamic behavior of the Internet, at least within the United States. This is now all within private hands; the NSF is completely out of the business. We could not generate a graphic today of Internet traffic flow; the information is proprietary—confidential with a competitive advantage to specific backbone providers. You cannot even find out how the various backbone providers interconnect ("peer") with each other, save though unreliable, heuristic external mapping techniques. If the Internet is the information superhighway, we have lost most of our access to data about the traffic flows upon it and the types of traffic that it is carrying.

Another example.You may recall that in the 1980s, the Council on Library Resources sponsored an extensive multisite study called *Users look at online catalogs* (Council on Library Resources, 1982), which was a watershed in understanding the impact of online catalogs. It provided data that countered many widely held opinions (for example, that users did not do subject searching). Results of this study guided the evolution of the next generation of online catalogs and provided a baseline for understanding how user behavior subsequently changed based on more experience with online catalogs. See, for example, the work of Chris Borgman (1986, 1996) on why online catalogs are hard to use and of Ray Larsen (1991) on the decline of subject searching. There's a great need to revisit such a study today, and to expand the study to also explore how online catalogs relate to Internet search engines. But it would be impossible to do such a study today, I believe. In the 1980s many of the key online catalogs studied were locally developed experimental systems that were run by universities. One of the things that the grant paid for was to instrument these systems and to develop data collection and analysis tools for them. Today, virtually all online catalogs are provided by vendors, and they have much more limited instrumentation and data collection capabilities.

And, of course, the Web search engines are almost entirely in commercial hands. Think about this carefully: Search engines are one of the principal tools that the public employs to find information in the digital age, yet the research community cannot examine or evaluate the kinds of queries submitted and the algorithms used to construct the databases that answer the queries or the algorithms used to evaluate the queries against these databases. A few researchers. for example, Steve Lawrence and his colleagues at NEC Research in Princeton, NJ, have done some excellent work trying to estimate empirically how much of the material on the Web the various search engines actually cover (see Lawrence and Giles 1998a, 1998b, 1999 and Giles, Lawrence, and Krovitz, 1998). The answer was not very much—perhaps 35 percent if I recall correctly—and this research finding became national news.

It gets worse. We are actually making the transition from print information to digital information, both in scholarly communication (books and journals) and in mass market information products (newspapers, magazines, and, more recently, books—so-called "e-books"). Other consumer media like sound recordings, images, and video are also moving to digital distribution. The primary system architecture in place today has users going directly to publisher Web sites for this information (or to third-party aggregators or systems like Napster in the case of digital music). All these systems are private and external to both the research community and the user base. There were some important early experiments by the research community in collaboration with publishers, one of the most notable being the TULIP project (Gusack and Lynch, 1995 and TULIP: Final Report 1996), where Elsevier Science Publishers worked with about 10 major U.S. universities to understand how journals in digital form would actually be used. TULIP sites built instrumented experimental systems and collected, published and evaluated actual usage data. Today, similar data from production systems are highly proprietary; universities and libraries are trying to negotiate contracts with their content suppliers that give them at least some access to data about how their user communities are actually using these materials. But the emphasis in these negotiations is management data, not the more detailed transaction logs needed to support research level analysis and evaluation.

The mass market case is even worse because institutions interested in seeing research are not a significant part of the marketplace and, thus, have little negotiating leverage. Basically, we have little access to real information about how users are using digital information. The federal government has mounted several large, important, and heavily used databases that could also be valuable sources of data. See the EDGAR database (Security and Exchange Commission, 2000), the U.S. Patent and Trademark Office's patent files

(2000), the Pubmed database (National Library of Medicine, 1998), and ERIC (The National Library of Education, n.d.). In most cases, privacy constraints on the government agencies prevent usage data about these databases from becoming resources for the research community.

Much of the locus of innovation has moved out of the universities and into operational commercial sites and systems. Amazon.com has done some wonderfully innovative work over the past few years in developing what I think can be fairly characterized as a digital library for book selection and acquisition. This system makes heavy use of recommender system (collaborative filtering) technology, various sorts of reviews, and other techniques that have otherwise seen rather limited production deployment. Certainly, the library community hasn't used them. There is some early experimental data such as the Movie Lens (Group Lens, 1999) recommender system datasets available for collaborative filtering researchers but nothing on the scale of the commercial systems. The Web auction sites such as E-bay have a wealth of data about the operation of auctions and reputation managers. The constellation of sites that make up the information systems that support the consumer and institutional financial markets—the exchanges themselves, the various online brokerages, and the online community sites that trade rumors and opinions about stocks—also hold a wealth of data. Yet as far as I know virtually all of this data, which represents many of the most innovative developments of the past decade, are essentially unavailable for research use.

In 1997, Hal Varian of UC Berkeley's School of Information Management and Systems chaired a workshop for the Computer Science and Telecommunications Board of the National Research Council (NRC) on research opportunities relating to economic and social impacts of computing and communications. The report of this workshop, published as *Fostering Research on the Economic and Social Impacts of Information Technology* (National Research Council, 1998), paints a very disturbing picture of the problems the research community faces in access to data. Read this to get a broader view of the situation, particularly as it relates to the diffusion and use of technology, as opposed to the more system-specific data that I've been emphasizing.

Just as a final point, let me note that there is some very controversial legislation that has been pending during the last few sessions of Congress (and that doesn't seem likely to go away, unfortunately) which could make the already serious problems with access to data much worse. This is generically called the "Database" bill, although in fact there are several competing bills, some of which are far worse than others, and they have varied from year to year over the past few years. Such legislation, by creating new proprietary rights in compilations of data of virtually all kinds, could not only damage scientific and scholarly inquiry in a wide range of fields, but would also make the problem of access to data to support measurement, evaluation, and analysis in information science even worse than it is. For more details, I invite you to read two

National Research Council (NRC) reports, *Bits of Power* (NRC, 1997) and the more recent *A Question of Balance* (NRC, 1999).

Ultimately, access to data is not just a problem for the research world. It's also a public policy problem. But clearly one thing that is needed is a search for new collaborations between industry and the research community are needed to try to ensure that the research community has access to data for analysis and evaluation while reaching compromises that honor the business concerns of industry. It will be difficult, but we must try to get access to data that support *important* measurement, evaluation, and analysis, rather than limiting our research to readily available data for systems and practices that do not reflect real concerns and activities.

DATA PROCESSING: TOOLS AND STANDARDS

As we try to deal with the problems of scale in today's networked information systems, a new focus on tools will be required. Current statistical and simulation packages leave much to be desired. A good evaluation of the available tools, followed by some systematic work in strategies for filling the gaps, would be an excellent project for the ASIS community.

Visualization has been one of the great breakthroughs of the 1980s and 1990s in dealing with very large datasets in a variety of scientific and engineering disciplines. Much can be done in applying these technologies to information science, and this has not been well explored. As a point of departure, I would commend to your attention the work of the networking community, particularly the National Laboratory for Advanced Networking Research (NLANR), the Cybergeography atlas efforts (Dodge, 2000), and Carl Malamud and his colleagues at mappa.mundi.net (Malamud, et al., 2000). From a completely different perspective, the efforts of the Electronic Cultural Atlas (2000) program led by Lewis Lancaster at the University of California, Berkeley, and the work of the Perseus Project at Tufts University led by Greg Crane (2000) offer other insights into how data visualization and geospatial organizations of datasets can change scholarship.

We need to bring these ideas, and these technologies, into measurement, analysis, and evaluation in information science.

Finally, standards will have a role to play in data collection and data analysis. Some useful work has been done by the International Consortium of Library Consortia (ICOLC) (2000) on possible standards for reporting usage data from publisher Web sites. We need to begin to examine where standards are needed and how they can facilitate comparative measurement, analysis and evaluation efforts.

INFORMATION RETRIEVAL AS AN EXPERIMENTAL SCIENCE: RELEVANCE, RECALL, AND TEST COLLECTIONS

I am not fond of the word "paradigm," in the sense of Thomas Kuhn's *Structure of Scientific Revolutions* (1970), and seldom use it. It's been hideously debased in the literature and the popular press. But, in the 1960s, we really did establish a paradigm for information science.

At that time a number of people—the late Gerry Salton's name is prominent, but he is only one of a number of pioneers, and I don't want to get sidetracked here about who should make this list—turned information retrieval research into a science. They established a framework for IR research that said that the key operation was the evaluation of a query against a database, and the right measures for query evaluation were relevance and recall. They defined how to compute them and established an experimental collection (the Cranfield collections and queries) which could be used to measure relevance and recall for a given query evaluation algorithm. This created a rigorous, quantitative experimental science of IR: One algorithm could be compared meaningfully to another. Their work was a bold and important achievement.

By the late 1980s, this accomplishment had soured. None of the assumptions were justifiable or realistic anymore. The test collections represented a few thousand records when real-world databases already had moved into the millions of records; today, in Web indexing systems, we are bumping up against the billion-page level in our databases. We have seen research papers and Ph.D. dissertations present algorithms that have improved performance to the third decimal place over the canonical collections when there was no reason to believe that this was anything other than statistical *noise*. There was considerable skepticism whether the performance improvements documented on the benchmark databases would scale to real-world applications. Worse, relevance and recall were perhaps useful measures in an environment of information poverty. Today, attention and time are the limiting factors most often; and the fact that there are 100,000 relevant records in the database and an algorithm finding 80,000 doesn't make much difference: The question is whether the first 20 satisfied the user's needs well enough.

The Text REtrieval Conference (TREC) work (2000), initiated by the National Science Foundation (NSF), Advanced Research Projects Agency (of the Department of Defense) (ARPA), National Institute of Standards & Technology (NIST), National Security Agency (NSA) and other organizations in the late 1980s supplanted the Cranfield databases with new benchmark databases that were at least large enough to have some resemblance to reality, even if the queries and content were perhaps a bit specialized. Scale effects were implicit in the databases, but not necessarily in the evaluation metrics. This was a breakthrough that revitalized much IR research by reconnecting it with the real-world information resources that had become commonplace in the 20 years since the Cranfield benchmarks were first established.

We need a systematic program to reassess our test collections and evaluation methodologies every few years. And we are still too focused on text. Video, images, and audio all need to find their way into the next generation of benchmark databases. Where do we get these databases and the benchmark queries? How should we define them?

TREC didn't help as much in expanding our repertoire of measurement and evaluation tools beyond relevance and recall in favor of new measures that are perhaps more appropriate in an environment of deceptive documents and document descriptions, information glut, massive duplication of content across distributed databases, and an economy of limited attention. We still haven't factored in the costs of searching multiple information resources, both in terms of human time and charges for using the various databases. There has been some interesting work in how to find the right database, or databases, to search and to decide how many candidate databases should be searched. See French, et al. (1999), for an overview of some of this. There is much more work to be done in these areas.

Furthermore, real-world IR happens now in a distributed environment with many databases, and with a multiplicity of auxiliary services such as entry vocabulary mapping systems, gazetteers, query expansion systems. The whole idea of architectures and reference models needs to come into our thinking in an explicit way as we develop new measures for retrieval quality and effectiveness. For networked information, however, the idea of system architecture is an absolutely fundamental one, driven by performance, trust, control, marketplace, economic, scaling, reliability and interoperability considerations: It proceeds, rather than follows, thinking about evaluation and measurement. For IR, architectural models that can underpin measurement and evaluation are still a relatively new idea; one of the first articulations that I'm familiar with can be found in the work of Michael Buckland and Chris Plaunt (see Buckland and Plaunt [1994] and Plaunt [1997]). We need to see a lot more work on how to conduct measurement and evaluation in real networked information environments.

QUERIES, SESSIONS, RELATIONSHIPS, AND USERS

The focus on queries that is part of the standard paradigm for IR is another fundamental error that has distorted our work on measurement and evaluation. It may have had its roots in the notion that every query was tremendously costly; thus, each query is carefully constructed and stands alone. This is no longer the case. Or, it may have simply been computationally tractable. It would be useful to try to reconstruct the thinking behind this part of the standard model. But whatever the origin of the idea, it's clear that it's no longer terribly useful. People today simply don't use IR systems that way, investing hours and consulting with experts to craft a single query that will be submitted at vast expense. Rather, they interact on an ongoing interactive, iterative and casual way with a variety of IR systems.

Online catalogs have received a considerable amount of critical abuse because it's easy for system operators to produce statistics about the distribution of result set sizes for queries, and if you look at these numbers of an appropriately instrumented online catalog like UC's MELVYL system you'll see that a substantial percentage of queries get zero results and a substantial percentage of queries produce enormous results (over, say, 1000 hits). People have seized on these numbers as proof that online catalogs are failures as retrieval systems and that they serve their users poorly in response to a large portion of queries.

Michael Berger (1994), then at the University of California Office of the President, did a very interesting Ph.D. thesis at the UC Berkeley School of Information Management and Systems. He went through a fair number of logs and tried to group the logs into sessions, rather than individual queries. His key insight was that the meaningful interaction was the *session* that a user had with the system, not the results of any single query. And he found that based on session-level analysis, online catalogs work much better than the query-based numbers might indicate. Users frequently recovered from zero or very large result queries, by refining or reformulating their searches as part of an interactive, iterative session with the retrieval system.

Query-based measures are easy. Session based measures are much harder, particularly in environments based on Web-based services that push session context and state management into cookies and other mechanisms and run stateless at the lower-level protocol level. And while it's easy to say what happened in response to a query in a mechanistic way (by measuring the size of the result set), determining whether a session is successful is much harder and more subjective; it involves making some judgement about the user's purpose. But here we have a beautiful example of a research direction that we need to pursue: measuring the encounter with an IR system rather than the subtransactions (queries) that are components of that encounter. This is an important caution in thinking about how to use system-generated data; the data that is easily collected, and that fits naturally into the system's view of the world may not capture the right experiences.

Berger's (1994) work was based on a painstaking and painful manual analysis. We need to learn how to do machine based session analysis so we can do it on a much larger scale. Though I don't know for sure, I have to believe that some of the more sophisticated commercial systems are doing this, but we need to make it routine for all kinds of information systems. One can imagine Amazon measuring success in terms of the number of books purchased per session.

This is just the starting point. Many users have access to more than one system. We need to begin to ask questions about whether the user, having had interactions with multiple systems, found the information he or she needed and, if so, how quickly and from what system. We need to understand how users work with a portfolio of available information systems.

There is the even more important question of long-term relationships with systems. Today we have the notions of personal computers, personal digital assistants, Internet appliances, "agents"—machines and systems that users have a long-term relationship with. These machines learn about the user over time, and mediate on behalf of the user with a world full of information resources. We have people who use information systems over a period of years, even decades, that occasionally migrate from one system to another for sometimes poorly understood reasons. We don't know much about how to design, evaluate, or measure such relationships and the systems involved in them. And we don't have research programs that focus on these fundamentally important questions.

We need to study the evolution of user understanding of systems, of system understanding of users, and of work practices in conjunction with systems. We need to evaluate not just sessions but relationships. There may well be a role for user studies here, as well, as they are intended to capture the user experience in interacting with his or her environment, and we can't directly capture the user experience since it is likely spread across multiple autonomous systems.

A few other related specific areas of inquiry are evident. For example, users will migrate from one *personal* system to another from time to time as a result of technology changes. How is this migration handled? How much re-learning has to take place? What are the penalties from the user perspective in moving from one system to another, the switching costs? How is information that has been learned about the user most effectively migrated from old to new systems?

CATALOGUING, METADATA, AND INFORMATION RETRIEVAL

Cataloguing practice has always, as far as I can tell, resisted any form of real evaluation. There are deeply held beliefs about what constitutes the *right* way to catalog a work, which seem to be largely independent of any systematic study of what the cataloguing is for or the way the cataloguing is used to support retrieval, particularly in an environment of electronic information, powerful retrieval systems, and new retrieval tools such as content-based access. There is a growing investment in conversion of special collections to digital forms and a growing need to describe novel types of works such as instructional materials, visual materials, or video recordings. In response, a diversity of new approaches to describing content—programs like the Dublin core metadata initiative[4] or the work of the Instructional Management System (IMS) on metadata[5]—have emerged. We are faced with the need to come up with a pragmatic, economically based engineering approach to developing metadata practices. This is a pressing and practical problem; it is now quite common to see proposals for digitizing collections of materials where a third to a half of the cost of the project is in the creation of metadata to organize and provide access to the collection as opposed to simply scanning or otherwise capturing primary content in digital form.

In the 21st century, more and more text will be directly available in digital form, either because it was created that way or improvements in optical character recognition (OCR) technology facilitating the conversion of scanned images of print pages into digital text. All of this text will be directly searchable. We are beginning to develop systems that provide similar automated access to the contents of sound recordings and images—systems that find pictures which are similar to other pictures, which share various computational characteristics (such as the relative amounts and arrangements of color or texture patterns), or that contain certain musical patterns. There's a large investment in research in this area today. It is possible to go further with just computationally-driven content based retrieval. Metadata sometimes adds more access—but when, how much, and when the improved access justifies the cost of the metadata creation—are questions that have no rigorous answers. These are some of the evaluation questions we must confront.

One of my great pleasures during last ten years has been the seminar I have taught with Michael Buckland at the School of Information Management and Systems at the University of California, Berkeley. Every year we discuss developments in metadata, and one of the key questions that Michael always asks is "What metadata actually makes a difference in user retrieval and selection decisions?" This is exactly the right question to help us start putting metadata creation on a rational economic and technical basis. We know almost nothing about how to answer it.

There's another side to the research agenda relating to measurement and evaluation of metadata, and that's understanding the practice of metadata creation and how it's changing over time. OCLC Research has a very useful program where they are periodically sampling metadata attached to Web sites and developing time series data. We need to know a great deal more about the practice of metadata creation, and how it is shifting from one year to another. Tom Baker (1998) of GMD has proposed a provocative way of thinking about how metadata usage evolves by analogy to the linguistic evolution of pidgins and Creoles. It would be useful to have the data, and the evaluation, to assess these analogies. Of course, this needs to be linked back to user searching behavior and, thus, to questions of the kinds of queries that users are constructing and the kinds of search services that use the evolving base of metadata.

SOCIAL AND BEHAVIORAL IMPLICATIONS OF INFORMATION AND INFORMATION SYSTEMS

There are many important questions about how social structures are established and function around information, its selection, and its use. Some of this takes us beyond measurement, analysis, and evaluation to modeling and simulation, but I believe that the questions are so important they deserve at least some very brief consideration here. Indeed, I believe that simulation and modeling are much underutilized complements to traditional measurement and evaluation approaches which can offer a great deal of new insight.

People have tried to build mathematical and statistical models of behavior for a long time, but they tend to be computationally intractable if they model reality in any detail. With inexpensive computation resources to conduct simulations, we have opportunities to experiment to try to understand causes and effects, rather than just look descriptively and analytically at individual cases through observation. There is work going trying to simulate societies and social processes, markets, and behavior on a large-scale. We need measurements and data collection to parameterize these simulations and to compare the results of modeling to reality. Because so much activity is happening inside IT-based systems, we have an unprecedented amount and detail of data potentially available to drive modeling and simulation.

There is a great flowering of interdisciplinary work in simulation and modeling that is potentially relevant to information science and to understanding how information is used. This ranges from the efforts of Epstein and Axtell (1996) and Axelrod (1997) in simulating society and behaviors like cooperation and competition. See also Gaylord and D'Andria (1998) and Prietla, Gaser, and Caley (1998). We have a whole array of work that tries to provide some insights into the behavior of people in groups with regard to various kinds of information. This includes recommender systems (collaborative filtering)[6] and mathematical models of the propagation of rumors and new ideas; a large body of related work, primarily in the area of epidemic modeling (Daley and Gani, 1999) is relevant here. Much of this work is highly rigorous, and lends itself to the construction of simulations and models though it needs to be adapted for information-related studies. Other efforts are provocative but more metaphorical—for example, the idea of *memes*—epidemics of ideas (Lynch, 1996). (Note: This is *another* Lynch, not me!) These are related developments in personalized media and advertising. Behavioral finance is another relatively young discipline that investigates how information is shared, and how this influences individual behavior and decision making, particularly in economic settings (Scleifer, 2000). We have a great opportunity to learn from this work and to absorb its methods, insights, and perspectives into information science.

To just give one specific example, there's a really disappointing book that came out a few years ago called *How Hits Happen*. (Farrell, 1998). While the book really doesn't get us very far, it's clear we really don't understand how popular or important works emerge and how social processes identify them. This is a central issue. It gets at how we can use social processes to help people to manage information overload. I'd argue that it's an information science question, or at least there is an information science perspective that can be taken on the question which should be very fruitful. It's an area that cries out for sophisticated measurement, simulation, and evaluation.

Identity and trust, in my view, are going to be critical components of the networked information infrastructure. We understand very little about identity, trust, and their relationships either at a technical level (think about Public Key Infrastructure [PKI] (Ford and Baum, 1997 and Feghhi, Jalilm and Williams, 1999), the PGP Web of trust (Zimmermann, 1995 and PGP Web of Trust Statistics, 2000), or at the deeper social level (the utility of reputation managers, for example, or even the question of the types of reputations we want to link to identities, and how we describe the components of these reputations). We need to begin to map trust patterns at PKI as they deploy, and to begin to understand and evaluate how users establish and rely upon trust relationships and reputation. In a recent paper for the *Journal of the American Society of Information Science*, or *JASIS* (Lynch, 2001), I've argued that trust and reputation need to be integrated into IR systems. Just as we've studied statistics and models of language and terminology and then applied this knowledge to the engineering and evaluation of IR, we are going to need similar fundamental studies in trust, reputation, and identity to underpin new work in IR.

Finally, we have a whole series of questions about how to define the quality and authority of information and how to integrate this into processes of IR and evaluation. We have questions about what measures of authority are effective and relevant to various kinds of users. This connects up to a rich body of work on citations and other forms of authority and to some of the more recent work on *infometrics*, the large-scale link structure of the Web and the like..

These questions are taking center stage as part of the debate about the validity of the Web as an information source and discussions about its appropriate role in the larger tapestry of information provision. As the role of publishers, referees and other gatekeepers and validators shifts in the networked information environment, it is gaining new urgency. Though we have a good deal of empirical practice in these areas, we are notably short on general theory or quantitative measures.

I think that the social and behavioral implications of information and information systems hold some of the most exciting questions in information science today and some of the most stimulating opportunities for interdisciplinary collaboration.

IN CONCLUSION: GRAND CHALLENGES AND PUBLIC POLICY

There's now a tradition in IT of defining "grand challenge" problems, problems that could have an enormous social payoff if we could marshal the technology to solve them. Examples are predicting weather and climate change, predicting the structure of proteins, and ensuring the viability of our nuclear weapons stockpile without the need for actual testing programs. Though these are very hard problems from an IT and computational science point of view, they are not framed (at the highest level) in terms of these technical challenges but rather in terms of broader results.

Ideally, grand challenges should be readily understood by the general public, and they should be able to capture the imagination of the layperson. They should also excite the scientists or other clients empowered by the breakthroughs in IT. Grand challenges have been used effectively over the past decade to communicate the importance of federal government support for research and development in IT and high-performance networking. The High-Performance Computing and Communication (HPCC) initiative and more recently the President's Information Technology Advisory Committee, or PITAC (2000), have used grand challenge problems as a way of both establishing goals and benchmarking progress in IT research programs. Grand challenge problems generally call for orders of magnitude computational and communications improvements or radical breakthroughs in algorithm design and data management rather than simply incremental progress.

I believe that the time is ripe for grand challenge problems in information science and networked information, particularly in areas related to evaluation, given the importance of the public policy choices we face today involving IT and the growing emphasis on accountability of our institutions.

Since we don't have any quantitative way to measure improvements in our ability to evaluate, I can't say that the grand challenge evaluation problems call for order of magnitude improvements in this ability. The grand challenge problems in measurement, analysis, and evaluation will certainly call for major conceptual breakthroughs and, perhaps, computational breakthroughs as well. I'm confident that significant progress on any of these will have far-reaching social and societal benefits.

In concluding this personal survey of research problems in evaluation and measurement, I want to frame a few of what I consider to be grand challenge problems (recognizing they are a little different from those familiar to information technologists and computational scientists). They are problems that will need new insights and techniques, not just massive improvements in our ability to compute or transfer data. Unlike many of the technical and disciplinary issues in information science and IR I've discussed earlier, these also have the characteristic that they reach beyond information science and demand extensive collaboration outside of our discipline, a property that they share with the grand challenge problems of IT. Unlike the grand challenge problems of computational science, the answers—the evaluations and measurements—as well as the problems themselves need to be at least somewhat comprehensible and persuasive for the lay public.

Evaluating Intellectual Property in the Digital Environment

For the last few years, I've had the privilege of serving on a National Research Council Committee on Intellectual Property in the Emerging Information Infrastructure. You may be familiar with the report *The Digital Dilemma: Intellectual Property in the Information Infrastructure* (National Research Council, 2000) that constituted the output of this committee. It was released in November 1999 and formally published by National Academies Press in January 2000. The work of the committee focused primarily on copyright in the networked information environment. My comments are not intended to summarize the committees findings comprehensively, and indeed go well beyond these findings and recommendations, though they build upon some of them. As a committee member, I want to be careful to distinguish my personal views from those of the committee as a whole.

There's a general agreement that intellectual property—copyrighted works, patents, etc.—is a key currency in the digital world and the new economy. No surprise there, although there's considerable debate about how intellectual property works within business and economic models, about when it generates revenue directly, and when it generates revenue indirectly (via advertising, promoting performance events, etc.).

I think some of the findings of the committee are rather startling and should serve as a wake-up call for those concerned with measurement and evaluation. Let me give a few examples.

In a stunningly craven act of appeasement to a few large media companies, Congress passed, with little public debate, the Sonny Bono Copyright Term Extension Act, (1998), which extended the copyright duration to the life of the author plus 70 years, or 95 years for corporately authored works.[7] Put another way, this extension, which is simply the most recent step in a secular trend towards lengthening copyrights, established a 25-year moratorium on the passage of works into the public domain. Leaving aside some of the obviously unjustifiable aspects of this legislation—in particular, that people who have already created works don't need further motivation to create the works they have already created (most especially if they are already dead)—we know almost nothing about the effects and social costs of various terms of duration for patents and copyrights. We don't know how extending the term encourages creation of new works or restricts the exploitation of protected but fallow works.

Related to this, we also have new legislative proposals (the Database bills) that may create a new set of rights in compilations of information. Again, we know almost nothing about the potential effects of such legislation in a systematic way although we have many positive and negative anecdotes.

We know little about the costs, benefits, and problems of various regimes for managing copyrighted works. In music, we have a compulsory licensing system that has been very important in making radio broadcasting work and in making music an almost ubiquitous part of our daily environment. What are the overhead costs of rights clearance, and how will they effect our ability to convert our cultural heritage into digital form? There has been very little study of these questions.

I want to draw your attention to one specific provision of the very complicated 1998 Digital Millennium Copyright Act, or DMCA (1998). The DMCA creates a new big-time crime: attempting to circumvent technical protection systems on digital content. With some specific exemptions, this is a crime irrelevant of the reason for which you are circumventing the protection system. Even if the use you make doesn't violate copyright law, the act of circumventing the protection system in order to make that use may still be a felony. Some reasonable concerns were raised about these provisions. For example, they could well represent the death knells of fair use, a vital provision for not just scholarship but intelligent discourse in a free society. Because of these concerns, the DMCA contains language mandating the Librarian of Congress conduct a periodic review and evaluation of the impact of technological protection measures and provides the ability to make exceptions to the anticircumvention provisions of the DMCA for certain classes of material if these are necessary for the public good. (At least, this is how I understand what is a very complex piece of legislation.)

My purpose in raising this is to point out that it's unclear what data need to be collected in order to support such a periodic evaluation or how such an evaluation might actually be conducted. This is a place where some help from the research community would, I think, be welcome.

Finally, one very important finding of the NRC *Digital Dilemma* report is that copyright is now much more than a narrowly legal issue to be argued about by attorneys representing large corporations. Copyright is becoming increasingly pervasive in the experience of every consumer and can only be fully understood through a multi-disciplinary perspective that includes not only law but also economics, psychology, business, and sociology. There appears to be a growing disconnect between social norms of behavior and law in the area of intellectual property. Just consider the emergence of Napster (2000) and similar systems for sharing music; my point here is not whether Napster is legal under current copyright law but to observe something more basic. Laws at odds with social norms create public policy problems. We know virtually nothing about what the general public believes about intellectual property, where it has acquired these beliefs, what may change them over time (including any actual or potential role for education about copyright and intellectual property), or about public behaviors with regard to intellectual property (which may or may not mirror beliefs about what is actually legal or fair).

Intellectual property law is intended to be a balance between creators and society, a pact that gives certain rights to creators for a limited time to motivate them to create, in exchange for which the public enjoys the benefits of their creativity. The rights are further not unlimited; certain specific societal interests are protected by provisions such as fair use and copyright deposit. It is clear that the digital world has upset this balance in complex ways. In the predigital world, intellectual property law does not seem to have been based on real measurement and evaluation. In the new digital world, we have the opportunity to do better and the *need* to make better use of real data, analysis, and evaluation because of the tremendous complexity, high stakes, and sometimes emotional nature of the decisions and problems we face today.

Providing the basis to take our intellectual property systems into the digital world in an informed way, and perhaps even to reconsider some of what are, in my view, ill-advised decisions that have been made in the early stages of this migration is surely a grand challenge problem.

In my view, the easiest and perhaps most productive place to start on this grand challenge is with comprehensive data collection and measurement. We need to measure before we can assess and evaluate.

Evaluating Libraries

We spend a substantial amount of money on libraries, e.g., public libraries funded by tax dollars, academic libraries funded by their parent academic institutions, and corporate and other institutional special libraries established to provide services to their organizations.

Libraries have invested a tremendous amount of work in developing measures of performance and quality. The Association of Research Libraries (ARL), for example, has worked very hard in this area over the years. Many of you will be familiar with the annual ARL statistical reports, which are in the research library ratings published in places like in the *Chronicle of Higher Education*.

These measures are based on traditional print collections and the activities that accompany them (e.g., circulation, materials processing, interlibrary loan). They clearly need major revision and rethinking to accommodate the networked information world, with its emphasis on access rather than collections, and work is underway on this difficult issue.

Key member institutions within the ARL are simultaneously undertaking a much more difficult challenge: to create ways of measuring the contribution of the library in advancing the research, teaching, and public service missions of the university. This, of course, raises the issue of measuring and evaluating universities themselves, which I'll discuss shortly. See http://www.arl.org/stats/newmeas/newmeas.html for information on the ARL programs.

Developing ways to extend traditional library performance measures into the networked information world is a difficult and important problem. Traditional library measures address how one library compares to another in various dimensions. There's an even harder problem, which has started to surface in the corporate world, but which is likely to be raised more broadly in the next decade or so, particularly in light of the growing range of commercial information service offerings.

The problem is that corporations are asking whether the ongoing investment in *having a library at all* is justified (as opposed to whether they are getting a good return on a given investment compared to other corporations making a similar level of investment, or whether their level of investment is comparable to that of similar organizations). This has led to attempts to understand the contribution that special libraries make to their organizations. The answers have been highly varied, ranging from a reaffirmed and even increased commitment to libraries in some corporations to the elimination or outsourcing of library services in other corporations. So far, there is not much open questioning of whether libraries are needed in academic institutions. Indeed, accreditation criteria, as well as the general weight of common wisdom says that one cannot have an institution of higher education without a library, and broad-based support for public libraries exists as an important public good.

But some states have gutted school libraries for K-12 over the past few decades without much discussion or remorse. In an age where more and more information is available via the Internet—either free or for license—questions about whether we really continue to need libraries, and whether the investments we make in them are justifiable, will surely be raised. The grand challenge in the area of libraries will be to address these questions with measurement and evaluation, not merely opinion, and to take the next step, which will be to discuss how we might determine appropriate levels of investment in library services. The exciting work of the ARL institutions to try to develop outcomes-based measures for library performance is a crucial first step in addressing this grand challenge. Addressing it for public libraries will be more difficult still because the purposes of public libraries are more diverse and less clear.

Evaluating Information Technology in Higher Education

For all of the problems and limitations of the current ARL statistics, it's important to recognize what they have accomplished. We have time series data, by institution, for these measures. This data allows university administrators to examine several key questions as they decide how much budgetary resource to invest in their libraries, and to evaluate the performance of library management in making use of the resources with which they are provided. Specifically, they provide answers to these questions:

- How much are we investing in our library compared to the institutions that we benchmark ourselves against?
- Given the rate of investment, how does this translate into library quality compared to other institutions making similar (or larger or smaller) investments?

Universities have been pouring money into IT for several decades. They would like to ask the same questions about IT investments that they can ask and largely answer about their libraries. We do not have the measures in place to allow us to respond to the same, very reasonable, questions about information technology. There are some techniques, like direct benchmarking against other organizations that have been of some help, though more outside of academic settings. The problems of measuring IT investment and results are complicated by a greater diversity of organization, mission, assignment of responsibility, funding and budgetary models, etc., when compared to libraries.

I will simply note in passing that many other organizations. including schools and government agencies, would like to ask and answer very similar questions about their investments in IT. This is not a problem unique to higher education. Indeed, the recent Government Performance Results Act (GPRA) has created a massive legal requirement for government agencies to perform regular assessments of their work. I have mixed feeling about this, which tie back to my earlier comments about the growing obsession with evaluation of all efforts. Though the requirement to perform such evaluation is a valuable discipline and is good accountability, such evaluation doesn't always make sense. Even when it makes sense, we sometimes have no idea how to go about it in a meaningful way. But evaluate we must.

A more important question points to the questions raised above, in some sense parallel with the question whether investment in libraries is justified in the first place. To some extent, comparisons are unimportant. They assume that, roughly speaking, everyone is doing the right thing to begin with. The key questions are the extent to which massive and ongoing investments in IT and networked information are improving teaching, learning, research, and public service.

Sometime in the 1990s, the stakes got much higher. Certainly, the availability of information technology began to have a transformative effect on research in specific, relatively narrow scholarly disciplines as early as the 1950s. By the 1960s, this began to be reflected in teaching as well as research to the extent that people were taught about the *use* of information technology in doing scholarship in specific disciplines, or in professional practice within professional schools. But there was little use of information technology in the actual teaching itself. Over the next few decades, the impact of information technology on scholarship and professional practice certainly spread, but in the 1990s, with the emergence of the Internet to broad scale public use and the ubiquitous diffusion of networks and personal computing the situation changed. We saw transformative uses of information technology in the conduct of scholarship, the communication of scholarship, and even in the practices of teaching and learning. This mirrored the transformative aspects of information technology on many other facets of professional and consumer life in the late 1990s. The current emphasis on technology-based distance learning and asynchronous learning are the most recent consequences of this transformation. The effects of these investments in information technology are now changing the whole way in which higher education operates.

Let me make this personal. Suppose you are a trustee of a university, a president or senior administrator in an academic institution, or a state legislator considering funding requests for your state university. You have a fiduciary duty and an obligation of accountability in making your decisions on investments in information technology. Or perhaps you are just an interested citizen and taxpayer trying to decide if your tax dollars are being spent wisely, or you are the parent of a college-aged child trying to select the right institution for your child's education. There are very reasonable questions that you can ask—indeed you should ask, you must ask, you are obligated to ask—about investments in information technology in higher education.

The answers we can supply today aren't good enough. We cannot currently measure outcomes and effects systematically with much success. We can talk about visions—for example, Appalachian schoolchildren coming home to surf the Library of Congress Web site looking for material on dinosaurs—and even possibly build systems that actually allow these things to happen. But we can't tell if the systems we build are making much difference, except by anecdote. Anecdotes still dominate the discussion, even if they are inspiring, graphic, specific stories about how IT has made a crucial difference on an individual level or how someone believes it has made a crucial difference.

I don't want to suggest that these problems haven't been looked at or that we haven't made progress. Some very rigorous and good work has been done at the level of individual courses or focused academic programs in understanding the impacts of introducing instructional technology. Ironically, a good deal of this work has been driven by the suspicion of instructional technology and IT. Traditional teaching and instructional methods have been used as a benchmark and new approaches have had to prove that they are better than the traditional ones. The measurements have been comparative against traditional techniques that were never evaluated well. A beautiful example that I came across recently was the Mathematics Emporium program at Virginia Tech, where they replaced much of the lower-division undergraduate math curriculum (things like linear algebra) by group-oriented, computer-based instructional approaches with what is evidently great success (they did a careful and extensive evaluation and benchmarked the new approach against traditional teaching of these courses). Still, evaluation at the level of individual courses, to me, has an anecdotal quality, though it is anecdote by course rather than by individual; it does not reach to broad evaluation of the changes in educational experiences.

On the instructional side, one way forward may be to generalize from individual courses to broader educational programs. We will have to be more precise about our many and diverse goals and include reaching new and historically underserved communities of learners, as well as the traditional student populations. I think that the aspect of contributions to improving research as opposed to teaching has not received enough attention though, of course, research productivity is notoriously difficult to measure. Finally, to echo a point that CNI's Joan Lippincott has made recently, IT isn't going to be optional in many disciplines; it's not just a tool for teaching but an integral part of a modern and relevant education in many disciplines and a fundamental part of the practice of these disciplines. This should change the way we think about technology in education and how to evaluate it.

This is my final grand challenge. We need to develop credible evaluation approaches that let us understand and measure how networked information and IT are changing—improving, we all hope—research, teaching, and learning within higher education from the broadest possible perspectives. The same questions apply to grade school education, of course, though here the educational objectives are even more confusing than they are in higher education.

ENDNOTES

1. The MELVYL system, which serves the nine campus University of California system, began as a union catalog and evolved to offer access to a large number of abstracting and indexing databases and full-text resources; it later formed the basis of much of the California Digital Library. See www.melvyl.ucop.edu.
2. Google, which can be found at www.google.com, is a commercial Internet search engine that was developed in part from work done at the Stanford University Computer Science Department. It was unique in that it considered the link structure of the Web as part of its algorithms for ranking pages in response to user queries.
3. This can still be found as part of the Cybergeography Atlas. See www.cyberspace.org/atlas/atlas.html.
4. For the Dublin Core, see http://purl.org/dc/.
5. For the Instructional Management System standards, see www.imsproject.org.
6. There is a comprehensive Web page on collaborative filtering which includes pointers to many papers. See http://www.sims.berkeley.edu/resources/collab/index.html.
7. For background on the Sonny Bono Copyright Extension Act, see http://www.public.asu.edu/~dkarjala/.

ACKNOWLEDGMENTS

I'm grateful to Chuck McClure for transcribing the original speech as a basis for preparing this, and to Nancy Gusack for additional editorial help. Chuck McClure, Cecilia Preston and Joan Lippincott provided valuable comments on drafts of the paper, and I owe a special thanks to Cecilia Preston for help with the citations.

ABOUT THE AUTHOR

Clifford Lynch has been the Director of the Coalition for Networked Information (CNI) since July 1997. CNI, jointly sponsored by the Association of Research Libraries and Educause, includes about 200 member organizations concerned with the use of information technology and networked information to enhance scholarship and intellectual productivity. Prior to joining CNI, Lynch spent 18 years at the University of California Office of the President, the last 10 as Director of Library Automation. Lynch, who holds a Ph.D. in Computer Science from the University of California, Berkeley, is an adjunct professor at Berkeley's School of Information Management and Systems. He is a past president of the American Society for Information Science and a fellow of the American Association for the Advancement of Science and the National Information Standards Organization. Lynch currently serves on the Internet 2 Applications Council; he was a member of the National Research Council committee that recently published *The Digital Dilemma: Intellectual Property in the Information Infrastructure*, and now serves on the NRC's committee on Broadband Last-Mile Technology.

Clifford Lynch
Executive Director, Coalition for Networked Information
21 Dupont Circle
Washington, DC, 20036
(202) 296 5098
(202) 872 0884 (fax)
E-mail: clifford@cni.org

REFERENCES

Axelrod, R. (1997). *The Complexity of Cooperation: Agent-Based Models of Competition and Collaboration*. Princeton, NJ: Princeton University Press.

Baker, T. (1998, December). Languages for Dublin Core. *D-Lib Magazine*. From http://www.dlib.org/dilb/december98/12baker/html.

Berger, M. G. (1994). *Information-seeking in the online bibliographic system: An exploratory study*. Doctoral dissertation, University of California, Berkeley.

Bishop, A. P.; Van House, N.; and Buttenfield, B. P. (Eds.) (In press). *Digital Library Use: Social Practice in Design and Evaluation*. Cambridge, MA: MIT Press.

Borgman, C. L. (1986). Why are online catalogs hard to use? Lessons learned from information retrieval studies. *Journal of the American Society for Information Science*. 37, 387–400.

Borgman, C. L. (1996). Why are online catalogs still hard to use? *Journal of the American Society for Information Science*. 47, 493–503.

Brin, S. (1998). Extracting patterns and relations from the Worldwide Web. *WebDB 1998*. pp. 172–183.

Brin, S. and Page, L. (1998). The anatomy of a large-scale hypertextual Web search engine. *Computer Networks and ISDN Systems*, 30 (1–7): 107–117.

Buckland, M. and Plaunt, C. (1994) On the construction of selection systems. *Library Hi Tech*. 12 (4): 15–28. From http://www.sims.berkeley.edu/~buckland/papers/analysis/analysis.html.

Chakrabarti, S.; Dom, B.; Kumar, S. R.; Raghaver, P.; Rajagopalan, S.; Tomkins, A.; Kleinberg, J. M.; and Gibson, D. (1999). Hypersearching the Web. *Scientific American*, 280 (6) p. 54 (7 pages).

Cleverdon, C. W.; Mills, J.; and Keen, E. M. (1966). Factors Determining the Performance of Indexing Systems, Volume 2: Test Results. Cranfield, England: Cranfield College of Aeronautics.

Council on Library Resources (1982). *Users look at online catalogs: Results of a national survey of users and non-users of online public access catalogs* (Final report). Berkeley, CA: Division of Library Automation and Library Research Analysis Group, Office of the Assistant Vice President—Library Plans and Policies, University of California Systemwide Administration.

Crane, G. (2000, September 19). Perseus Project. From http://www.perseus.tufts.edu.

Daley, D. J. and Gani, J. (1999). *Epidemic Modeling: An Introduction*. Cambridge, MA: MIT Press.

Digital Millennium Copyright Act of 1998, Pub.L. No. 105–304.

Dodge, M. (Ed.). (2000, September 7). An atlas of cyberspace. From http://www.cyberspace.org/atlas/atlas.html (September 19, 2000).

Epstein, J. M. and Axtell, R. (1996). *Growing Artificial Societies: Social Science from the Bottom Up*. Cambridge, MA: MIT Press.

Farrell, W. (1998). *How Hits Happen: Forecasting.Predictability in a Chaotic Marketplace*. New York: HarperBusiness.

Feghhi, Jakl, Feghhi, Jalil, and Williams, Peter. (1999). Digital Certificates: Applied Internet Security. Reading, MA: Addison-Wesley.

Feigenbaum, J. and Kannan, S. (2000). Dynamic Graph Algorithms. In, *Handbook of discrete and combinatorial mathematics*. (pp. 1142–1151). Boca Raton, FL: CRC Press.

Ford, W. and Baum, M. S. (1997). *Secure Electronic Commerce: Building the Infrastructure for Digital Signatures and Encryption*. Upper Saddle River, NJ: Prentice-Hall.

French, J. C.; Powell, A.; Callan, J.; Emmitt, T.; Prey, K. J.; and Mou, Y. (1999). Comparing the Performance of Database Selection Algorithms. *Proceedings of SIGIR 1999*, 74–81.

Gaylord, R. J. and D'Andria, L. J. (1998). *Simulating Society: A Mathematica Toolkit for Modeling*. New York: Springer-Verlag.

Gibson, D.; Kleinberg, J.; and Raghaver, P. (1998). Inferring Web communities from link topology. *Proceedings of the 9th ACM Conference on Hypertext and Hypermedia*. 225–234.

Giles, C. L.; Lawrence, S.; and Krovetz, B. (1998, June 19). Access to information on the Web. *Science*, 280, 1815+.

GroupLens. (1999, December 9). MovieLens: Help/FAQ. From http://movielens.umn.edu/help/index.html (September 18, 2000).

Gusack, N. and Lynch, C. A. (Eds.). (1995). Modes of Communicating Information and Knowledge [Special issue]. *Library Hi Tech*, 13(4).

International Consortium of Library Consortia. (2000, March). From http://www.library.yale.edu/consortia (September 19, 2000).

Kuhn, T. (1970). *Structure of scientific revolutions*, 2nd ed., enlarged. Chicago, IL: University of Chicago Press.

Lancaster, L., et al. (2000, July 18). The Electronic Cultural Atlas Initiative. From http://www.ias.berkeley.edu/ECAI (September 19, 2000).

Larson, R. R. (1991). The decline of subject searching: Long-term trends and patterns of index use in an online catalog. *Journal of the American Society for Information Science*. 42, 197–215.

Lawrence, S. R. and Giles, C. L. (1998a, April 3). Searching the World Wide Web. *Science*, 280, 98–100.

Lawrence, S. R. and Giles, C. L. (1998b, July 10). Searching the Web, continued—Response. *Science*, 281, 177.

Lawrence, S. R. and Giles, C. L. (1999, July 8). Accessibility of Information on the Web. *Nature*, 400, 107–109.

Lynch, A. (1996). *Thought Contagion: How Belief Spreads Through Society: The New Science of Memes*. New Yorks: Basic Books.

Lynch, C. A. (2001). When documents deceive: Trust and provenance as new factors for information retrieval in a tangled Web. *Journal of the American Society for Information Science*. 52:1, 12–17.

Malamud, C., et al. (2000). Mappa.Mundi Magazine. From http://mappa.mundi.net (September 19, 2000).

Moen, W. E. (2000 July 31). Z39.50: Projects, presentations, and resources. From http://www.unt.edu/wmoen/Z39.50.htm (September 14, 2000).

Napster. (2000). From http://www.napster.com (September 18, 2000).

National Library of Education. (n.d.). The Education Resources Information Center. From http://www.accesseric.org. (September 18, 2000).

National Library of Medicine. (1998, January 9). The NLM PubMed Project. From http://ncbi.nlm.nih.gov/PubMed/overview.html (September 18, 2000).

National Research Council (1997). *Bits of power: Issues in global access to scientific data*. Washington, DC: National Academy Press.

National Research Council (1998). *Fostering research on the economic and social impacts of information technology: Report of a workshop*. Washington, DC: National Academy Press.

National Research Council (1999). A *Question of balance: Private rights and the public interest in scientific and technical databases*. Washington, DC: National Academy Press.

National Research Council (2000). *The digital dilemma: Intellectual property in the information age*. (2000) Washington, DC: National Academy Press.

PGP Web of Trust Statistics. From http://bcn.boulder.co.us/~neil/pgpstat (September 30, 2000).

President's Information Technology Advisory Committee. (2000) From http://www.ccic.gov/ac (September 18, 2000).

Plaunt, C. (1997). A *Functional Model of Information Retrieval Systems*. Doctoral dissertation, University of California, Berkeley.

Prielta, M.; Gaser, L.; and Caley, K. (Eds.) (1998). *Simulating Organizations: Computational Models of Institutions and Groups*. Cambridge, MA: MIT Press.

Schatz, B. (1997). Information retrieval in digital libraries: Bringing search to the net. *Science*, 275, 327–334.

Scleifer, A. (2000). *Inefficient Markets: An Introduction to Behavioral Finance*. Oxford: Oxford University Press.

Security and Exchange Commission. (2000, August 28). EDGAR Database. From http://www.sec.gov/edgarhp.htm (September 14, 2000).

Sonny Bono Copyright Term Extension Act of 1998. Pub. L. No. 105–298.

Text REtrieval Conference (TREC). (2000, August 21). From http://trec.nist.gov (September 18, 2000).

TULIP: Final report. (1996). New York: Elsevier Science.

United States Patent and Trademark Office. (2000, September 18). Home page. From http://uspto.gov/Web/menu/pats.html (September 18, 2000).

World Wide Web Consortium (2000 August 8). Web Accessibility Initiative. From http://www.w3.org/WAI (September 14, 2000).

Zimmermann, P. R. (1995). *The official PGP user's guide*. Cambridge, MA: MIT Press.

About the Editors

Charles R. McClure is the Francis Eppes Professor of Information Studies and Director of the Information Use Management and Policy Institute at Florida State University http://www.ii.fsu.edu. McClure has written extensively on topics related to planning and evaluation of information services, information resources management and Federal Information Policy. He is the co-author (with John Carlo Bertot) of *Public Libraries and the Internet 2000*, funded and published by the National Commission on Libraries and Information Science (see http://www.nclis.gov) and is currently completing a study funded by the U.S. Energy Information Administration, the Government Printing Office, and the Defense Technical Information Center to produce performance measures that assess Federal Web sites. McClure is also President of Information Management Consulting Services, Inc. Additional information about McClure can be found at http://slis-two.lis.fsu.edu/~cmcclure.

E-mail: cmcclure@lis.fsu.edu

John Carlo Bertot is Associate Professor in the School of Information Studies and Associate Director of the Information Use Management and Policy Institute at Florida State University http://www.ii.fsu.edu. Bertot was the co-principal investigator for the National Leadership Grant funded by the Institute of Museum and Library Services (IMLS) to develop national public library statistics and performance measures for the networked environment that made this manual possible. This effort led to the book *Statistics and Performance Measures for Public Library Networked Services*, published by the American Library Association. At present, Bertot is co-principal investigator for an IMLS National Leadership Grant to develop a national model for collecting public library network statistics and performance measures, as well as an Association of Research Libraries (ARL) project to develop measurement tools for networked services and resources in ARL libraries. Bertot continues to work with public and other libraries to develop, plan, and evaluate network-based services through a variety of projects. He is also the President of Bertot Information Consultant Services, Inc. Additional information on Bertot is available at http://slis-two.lis.fsu.edu/~jcbertot.

E-mail: jcbertot@elis.fsu.edu

Index

A

D

M

N

O

P

Q

R

S

T

U

Z